★ ★ ★

"Stanton's straightforward history recounts the hard-won and often misunderstood accomplishments of the elite counterinsurgency force that performed a multifaceted role throughout the Vietnam War. . . . Included is information on SF Medal of Honor recipients and MIAs."

—*Publishers Weekly*

"Stanton's style is powerful and evocative. His presentation is commendably balanced and masterfully delivered—the soaring triumphs and crushing defeats, heroism and cowardice. Nineteen of undoubtedly the best black and white maps in print supplement his text, while twelve charts capture a wealth of detail. . . . No library on the war in Vietnam is complete unless it contains *Green Berets at War.* Given today's renewed emphasis on special operations and low-intensity conflict, discerning readers will find priceless insight into the correct application of Special Operations Forces, especially in counterinsurgency operations. Rarely does a combat history provide such utility for tomorrow."

—*Military Review*

"*Green Berets at War* . . . provide a unique perspective on the Vietnam War, differing from those accounts that deal with the larger war or see it from the viewpoint of a specific individual. . . . Stanton presents a balanced view, though, not just a book of hero worship. He also discusses, for example, instances of misuse of the Special Forces, their manpower problems, and the double-agent murders that tarnished their image."

—*Sea Power*

"Written in easy-to-read but well-documented style, . . .*Green Berets at War* successfully combines scholarly research with high adventure, and belongs on every vet's bookshelf. Very highly recommended."

—*Soldier of Fortune*

Green Berets at War

U.S. Army Special Forces in Southeast Asia 1956–1975

Shelby L. Stanton

PRESIDIO

Published by Presidio Press
505 B San Marin Drive, Suite 300
Novato, CA 94945-1340

Presidio Press cloth edition published in 1985
This paperbound edition published in 1995

Library of Congress-in-Publication Data

Stanton, Shelby L., 1948–
  The Green Berets at war
  Includes bibliography and index.
    1. United States. Army. Special Forces-History.
2. Vietnamese Conflict, 1961-1975–Commando operations.
I. Title.
UA34.S64S73   1986   356'.167'0973   85-19441
ISBN 0-89141-238-7 (cloth)
ISBN 0-89141-574-2 (paper)

Printed in the United States of America

To those soldiers assigned or attached to U.S. Army Special Forces who sacrificed their lives in Laos, Thailand, Cambodia and Vietnam.

(U.S. Army)

Contents

Foreword

Several books have been written on the exploits of U.S. Army Special Forces in Indochina, both as fact and fiction. Captain Stanton's *The Green Berets at War,* however, represents the only authoritative and detailed Special Forces battlefield history of the Vietnam War.

Captain Stanton served with distinction as a Special Forces officer assigned to the 46th SF Company in Lopburi, Thailand. As the chief agency operations officer working with the Deputy Chief, Joint U.S. Military Advisory Group, I briefed Stanton and other Special Forces commanders sent into combat in Laos late in the war.

Following his own experience with years of intensive research, Shelby Stanton has now written this comprehensive history of Army Special Forces throughout Southeast Asia, including the early struggles at Plei Mrong and Hiep Hoa, the devastating battles of A Shau and Lang Vei, as well as the intense combat during the Tet Offensive in 1968.

It was with deep humility, but with considerable pride, that I served as the first commander of those valiant officers—many of whom forfeited career advancement to serve in the Special Forces—and of the noncommissioned officers who were truly the backbone of the U.S. Army Special Forces in Vietnam. Few men have served their country with greater devotion and dedication, or in a more professional manner. Captain Stanton captures this spirit of duty and sacrifice in his accounts of the battles that Special Forces fought during that conflict. His book is a tribute to the outstanding contribution that SF made in the most protracted and controversial war in the history of the United States. *The Green Berets at War* is a book which every Special Forces soldier will cherish, and in which he will take deep pride.

Since Captain Stanton takes up the story of the Army Special Forces in the Pacific starting with the year 1956, I would like to give a brief overview of the origin and development of Special Forces. When General William J. "Wild Bill" Donovan's Office of Strategic Services (OSS) was demobilized after World War II, the United States lost its capability to conduct unconventional warfare. The vast experience gained by American personnel involved with the World War II resistance movements worldwide was irretrievably lost. Unfortunately for America, this occurred at the same time that communist expansionism was being manifested throughout the newly emerging and Third World countries of Asia, Latin America, Africa and the Middle East in support of so-called national wars of liberation. Eastern European countries which had been occupied by Soviet forces at the end of World War II, as well as most of Asia, fell under communist control. Without a capability to support resistance movements in those countries, opposition eventually withered and those nations fell under the firm grip of either the Soviet Union or the People's Republic of China. To block further communist expansion, American national defense policy relied on containment backed up by strategic nuclear deterrents. This policy resulted in a proliferation of collective or bilateral defense treaty organizations which all involved large numbers of U.S. and allied conventional units supported by an arsenal of nuclear weapons. These forces were totally unsuitable for the grassroots wars of liberation which cropped up throughout the Third World.

The Greek Civil War, the Hukbalahap Guerrilla War in the Philippines further highlighted the necessity for a national defense policy aimed at countering communist expansionism using an alternative to massive conventional intervention or atomic annihilation. Such a requirement also received impetus during the Korean War, when bands of South Korean irregulars were formed behind the lines in North Korea and conducted sabotage, ambush and intelligence collection operations, and established escape and evasion nets for the rescue of downed American pilots in MIG Alley.

As a result, on June 20, 1952, the first contingent of volunteers assembled on Smoke Bomb Hill at Fort Bragg, North Carolina, to be organized into the 10th Special Forces Group under the auspices of the Army Chief of Psychological Warfare. These volunteers were trained for infiltration deep into enemy territory by land, sea or air to conduct unconventional warfare—guerrilla warfare, sabotage, and escape and evasion. Although this original contingent included a smattering of former OSS men and individuals who had served with other guerrilla and resistance groups in World War II, the majority had no previous unconventional warfare experience. They were, however, outstanding paratrooper-qualified officers and non-commissioned officers who were dedicated and highly motivated. These professionals brought with them their skills in operations, intelligence, demolitions, communications, light and heavy weapons, and medicine. Capable of operating independently as small teams for extended periods in hostile territory with minimal support, they were taught to organize, train, and equip guerrilla forces, conduct sabotage operations, support resistance movements and to evade, and if necessary, escape from enemy forces. These elite troopers adopted the insignia of the Trojan Horse as their symbol, and *De Oppresso Liber* (To Liberate from Oppression) as their motto.

In November of 1953, the 10th Special Forces Group, which had completed over a year of training at Fort Bragg, deployed to Bad Tolz in Germany. There the group prepared to support resistance movements and organize guerrilla forces in the Soviet-dominated Eastern European satellite countries and, if indicated, throughout Africa and the Middle East. On the departure of the 10th SFG for Germany, the 77th Special Forces Group was activated at Fort Bragg and cadred by members of the 10th SFG. In 1957 the 1st Special Forces Group was activated on Okinawa to support unconventional warfare missions in the Far East. By 1961, Special Forces teams from both the 77th and 1st SFGs were operational in Korea, Taiwan, the Philippines, Vietnam, Laos, Thailand, and other nations, primarily as mobile training teams for indigenous counterparts.

By the time John F. Kennedy became President of the United States on January 20, 1961, the communist-supported national wars of liberation conducted along the periphery of the Soviet Union and Red China, as well as in Africa, the Middle East, Latin America, and Southeast Asia, had assumed major proportions. Embarrassed by the abortive Bay of Pigs operation in Cuba, which aimed at preventing the establishment of a communist regime in the Western hemisphere, and confronted by imminent communist insurgency in Laos and South Vietnam, President Kennedy sought an alternative to committing regular forces in these areas. Later that year, during a visit to the U.S. Army Special Warfare Center at Fort Bragg, Kennedy found his answer. After discussions with the young, dynamic and highly articulate advocate of unconventional warfare and counterinsurgency operations, Brigadier General William P. Yarborough (the commander of the Special Warfare Center), Kennedy observed the capabilities of Special Forces troops at Fort Bragg. The President was determined to expand these forces and commit them to fight communist-inspired insurgencies anywhere in the world. He authorized the green beret as their official headgear, describing it as a symbol of excellence, a mark of distinction, and a badge of courage.

Upon his return to Washington, President Kennedy instructed the Secretary of Defense to improve America's paramilitary and unconventional warfare capabilities. Kennedy also advised him that the United States needed a greater ability to combat communist guerrilla forces, insurgency, and subversion. Counterinsurgency became a buzz-word in Washington, and the Army Special Forces was predestined to be committed to a protracted war in Vietnam that no one in Washington could foresee at the time.

The Army Special Forces lost its champion and foremost advocate of counterinsurgency and unconventional warfare on November 22, 1963, when President Kennedy was assassinated in Dallas, Texas. However, by this time, many of his directions had been implemented. In addition to the 10th SFG in Germany, the 1st SFG in Okinawa, and the 77th (later redesignated the 7th) SFG at Fort Bragg, the 8th SFG had been activated in Panama, the 5th SFG was already sending personnel to Vietnam, and the 3d and the 6th SFGs were activated at Fort Bragg with African and Middle Eastern priority (Captain Stanton includes a chart in Appendix E of this book which details the global posture of Special Forces a year later, in 1964). Elements of the 1st, 5th, and 7th SFGs, under the command of U.S. Army Special Forces (Provisional), Vietnam, had been involved in Southeast Asian fighting since early 1962. The United States had finally regained its capability to conduct unconventional warfare and counterinsurgency operations.

George C. Morton *
Colonel, U.S. Army (Retired)
Alexandria, Virginia
June 17, 1985

* Editor's Note: Colonel Morton was the first commander of U.S.
Army Special Forces Vietnam (Provisional)

Introduction

The writing of *The Green Berets at War* actually began during the author's own Special Forces service, and was given direction by the hundreds of comrades interviewed both during and after the war. Finally, four years were spent researching the Special Forces records which survive in various official archives, in order to produce a definitive and accurate account of the wartime exploits of this vital Army fighting formation.

The author must pay foremost acknowledgement to the Army Special Forces veterans who shared their first-hand knowledge, as well as those unsung troopers and military historians who duly filed after-action and team reports, often under adverse field conditions and sometimes in the midst of combat. The following individuals spent their valuable time and offered crucial assistance during the book's review process: Brig. Gen. Donald D. Blackburn (USA Ret), former commander of the 7th Special Forces Group and MACV-SOG; Gen. George S. Blanchard (USA Ret), former senior officer in the Army Special Warfare Directorate; Vincent H. Demma, Army historian in the Office of the Chief of Military History Southeast Asia branch; Dr. John H. Hatcher, Archivist of the U.S. Army; Maj. Gen. Michael Healy (USA Ret), former commander of the 5th Special Forces Group; Thomas E. Hohmann of Army Declassification Review; Col. Donald E. Lunday (USA), Chairman of the Army War College Department of Military Policy; Col. George C. Morton (USA Ret), former commander of U.S. Army Special Forces, Vietnam (Provisional); Maj. William C. North (USA), Office of the Deputy Chief of Staff, Operations; Col. Rod Paschall (USA), Director of the U.S. Army Military History Institute at Carlisle Barracks; Wanda Radcliffe, Chief of Army Declassification and Reference Support; Sergeant First Class Gordon Rottman (Texas Army NG), the author of the highly recommended uniform booklet, *U.S. Army Special Forces, 1952–84* (London: Osprey Publishing, 1985); Maj. Clyde J. Sincere, Jr. (USA Ret), former commander of II CTZ Mike Force; Maj. Gen. John Singlaub (USA Ret), former commander of MACV-SOG; Col. John Schlight (USAF Ret), Chief of the Southeast Asia Branch, Army Office of the Chief of Military History; Lt. Col. John F. Sloan (USA

Ret), editor of The International Military Encyclopedia; and Lt. Gen. William P. Yarborough (USA Ret), former commander of the Army JFK Center for Special Warfare. I also wish to acknowledge my editor, Adele Horwitz; the encouragement of my father, Samuel Shelton Stanton; and the loving cooperation of my wife, Kathryn.

While this book has been devoted to recording the factual history of U.S. Army Special Forces combat operations throughout Southeast Asia from 1956–1975, these pages actually represent only a brief summary. Many important battles and events could only be touched upon, and other gaps remain due to continuing classification restrictions. In many ways, perhaps the entire story of the Army Special Forces in Asia may never be told, but it is hoped that this book provides a start.

Shelby L. Stanton
Captain, U.S. Army, Retired
Bethesda, Maryland
17 June 1985

CHAPTER 1

OKINAWA

1. A Special Pacific Mission

In 1956 the Pacific had been an active U.S. military region for fifteen years and had witnessed two major American wars. The U.S. Pacific Command's area of responsibility was vast, extending roughly from the Arctic to the Antarctic and from California to India, and crucial to U.S. national interests. This importance was elevated by the fact that the United States was on the threshold of a new era in Pacific strategy. Highly classified Pacific-based Army Special Forces units were being formed in anticipation of this new direction.

The 14th Special Forces Operational Detachment (Area) (Airborne), commanded by Lt. Col. Albert "Scott" Madding, was secretly activated on 2 April 1956 under a cover designation as the 8251st Army Unit. His sixteen-man detachment had a dangerous and unusual mission: in the event of general war, Madding's detachment would lead Asian resistance forces against Sino-Soviet forces expected to overrun the rim of Asia. This kind of fighting was labeled *unconventional warfare,* a little-understood Army term defined as guerrilla warfare, escape and evasion, and subversion.

Since the Special Forces would organize, train, and control indigenous Asian populations in its anticipated wartime mission, the detachment began organizing three mobile training teams, each consisting of one officer and six sergeants, which would be sent to the Military Assistance Advisory Groups (MAAG) in Taiwan, Thailand, and South Vietnam. There they would spend two or three months training allied forces in unconventional warfare tactics and techniques. The first mobile training team was deployed that September.[1]

Several other Special Forces detachments had been secretly formed closer to the Asian continent on 1 April 1956. The 16th Special Forces Detachment (District B) (Airborne) and its subordinated 12th and 13th Special Forces Detachments (Regiment) (Airborne) had been activated at Camp Drake, Japan, just north of Tokyo, as Detachments A, B, and C of the 8231st Army Unit under Lt. Col. Jack T. "Blackjack" Shannon. The 8231st Army Unit was a miniscule part of the Army machinery in the western Pacific, which was geared to fling back Chinese and Soviet armies venturing into South Korea and invading Taiwan or Japan itself. Secretive special mission units were an unwelcome complication to the high-ranking officers at Pacific Command, who were told to program them into war plans to organize behind-the-lines guerrilla fighters after nuclear exchanges.[2]

Throughout the latter 1950s the U.S. military was coping with the difficult task of surviving and winning a major nuclear war. The grandiose Pacific war plans envisioned continental-scale actions, with plenty of atomic blasting, followed by rolling drives into North Korea and Manchuria "to pin certain Chinese armies," while the paratroopers of the 82d Airborne Division held Bangkok and the 1st Marine Division defended Saigon. Special Forces were intended to supplement the general scheme of atomic warfare, by being inserted into enemy-held territory to develop partisan bands capable of resistance and disrupting rear areas.[3]

The Pacific Command's ground warfare concerns covered five major categories, of which Special Forces played a relatively small part in the final list of priorities. Foremost were maintaining the Eighth Army defenses in South Korea at a high state of readiness, keeping the 3d Marine Division and the 25th Infantry Division in fighting trim as the strategic Pacific reserves, developing a forward base on Okinawa, completing the movement of atomic-capable units into Korea, and developing effective indigenous armies in friendly countries to assure their capability for integrated action with U.S. forces in event of general war.[4]

Although the threat of all-out war, coupled with declining troop strength and dwindling funds, made it imperative to be as resourceful as possible in damaging the enemy, most Army field commanders still had little use for unconventional warfare. The planners of U.S. Army Pacific, like other Army commands, considered Special Forces an unwanted, long-shot scheme forced upon them by the cuts in regular units, which had mandated odd approaches toward responding to major attack. At best, they saw Special Forces as representing a possible unorthodox solution to maximize losses and cause discomfort to the enemy at minimal cost. At worst, they viewed Special Forces doctrine as a crackpot "non-Army" method of fighting a war.

The Special Forces was composed of a small number of specially selected and highly trained soldiers. Unconventional warfare, by its very nature, demanded rugged individuals who were able to master critical military skills needed to train and lead guerrilla warriors, to be inserted anywhere in the world by any means of transportation, to survive the most hostile environment, and to take care of themselves and others under harsh combat conditions. At the same time, these individuals had to be independent thinkers, able to grasp opportunities and innovate with the materials at hand. In order to control and lead irregular partisan fighters, they had to understand people, languages, and foreign cultures. Most important, the Special Forces warriors had to possess the intelligence, knowledge, tact, and acumen to successfully transform ordinary civilians into an effective military threat to a strong and cunning occupation army.

The ideal Special Forces material was composed of individuals who demonstrated a mastery of the mental discipline and physical hardiness needed to reach and impart expert skills to natives behind enemy lines. Reliability under pressure, an ability to survive isolation, and bravery in adversity were routine requirements for survival under such circumstances. In addition to recruiting rugged individuals possessing these attributes from regular army formations, the Army Special Forces were able to attract a proven lot of hardy, versatile volunteers from Finland and other European countries through the Lodge Act; Public Law 957 of the 81st Congress, sponsored by Henry Cabot Lodge, Jr.

Regardless of his background, each Special Forces volunteer underwent strenuous physical conditioning, including paratrooper training, and was extensively tested to determine his best skills and abilities. He then received comprehensive instruction in one of five areas: intelligence, weapons, demolitions, medicine, or communications. Special Forces radiomen completed a minimum of four months' communications training. Weapons leaders started with two months of weapons training then continued to master multiple types of allied and communist rifles, grenades, bazookas, and crew-served weapons. Demolitions men took four months of intensive training in plastic explosives, dynamite charges, fuses, and other compounds applied with engineering precision to destroy everything from railroads to bridges. The medical specialists completed thirty-nine weeks of rigorous instruction in the medical field and became practically qualified as field surgeons. Senior noncommissioned officers became team and intelligence sergeants after taking extensive advanced intelligence and operational training.

Special Forces troopers found that their training had just begun after completing their basic skills courses. All Special Forces soldiers had to have a working knowledge of at least one other language in addition to English. Certain individuals were selected as experts in advanced techniques of underwater operations, high-altitude low-opening (HALO) parachuting, and hand-to-hand combat. After passing an additional seven weeks of preliminary branch training under the Special Training Group at Fort Bragg, North Carolina, qualified Special Forces personnel were assigned to the Special Forces Operational Detachments A, or A-Detachments, commonly known as the A-Teams.

Each Special Forces A-Detachment was a self-sufficent group of expertly trained, robust soldiers who constantly worked together to perfect both team capabilities and individual fighting proficiency. Every team member was cross-trained in another specialty, so he could perform that job under emergency conditions. Teams participated in specialized training in mountain, cold-weather, and jungle warfare. Basic underwater training and submarine operations were conducted with the U.S. Navy. Unlike conventional ranger and long-range patrol units, the Special Forces teams had to learn to work effectively with natives of other countries. Such aptitude could be gained only during team expeditions or when stationed in foreign countries.

Many senior officers intensely disliked this strange collection of soldiers but realized that stripped-down conventional resources left them no choice but to hope that Special Forces-led guerrilla outfits would disrupt the rear areas of communist forces, while the United States rushed in reinforcements for the counterattack. The anticipated difficulty of defending U.S. ramparts in the Pacific led to the creation of the 1st Special Forces Group (Airborne).

2. The 1st Special Forces Group Takes Charge

On 24 June 1957 the headquarters and headquarters company of the 1st Special Forces Group were activated at Camp Drake, Japan, near Tokyo. On the same day the company's subordinated 248th Quartermaster Detachment (Special Forces Parachute Rigging) was raised.[5] A week later the U.S. Army Pacific assumed operational control over all Special Forces units in Hawaii and the Orient and ordered them concentrated on Okinawa. The 14th Special Forces Detachment flew out of Hawaii on 2 July and arrived in Okinawa on 5 July. On 14 July the 1st Special Forces Group arrived and took control over the 12th, 13th, 14th, and 16th SF Operational Detachments stationed there. On the first anniversary of the group's formation, 24 June 1958, the fifteen-man 15th Special Forces Operational Detachment (Regiment) (Airborne) was activated as the fifth operational team under its command.[6] The group reached its full authorized strength of sixteen officers and ninety-nine enlisted men at that time.

Okinawa was chosen as the home of Pacific-based Special Forces in consonance with its perceived advantages as an advanced citadel of the U.S. Pacific defenses. Not only would hostile powers have to mount a major military effort to seize the island, resulting in direct confrontation with America, but its base activities were immune to creeping insurgency and other problems vexing Asiatic facilities. Okinawa had been revitalized as a forward strategic location since 2 January 1953, when Brig. Gen. David A. D. Ogden announced, "I was sent down from Japan to develop Okinawa as a major base in the defense of the Pacific." Increased Japanese pressure to get U.S. military forces out of their country after the Korean War hastened Okinawa's development as a major bastion past 1955, when elements of the 3d Marine Division began transferring to the island.[7]

Okinawa was an excellent Special Forces operating base. Its proximity to Special Forces Asiatic responsibilities was ideal, since Okinawa was located less than a thousand miles from Taiwan, Korea, most of Japan, the Philippines, and important areas of China. The Special Forces was initially hindered by chronic shortages of critical communications and other equipment, but these were the normal growing pains of any organization. The Special Forces was glad to have a home so close to operational areas, even if the available parachute drop zones were extremely hazardous. Col. Frank Mills, an

OSS veteran of World War II, took over the 1st Special Forces Group in 1959. On 24 March 1960 the group was moved into new compounds in the vicinity of Kadena Air Force Base at Bishigawa, Hizagawa, Yara, Matsuda, and the Ryukyu Army Ammunition Depot (Chibana).[8]

The 1st Special Forces Group immediately began raising more mobile training teams, which would teach American concepts of unconventional warfare to cadres from Korea, the Philippines, South Vietnam, Taiwan, and Thailand. These cadres were then encouraged to form indigenous Special Forces units in their own countries. During the first year of the group's existence, ten mobile training teams were dispatched on these sensitive initial missions with strict orders to avoid newspaper publicity. Reporters were soon on the story, however, thanks to a few braggarts. Pacific Command was aghast to read a major 9 October *Manila Chronicle* article quoting a Special Forces captain, who stated that countries received classified equipment in exchange for participating.[9]

The first Special Forces personnel arrived on Taiwan in February 1957. The 77th Special Forces Group at Fort Bragg, North Carolina, had dispatched Mobile Training Team 1A on a six-month temporary-duty assignment to train fifty Chinese officers in all aspects of Special Forces operations and techniques. Commanded by Lt. Col. Eugene "Mike" Smith, the team consisted of six officers and six sergeants. Shortly after their arrival in Taiwan, the team was joined by Maj. Donald "Paddy" O'Rourke, M. Sgt. Henry "Hank" Furst, and Sfc. Everett C. White from the 14th Special Forces Operational Detachment in Hawaii. The reinforced team conducted intensive training for six months and was then reassigned to the newly activated 1st Special Forces Group on Okinawa. The Chinese cadre subsequently created its own Special Forces training center at Lung Tan, about fifty miles south of Taipei.

Another major priority was the training of the Korean Special Forces cadre. Although the Korean government had appropriated an area southeast of Kimpo Airfield as the site of the future training center, the Korean special warfare aspirants were sent to Okinawa because of the lack of facilities. The Special Forces could not obtain any Air Force aircraft for the cadre to use in jump training. Finally, it was necessary to borrow a C-46 aircraft from the Korean Air Force, and on 14 May 1958 the first seventy members of the Korean Special

Forces earned jump wings. Six others, who had suffered minor injuries, qualified as paratroopers later. Advanced instruction was given in Korea by the group's Mobile Training Team 12A, and the cadre completed this rugged course on 20 August 1958. The Korean Special Forces began instructing its first trainees in October. By the end of the year, the 1st Korean Combat Group (Airborne) had 290 parachutist-qualified members. After the 1st Special Forces Group vehemently complained about the lack of air support, the Pacific Command ordered the Air Force 315th Troop Carrier Division to meet future group aerial requirements.[10]

The 1st Special Forces Group was also busy refining its own capabilities. Advanced unit training was regularly held in Korea and Taiwan and planned for the Philippines, Thailand, and South Vietnam. Increasing numbers of personnel completed advanced jungle training at the British Far East Land Forces Training Center at Kota Tinga near Johore Bahru, Malaya, where they were given special instruction in jungle survival, tracking, traps, and antiguerrilla tactics. The Seventh Fleet provided submarines and destroyers for amphibious infiltration exercises on Miyako Jima. On Okinawa itself the group continued intensive training in another key commando mission assigned them by Pacific Command; infiltrating and emplacing the T-4 Atomic Demolition Munition.[11]

In 1959 the Pentagon decided to back up the 1st Special Forces Group in case of war by forming a reserve Special Forces group in Hawaii. On 1 June 1959 the U.S. Army Special Forces Detachment (Provisional) was formed accordingly. The unit was highly classified and initially created as a classified adjunct to the Hawaiian Reserve Training Battle Group (known officially as the 4995th Army Reserve Augmentation Unit). Between 17 and 27 October thirteen officers and twenty enlisted men were ordered to active duty and conducted parachute training near Seoul, Korea.

This reserve unit became the basis of the 329th Special Forces Operational Detachment, which was organized by the Hawaiian U.S. Army Advisor Group on 5 November 1959. By the end of the year, the detachment had 18 officers, 2 warrant officers, and 35 enlisted men out of a total authorized strength of 148. The 329th Special Forces Detachment received its first annual active duty training on Okinawa 15 to 27 August 1960, but typhoon conditions canceled planned tactical exercises on Taiwan and in Korea. This detachment served as the basis for the Army Hawaiian Reserve 24th Special Forces Group, organized at Fort De Russey, Hawaii, on 6 January 1961.[12]

The 1958 Taiwan Crisis disrupted Joint Chiefs of Staff hopes to field test combined U.S. and allied Special Forces units on a global basis. The first combined Special Forces training exercise in the Pacific was HSIEN JUNG, played out in Taiwan from 8 to 29 May 1959, simulating unconventional warfare in mainland China. The 1st Special Forces Group jumped in 86 troopers in conjunction with 860 members of the new Special Warfare Center on Taiwan.[13]

Throughout the year Mobile Training Teams continued active operations with the 1st Korean Combat Group, the Philippine Ranger Battalion, and French instructors in Laos. On Okinawa the group opened an eight-week ranger training course for Indonesian National Police officers in January. When not absent on foreign duty, the group's detachments conducted extensive training in atomic demolitions, amphibious infiltration and exfiltration, small-boat handling, parachuting, mountain climbing, and submarine operations. Depending on their area of anticipated wartime assignments, teams also studied either Vietnamese, Chinese Mandarin, Korean, French, or Thai. During Operation KEYSTONE in February, the group joined the Marine 3d Reconnaissance Battalion to wage mock guerrilla battles against the Marine division on the island. Group instructors also taught survival, escape, and evasion in Hawaii to the soldiers of the 25th Infantry Division.[14]

On 1 November 1959 the 1st Special Forces Group was increased to an authorization of 35 officers and 213 enlisted men, and internally transformed with the inactivation of the 12th to 16th Special Forces Operational Detachments. To take their places the group formed four "C" command detachments, each oriented toward creating a separate operational base for guerrilla operations in case of war. Special Forces Detachment 101 was programmed to have its base established in Southeast Asia, 202 in China and adjacent areas, 303 in Korea and Manchuria, and 404 in Okinawa and Japan.

On the last day of 1959, the Department of the Army designated the group as part of the combat arms regimental system, with all special forces groups honorarily becoming part of the 1st Special Forces, which became effective on 30 September 1960. Thus, the group became the 1st Special Forces Group (Airborne), 1st Special Forces. The group's authorized strength was increased to forty-nine officers and 315 enlisted men on 4 October 1960, the same date that it in-activated the 248th Quartermaster Detachment. By the end of the year the group was up to strength, posting forty-eight officers and 319 enlisted men in twenty-six operational detachments.[15]

3. Expanding Special Forces Commitments

During 1960, the group was still largely focused on the Korean and Taiwan fronts. Exercises, such as July STRIKEBACK, October BEACON, and December SPRINGFIELD, usually involved group teams from Special Forces Detachment 303, infiltrated into the area between Seoul and Taegu to rehearse ground reconnaissance and long-range communications. In the fall of 1960, a permanent group pres-ence was maintained on the peninsula with the transfer of three-man Special Forces Detachment 40 to Korea. When the detachment was brought up to strength a year later, Mobile Training Team 12 was finally phased out. In February 1961 KOREA 61-I pitted six Korean reserve divisions against three Korean and three U.S. Special Forces detachments deployed as guerrilla bands. KOREA 61-II followed that fall, but by that time developments in Laos had shifted group prior-ities to Southeast Asia.[16]

The group headquarters and 115 troopers jumped into combined U.S.-Taiwan Special Forces annual Exercise KUN LUN during May–June 1960, which ranged over one-third of Taiwan. That fall the group's eight-man Special Forces Detachment 26 was permanently transferred to Taiwan. However, December Exercise HSIUNG-SI (MALE LION) was destined to be overshadowed by other events. Combat alerts forced postponement of Exercise AUMEE, which had been projected for the spring of 1961.

During this time group training of other foreign armies was es-calating. Selected members of the Indonesian National Police Mobile Brigade underwent ranger training at Matsuda, Okinawa, from 10 April until 4 June 1960. In September ten Thai Border Patrol Police (BPP) began a ten-week ranger course on Okinawa. On 27 March 1961 the group dispatched MTT Thailand-A to that country to train sixty more Border Patrol Police in ranger operations, followed by another team in April. The Ranger Mobile Training Team, attached to U.S. Mil-itary Assistance Advisory Group Vietnam to conduct ranger training for the Vietnamese Army (ARVN) and Civil Guard, was expanded from two officers and two sergeants to a nine-man contingent during 1961.

The relatively obscure Exercise DALLAS II, held in northern Thailand during November 1960, proved to be of critical historical importance. Between 11 and 15 November 1960 the 315th Air Division brought 161 men of Col. Frank Mills's group headquarters and fifty tons of equipment and supplies from Okinawa into the Koke-thiem and Chiang Mai airfields. An operational base was established under tentage at Lopburi, the budding Thai Special Warfare Center being built by the brilliant Maj. Tienchai Sirisumpan. Five group teams, along with five detachments from Major Anek's Royal Thai Ranger Battalion, were deployed into northern Thailand around Chiang Mai. They acted as guerrilla bands facing a battalion of the Thai 7th Regimental Combat Team, which simulated an advancing Chinese army. The regiment set up a counterinsurgency operations center at Ban Don Kaeo, eight miles north of Chiang Mai, jointly staffed by Detachment 101 and its four teams.

Exercise DALLAS II had problems. For example, in an effort to ease parachute recovery and jump-injury evacuation, seven detachments were parachuted near a populated area in broad daylight. The 7th Thai Regiment used information from local farmers to promptly begin tracking the teams. The 19 November resupply mission for all detachments became a comedy of errors. On one drop zone the aircraft miscalculated altitude, and the bundles smashed into the ground before the parachutes deployed. A parachute-delay timing device that was activated prematurely over another resupply point caused the bundles to miss completely the small drop zone.

Nevertheless, the mixed U.S.-Thai guerrilla teams were able to move in and destroy five of seven targets. At the same time, the potential cost of such operations quickly became apparent. Patrols from the 7th Thai Regiment forced one team near Mae Rim into an area where they nearly captured it. Although the Thai soldiers uncovered the Special Forces cache of equipment, the 45th Special Forces Detachment was able to evade the strike force in the dense jungle. A Thai Ranger team was surprised and captured at Chiang Dao on 18 November, and the next day relentless pursuit bagged another Thai Ranger team near Chom Thong. A member of the 41st Special Forces Detachment was taken prisoner as he was making a reconnaissance of the main railroad bridge east of Lamphun on 18 November.

DALLAS II, which ended with the scheduled ambush of a regimental convoy on 23 November, was one of the 1st Special Forces Group's great precombat lessons in fighting through the tropics of Southeast Asia. The wargame provided additional training and staff experience to a group destined to become embroiled in adjacent battlefields within a year.[17]

The group was also involved in testing American response to local governments in trouble. During 11 to 22 February 1961, half of the group (136 personnel) was sent to Clark Air Force Base in the Philippines during Exercise LONG PASS. The Special Forces soldiers donned guerrilla-type clothing and used Filipino civilians at Clark Field to simulate a dissident native battalion, resisting American forces airlanded to assist a threatened local government. One opening success was gained when umpires assessed 75 percent casualties against the 53d Aviation Detachment and a company of the 2d Airborne Battle Group, 503d Infantry, after they helicoptered into a position parallel to and only a thousand yards from the "aggressor" Special Forces front. The Special Forces guerrilla battalion then fell back, remaining quiet and concealed during daylight, and striking advancing forces at night with stay-behind sabotage and ambush teams. Although the accompanying field problem was an additive to the major mobility purpose of the exercise, it was deemed an important preview of group capability. At the time, guerrilla fighting was expected to be the actual wartime role of Special Forces.[18]

The 1st Special Forces Group sent three teams from Special Forces Detachment 101 into Thailand on another exercise, RAJATA (named to honor the supreme commander of the Royal Thai military forces), which was played out against a command post of the 3d Marine Division 25 April to 9 May 1961. During the scenario, Special Forces Detachment 101 established a combined base at Lopburi and parachuted two of its teams into remote Sakhon Naknon and Muang Loi of eastern Thailand. The wargame was ostensibly designed to test joint Southeast Asia Treaty Organization reaction to a request for counterinsurgency assistance from Laos. To the Special Forces, its real value was the opportunity to reconnoiter a large portion of northeastern Thailand.[19]

On 28 March 1961, in his message to Congress on the defense budget, President John F. Kennedy recommended that the U.S. Army Special Forces be expanded in conjunction with related counterinsurgency forces. He had been very impressed by the "appearance and demeanor" of the Special Forces soldiers and believed that their presence in other countries could project a positive national image of great political benefit. He also considered the small number deployed around the world insufficient to have the desired impact. The Army approved a 3,000-man increase in counterinsurgency forces on 15 June 1961 as an initial step to implement President Kennedy's guidance.[20]

During 1961, Col. Noel A. Menard took over the 1st Special Forces Group. Widely respected throughout the Special Forces ranks as an outstanding leader of great integrity, he was a military academy graduate (USMA, 1937) and the first colonel selected to command a second group; he had previously commanded the 77th Special Forces Group from 1956 to 1957. He was ordered to expand his group, but additional Special Forces–qualified soldiers from the United States were not forthcoming. The Laotian situation was worsening, and more teams were required in many Asian areas. The group had no choice but to recruit 130 soldiers from regular line units in U.S. Army Pacific. They were transferred to the group before September. This brought group strength totals to sixty-six officers and 402 enlisted men. Of the 150 who were not Special Forces–qualified, 50 were learning "on the job" in A-Teams, and the rest were being taught at headquarters level. Forty-five nonjumpers had been rushed through a basic airborne course conducted by the group on Okinawa from 17 to 28 July 1961.[21]

Colonel Menard's 1st Special Forces Group was frantically trying to absorb the additional manpower when it was slated for combat duty on 16 September 1961. On that day Colonel Menard was officially informed that his group was assigned a portion of the White Star Mobile Training Team mission in Laos. All group priorities were realigned toward preparing the first detachments, scheduled to be in Bangkok on 15 October. Company D was formed into two B-Detachments and three A-Detachments. Company A was stripped to provide three more A-Detachments that were ordered into Laos on 1 December. The group was informed that its slice of the White Star requirement would amount to 412 men by April 1962: a total of twenty-four A-Detachments, four B-Detachments, and a control detachment.[22]

DALLAS III, scheduled as a grand-slam followup to the previous year's wargame in Thailand, became instead a muted U.S.-Thai counterinsurgency maneuver. Held in the same Chiang Mai vicinity from 26 November to 15 December 1961, the entire 7th Thai Regimental

Combat Team again tackled guerrilla teams formed by elements of Special Forces Detachment 101 and Royal Thai Ranger Battalion. Three Special Forces teams and Lieutenant Colonel Anek's Ranger Battalion led native guides and hill tribesmen against the 7th Thai Regiment and three other group teams. Sixty-nine Thai Border Patrol Police joined the fray, but the entire event was overshadowed by events in Laos.

By the end of the year, the 1st Special Forces Group had mushroomed to 123 officers and 586 enlisted men. Most of these had no Special Forces experience; scores were not even parachutists, and 334 soldiers lacked any Special Forces qualifications whatsoever. Even with these new men, Colonel Menard's group was spread thin. A full detachment was permanently stationed in Korea with the 1st Korean Special Forces Group, and another was performing fulltime service with the Taiwan Special Warfare Center. A ranger and a medical mobile training team were fully engaged in Vietnam, and they were joined 11 December 1961 by two Special Forces mobile training teams that arrived, in response to a Central Intelligence Agency request, to instruct the cadre of the South Vietnamese 77th Group of the Presidential Palace's Topographical Exploitation Bureau in long-range patroling, weapons, and demolitions. In addition, Menard had twenty-four officers and ninety-four sergeants providing leadership and assistance to the Forces Armées de Laos on the Laotian battlefront. The 1st Special Forces Group was at war.[23]

Notes

1. CGUSARPAC Message RJ61953, Subject: Concept of Pre–D Day Employment of 14th Special Forces Operational Detachment (Airborne), dtd 23 May 1958; DA Ltr AGAO-O(M) 322 (16 Mar 56) DCSPER, Subject: Activation of Unit.

2. All four of the Special Forces detachments organized in the Pacific during 1956 had been redesignated from previously active Special Forces detachments (SFOD) that served at Fort Bragg, North Carolina, from 15 August 1952 until 24 September 1953. However, the 12th SFOD, Area; 13th SFOD, District A; 14th SFOD, District A; and 16th SFOD, District B, had all been inactive for a span of three years and had no connection other than lineage consideration.

3. CINCPAC OPLAN 1-59 and OPLAN 32-59. At the time many war plans were designated to cover a general war, a limited war, and a war of withdrawal (reference EUSA OPLAN 60-58 and 61-58, Defense of Korea).

4. U.S. Army Pacific, *Annual History,* FY 58, p. 39, 40.

5. The 248th Quartermaster Detachment had been originally formed at Camp Lee, Virginia, as the 248th Quartermaster Laundry Section. It had shipped to England on the *Queen Mary* and arrived in France on the day of the German Ardennes counteroffensive, 16 December. After European service, the detachment was sent to Okinawa, where it was inactivated 30 January 1946. The laundry detachment was reactivated at Fort Lee on 12 April 1946 and arrived at Pusan, Korea, 4 February 1952. During the Korean War, it was awarded two Korean Presidential Unit Citations. The detachment was inactivated there on 21 February 1955 and reactivated as a Special Forces parachute rigging detachment for service with the 1st Special Forces Group on 24 June 1957.

6. The 15th Special Forces Operational Detachment, District A, (Airborne) had previously existed at Fort Bragg from 6 February to 24 September 1953.

7. Hq, USARYIS, *Command Historian Papers;* and Ralph W. Donnelly et al., *A Chronology of the United States Marine Corps,* Vol. III.

8. TAGO, *History Card* for 14th SFOD, completed in 1959; USARYIS/IX Corps, *Staff Office Report,* 1 January–31 March 1960 (Annex 185) and April–June 1960 (Annex 186).

9. U.S. Army Pacific, *History, 1st Half FY 59,* Annexes 42 and 43.

10. Eighth U.S. Army, *Annual History, 4th Installment, FY 58,* p. 69; and U.S. Army Pacific, *Annual History,* FY 58, Annex 4, Documents 89 and 90.

11. GHQ Far East Land Forces to CINCUSARPAC Ltr dtd 19 Aug 58, Subject: Jungle Warfare Course; USA Ln Ofc, US Con Gen, Singapore Ltr dtd 10 Mar 59, Subject: Jungle Warfare Courses, FARELF Training Center;

Memorandum for Record by G3, USARPAC, Subject: Air Drop of T-4 Training Device.

12. USARPAC *Annual History for 1959*, Annex 105; and General Orders 17 and 29, HQ USA Advisor Group (USAR) Hawaii, 1 Jun 59 and 5 Nov 59; USARYIS/IX Corps, *Staff Office Report*, July–September 1960 (Annex 188); TAGO, *Unit Historical Card* for 24th Special Forces Group.

13. U.S. Army Pacific, *Annual History, 2d Half FY 59*, Annexes 9, 31, and 165.

14. USARYIS/IX Corps, *Staff Office Report*, January–March 1959 (Annex 160).

15. TAGO, *Unit Historical Card*, Hq and Hq Co, 1st Special Forces Group, 1st Special Forces, and DA *Lineage and Honors* statement for the 1st Special Forces Group, 1st Special Forces; USARYIS/IX Corps, *Staff Office Report*, July–September 1960 (Annex 188).

16. USARYIS/IX Corps, *Staff Office Report*, October–December 1960 (Annex 189).

17. Headquarters, 1st Special Forces Group, *Final Report, Exercise DALLAS II*, dtd 11 December 1960.

18. USARYIS/IX Corps, *Staff Office Report*, April–June 1960 (Annex 186); and USARPAC, *Annual History, 1 July 60–30 Jun 61*.

19. USARYIS/IX Corps, *Staff Office Report*, January–March 1961 (Annex 473).

20. Office of the Assistant Chief of Staff, G3, U.S. Army Pacific, *Staff Office Report*, October–December 1961.

21. Headquarters, 1st Special Forces Group, *Operational Readiness Report*, dtd 26 September 1961.

22. DA Message 902015 dtd 5 Sep 61; CHMAAG Laos Messages ML OPT 4049 dtd 2 Sep 61 and ML OPT 5182 dtd 28 Oct 61; CINCPAC Messages DTG 021916Z Nov 61 and DTG 011948Z Dec 61; USARPAC Message RJ 98969 dtd 7 Nov 61.

23. USARYIS/IX Corps, *Staff Officer Report*, October–December 1961 (Inclosure 28).

CHAPTER 2

LAOS

1. Special Forces in Laos

Laos had achieved full independence under the Geneva Accords of 1954, but its national defense remained under the control of French military forces, which had been permitted to remain as advisors. The United States was an important partner in this arrangement, since it bankrolled the majority of Laotian army salaries, food, clothing, and equipment after 1 January 1955. Basic United States–Asian strategy was hinged on retaining Laos as a buffer state between communist North Vietnam and friendly Thailand. The Geneva Agreement prohibited the presence of American military personnel in Laos, so in December 1955 the United States established a Programs Evaluation Office (PEO) instead of a Military Assistance Advisory Group in the capital of Vientiane. The PEO was manned by "civilians," officers retired or put in reserve status for staffing purposes, to monitor how American-furnished material was being used.

PEO inability to survey the material in the field prevented any real accountability. Brig. Gen. Rothwell H. Brown (Retired), who took over the PEO in February 1957, was chagrined to learn that the French had been arbitrarily dumping thousands of American 105 mm shells, left over from the Indochina war, into Laos, where no 105 mm artillery tubes existed, and that most equipment was simply rusting or rotting in receiving centers. As a result, Brig. Gen. John A. Heintges, an active duty officer, was appointed prospective PEO chief and conducted a survey in November 1958.[1]

General Heintges found Laos to be a political quagmire. Prince

Souvanna Phouma's efforts to unify the nation under a coalition government had failed, and the North Vietnamese–backed Pathet Lao forces led by his half-brother, Prince Souphanouvong, controlled the northeastern portion of the country. The widely dispersed Armée Nationale de Laos was poorly organized and inadequately trained. The French officers and sergeants appeared indifferent, exhibiting an aloof colonial attitude that precluded any real Laotian combat improvement.

General Heintges's recommendations led to meetings between the United States and France in Paris during May 1959. There a joint U.S.-French military training plan for Laos was agreed upon. Since the French insisted that their honor mandated all tactical training responsibilities, the United States consented to provide only technical training. This combined training plan called for eight-man U.S. technical field training teams working in cooperation with French tactical advisory teams of identical size.[2]

The Laotian mission called for basic military training on an infantry battalion level in a conventional military environment. Many Pentagon officers deemed this task more appropriate for regular Army and Marine advisors than for Special Forces, which was primarily oriented toward unconventional warfare techniques designed to raise guerrilla forces behind enemy lines. However, since the Special Forces was trained to survive and operate in remote, undeveloped areas and was already organized along team lines, General Heintges secured its use.

The 77th Special Forces Group (designated the 7th Special Forces Group on 6 June 1960) at Fort Bragg, North Carolina, had been the Special Forces global response force since September 1953. The group was ordered to form secretly twelve initial teams, which would be sent to Laos for six months' duty disguised as contracted civilian specialists. Their payment, records support, and other cover functions were provided by the 902d Counterintelligence Corps Group stationed at Fort Myer, Virginia, in the Military District of Washington.[3] Each field training team (FTT) was a scaled-down Special Forces A-Detachment, consisting of a team leader and his assistant, two light-weapons and one medical specialist, one medical aidman, one radioman, and one motor maintenance specialist. This latter expert on each team had to be taken from the 82d Airborne Division, since Special Forces organization did not contain engine maintenance personnel.

The first twelve teams and a control team arrived in Laos during the last week of July 1959, just as the rainy season started and the Pathet Lao resumed active operations in the jungled mountains of northeastern Laos. Thai interpreters were hired "on loan" from the Royal Thai Army, and the control team was posted to Vientiane to provide Special Forces logistical support. The other teams were sent out three each to four rear-area training sites (Luang Prabang, Vientiane, Savannakhet, and Pakse) as part of the Laotian Training Advisory Group, Programs Evaluation Office. Special Forces field training teams were named instead of being numbered prior to March 1961. Many of these early teams used the last name of their commander, but some adopted such lively titles as Team Monkhood or Team Footsore.

Until the U.S. Military Assistance Group in Laos surfaced in the spring of 1961, the initial Special Forces soldiers wore civilian clothing and carried civilian identification cards. The Special Forces personnel lacked the normally issued RLG (Royal Laotian government) identification cards authorizing them to accompany units of the Armée Nationale de Laos. This civilian cover would later cause considerable State Department concern about the applicability of the Geneva Convention terms, after several Special Forces personnel were captured in action. The only legitimate authority for their presence in Laos, and thus their military status as proper prisoners of war, was a single letter from the Laotian Ministry of National Defense on file in Vientiane.[4]

The Special Forces training efforts in Laos got off to an uneven start because of allied infighting and Laotian lethargy. The carefully prepared Special Forces programs of phased instruction were eradicated by Laotian hesitation to offend their French advisors by cooperating too closely with the new foreign advisors. Initially, the Laotians cited the Pathet Lao offensive as sufficient reason not to release selected soldiers for planned cadre development. However, the military threat receded after scattered fighting and light casualties, since the Pathet Lao forces chose to withdraw into North Vietnam during October rather than to push on into Sam Neua. Afterwards, the required Laotian officers and sergeants still were not provided to the Special Forces training teams because the armed forces were heavily involved in political activities prior to the 1960 spring elections.

Since September, the field training teams had been forced to dispense with scheduled cadre processing. Individual teams taught whomever was made available. A discordant array of cadre, police, recruit, bataillon volontaire, and line unit instruction was conducted simultaneously. The Laotian officer corps members did not respond well to being retrained by the Americans, since they considered their French military and battlefield experience adequate reason to avoid further instruction. Other secret Laotian training programs, such as the ERAWAN Program in Thailand started in November 1959, and a jungle warfare course for officers in Malaya initiated in January 1960 barely sputtered along.

Special Forces complications in securing trainees were compounded by friction between the Americans and the French. The Programs Evaluation Office not only considered the French incompetent but suspected they were poisoning Laotian opinion against American instruction. The French were accused of taking their better officers to fight in Algeria, promoting Laotian officers on the basis of family status or lingering colonial considerations instead of on soldiering qualities. The French were also accused of having lost too much prestige by their defeat at the hands of the Viet Minh to command Laotian respect. For their part, the French viewed the Americans as unwelcome upstarts who did not comprehend the complexities of Southeast Asian warfare.

Many joint training efforts were hampered by constant bickering and disputes over authority. For instance, the French allowed Special Forces to use paper bull's-eye targets on firing ranges, but considered employment of mechanical pop-up targets as tactical training, and thus their exclusive prerogative. Special Forces chafed at the restrictions and sought training sites away from the centers. The Special Forces field training teams and the French Military Mission were soon working independently, while the nonchalant Laotians simply avoided any involvement not forced upon them.

The field training teams rotated normally throughout this early period, which lasted until the summer of 1960. The first Special Forces contingent was relieved on 13 to 17 January 1960 by a new set of teams, which in turn was replaced by another group arriving in Vientiane on 29 June. They arrived just prior to the turning point in United States–Laotian relations, which would transform Special Forces soldiers from instructors into combat advisors.

On 9 August 1960 Capt. Kong Le, the commander of the crack 774-man 2d Bataillon de Parachutiste posted to the mud flats outside

Vientiane after hard fighting on the Sam Neua front, staged a coup d'état while most Laotian governmental officials and military leaders were in Luang Prabang. Kong Le and most of his paratroopers had received Special Forces training and were considered the best troops in the army. Kong Le himself was a graduate of the CIA-sponsored Philippine scout and ranger school and had a deep hatred of high-level corruption. He announced that he desired a united Laos free of foreign influence, demanded the establishment of a coalition government under Prince Souvanna Phouma and a return to strict neutrality. The period immediately following Kong Le's coup was characterized by confusion about what was going on.[5]

Although Prince Phouma was installed with royal assent, civil war erupted, and France and the United States found themselves at odds on major policy. Both nations ordered the majority of their training assistance stopped when the coup occurred. France favored the new neutralist government of Prince Phouma, but the United States vacillated. Although Capt. Kong Le hurriedly raised formations around Vientiane (ten battalions by December, assisted by Soviet aerial delivery of supplies, including a battery of North Vietnamese artillery), he controlled little territory outside the city. Gen. Phoumi Nosavan gathered anticoup forces for a march on the capital.

While the Programs Evaluation Office in Vientiane retained relations with the legal government, the United States established a "rebel MAAG" under the Deputy Chief of PEO, Col. Albert Brownfield. Located at Savannakhet, over 200 miles downriver from Vientiane, Brownfield's headquarters actively assisted Gen. Phoumi Nosavan's countercoup forces. Before Gen. Phoumi Nosavan could get moving, some of his line troops were trounced by tough Kong Le paratroopers led by Pathet Lao commanders. Colonel Brownfield decided to invigorate the countercoup command with the rebel MAAG Special Forces team. Finally released from all tripartite training restrictions, the Special Forces enjoyed a new freedom of action as operational advisors instead of as technical trainers.

The countercoup advance toward Vientiane started on 25 November 1960, spearheaded by Special Forces officers and sergeants with the forward units. Gen. Phoumi Nosavan's Groupement Mobile 1 (roughly equivalent to a brigade) fought through heavy resistance, stormed across the Ca Dinh River, and recaptured the key town of Paksane. On 13 December 1960 Special Forces soldiers jumped into the critical communications crossroads of Ban Tha Deua with the 1st and 3d Bataillons de Parachutiste and pushed aside light opposition. Two days later Vientiane was surrounded. The battle for the capital began, during which the U.S. embassy was hit by artillery fire and burned out. The capital fell after sharp rearguard fighting on 17 December 1960, and a new Laotian government was declared by the victors.[6]

Groupement Mobile 15 of the new Forces Armées de Laos continued the pursuit of Kong Le's forces retreating away from Vientiane north along Route 13. This northward advance was coordinated with a Groupement 11 thrust south down Route 13 from Luang Prabang. Both drives were aimed at cutting off Kong Le at the vital junction town of Sala Phou Khoun, where the road joined east-west Route 7 leading to North Vietnam. Groupement Mobile 15 breached the main Kong Le defenses along the Nam Lik in a Special Forces–directed river assault crossing on 12 January. Four days later the Soviet airhead of Vang Vieng was captured, along with considerable quantities of materiel. Sala Phou Khoun was finally reached on 4 February 1961, but the Kong Le–Pathet Lao forces withdrew safely along Route 7 toward the Plaine de Jarres. That critical area of grassy, rolling hills had been seized weeks earlier by Soviet-airlifted Pathet Lao forces advancing in concert with North Vietnamese troops moving down Route 7 from the east. The bulk of Kong Le's troops had escaped Gen. Phoumi Nosavan's trap, and the Pathet Lao remained in control of northeastern Laos.

Further action against the Pathet Lao fizzled out. On 7 March 1961 the Pathet Lao counterattacked and drove Groupement 12 (the new number of the old Groupement 15) back to the Nam Lik riverline. The groupement withdrew toward Vang Vieng but was closely pursued by two Pathet Lao battalions, which attacked early on the morning of 22 April. Capt. Walter H. Moon's four-man Field Training Team FTT-59 of the 7th Special Forces Group was attached to the 6th Bataillon d'infanterie at Ban Pha Home, about thirty miles north of Vang Vieng. The battalion was subjected to a heavy and accurate artillery barrage and was rapidly flanked.

Shortly after the battalion commander announced that they were cut off, the perimeter collapsed and the Pathet Lao quickly overran the battalion positions. Sfc. John M. Bischoff and Sgt. Gerald M. Biber jumped aboard an armored car, heading south on Route 13, along with some Laotian soldiers, in an effort breakout. They crouched behind the turret, but the car came under heavy grenade attack. Sergeant Bischoff fired a machine gun from the vehicle until he was shot through the neck and killed. Sergeant Biber had already been wounded and was apparently killed by stick grenades thrown against the armored car. The vehicle was halted and its crew captured.[7]

Sgt. Orville R. Ballenger escaped through the jungle and linked up with some Laotian soldiers. They found a boat and were going downriver when they were surprised and captured by the Pathet Lao seven days later. Sergeant Ballenger was eventually released on 15 August 1962 as part of the peace talks. Capt. Walter H. Moon was captured in the initial attack. He tried to escape twice during his confinement, and on the last attempt was wounded in the chest and head. His head injury caused him to become mentally unbalanced, and after several months of persecution, he was executed in his prison quarters by a Meo guard and Pathet Lao officer.[8]

Vang Vieng fell to the Pathet Lao as Groupement 12 made further forced withdrawals during the early morning hours of 23 April. An uneasy truce was arranged on 3 May 1961, and the Special Forces entered a year-long span of raids, limited counterattacks, and bitter fighting for certain locations, known as the "Cease-Fire Period." This proved to be the most crucial period of Special Forces presence in Laos as the WHITE STAR Mobile Training Teams.

2. WHITE STAR

Just days before the loss of Team Moon (but unknown to them), the U.S. Military Assistance Advisory Group Laos had been formally established on 19 April 1961. The Special Forces soldiers were allowed to put on their green berets and full uniforms, and the Special Forces teams were redesignated as WHITE STAR Mobile Training Teams. This change was possible because the Mission Militaire Française d'Instruction pres le Gouvernement Royal du Laos had been withdrawn during the fall of 1960 after the Kong Le coup. The PEO requested nine more eight-man Special Forces teams to fill the gap left by the French withdrawal and to help activate four new Laotian battalions. Three of these new teams, FTT-63, FTT-64, and FTT-65, arrived in March, but they were merged into veteran teams to provide extra manpower and to replace losses.

The twelve Special Forces field training teams had eleven men each by the end of spring. Total authorized Special Forces strength in Laos, including the twenty-two man control team, added up to 154.[9] The authorization of twelve additional Special Forces intelligence specialists on 16 August boosted team levels to normal A-Detachment twelve-man complements. These teams were then split to enable more battalions to be advised, but the smaller six-man elements were found to be inadequately manned for dual training and combat advisory responsibilities.

Many WHITE STAR teams moved from the training centers into the field as conventional operational advisors. Other teams served as the first instructors for newly opened Laotian military schools. Still other teams specialized in forming and equipping Meo and Kha tribal shock companies. In addition to providing combat advice, Special Forces advisors coordinated aerial resupply missions, insured radio communications, and provided medical assistance. Special Forces personnel also acted as the "eyes and ears" of MAAG Laos, gathering intelligence and reporting how equipment and supplies were being used. They also performed critical civic action missions. Despite the reluctance of some Laotian commanders, Special Forces presence was established in most line battalions of the Forces Armées de Laos.

WHITE STAR strength continued to grow upward through the summer as more advisors were placed into the Forces Armées du Royaume, so named by the King in September 1961. By late October 300 Special Forces personnel were in Laos and another 112 were being prepared for overseas deployment at Fort Bragg and Okinawa. The Special Forces used part of this increase to expand development of the Meo and Kha tribal forces.

The Meo, ethnically related to the Chinese, were primitive, semi-nomadic mountaineers who had been driven from many of their native areas by the fighting in northern Laos. The Meo were held in low regard by both the Laotians and Vietnamese, and the Central Intelligence Agency was able to capitalize on Meo resentment against both groups by arming them against the North Vietnamese–sponsored Pathet Lao. The majority of the 8,000 armed Meo warriors were led by Col. Vang Pao, who relied on tough, secretly imported Thai Police Aerial Reinforcement Unit (PARU) teams to advise and direct his scattered forces, loosely called Groupement B.

In late 1961 the Central Intelligence Agency began using WHITE STAR teams to train the growing number of Meo 100-man "Auto

Défense de Choc" (shock) companies. Special Forces experts favored dispersing Meo guerrillas throughout the highlands to ambush and raid Pathet Lao forces. The Meo tribesmen were excellent warriors and were converted into irregular units that were able to defend and capture key military territorial objectives. The CIA gave Special Forces a great deal of material support and allowed them maximum flexibility. In May 1962 a Meo training center was established by Special Forces at a fortress known as Site 20, at the foot of Phu Bia Mountain, and six WHITE STAR mobile training teams (FTT-3, 14, 19, 33, 40, and 41) were involved in the Meo program.[10]

The Special Forces exercised total control over training the Kha tribal groups in Operation PINCUSHION under Team BA. The Kha tribes were scattered throughout Laos but were especially prevalent in the south. The Special Forces teams began forming special Kha shock companies in December 1961 to clear the Bolovens Plateau region, with the eventual target of slashing into the Ho Chi Minh trail network, which braided through much of southeastern Laos. Kha patrols had the potential of gathering intelligence and disrupting this supply route to the Viet Cong in South Vietnam.

Any program to organize and arm the Kha tribal groups was viewed with displeasure by the Laotian government. Special Forces Lt. Col. Arthur D. "Bull" Simons obtained the initial money and material from the CIA. The K-1 Kha Hune tribal Auto Défense de Choc company, popularly known as the "Kha Maquis," was formed on 13 December 1961. MAAG reluctantly recognized the program in January 1962 but left WHITE STAR on its own. By the end of May, the twelfth Kha Auto Défense de Choc company was being raised from refugees at Saravane.

Ten WHITE STAR teams were rapidly fielding Kha combat units (FTT-4, 6, 12, 16, 17, 18, 25, 42, 45, 48) in several different locations on or near the Bolovens Plateau. Unfortunately, the U.S. government considered the latest Special Forces irregular force too independent of the Laotian government. On 1 June 1962 MAAG pulled in the reins, just as the Special Forces–led Khas were starting to move against the Ho Chi Minh trail. Placed under MAAG auspices, the promising Kha tribal program was abandoned that fall.[11]

The WHITE STAR mission reached its peak strength, 433 Special Forces personnel, in July 1962 as the Cease-Fire Period ended. Since the previous April, WHITE STAR had trained and advised the Forces

Armées du Royaume, staffed Laotian military schools, and conducted successful Meo and Kha unconventional warfare programs. WHITE STAR soldiers had quickly discarded the green beret in the field, as it offered no protection from either the weather or insects falling from jungle vegetation down the back of the neck. Instead, the Special Forces soldiers wore locally purchased, wide-brimmed Australian "bush hats" in camouflaged fabric. They carried M1 and M2 carbines and some M3 .45-caliber submachine guns, as well as Bren light machine guns and Sten/Owen carbines. The Laotian soldiers were armed with M1 rifles, Thompson submachine guns, and Browning automatic rifles, which were obsolete compared to the AK-47 and other lightweight, fully automatic Sino-Soviet weapons being used by the Pathet Lao.

The Special Forces soldiers found inadequate maps and lack of supplies to be routine problems. Greater crises resulted because the Laotian officers considered it a grievous loss of face to follow suggestions from lower-ranking American officers or sergeants. The Special Forces advisors were distressed by the lack of leadership that caused many Laotian units to perform poorly on the battlefield. There were repeated instances of disorderly retreat at the mere sound of enemy fire, or panic after only a few casualties. Physically unharmed Laotians, who suffered the "loss of friendly spirits" because of the close passage of a bullet or a nearby mortar explosion, were considered priority evacuation cases by their comrades. They were taken as quickly as possible to a temple where Buddhist priests could restore the spirit to its proper position of protection.[12]

WHITE STAR FTT-40 and FTT-41 were typically frustrated in their efforts to assist Laotian operations during the Nam Beng Valley campaign waged over the winter of 1961–1962. FTT-40 had been helicoptered into Muong Houn in late September 1961 to advise the 3d Bataillon d'infanterie, reinforced at the time with a volunteer (militia) battalion and a special battalion of Chinese mercenaries under "General Lu." After intensive last-minute training, the polyglot task force headed up the valley toward the objective of Muong Sai. On 26 December the Laotian infantry and the Chinese were surrounded on Hill 1378, just short of the town, as the team was trying to keep the militia moving up the road.

The Laotians and Chinese managed to fight their way off the hill but were chased sixty miles down the road until they were across the

Mekong River. FTT-40 found itself in a village on the last day of the year with one local militia company. The entire company ran off, hid their weapons, and changed clothing. The Pathet Lao regulars were rapidly approaching, and the Special Forces soldiers had no choice but to radio for helicopters to take them out.

The team spent more than a week rounding up 250 deserters in the nearest city, Luang Prabang, then escorted them to the shaken 3d Bataillon d'infanterie in order to rebuild it. The new battalion commander, Major Bong, stayed drunk and put armed guards around the team members. After several days the team leader threatened to leave. Faced with the possible withdrawal of American aid, Major Bong "began to lay off the bottle and take hold." The battalion was still in bad shape. Its heavy weapons consisted of only two 81mm mortars (one with no sighting device) and a 75mm recoilless rifle, which was unserviceable. There was a shortage of basic ammunition, and no medical supplies at all.

Despite the battalion's deplorable condition, Major Bong was promoted to lieutenant colonel and the battalion was ordered back into the Nam Beng Valley. FTT-40 was replaced by FTT-41 on 2 February 1962, and the 3d Bataillon d'infanterie had advanced as far as the original jumping-off point at Muong Houn by early March. On 1 April the Pathet Lao started counterattacking. Colonel Bong moved his command post with FTT-41 to the airstrip south of town. Shortly after two o'clock on the morning of 3 April, the team was suddenly awakened by the sound of automatic weapons. One Special Forces soldier opened his eyes to see the upper walls of their grass hut being peppered by bullets. Sergeant Miller dashed out, looked around, and reported back that Bong and his staff had already run away.

The team discarded all its equipment except for a radio and each man's rifle. They broke brush as they moved to the Nam Beng, avoiding any trails, and waited for rescue helicopters. At 10:00 A.M. on 4 April, FTT-41 was extracted and returned to Luang Prabang. Although it was customary not to return the same team to a unit that had deserted it under fire, FTT-41 was back with the 3d Bataillon d'infanterie on 29 April 1962, since a new Laotian commander was put in charge. The battalion was again ordered to take Muong Houn. The team was unable to fulfill its training role because the new commander refused to allow his men to undergo instruction. A thirty-minute Pathet Lao mortar barrage on 9 May caused the battalion to scramble south back across the Mekong River.

There was no discourse between the Laotian commander and the Special Forces team, which ambled along and followed him. After walking farther south for an hour, the commander asked a native if there was a suitable place on the mountain for a helicopter landing site. After he heard there was none, he turned around, and the battalion reversed its direction and moved toward the Mekong River again. On 11 May FTT-41 was informed by the battalion commander that he could no longer control, feed, or resupply his men with ammunition. The battalion then moved and reached Muong Hong Sa on 5 June so the commander could attend a celebration. In his final report the team leader stated that the operational utilization of FTT-41 had been a complete farce. The only contribution the Special Forces was allowed to make was to call in helicopter transport and to give away its radio batteries.

Just north of the Nam Beng Valley, at Nam Tha, FTT-2 and FTT-3 had a similar degree of noncooperation. FTT-2 had been assigned to the 2d Bataillon d'infanterie in October 1961. The next month the battalion was ordered to take Ban Na Mo twenty miles to the east, which it reached after three days. There the Pathet Lao occupied an old, ruined French outpost on the high ground, and the first attack against it was repulsed. The Pathet Lao abandoned the fort during the night, and the 1st Bataillon took possession of Ban Na Mo on 2 December. The 2d Bataillon from Nam Tha, escorted by FTT-3, joined the 1st Bataillon at the town on 11 January 1962.

The 2d Bataillon moved farther east and was told to prepare to advance south on Muong Sai within three days. Muong Sai had been the target of the previous Nam Beng Valley drive from the opposite direction just three weeks earlier, and the Special Forces advisors wondered why nothing had been coordinated. The battalion occupied new hillside positions on the afternoon of 20 January in anticipation of attack orders. The team leader of FTT-3 was flown by helicopter to Team BB headquarters at Luang Prabang, where he was instructed to discourage any Laotian plans to reattack Muong Sai.

When the team leader returned to the battalion's forward lines, they were already under sporadic 120mm mortar and recoilless rifle fire. The Pathet Lao aim was so poor that most of the shells sailed over the battalion positions into the valley behind them, and there were no casualties. Since the battalion commander refused advice to send out patrols, no one knew what was in front of them. On the morning of 21 January, half the battalion suddenly bolted to the rear, and the company in front of the command post began exchanging rifle fire with the Pathet Lao. The team leader tried to get the battalion to use its 81mm mortars, but the commander was afraid that firing the weapons would give away the location of his command post.

Later that morning the Laotians from the company in front of the battalion headquarters began drifting through the area. When the team leader went to the battalion commander for an explanation, he found the Laotians tearing down their tents and moving away. Rifle fire crackled through the foliage overhead, and FTT-3 frantically destroyed their own equipment as they heard the unopposed Pathet Lao yelling and climbing the hill.

Directly to the west, the 1st Bataillon abandoned the fort at Ban Na Mo the same morning after an abrupt but inaccurate mortar barrage. FTT-2 tried in vain to get the battalion to reoccupy the outpost, and all control vanished when retreating members of the 2nd Bataillon were seen coming from the east. The FTT-2 team leader asked the arriving battalion commander about the fate of FTT-3 and was told that an entire company was with FTT-3 at a designated rallying point and that everyone was safe. The two battalion commanders then walked along the trail together, followed by their men.

After an hour's march, everyone sat down and rested. The Special Forces used this opportunity to scan the fort with binoculars and spotted four or five people wearing khaki uniforms and white hats on the outpost position. The Laotians insisted that these were Viet Minh, and the news soon had the entire column retreating again. Both battalion commanders left FTT-2 behind trying to pack up the team radio. The team leader kept six tahans (village militiamen) and a light machine gun with the team, waited until more Laotians passed by, and ascertained that FTT-3 was not far behind. About 4:30 P.M. FTT-3 came up the road guarding the rear of the Laotian withdrawal, and the Special Forces soldiers linked up. The helicopters were seen overhead, but radio contact failed. Red smoke grenades were pitched, and the helicopters directed them to a small clearing on a ridge where both teams were extracted.

On 24 January 1962 both Laotian battalions regrouped on Hill 1620 about seven miles closer to Nam Tha. FTT-1 was assigned to the headquarters of Groupement 11, in charge of the hill defenses. The groupement commander became dismayed after a small 2d Bataillon firefight with a probing Pathet Lao patrol the next day. He informed the FTT-1 team leader that he had no faith in his men, expected to be attacked en masse the next morning, and was already planning a withdrawal. The team leader suggested that an AT-6 aircraft bombing strike could improve the situation, but the groupement commander declined.

The front collapsed shortly before noon on 26 January when desultory rifle fire sent the 1st Bataillon fleeing in disarray toward Nam Tha. Shortly afterwards, their sister battalion also fled the hilltop. Two days later a new team, FTT-14, found that the 2d Bataillon d'infanterie was missing a quarter of its personnel and all crew-served weapons.

The Laotian government began shoring up the road defenses of Nam Tha with fresh new battalions airlifted in from secret Project EKARAD training in Thailand (the 28th and 30th Bataillons d'infanterie). After the Nam Tha airstrip was shelled by Pathet Lao artillery, the 1st Bataillon de Parachutiste was jumped in on 12 February 1962. The paratroopers advanced, enabling American planes to land three 105mm howitzers with their assembly team of Filipino technicians on 6 March. In the same month Groupement Mobile 15 (Airborne) headquarters and its 55th Bataillon de Parachutiste were jumped into the Nam Tha front. The groupement's third paratrooper battalion, the 11th, arrived on 16 April. American advisors considered the paratrooper force well disciplined and good fighters. On the first of May, more than nine Laotian line and volunteer battalions were deployed in front of Nam Tha.

The paratroopers were decimated in mid-April fighting retaking Hills 1620 and 1860. Although the eastern line was still strong, the Laotians decided to retreat after they perceived a threat on the town from the north. The planned retrograde movement fell apart because two of the paratrooper battalions had been reduced below their ability to function effectively and the rest of the Laotians ran for the rear. When the Pathet Lao attack came on 5 May the 1st Bataillon de Parachutiste was able to delay for only six hours. During the entire episode, the WHITE STAR team at Nam Tha (FTT-1) was not informed of any events. The team learned of the battle when a wounded paratrooper seeking medical treatment drifted into the town.

The team leader sought information from Brig. Gen. La Patham-mavong but was told nothing except to make sure helicopters were available the next morning. Before dawn on 6 May, shellfire began falling into the outskirts of town, and at 7:00 A.M. the Laotians began spiking their howitzers. FTT-1 destroyed all its equipment and both jeeps and evaded to the emergency pickup point, where helicopters rescued them at nine o'clock that morning.

The entire Laotian force streamed past Nam Tha and headed for the Thai border at Ban Houei Sai, fifteen miles farther west along the road. There the Laotians commandeered the ferry and every boat or raft to get across the Mekong River. Several Special Forces teams volunteered to go back into Laos and patrolled some distance toward Nam Tha. After encountering no resistance, they attempted to get the Laotians to come back across into their own country. The Laotians refused. Groupement 15 was not successfully reassembled until between 15 and 25 May 1962, when it was flown back to the Laotian airborne training center at Seno from Thailand and reequipped. Northwestern Laos had been lost.

On 12 June 1962 the three princes of Laos agreed on a coalition government and signed a declaration of neutrality on 23 July. Under its terms all foreign military personnel were ordered withdrawn from the country by 6 October 1962. The forty-eight WHITE STAR Mobile Training teams were withdrawn from Laos from 21 through 28 September, the four B-Detachments left from 27 September through 2 October, and Team Control departed 6 October 1962. On that day the Special Forces WHITE STAR mission in the Laotian conflict ended, except for a clandestine Special Forces presence that was maintained with the Meo tribesmen and supported by Air America.

The Special Forces had completed its first Asian combat assignment under difficult conditions, aggravated by the lack of French cooperation and shifting directions caused by internal changes within the Laotian government. The Special Forces advisory effort during the Laotian emergency had rapidly expanded past initial Pentagon expectations. The Special Forces had arrived in Laos as technical instructors, but became full-fledged operational military advisors on a conventional battlefield.

The most important result was the new role Special Forces had assumed as an instrument of national policy. By virtue of President Kennedy's belief in its individual and collective excellence, the Special Forces became the principal counterinsurgency force of the United States. The wartime Special Forces was forged in the jagged Laotian mountains and forest plateaus in direct contrast to its intended wartime mission as guerrilla cadre. In Laos it fielded armed hill tribes and regular units against standard combat formations fighting a civil war. In Laos, as in Vietnam, Special Forces soldiers were employed as elite troops able to execute long-range special missions, to lead normal infantry, and to train remote, indigenous minorities. Actual missions against true enemy guerrilla bands were rare, and the Special Forces was never allowed to penetrate denied areas to establish guerrilla units.

While the Special Forces soldiers performed admirably under dangerous and frustrating conditions, their sponsored Forces Armées du Royaume did not fare well on the battlefield. Some of this could be attributed to hasty team preparation, the language barrier, and the six-month rotational tours that gave teams too little time to reach their goals. However, most of the blame belonged to larger considerations outside Special Forces control. These included operational constraints, fluctuating U.S. policy, refusal of Laotian officers to heed Special Forces advice, and the generally low fighting spirit of the Laotian soldiers compared to that of the Pathet Lao.

The Laotian conflict also produced the first Special Forces breach with the regular Army advisory command structure. In the standard Special Forces organization, B-Detachments were designed to serve as intermediary headquarters between the A-Detachments and the C-Detachment. With this in mind, four B-Detachments (Teams BA thru BD) were sent to Laos to help the C-Detachment (Team Control) in Vientiane control the growing number of WHITE STAR field training teams, forty-eight of which (FTT-1 through FTT-48) were in country at the peak of Laotian operations. The Special Forces effectively used this structure to circumvent the MAAG regional advisors, since B-Team commanders could deal directly with Team Control at the highest MAAG level. The ability of Special Forces to interact directly with other agencies, such as the Central Intelligence Agency and the Defense Intelligence Agency, also allowed Special Forces to avoid regular MAAG channels.

For Special Forces, the lasting legacy of Laos was not manifested in the combat results or the inconveniences of higher advisory superstructures, but rather in the combat experience gained and relationships established between other U.S. military components and governmental agencies. For example, the Special Forces interacted directly with the regular Army advisory group, the embassy, and the Central Intelligence Agency. The Special Forces also experienced the frustrations and inherent complexities of leading native forces in an actual combat environment. Valuable jungle warfare knowledge was gained in conjunction with terrain and climatic familiarization in a region of the world, Southeast Asia, that would engage Special Forces efforts throughout the next decade. Finally, the chance to actually test weapons, communications, and operating systems in combat provided an excellent opportunity to improve techniques: an experience that could not be duplicated in sterile training situations.

Notes

1. U.S. Program Evaluation Office, *U.S. Operations Mission to Laos*. General Heintges was a colorful West Pointer who had been wounded during heavy fighting in Italy during World War II.

2. RAC-T-435, *Case Study of U.S. Counterinsurgency Operations in Laos, 1955–1962*.

3. The 902d Counterintelligence Corps Group had been activated as the 902d Counterintelligence Corps Detachment at Hollandia, New Guinea, on 23 November 1944. It was disbanded on Luzon in the Philippine Islands on 22 July 1945 and later served briefly as a reserve component at Fort Smith, Arkansas. The detachment was activated in the regular Army on 8 January 1952 at Fort Holabird, Maryland, and redesignated as a group on 15 December 1957. On 25 July 1961 it became the 902d Intelligence Corps Group. The 902d directly supported all Special Forces operations throughout the Laotian emergency.

4. CHMAAG Laos Message L-OPT 1756, dtd 27 April 1961.

5. Headquarters, U.S. Army Special Warfare Center Study, *Laos*, dtd 16 February 1961.

6. The U.S. embassy was destroyed on 15 December 1960, and the American personnel made their way to Nong Khai, Thailand, about ten miles away. Three U.S. soldiers were wounded by mortar and machine gun fire.

7. Reports as to the deaths of Bischoff and Biber came from Laotian survivors and were contradictory. The account of Bischoff's death was told by Captain Siduene to Sergeant Ballenger while both were prisoners.

8. ACSI-SC Memorandum for Chief, Security Division, Subject: Released American Prisoners from Laos, dtd 29 August 1962; CHMAAG Laos Message ML-OPT 1679 dtd 23 Apr 61; Secretary of State Message DA IN 256360 dtd 17 August 1962. Details of Captain Moon's death were related by Grant Wolfkill, an NBC correspondent captured after his helicopter went down because of engine failure. The Pathet Lao were convinced he was a colonel and placed him in the room next to Moon. Wolfkill could see through a crack in the fiberboard wall.

9. DA Cable to CINCPAC, dtd 21 April 1961. DA Message PEO-OPT 627 dtd 13 Feb 61, planned the nine teams (FTT-63 through FTT-71) to arrive in three increments and be sponsored by Teams Control, Thrower, Moon, Rachui, McCollum, McWhinnie, Lamar, Metcalf, and Garrison. The Special Warfare Center at Fort Bragg also dispatched a twelve-man Psychological Warfare Team under Lt. Col. Charles A. Murray from the United States to Laos on 28 January 1961. USCONARC Message 101959Z Jan 61. The WHITE STAR mobile training teams, however, retained their field training

team letter-number designations, such as FTT-48, and were only rarely initialed as WSMTT.

10. CINCPAC, *Weekly Intelligence Digest* for years 1959 through 1962.

11. WHITE STAR Mobile Training Teams, MAAG Laos, *Kha Guerrilla Warfare Program in Bolovens Plateau and Saravane Area.*

12. RAC-SP-1 (SEA) Staff Paper, "Suitability and Effectiveness of Weapons and Equipment Used in U.S.-Supported Operations with the Royal Laos Army," September 1962.

CHAPTER 3

VIETNAM ASSIGNMENT

1. Special Forces in Vietnam

The Laotian emergency overshadowed the expanding Army Special Forces combat presence in the divided lower half of the country directly to the east of Laos: South Vietnam. Special Forces Laotian experience was directly infused into Vietnam's rice fields and misting rain forests. There the Army's Special Forces would become engaged in its first major war and would carve out an extraordinary battlefield reputation under the most adverse geographical and political conditions.

Initial Special Forces efforts in South Vietnam, as in other eastern Asian countries, were directed toward training the cadre of indigenous units that needed expertise in unconventional warfare tactics, such as raiding or long-range patrolling. The South Vietnamese had no Special Forces of their own. Early in 1957 seventy selected officers and sergeants of the Army of the Republic of Vietnam (ARVN) received parachutist training in Saigon and communications instruction in Vung Tau. They were then regrouped in Nha Trang, where fifty-eight underwent four months of commando training taught by the first Special Forces personnel introduced into Vietnam, two officers and ten sergeants from the 14th Special Forces Detachment, during the summer and fall. During that mission, Capt. Harry G. Cramer, a regular Army officer (USMA, 1946) was killed in a training accident on 21 October 1957 near Nha Trang. He was the first Special Forces soldier to be killed in Vietnam.

Forty-four of these trainees formed the nucleus of the Vietnamese 1st Observation Group (also referred to as Reconnaissance Joint Unit

I), activated at Nha Trang on 1 November 1957 under the control of the Presidential Liaison Office, or "Sixth Office," a former French counterespionage unit. This component, later redesignated the Topographical Exploitation Bureau of the Presidential Palace or Presidential Survey Office, was answerable only to President Diem. During 1958, the Vietnamese 1st Observation Group conducted field training exercises under Special Forces direction and expanded to 400 men by December. With it the Special Forces hoped to have an anticommunist guerrilla cadre in case of global war, which, at the time, was imagined to include China's early consumption of southeastern Asia.

The 1st Observation Group remained politically oriented during the Diem regime with a special intelligence mission. It was arrogant and occupied a privileged status divorced from the constant field service performed by other segments of Saigon's national defense apparatus. Actual combat missions were few and far between. In 1960 it briefly sojourned into the swamp forests of southernmost Vietnam. During the next two years, the group occasionally poked along the Laotian border in Operation LEI-YU under the CIA-sponsored PACIFIC OCEAN Project.

In November 1961 the Vietnamese 1st Observation Group was redesignated the Vietnamese 77th Group, in honor of the American Special Forces group of the same number, which had since been renumbered the 7th Special Forces Group under the combat arms reorganization in the United States. On the last day of the month, four officers and twenty-four enlisted soldiers of the 1st Special Forces Group arrived in Vietnam to teach weapon techniques, medical and demolitions training, long-range patrolling, and guerrilla-oriented operations to selected Vietnamese 77th Group personnel. These agents were used in cross-border raids into North Vietnam and Laos. The bulk of the group remained aloof and out of harm's way.[1]

Since the Army had dispensed with ranger formations after the Korean War, the Special Forces was also charged with ranger training requirements in foreign lands. Ranger training was a specialized but conventional infantry task and one of the constant peculiarities that blurred the line between unconventional Special Forces doctrine and its actual field practice, that is, using members of Special Forces as ordinary military instructors. The Special Forces was directed to train sixty ARVN ranger companies. To accomplish the task, three ranger centers were established in May, 1960: at Da Nang, Nha Trang, and

Song Mao. They were staffed by twelve Vietnamese graduates from ranger school at Fort Benning, Georgia, but were actually run by thirty instructors from the 7th Special Forces Group. Early in 1961 these personnel were replaced by a nine-man mobile training team with four personnel from 1st Special Forces Group and five soldiers from the 25th Infantry Division. The four Special Forces personnel were deployed to Da Nang and Nha Trang to supervise ranger cadre development, while the other soldiers went to Song Mao, northeast of Saigon, to support preparations for the Civil Guard program. For the next two years rotating Special Forces mobile training teams from Okinawa gave ranger instruction.[2]

In Vietnam, unlike Laos, regular Army and Marine advisors of the Military Assistance Advisory Group Vietnam trained the line units of the South Vietnamese military and advised the strategic hamlet program. Special Forces advisors were reserved for clandestine, paramilitary, and special unit projects. These were initially controlled by the Central Intelligence Agency's Combined Studies Group, which operated as a staff section of MAAG Vietnam.

In actual fact the MAAG Vietnam strength of 1,062 personnel as of 12 December 1961 was surpassed by an additional 1,209 military and civilian personnel working under the headquarters on classified projects. With the creation of U.S. Military Assistance Command Vietnam (MACV) under General Harkins on 8 February 1962, the CIA Combined Studies Group staff section was reattached to the new joint MACV command effective 1 May 1962. Although later Special Forces efforts were conducted largely independent of CIA control after the conclusion of Operation SWITCHBACK, these three tasks (special unit, clandestine, and paramilitary projects) constituted the triplex Special Forces mission throughout the Vietnam War.

Special unit training encompassed ARVN ranger and Vietnamese 77th Group training and merged into ongoing clandestine raiding missions. For example, as early as 1961, the Central Intelligence Agency retained one reinforced Special Forces A-Detachment at Thu Duc outside Saigon, which was dedicated entirely to secret agency cross-border operations. Missions into North Vietnam and Laos were conducted on an increasing basis, and by 1963 an average of four teams trained by CIA and Special Forces entered North Vietnam each month to conduct harassment and psychological operations.[3]

Regardless of these special and ranger mission requirements, the primary assignment for Special Forces in Vietnam evolved in conjunction with the burgeoning paramilitary program, an emergency expedient developed to help Saigon maintain order in the provinces. This program had its roots in early American efforts to beef up President Diem's regular army, the ARVN, by forming a wide variety of paramilitary, or nonregular, groups to render an armed presence at the village level. The most important of these paramilitary outfits were the Civil Guard and Self-Defense Corps (later renamed the Regional Forces and Popular Forces, respectively), which existed as a fulltime but ragamuffin constabulary in the provinces. The retitled Regional Forces/Popular Forces, or RF/PF, were popularly known as the Ruff-Puffs. The Viet Cong, increasingly able to challenge and defeat the ARVN in open combat, usually made short work of the poorly trained, and poorly equipped static security forces. By late 1961 the Saigon regime had lost all real control over many rural provinces. The CIA estimated that roughly half of the country's western highlanders were probably Viet Cong sympathizers.[4]

2. The Montagnards

The western highlands, the frontier fringes, and the interior of Vietnam were inhabited by several minority groups. Most had been pushed out of the more fertile regions of the country by the Vietnamese over the course of history. Others were armed religious splinter parties or long-standing opponents of Vietnamese mainstream culture. Basically, the Saigon regime held all minority groups in contempt as either primitive savages or potential dangers to the central government, even as paramilitary fighters, and deliberately excluded them from all defense efforts. The United States insisted that the rapidly deteriorating military situation left South Vietnam no choice but to utilize all available manpower, if only to keep territory from falling under VC domination by default. The South Vietnamese continued to resist mobilization of such resources.

One of the largest minority groups, the isolated Montagnards, "mountain people," had been identified by the Central Intelligence Agency as potential anti–Viet Cong allies. In late 1961 Col. Gilbert B. Layton, a CIA officer serving as Chief of the Combined Studies Division, MAAG Vietnam, conceived the Civilian Irregular Defense Group (CIDG) program as a means to win over the Montagnards. In 1961, with the assistance of David Nuttle, an unwitting

International Voluntary Services (IVS) official who was engaged in an agricultural project with the Rhade tribe in Darlac Province, Colonel Layton commenced development of Rhade allegiance. Later in the same year he turned to the Special Forces soldiers, who were gaining success with Meo and Kha tribesmen in the Laotian conflict, to provide the required training and advisors. The CIDG program was destined to be the most crucial Special Forces task throughout the Vietnam War. The program's primary objective was blocking VC encroachment into Vietnam's backcountry by developing the loyalties and fighting abilities of various native contingents.[5]

The Montagnards were fundamentally village-level aborigines scattered in more than a hundred different tribes that relied on hunting or slash-and-burn farming. Their most significant common traits were a deep hostility toward the Vietnamese and a strong desire to be left alone. Under French rule the Montagnards had lived in a large territory under a French commissioner, similar to an Indian preserve in the United States. It included Kontum, Pleiku, and Darlac provinces. Since the French had generally protected the Montagnard land (*Pays Montagnard Sud*) from the Vietnamese, the tribesmen liked Caucasian people. During the First Indochina War, the French had used, with some success, this trust to employ guerrilla bands of "Montagnard Maquis" against the Viet Minh.

The Montagnard tribes (see map) represented a diversity of ethnic Mon-Khmer and Malayo-Polynesian peoples who occupied the rugged length of the Vietnamese western highlands. The tribes included the physically hardy Bahnar in the upper Kontum area, the secretive Bru in the northern mountains, the coastal Cham, the migrating Halang, the betel-chewing lowland and upland Hres, the quarrelsome Jarai in the Pleiku region, the warlike Jehs, the hostile Katu, the slave-holding Koho, the forest-dwelling Mnong, the polytheistic Raglai, the physically strong Rengao, the friendly Rhade in the savanna of Darlac Plateau, the jungle-dwelling Sedang, and the witch-fearing Stieng.

The Special Forces found the Montagnard aborigines incredibly simplistic and superstitious. To gain their allegiance, the Special Forces soldiers carefully learned tribal customs and studied the local dialects, ate the tribal food, endured the cold, mixed indigenous garb with their uniforms, and participated in the rituals and ceremonies. Many senior MACV officers viewed this latest rugged and independent Special Forces effort with extreme displeasure, but the CIA heartily approved. Montagnards accepted only those who shared their lifestyles and dangers. The Special Forces hardships were rewarded as the Civilian Irregular Defense Group program became firmly anchored in the remote jungled periphery of western Vietnam.

In Montagnard culture, village chieftains were elected by the people, sorcerers and shamans held exalted positions, and justice was meted out with alcohol payments for offenses and livestock fines for serious crimes. Disputes were settled by seeing which party became drunk first or which individual came to the surface first after being dunked in a stream. Beatings or imprisonment were practically unknown, but slavery existed among some groups for unpaid debts or witchcraft.

The females dominated the society, since most Montagnards were matrilineal. Women owned all property, the girl or her family chose the husband, and the children took the mother's name. The woman of the house greeted a guest before the husband was allowed to speak. Marriages were typically arranged by matchmakers; they included dowry, and husbands belonged to the wife's family. Thus, young men engaged to little girls had to work for the in-laws until the girls were old enough for marriage. When a wife died before the husband, the family had to find another wife for the son-in-law from the other girls of the family or pay twice the dowry.

Clothing usually consisted only of loincloths. Wealth was indicated by the colors and embroidery of the clothing, or the silver, brass, and glass-bead jewelry worn. Bahnar Montagnards traditionally filed their upper teeth in adolescence. The Montagnards loved alcohol and rice wine. The Raglai tribe stayed inebriated from December to April, following their harvest. Montagnards ate the swidden rice and corn they raised as well as whatever they could find, fish, or hunt. They were brave hunters and skilled in the use of poisons. Meals included wild plants, roots, lizards, snakes, and rats. Livestock was bred as much for sacrificial purposes as for food.

The animistic Montagnards worshiped spirits and ghosts, and taboos and superstitions governed every act. For example, choosing a time for a religious ritual required a ritual in itself. Some evil deities were accorded two souls, or aspects, the first aspect appearing normal while the second aspect was a night devil that ate corpses or killed living persons for the same purpose. Exorcisms, sacrifices, and individual purification rites were common. Deaths were announced by

drumbeat, and long elaborate mournings were marked by the ritu-
alistic slaughter of cattle, pigs, and chickens. The mourners often
burned or scarred their own flesh, and the tombs were then abandoned. The most feared death was one that occurred away from the
village.

3. The Buon Enao Experiment

The largest tribes of the Montagnard people were the Rhade and
Jarai, and the Rhade were considered the most advanced. Many Rhade
were combat veterans of previous wartime service under the French,
and the Rhade-inhabited Darlac "Lake" Province was considered a
major danger zone in the war against the Viet Cong. For these reasons
the Rhade were chosen as the pilot tribe for the civilian irregular defense program.

Special Forces Capt. Ronald A. Schackleton's Detachment A-113
from 1st Special Forces Group had been preparing for Laotian duty.
Captain Schackleton was told instead to report to Vietnam with half
his team. They dressed in civilian clothing, linked up with a counterpart Vietnamese team composed mostly of area natives, and established a trial civilian irregular defense organization at the Rhade
village of Buon Enao, just to the northeast of Ban Me Thuot, on 14
February 1962. A paid, fulltime volunteer strike force guarded Buon
Enao while the village defenders were trained. In the CIDG scheme,
once an area development center like Buon Enao was created, a secure base existed from which Special Forces could expand its operations. From the base, visits were made to surrounding hamlets, which
were encouraged to join the program. Welcome supplies and medicine always accompanied the Special Forces soldiers, who displayed
a great sense of tact and understanding for the local customs.[6]

From Buon Enao the program was actively expanded to neighboring villages. Recruits were obtained from the local village leaders,
screened for Viet Cong, and trained at Buon Enao while strike force
personnel garrisoned their villages. After these hamlet militia had been
trained, they were issued weapons and sent back to their villages.
Hamlet militia were unpaid, and the villages were only lightly defended.

The villages relied on security by patrolling, ambushes, local intelligence, and a simple alert system. In case they were attacked, the
defenders could ask for additional help from the centrally located strike
force. A strike force, consisting of paid, fulltime local soldiers who

had received advanced training, was organized for easy combination with other strike force units into a composite platoon or company for larger missions. Strike forces continuously patrolled their own areas, usually escorted by Special Forces patrol leaders, and checked hamlet defenses and weapons.

The Buon Enao complex was the trial balloon of the CIDG program, and many of the later camp development concepts originated there. MACV was stunned by the rapid success, the South Vietnamese declared Darlac Province secure, and the Montagnards' simple clustered long-house villages were visited by a succession of important dignitaries. In no time at all the impecunious Montagnards had given away as favored souvenirs all the locally made bracelets. Col. George C. Morton, the special warfare chief of MACV, rushed crates of World War II–era brass rifle-cleaning rods to Buon Enao from Okinawa, and soon the Special Forces had the Montagnards happily hammering out hundreds of bracelets to meet the seemingly insatiable demand.

The Special Forces teams seemed tailor-made for the Montagnard CIDG task, and Colonel Morton seized upon the opportunity to press for a larger commitment of Special Forces detachments and special warfare air elements during June. In July a joint unconventional warfare committee was established by Brig. Gen. Gerald Kelleher, the MACV operations officer, and Colonel Morton actively championed an increased Army Special Forces role despite intense pressure from the other services to get into the act. That month he sent a letter to Lt. Col. Ralph Kinnes of the Pentagon Special Warfare branch that expressed his concerns: "Again, I want to read you in on the latest developments here, because if you don't move fast, either 'Air Commandos' or 'tailored USMC guerrilla fighters' will be encroaching in a field that belongs to the Special Forces of the U.S. Army."[7] Colonel Morton was already formulating the creation of an entire provisional Special Forces group within the country.

By August five A-Detachments had organized over 200 villages containing 10,000 Rhade tribesmen. The Buon Enao complex CIDG project included A-113 at Buon Enao, A-213 at Buon Ho, A-214 at Buon Mi Ga, and A-334 at Buon Dan Bak from 1st Special Forces Group, and A-2 at Ban Don from the 5th Special Forces Group. That same month Captain Schackleton's detachment returned to Okinawa and was replaced by Capt. Terry D. Cordell's Detachment A-334.

Captain Cordell was an outstanding officer who immediately won the continued loyalty of the Rhade. Despite the fact that Buon Enao had now become a major Viet Cong target, he continued expansion of the project. In mid-October the Viet Cong launched a multidirectional attack against the Buon Enao complex. Captain Cordell flew over the battlefield on 15 October 1962 in an Air Force FARMGATE T-28 aircraft from Ban Me Thuot in order to direct fire support. He was shot down in flames in full view of his camp strike forces, and the Rhade were so enraged at the loss of their leader that they immediately counterattacked and defeated the Viet Cong.[8]

Colonel Morton realized the critical importance of Rhade loyalty and smooth Presidential Survey Office relations to the future of the Special Forces movement. He selected another outstanding officer, Capt. Curtis D. Terry, from Detachment B-110 at Hoa Cam, and placed him in charge of Detachment A-334, with additional duties as overall coordinator and director of Buon Enao project. Fortunately, the Rhade immediately took to the new captain, whom they called "Captain Terry." The Rhade experiment continued to enjoy a succession of superb Special Forces leadership while the highly proficient detachment sergeants solidified Rhade military development.[9]

4. The CIDG Program Gets Underway

The Special Forces became active in a kaleidoscopic array of other early irregular programs as the number of teams in country multiplied during 1962. Camps Tra My (A-4) and Phu Hoa were established in northern Quang Tin and Quang Nam provinces during October and December, respectively. Camps Mang Buk (A-15), Ba To (A-1), and Tra Bong (A-123) were built in Quang Ngai Province during May, October, and December. Camp Cung Son (A-311) in Phu Yen Province was opened in May, and Camp Van Canh (A-3) in adjacent Binh Dinh Province was started during November. Detachment A-312 began Camp Bon Sar Par, Darlac Province, in April, and A-331 initiated Camp Dam Pau in the Serignac Valley of Tuyen Duc Province. Camp A Cham was set up at Phuoc Thien (Phang Rang) by A-133 in May.

The major Special Forces training center was located at Hoa Cam in Da Nang and operated from January 1962 until it was turned over to Vietnamese authorities in May 1963. By August 1962 a control B-Detachment, B-110 from the 1st Special Forces Group, was stationed at Hoa Cam to supervise the three A-Detachments (A-313, A-322,

and A-324) instructing camp forces, district volunteers, Force Po-
pulaire, rangers, trailwatchers, mountain scouts, village health workers, and Republican Youth. Other special training was being performed at the same time by Capt. Edward E. Langbein's A-233, which
was teaching advanced reconnaissance techniques to the Vietnamese
77th Group at Song Mao.

The Special Forces also trained the blue-uniformed Republican
Youth from the strategic hamlet program, who were used in the hamlet militia and CIDG efforts. On 4 April 1962 a thirty-one-man Republican Youth volunteer group took up positions near the hamlet of
An Chau, about twelve miles from Da Nang. They were escorted by
four Special Forces trainers and an interpreter. The *3d Company, 7th
Viet Cong Liberation Battalion,* suddenly attacked the Republican Youth
site at 7:00 A.M. on 8 April, firing automatic weapons and closing
in from three directions. They were wearing mixed khaki uniforms
and native attire, with pith helmets and odd-colored berets. Two assaults on the command post were repelled, but the third VC charge
carried the field. The VC occupied the area for twenty minutes then
withdrew along a trail into heavy underbrush.

All four Special Forces advisors had been captured. Sfc. Francis
Quinn and Sgt. George E. Groom had their hands bound but tried to
assist Sp. 5th Class James Gabriel, Jr., who had been wounded in
the stomach and arm, and S. Sgt. Wayne E. Marchand, who was
crippled by a badly mangled leg. The Viet Cong were impatient with
the wounded Americans who could not keep up with the withdrawal.
The Republican Youth radio operator, who had gone over to the Viet
Cong when the post was overrun, shot both through the head. They
were later found in the trail at the point of execution, one body lying
atop the other.

When helicopters were heard overhead, Sergeants Quinn and Groom
tried to slow down the retreat, causing confusion, during which four
Republican Youths were released and one escaped. The helicopters
were unable to locate the withdrawing VC because of the heavy clouds
clinging to the foothills. Operation THAI PHIEN, a joint American-
Vietnamese effort that was launched three days later to rescue the
captives failed to locate the prison camp in the heavy rain forests.
The prisoners were subjected to daily political lectures but were not
mistreated or tortured. On 1 May the Viet Cong released Sergeants
Quinn and Groom with no explanation near An Dinh, ten miles south-

west of their point of capture. The Special Forces had sustained its first combat losses, less than three months after becoming involved in the CIDG program.[10]

At the southern end of the country, Special Forces was assisting another band of President Diem-backed irregulars—the "Fighting Fathers," a group of Catholic priests who raised sizable armed contingents to fight the Viet Cong. One of the most well known was Fr. Nguyen Lac Hoa. Father Hoa had also been a lieutenant colonel in the Chinese army previous to the communist takeover. After seeking asylum in several other Southeast Asian countries, he was welcomed to Vietnam by President Diem, a fervent Catholic, who gave him land along the Gulf of Thailand's Delta coastline. In 1960 Father Hoa was entrusted with clearing the Viet Cong out of an entire district within An Xuyen "Peaceful Streams" Province.

Initially, Special Forces support for Father Hoa and his Hai Yen (Sea Swallow) boys was clandestine and consisted of a Taiwan Special Forces team sheep-dipped as Cholon Chinese and sent to assist his anti–Viet Cong clearing campaign. During mid-1962, as part of the price paid for Diem's support of the CIDG program, the Special Forces became openly involved in Catholic Youth activities. Captain Henry's A-333 from 1st Special Forces Group was posted to the Catholic Youth camp at Du Tho at Soc Trang in August, and Captain Farrington's A-14 from 5th Special Forces Group opened Chau Lang camp on 25 October 1962.

In 1962 the war was still a backwater affair, and local Vietnamese military commanders often treated the Viet Cong haphazardly, as more of a nuisance than as a formidable threat. Special Forces attempts to counter the Viet Cong forces that were building up around Long Phu, a fortified Catholic Youth village, were negated by Vietnamese indifference. Just before the village was attacked, a strike force company from A-333, escorted by Lieutenant White, swept the entire vicinity for two weeks. The Vietnamese soldiers were under orders not to fire first at fleeing Viet Cong suspects. The rule was imposed because the local Vietnamese, who often had been forced to contribute labor, usually ran away at the sight of a military patrol. For days, no action was taken despite numerous VC sightings. While crossing an open rice field, the strike force was engaged by rifle fire. The Vietnamese lieutenant ran away with half of the men, leaving no one to give orders. Three more shots rang out in their direction. Lieutenant

White ordered a light machine gun crew to cover the woodline, but they refused to fire on four Viet Cong leaving their positions. A Viet Cong suddenly stood up with rifle aimed at Lieutenant White, who fired first. The VC fell dead into the canal, but the others escaped in boats.[11]

The area had been infested with Viet Cong. Just days later, on the night of 30 October 1962, Long Phu was attacked. A Viet Cong assault battalion, clad only in shorts and unarmed except for crude homemade bombs, rushed the village under the blare of bugles. Father Tong's Catholic Youth defenders were unable to prevent the swift infantry from capturing their mortar and a few buildings. Aircraft arrived overhead and dropped flares, a tactic that startled the Viet Cong, and Sergeant Tung of the Vietnamese 77th Group led a Catholic platoon around behind the attackers. Tung's men opened fire when the VC were suddenly silhouetted in the flarelight. This tactic broke the assault. Captain Aldrich's Detachment A-8 garrisoned Long Phu (also called Tra Lang) commencing 6 February 1963, and the Special Forces officially assumed advisory and support responsibilities for the Catholic Youth program on 29 August 1963.[12]

Although technically part of the CIDG program, the Special Forces also built border surveillance camps where no real native population base existed for CIDG recruitment. Beginning in the summer of 1962, these camps were hacked out of the mountainous jungle close to North Vietnam, Laos, and Cambodia. A campsite at Khe Sanh, in the sparsely Bru-populated northwestern corner of the country, was opened on 8 July 1962. It would later become a major Marine combat bastion and the scene of one of the pivotal battles of the Second Indochina War. In August Dak To (A-332) and Dak Pek (A-13) were set up as border-monitoring points in the Sedang-inhabited hinterland of Kontum Province. These remote and isolated camps were intended as bases for the trailwatchers, special Montagnard companies formed to help watch South Vietnam's rugged frontier.

Closely akin to the trailwatchers were the mountain commandos, later designated as the mountain scouts, which had been first formed in November 1961. Mountain scout teams also received special training at Hoa Cam, and after December 1962, at Plei Yt in Pleiku Province under A-16 of 5th Special Forces Group. The upland Sedang were the first mountaineers to receive this kind of military training from the Special Forces. However, upon completion of their training, the mountain scouts were turned over to the control of the province chiefs, who misused them as drivers, hunting guides, and district intelligence agents. The Special Forces advisors later found it impossible to regroup the mountain scouts under their own control as an adjunct to the border surveillance mission.[13]

The Saigon regime remained hostile toward the CIDG program, which, apart from ethnic Vietnamese paramilitary entities such as the Republican or Catholic Youth forced upon the Special Forces at Diem's insistence, aimed at securing minority elements. The South Vietnamese government considered the arming and organizing of large segments of the non-Vietnamese population within the country a political menace. Under great pressure from the United States, President Diem reluctantly consented to support the CIDG effort.

Language difficulties and the poor quality of the trainees greatly hampered Special Forces CIDG efforts in the field. Arriving hamlet militia and strike force recruits frequently had to be fed for two weeks just so they would have the strength to go through the required instruction. Valuable training time was spent on the most basic fundamentals of sanitation. Vietnamese response to the program was tardy, inadequate, and sometimes openly hostile. The district chief in the Khe Sanh area of Quang Tri Province so frightened the natives with tales of Viet Cong reprisals that the tribesmen asked him to collect their weapons, to avoid provoking VC anger. The Darlac Province chief largely negated the Buon Enao success by collecting Rhade weapons after the Special Forces turned over the camps to government authority. There were even occasional cases of Vietnamese refusal to give emergency medical supplies to Special Forces personnel.[14]

One of Diem's tricks to disrupt the CIDG program was turned into an asset. He emptied the Saigon jails of city thugs, violent criminals, and military deserters and gave them to Special Forces in a special "noncontract deal." These unsavory characters were shipped to remote Special Forces camps, where they were ordered shot if caught escaping. The Special Forces soldiers were tough enough to win the respect of these hoods and kept most of them in line. They were turned into valuable gunhands who were naturally adept at counterterror tactics against the VC. They mutilated Viet Cong dead. They paid shopkeepers by leaving a round of ammunition on the table, which forced Special Forces soldiers to pay debts to local merchants with team funds and lecture them on civilized warfare. Privately, Special Forces welcomed this tough approach to waging guerrilla war.

Nevertheless, Special Forces detachment efforts were primed with readily available CIA funding to spark the CIDG program, which rapidly spread throughout the Montagnard territories of the western highlands. This was accomplished despite the misgivings of the South Vietnamese authorities, who feared that the newly armed and organized hill tribe forces might turn this power against the government as well as against the Viet Cong.

Pentagon unconventional warfare experts proclaimed that CIDG implementation was the key to security and stability within South Vietnam. They held that the CIDG paramilitary program was capable of winning over the tribal groups, strangling remote Viet Cong area redoubts, and providing a reasonable degree of border control. This may have been true if the Vietnam battlefield was confined to a simple struggle between partisans and government police. Instead, the civil war exploded into a major confrontation between national armies, which hopelessly outclassed the ability of rifle-toting local natives to influence the outcome.

The increased Special Forces commitment was formalized in the creation of U.S. Army Special Forces Vietnam (Provisional) during September under the leadership of Colonel Morton. He laid the foundations of the Special Forces effort in Vietnam and supervised the turnover of the CIDG program from CIA to Special Forces auspices during Operation SWITCHBACK, which was completed by July 1963. At that time the Special Forces had, in one way or another, become involved in almost every conceivable Vietnamese paramilitary activity. Seven years after the first detachments had been organized in Hawaii and Japan, the Special Forces had evolved from a small, specialized guerrilla warfare cadre into the spearhead of an all-out American military training and advisory effort in a major combat theater.

Notes

1. 5th Special Forces Group S3 reading file, Fact Sheet on Vietnamese Special Forces History with attachments, dtd 18 Nov 69.
2. USARPAC G3 MHD Files, Vietnam MTT, *After Action Report,* dtd 26 May 1961. During 1963, the ARVN contained seven ranger battalions (11th, 21st, 31st, 32d, 33d, 34th, and 41st) and forty-six separate ranger companies. The 22d, 35th, and 36th ARVN Ranger Battalions were composed of Montagnard scout companies.
3. HQ CINCPAC Agenda, Secretary of Defense Conference, *Summary of U.S. Personnel in Vietnam,* Document 8K, dtd 19 December 1961; Headquarters, USARPAC Office of the Assistant Chief of Staff G3, *Staff Office Report,* April–June 1962; USASF(P)V Report, Subject: Debriefing of Col. George C. Morton, dtd 6 Nov 63.
4. DA Office of the Deputy Chief of Staff for Military Operations Report, Subject: Special Warfare Field Visit to Vietnam and Okinawa, dtd 19 February 1963.
5. USARPAC G2, *Intelligence Bulletin,* May 1961; and Headquarters, 5th Special Forces Group, *Debriefing* of Col. George C. Morton, dtd 6 November 1963.
6. Research Analysis Corporation Technical Memorandum RAC-T-477, *U.S. Army Special Forces Operations Under the Civilian Irregular Defense Groups Program in Vietnam,* dtd April 1966.
7. Headquarters MACV J3 Ltr, dtd 19 Jul 62.
8. In memory of Captain Cordell, the first Special Forces officer killed in combat in Vietnam, an academic building at the U.S. Army Transportation School, Fort Eustis, Virginia, is named Cordell Hall. At The Citadel in Charleston, South Carolina, where he graduated in 1957, a company of airborne ranger-qualified cadets is designated The Cordell Airborne Ranger Company.
9. Headquarters, USASF(P)V Ltr, dtd 3 Nov 62.
10. Sp5 Gabriel and SSG Marchand were from Company C, and SFC Quinn and Sgt. George A. Groom were from Company A, 1st Special Forces Group; USARYIS/IX Corps, *Staff Office Report,* April–June 1962, Annex 277; details extracted from CINCUSARPAC Message RJ92563, dtd 10 April 1962; CIA Information Report DA IN 219901, 220329, and 221453, dtd 10, 11, and 14 April 1962; CINCUSARPAC Msg RJ 93049, dtd 2 May 1962; DA IN Msg 226373 dtd 22 May 1962. The Special Forces Gabriel Demonstration Area at Fort Bragg, North Carolina, is named in honor of Sp5 James Gabriel, Jr.
11. CSD-177, Memorandum for Record, Subject: Clarification of Information Contained in CSD-156, dtd 9 November 1962.

12. USMACV Memorandum, Subject: After Action Report on Fight at Long Phu, III Corps, dtd 2 Nov 62; and 5th SFG, *Synopsis of the USASF Sector/ Subsector Advisory Role,* dtd 1 December 1968, Section V.

13. MACV J32, *Status Report,* Integration of Mountain Scout Program Personnel, dtd 23 Dec 63.

14. RISFC Report, S. Sgt. B. I. Luttrell to Commander, 1st Special Forces Group, dtd 4 Oct 62.

CHAPTER 4

OPERATION SWITCHBACK

1. SWITCHBACK to Special Forces

Special Forces presence in Vietnam rapidly expanded as the CIDG program blossomed. In April the Central Intelligence Agency asked the Defense Department for an additional modified B-Detachment and four more A-Detachments, totaling sixty-eight troopers, for CIDG purposes. The CIA hoped that this new request could be met with Special Forces resources in the United States. The Pentagon replied that the Latin American and Caribbean commitments prohibited a stateside task force of that size and directed CIA attention back to the 1st Special Forces Group.[1]

An additional eight A-Teams had been committed by 23 April 1962, and the CIA requested another sixteen A-Teams in June. At that time, the able and highly articulate CIA Chief of Station John "Jocko" Richardson recommended to Desmond "Dez" Fitzgerald, Chief of the Far East Division at CIA headquarters in Langley, Virginia, that the military take over the entire CIDG program. That decision was based on National Security Action Memorandum (NASM) #57, promulgated after the ill-fated Bay of Pigs operation in Cuba in April 1961. NASM #57 stated in essence that whenever a secret paramilitary operation became so large and overt that the military contribution, in terms of manpower and equipment, exceeded the resources contributed by the CIA, the operation should be turned over to the Department of Defense.

In July 1962 Secretary of Defense Robert S. McNamara mandated a meeting of Defense Department, CINCPAC, CIA, State Department, and MACV officials at Camp H. M. Smith in Hawaii for the purpose of considering the military takeover of the CIDG and other paramilitary programs being conducted by the CIA in Vietnam. Gen. Paul D. Harkins, the commander of MACV, attended the conference accompanied by Col. George C. Morton, the Chief of the Special Warfare Branch, J-3 MACV. Colonel Morton successfully pleaded the case for a greater Special Forces role in the area. As a result of that conference, the Department of Defense agreed to accept responsibility for the program from the CIA on a phased basis over a one-year period and to give the Special Forces entire CIDG responsibility.

The Special Forces was given the authority to pay CIDG forces, make a wide range of purchases without accountability, draw directly on Okinawa for equipment, weapons, and ammunition, and to set up its own separate command in Vietnam for control purposes. The transition of the CIDG program from civilian to military control was coded Operation SWITCHBACK, which was to be completed by 1 July 1963. On that day it was visualized that Special Forces would assume control over 50,000 irregulars and fourteen fortified camps and be prepared to expand that force to 125,000 irregulars and forty-nine camps within another year. Operation SWITCHBACK was an ambitious undertaking. High-level directives to produce quantitative results rushed and weakened the careful preparation that had insured early CIDG success.[2]

The magnitude of the escalating CIDG program quickly outpaced the 1st Special Forces Group capability to support it, even though the group had been expanded to 213 officers and 778 enlisted men assigned by the end of June 1962. On 16 August the U.S. Army Pacific notified the Pentagon that the projected Special Forces headquarters, one C-Detachment, and half of the sixteen A-Detachments scheduled for Vietnam would have to come from the United States.[3]

Col. George C. Morton, the highly respected Chief of the Special Warfare Branch on the MACV staff, was appointed as the Special Forces commander in Vietnam effective 1 September 1962. Colonel Morton was a World War II company commander of the 86th Infantry Division who had later served as a battalion commander in the post-war 511th Airborne Infantry Regiment. During the Korean War, he had been stationed in Greece as the senior Special Forces advisor to the Royal Hellenic Raiding Forces and was involved in stay-behind operations in northern Greece on the Bulgarian, Yugoslavian, and Albanian borders. He was a well-known expert on special warfare and had taught joint airborne and special operations courses at the U.S. Air Force Air University.

The 5th Special Forces Group at Fort Bragg, North Carolina, readied a seventy-six-man command and support element for Vietnam duty, simply labeled as the Headquarters Detachment, 5th Special Forces Group (Provisional). The six-man advance party of that detachment was flown out of Pope Air Force Base next to Fort Bragg on 29 August 1962 and arrived in Saigon on 5 September. On that date Colonel Morton created his tentative headquarters of ·U.S. Army Special Forces Vietnam.

The first large contingent of stateside Special Forces personnel arrived in Saigon 14 and 15 September 1962 on temporary six months' duty. The seventy-two men were formed into one C-Detachment and four A-Detachments. On 8 November the rest of the Headquarters Detachment, 5th Special Forces Group (Provisional), landed in Saigon aboard five C-130 aircraft on permanent change-of-station orders to Vietnam. Upon their arrival MACV formally established the Headquarters, U.S. Army Special Forces Vietnam (Provisional).

Colonel Morton retained fourteen officers and forty-three enlisted men with him in Saigon, where a joint CIA–Special Forces tactical operations center was established in an old four-story apartment building on Tran Hung Dao Street in the Cholon district of Saigon, adjacent to the MAAG-Vietnam compound. This enabled Colonel Morton and his staff to maintain close coordination with Col. Gilbert Layton, Chief of the CIA Combined Studies Division (CSD), and with Col. Gil Strickler, Layton's deputy who controlled the critical support and logistical aspects of Operation SWITCHBACK.

Colonel Morton's Cholon tactical operations center was deliberately kept "low profile," although a large painting of a green beret decorated the otherwise nondescript sign hung over the main entrance. Visitors who entered the innocuous building were met by a pretty receptionist, who occupied a well-furnished street-level office devoid of military trappings. Many Vietnamese mistook the green beret logo and interior for a restaurant parlor and attempted to make dinner reservations. Little did they realize that past the charming, *ao dai*-skirted secretary, behind the wall on the ground floor, were stacks of machine guns, automatic rifles, and munitions crates, and upstairs Special Forces personnel were busily issuing joint CIA–U.S. Army

Special Forces Vietnam (Provisional) memorandums, keeping both the agency and General Harkin's MACV headquarters informed of the progress of Operation SWITCHBACK.

Lt. Col. Eb Smith and eighteen enlisted men of his C-Detachment, which was used to augment Morton's understrength headquarters, were posted to coastal Nha Trang. There they commenced development of the Special Forces Operations Base (SFOB), which Colonel Morton planned to occupy in February 1963. The pleasant beachfront town had been selected as the headquarters because it was located in a central location ideal for controlling the 530 Special Forces soldiers in four B-Detachments and twenty-eight A-Detachments that were scattered the length of the country by the end of the year. A huge, white, hilltop Buddha overlooked Nha Trang's attractive villas and the tree-lined promenade, Beach Road, which gently curved along four miles of sandy beach. Morton moved his command element to Nha Trang on 12 February 1963. Late construction at Nha Trang caused inconveniences, but by the SWITCHBACK completion date three warehouses, a parachute-packing facility, and four ammunition bunkers had been completed.[4]

Nha Trang's bikini-clad beach girls and dazzling white Special Forces logistical complex did not keep Colonel Morton tied down. Leaving the operations of the SFOB to his deputy, Lt. Col. George Callaway, he constantly shuttled unannounced from one remote A-Detachment camp to the next, keeping his aircraft and jeeps idling on dirt airstrips or roadways in steaming mountain jungle or grassy plains while he coordinated with his young captains and battle-hardened operations sergeants. The Viet Cong had put a high price on his head, and their assassins and kidnappers were desperate to kill or capture the circuit-riding Green Beret chieftain. The closest they came was when his jeep stalled in dense scrub brush along a narrow trail between Gia Vuc and Quang Ngai, but Morton's "shotgun" sergeant finally restarted the vehicle before the Viet Cong could close the trap.

2. The War Heats Up

In the first month of 1963, the CIDG border surveillance camp at Plei Mrong, located on the highland plateau of Kontum, became the first Special Forces camp assaulted in Vietnam. Capt. William P. Grace III of the 1st Special Forces Group established the campsite with his Detachment A-314 at the beginning of the dry season, on the first day of November. Throughout the winter the humid days slipped into cold, starry nights, with temperatures ranging from 88 to 39 degrees Fahrenheit.

The Jarai Montagnard natives grew rice, Indian corn, and tobacco and possessed some water buffaloes, cows, hogs, goats, ducks, and chickens. The Jarai hunted deer and other animals and feasted on the abundant field rats, a delicacy. The detachment had initiated a village defense program at Plei Mrong on 27 December after six skirmishes with local Viet Cong, the discovery of several caches, and one truck mining. The recruits were placed inside the camp for hamlet militia training.

The Viet Cong in the area were considered unsophisticated, belonging to no particular unit, and were armed with a motley assortment of American weapons. They led Montagnards, who were tired of being mistreated and cheated by the Vietnamese. They used a simple system of vines to ring gongs and rattle bamboo drums to warn them of approaching soldiers. Call signs consisted of hand clapping, and information on Americans was gained by children and VC mistresses.

The Plei Mrong Special Forces camp had very strained relations with the Vietnamese. Captain Grace considered the youthful camp commander, LLDB Aspirant Hanh, irresponsible and incapable of performing his job. Mr. Pirout, the local secretary of Montagnard affairs, was responsible for checking militia trainees for VC connections. The detachment had already placed him in a week's confinement for failing to screen out VC infiltrators when the camp was opened. The district chief was a PSO officer, Captain Hung, whose fear of ambushes kept him off the road and away from the camp. He was related by marriage to the Pleiku Province chief, Mr. Chu. Their reports to Saigon accused the Special Forces of undermining the government.

Camp Plei Mrong's defenses were reasonably good for that stage of the war. The rectangular perimeter was completely surrounded by two double barbed-wire fences. The outer fence was interlaced with broken glass and three-inch-high steel spikes, and the ground between the two fences was filled by M-14 antipersonnel mines and wooden punji stakes. A ring of trenches and fighting positions had been dug fifteen yards inside the fencelines, interrupted only at the two camp gates.

On the morning of 2 January 1963, Captain Grace helicoptered half the detachment and a strike force to conduct an operation across the Krong Bolah River. Lieutenant Leary, the executive officer, wisely moved two supporting 155mm howitzers, from the 37th ARVN Artillery Battalion, inside the camp perimeter to afford better security and communications.

On 3 January at 1:30 A.M. in the pitch blackness, a reinforced Viet Cong company raced through a twelve-foot gap in the Plei Mrong fenceline, cut by pro-VC hamlet militia trainees inside. The assaulters turned toward the ammunition bunker and the militia tents and opened fire with rifles and Browning automatic rifles. They ran along the eastern trenchline, hurling potato-masher-type hand grenades and blocks of TNT. The trainees in the tents either joined the Viet Cong, scrambled into the trenches to fight alongside the camp defenders, or were killed by VC grenades and TNT bombs pitched into the tentage.

The camp strike force soldiers manned defensive positions and returned fire against the Viet Cong onslaught. Four Special Forces soldiers jumped into the 81mm mortar pit, where the weapon had been sabotaged. Lieutenant Leary and the radio operator ran into the communications bunker and tried to contact Detachment B-210 in Pleiku.[5] All attempts failed as the antenna had been cut in half by VC fire. The radio operator desperately changed crystals and moved to an alternate radio in another bunker.

The liaison officer from the 22d ARVN Division at Plei Mrong was Second Lieutenant Bao, a distinguished combat veteran of nine years' service and a graduate of both the British Malayan jungle school and American transportation school at Fort Eustis, Virginia. He spoke excellent English and soon had the ARVN artillery communications network working with both divisional and B-Detachment levels. Unfortunately, II Corps insisted on keeping the 22d ARVN Ranger Battalion, only twenty-two miles away in Pleiku, "in reserve." Lieutenants Leary and Bao directed the battle with the artillery radios and lobbed grenades from behind the barricades.

The battle was confused and ugly, with VC sympathizers among the camp defenders killing CIDG personnel and trainees from the rear trenches. Automatic weapons fire and blinding explosions rocked the camp for 2$^1/_2$ hours. Two determined Viet Cong assaults were repulsed in front of the Special Forces mortar position. The Viet Cong blasted the length of one trench with a 57mm recoilless rifle, but its occupants were already dead or wounded from previous VC dynamiting. ARVN artillery destroyed the recoilless rifle after it was brought forward. Another Viet Cong assault was made by a fresh VC company using sappers armed with bangalore torpedoes on the other fenceline. It was defeated, and shortly after four o'clock that morning, the Viet Cong retreated from the camp carrying their dead and wounded.

Aircraft illumination had been desperately needed throughout the action, but the lack of airstrip lights prevented the aircraft at Pleiku from taking off. A C-47 flareship finally arrived over the camp at 5:10 A.M., and the American B-Detachment and MAAG personnel in Pleiku could see the flares floating over Plei Mrong on the horizon. One final VC probe against the perimeter was defeated at 6:00 A.M. An hour later medical evacuation helicopters arrived from Kontum.

The battle of Plei Mrong had been a harrowing ordeal, and the Viet Cong had almost succeeded in overrunning the camp. Losses had been grievous. Twenty-nine camp defenders had been killed, seventy-three were missing, and thirty-eight were wounded. Additionally, all four Special Forces soldiers in the weapons pit had been wounded. Later investigations revealed that the Viet Cong had had the cooperation of at least thirty-three penetration agents in the strike force as well as the apparent complicity of a larger number of other hamlet militia trainees.[6]

At the end of that month, the U.S. Army Special Forces Vietnam (Provisional) assumed operational control over the civilian irregular defense group effort. The Special Forces formally absorbed the remaining logistical and other aspects of the CIDG program on 1 July 1963, and Operation SWITCHBACK terminated as scheduled. All SWITCHBACK goals had been exceeded by wide margins. The Special Forces had trained 52,636 hamlet militia, 10,904 strike force soldiers, 515 village medical workers, 946 trailwatchers, and 3,803 mountain scouts. Thousands more militia and strike force trainees were undergoing instruction. Special Forces had extended the CIDG program to 879 villages throughout Vietnam. Roughly seventy A-Detachments, nine B-Detachments, and one control C-Detachment had served or were serving six-month tours in Vietnam. All these were on temporary duty, and on 12 April Colonel Morton requested that future B- and C-level detachments be sent to Vietnam on permanent orders. Special Forces was in Vietnam to stay.

During the last six months of the SWITCHBACK period, January through July 1963, Special Forces involvement in the war had steadily increased. While Plei Mrong remained the single instance of an open assault on a CIDG camp, there had been 372 patrol contacts, 94 probes and mortar attacks against camps, and 11 known infiltrations of Special Forces camps. The three most frequently engaged camps were Gia Vuc (A-729) in northern Quang Ngai Province, opened by Captain Carr during February 1963 to enlist the Rhe tribal group in the CIDG program, and Captain Dutton's Chau Lang (A-734) and Captain Lewis's Tan Phu (A-20) camps in the Delta marshlands.

Special Forces casualties continued to increase. S. Sgt. Robert J. Hain of Detachment A-132 was killed by a sniper on 6 May 1963 near An Diem. On 29 May A-114 at Son Ha in Quang Ngai Province lost its commander, Capt. James H. Brodt and Special Forces Pfc. Neil K. MacIver in a violent firefight. The rising toll of Special Forces dead, wounded, and injured was matched by serious health problems such as hepatitis and malaria in the tropical climate. During June, one A-Detachment had to be rushed from Okinawa to Vietnam on emergency orders to replace a stateside detachment that had been all but wiped out by disease, and most of its members had been medically evacuated to Clark Air Force Base in the Philippines.

Colonel Morton's Special Forces strength in Vietnam at the conclusion of Operation SWITCHBACK on 1 July 1963 was exactly 646 personnel. This total included 122 at the headquarters (98 permanently assigned and 24 in a temporary duty C-Detachment) and 524 on temporary duty with the four B-Detachments and thirty-seven A-Detachments in the field. A civil affairs mobile training team and four Army engineer control and advisory teams attached to Special Forces headquarters increased total strength to 674. In addition, two Navy Seabee Technical Assistance Teams had been assigned to the provisional group since January and had been performing invaluable engineer support. With one exception, these detachments were involved with various aspects of the CIDG program. One A-Detachment (A-413) was under CIA control at the top-secret deep-penetration mission site in Long Khanh Province. Of the others, 5-1/2 A-Detachments were charged with border surveillance, a like number with mountain commando activities, and fourteen with various Diem-approved CIDG missions.[7]

Throughout the tenure of U.S. Army Special Forces Vietnam

(Provisional), Viet Cong military action against the Special Forces intensified. Ambushes, road mines, and patrol clashes became more frequent. The Viet Cong possessed excellent intelligence nets of informants, who were aided by careless open and uncoded Vietnamese radio traffic. For example, in July 1963 a VC mortar barrage struck Can Tho when the control headquarters was in the midst of staging teams into the Delta. Fourteen Special Forces troopers in two deploying teams were wounded and evacuated to the 8th Field Hospital set up in tents at Nha Trang.

Multiple combatant casualties were still a rarity in Vietnam, and Colonel Morton could scrounge up only five Purple Heart medals in all of Vietnam for bedside presentation by the Army Chief of Staff to the fourteen. As Gen. Earle G. Wheeler walked down the row of cots pinning a Purple Heart on each wounded soldier, Colonel Morton followed behind taking off the medals and replacing them on the awards tray held by the chief nurse, Maj. Louise Bitter, so that there would be enough awards.

Camps were especially vulnerable when detachments were being exchanged. The Loc Ninh border surveillance camp was located beside a French rubber plantation's asphalt airstrip near Cambodia and was garrisoned by one local Stieng and two Cambodian CIDG companies. On 17 July 1963 Capt. Robert K. Mosier arrived at Loc Ninh with his Detachment A-22 of the 5th Special Forces Group to relieve Capt. Laurence E. Hackley's A-18 from the same group. The next day a medical team was sent to the nearby village of Srok Thom, and later that same morning the two detachment commanders decided to visit their village aid station. They drove off in two jeeps, along with LLDB camp commander Captain Yem and several others.

The Viet Cong ambushed both jeeps along a straight stretch of dirt road just outside Xom Bung hamlet. Captain Hackley, driving the second jeep, and M. Sgt. Jack. L. Goodman, the A-18 operations sergeant sitting beside him, were hit by several bullets and grenade fragments. They crawled across the road to a shallow ditch, but both had been mortally wounded. Captain Mosier was killed getting out of the same jeep, and fell over his executive officer, Lieutenant Barbee. The lieutenant and Captain Yem, who had been hit in the hip, ran into the nearest hootch. They defended it with rifle fire until automatic weapons and exploding grenades forced them to retreat back to another house.

First Lt. James W. Gasaway, the A-18 detachment executive officer, heard the firing and boarded fifty Cambodians on a truck. He sped to the ambush site within ten minutes, just as the Viet Cong were advancing toward the second house and about to finish off the wounded CIDG soldiers lying around the jeeps. The Viet Cong hastily withdrew, but their ambush mission had been completed.

3. President Diem and Vietnamese Special Forces

While the Special Forces wanted CIDG emphasis shifted to the border and Montagnard efforts, President Diem insisted on using Special Forces resources on pet projects sponsored by his regime. Consequently, Colonel Morton had been forced to appease the powerful minister of finance under Diem, Nguyen Van Buu, a multimillionaire who had insisted on placing many Special Forces teams in areas convenient for protecting his varied landholdings and industrial pursuits. This abuse of the Special Forces CIDG program had already given rise to the "cinnamon soldier" camps in the midst of Buu's cinnamon plantations of Quang Ngai Province's Tra Bong Valley and the "shrimp soldier" camps at Long Hai and Vung Tau. The Special Forces support of the Catholic Youth program led by a number of combative parish priests was another Diem-imposed sideline.

One of the most frustrating elements of the Diem regime, as far as Special Forces was concerned, was the Presidential Survey Office. Finally, as a result of the increased Special Forces support rendered to Diem's projects, Chief Le Quang Tung's Presidential Survey Office headquarters in Saigon was directed to conform the 77th Group in harmony with American desires. The group's realignment along American Special Forces organizational lines was completed with the establishment of the Luc Luong Dac Biet, or LLDB (which translates into Airborne Special Forces), on 15 March 1963. The 31st Group had been formed on 1 February 1963 but remained in training under Special Forces guidance throughout the year. The 77th Group was the only actual LLDB organization in the field. All LLDB officers were Presidential Survey Officers (PSO).

Under President Diem the LLDB served as a palace guard. The few highly experienced combat veterans were outnumbered by scores who had obtained their position through the influence of relatives or the payment of bribes. Graft, corruption, and misbehavior were even more pronounced than in the regular army. Placed alongside Special

Forces teams primarily as spies for Diem, the LLDB rarely exhibited any initiative hunting Viet Cong and resisted American advice. Since Diem's internal actions hinged largely on his Presidential Survey Office reports, the LLDB carried the stigma of his political repression. After the collapse of the Diem regime, the LLDB was mistrusted by the national leaders who followed. Additionally, Vietnamese society did not place high esteem on service with savage natives in the remote backcountry. Under the circumstances, the quality of incoming LLDB officers and personnel continued to slip throughout the war.

The Special Forces was saddled with advising the same kind of incompetent indigenous leadership that had hindered its efforts in Laos. Since they were advisors, the Special Forces were forced to plead and cajole LLDB personnel into action. In most cases the Special Forces actually performed all the camp administration and training and actually led CIDG forces in the field. The Special Forces advisory objective in Vietnam was stated as assisting the LLDB to the point that the Vietnamese would be capable of running the CIDG program on their own, freeing Special Forces to turn to other matters. The goal of their "working themselves out of a job" was never reached. After Diem, the Saigon regime deliberately kept the LLDB at a substandard level and obstructed the civilian irregular defense group concept.

Detachment A-19's experiences were typical of the wide variation in the quality of their LLDB counterparts. The A-Team, under Capt. Jay H. Kidder of the 5th Special Forces Group, had established a CIDG camp in the canal-laced rice paddies at Hiep Hoa west of Saigon near Cambodia during February 1963. As the team outprocessed from Vietnam six months later, Captain Kidder wrote:

Since commitment Camp Hiep Hoa has had three Vietnamese officers as camp commander (PSO). The first of these, an Aspirant, had experience and was mission conscious in every respect. He was replaced by a "diamond in the rough," a "living jewel," an ass. The most crooked, inconsiderate, incompetent, ineffective soldier in the Vietnamese army. His selfish, cowardly composure set the detachment mission back three months. His cowardice is only superseded by his corruption and graft. He is a menace to Special Forces and is dangerous to either side he works for. However, he does sit a chair well. This man was replaced by the current PSO, 1st Lt. Luu. He promises to be an asset to the camp. He has cooperated fully in every respect, coordinates and works closely with American SF. In operations he participates completely, is very experienced, and has common sense. In training he has as yet to be observed; however, it is positive he will perform as a commander, doing his duty well. Camp management he realizes as one of his responsibilities and has accepted and performed well.[8]

While junior officers and team sergeants wrestled with the activities of the LLDB counterparts, the American high command considered how best to redirect Special Forces efforts toward military objectives more in line with MACV campaign plans. General Paul Harkins wanted Special Forces in a reconnaissance role along the border of South Vietnam, while his MACV staff officers insisted on closer control of Special Forces enterprises under the direct scrutiny of corps senior advisors. On 1 November 1963 President Ngo Dinh Diem was slain in a coup d'état, and all vestiges of his power were quickly dismantled.

Colonel Morton was immediately whisked out of country. He was sent to Fort Bragg, where he served as assistant commandant of the Special Warfare School, then he retired to join the CIA. He returned to Southeast Asia in 1966 as an agency paramilitary officer in Vietnam, Laos, and Thailand. From 1968 to 1973 he served as CIA Chief of Operations at Udorn Base for a 30,000-man, U.S.-sponsored irregular force fighting in Laos. In his absence, MACV had moved rapidly to tighten its grip on Special Forces, while the demise of Diem allowed redirection of Special Forces efforts toward Vietnam's forbidding frontiers.

Notes

1. DA Msg 909466, dtd 6 Feb 62; USARYIS Msg IXC-3024, dtd 13 Feb 62; CINCPAC Msg RJ 91339, dtd 21 Feb 62; CHMAAGV Msg MAGPE-1243, dtd 23 Feb 62; MACV-15 Msg, dtd 28 Feb 62; DA Msg 912697, dtd 13 Apr 62.

2. DA Msg 309962, dtd 17 Jul 62, and DA Msg 917028, dtd 19 Jul 62; USARYIS Ltr, Subject: Operation SWITCHBACK, dtd 25 Sep 62, Tab A.

3. Through the first half of 1962, Vietnam inroads into 1st Special Forces Group had been severe. On 2 February 1962 a full detachment from 1st Special Forces Group arrived in Vietnam for CIDG expansion, followed by thirty-two more personnel for CIDG purposes at the end of March. Six officers and twenty-six enlisted men landed on 2 May to train Montagnard mountain scout companies and special battalions. On 15 May two A-Teams reported into Vietnam to instruct ranger basic and advanced courses. On 28 May a tactical operations center for Special Forces elements in Vietnam was put into operation by two officers and nineteen enlisted men (augmented by six more on 19 June), two A-Teams arrived to participate in the village defense program, and two officers were sent to Saigon as CIA case officers. USARYIS/IX Corps, *Staff Office Report*, April–June 1962, Annex 277.

4. U.S. Army Special Forces Vietnam, *Staff Office Report*, October–December 1962; CSD/SF/JOCG SWITCHBACK No. 3, Subject: Monthly Progress Report, Operation SWITCHBACK, dtd 9 Jan 63; HQ USASFV, *Semi-Annual Status Report*, dtd 30 June 63, Annex A.

5. Detachment B-210, from Company B of the 1st Special Forces Group, was the first B-Detachment in Vietnam, serving from November 1962 until 6 May 1963. B-210 was commanded by Maj. Walter T. Little and commanded all Special Forces elements in II Corps Tactical Zone.

6. The narrative was primarily extracted from Detachment B-210, *After Action Report*, dtd 6 January 1963; Detachment A-314, *After Action Report*, dtd 5 January 1964; and Detachment A-314, *Area Assessment*, dtd 21 February 1963.

7. USASF(P)V, *Semi-Annual Report*, dtd 30 June 1963; USASF(P)V, *Monthly Progress Report*, dtd 10 July 1963.

8. Detachment A-19, *Debriefing*, dtd 2 July 1963, Inclosure 3.

CHAPTER 5

MOVE TO THE BORDER

1. Special Forces Shifts to the Border

The demise of the Diem regime in November 1963 radically altered Special Forces direction in Vietnam. From the beginning, MAAG-Vietnam, followed by MACV, had made a concerted effort to bring Special Forces activities in Vietnam under its direct control. This had been largely negated because the LLDB had existed apart from the Vietnamese armed forces structure, which allowed the Special Forces an excellent excuse to remain independent and allied with the CIA. Now that Diem was slain, MACV ordered Special Forces emphasis shifted to the border and began a major effort to terminate all projects instituted at the request of Diem. Col. Theodore Leonard, an infantry officer who served in World War II, was placed in charge of U.S. Army Special Forces Vietnam (Provisional), despite the fact that he had no previous Special Forces experience. He was installed with directives to place all Special Forces under operational control of MACV senior corps advisors.

Events in the country swiftly engulfed U.S. military direction as the Viet Cong intensified the level of combat on the battlefield. Additionally, a major problem arose within Special Forces jurisdiction when the Montagnards revolted.* These factors impacted directly on Special Forces operations. Coupled with the new MACV relationship, they reshaped Special Forces utilization. The provisional Special Forces organization in Vietnam bore the brunt of the martial whirlwind that pitched America into the Second Indochina War.

The Central Intelligence Agency's desire to detect and prevent

Viet Cong troop and resupply movement across the international border rivaled the emphasis on recruiting native minorities. South Vietnam's 900-mile boundary extended from the South China Sea across the Demilitarized Zone (DMZ) on the 17th parallel, turned sharply south and followed a 75-mile escarpment dominating the Khe Sanh plains, twisted through 180 miles of verdant mountains and broken savanna along the Laotian border, fringed Cambodia for another 210 miles through rolling and partially jungled highlands from Dak To to Loc Ninh, then zigzagged the final 250 miles across the Delta's alluvial ricelands to the coast. The majority of its rugged terrain afforded little or no native population potential for area development.

The Special Forces was thrust into full-scale frontier security on 1 November 1963, the date of Diem's death, when the Central Intelligence Agency turned over its border surveillance responsibilities to the provisional group. Gen. Paul D. Harkins of MACV directed Special Forces to (1) recruit and train border surveillance personnel, (2) establish intelligence nets "to detect infiltration *prior to or during* the crossing phase of an infiltrating element," (3) gain the border zone population's loyalty to the South Vietnamese government, (4) "*gain control* of the international border and entry into Vietnam by gradually expanding initially small areas denied to the Viet Cong," and (5) "conduct guerrilla warfare—long-range patrol activities in the border control zone to deny the border areas to the Viet Cong by detection, interdiction, harassment, and elimination of the infiltration routes parallel to or through the border control zone."[1]

Col. Theodore Leonard formally took over the U.S. Army Special Forces Vietnam (Provisional) group six days later on 7 November 1963. His tenure of command was dominated by the construction of new camps in the remote hinterland of Vietnam. The original CIDG minority development goals shriveled as Special Forces were moved westward to cover the Viet Cong infiltration routes. Although unconventional warfare titles were used, such as the CIDG light guerrilla companies, border zone reconnaissance and interdiction were ordinary military attempts at area control.

A few CIDG camps had been built at great expense in the arboreal wilderness and man-high grasslands along the Laotian and Cambodian borders during the SWITCHBACK period. Border screening meant planting more camps in the narrow valleys along the very spine of the Chaine Annamitique, on the red clay of the jungled highland plateaus, or in the trackless, snake-infested marshlands of the Delta. The frail campsites baked in the tropical sun under a vault of endless Delta sky or were drenched by chilling monsoon rains from clouds masking the peaks of razor-backed mountains. The patrols clambered through thickets of vine and bamboo in triple-canopy jungle, brushing against Indochinese tigers and Viet Cong murder squads.

No military mission was more difficult or potentially more dangerous than border duty, and the Vietnamese sent only their outcasts when the Special Forces imported strike forces into some frontier compounds. The northwestern outposts, in close proximity to North Vietnam and the dreaded A Shau Valley, were the most feared assignments. Friendly natives were scarce, and in the absence of indigenous CIDG manpower, the Special Forces asked for lowland Vietnamese "volunteers" to man camps placed deep in hostile territory. Camps A Ro and Ta Ko were garrisoned by dragooned city toughs from the waterfronts of Hue and Da Nang, tailored into infantry patrol companies, and sent off to march and die by the town authorities.[2]

The Special Forces sergeants sweated compass readings as they led daily patrols from forward-operating bases clinging on the jungled aprons of unknown hills. Years later some of them were finally given numbered identifications after aerial mapping determined their heights. The hostile Katu and Bru tribesmen kept their distance, and chance encounters with wandering families only gave the Vietnamese hoodlums a chance to kill somebody. Most Special Forces attempts to convert Katu and Bru Montagnards into CIDG failed. Camp An Diem, established in March 1963 to contact the Katu, was closed out barely a year later by Captain Griffin's Detachment A-224 on 11 July 1964. Camp Ta Ko lasted only from 1 September 1964 until abandoned by Captain Moon's Detachment A-324 on 5 February 1965. Camp A Ro, initially established by Captain Toughey's composite detachment on 6 June 1964, was shut down by A-414 on 24 April 1965.

By June 1964, Colonel Leonard presided over eighteen camps and sixty-four CIDG companies posted on border surveillance missions. Although a few of the camps could be reached by road or boat in favorable weather, nearly all (90 percent) of the ammunition, food, supplies, and personnel had to be flown in or airdropped to these isolated sites. He realized that such a limited number of camps was insufficient to conduct effective border surveillance, even though ten more teams were moved to the border through the summer. By the end of the year, Special Forces averaged only one camp per thirty miles of border.

Border screening was dangerous, and tangible results were mixed. Most Viet Cong infiltrators simply bypassed camps, sought alternate routes, and avoided large CIDG company-size patrols. Special Forces advisors, hard-pressed to get the LLDB into the field in the first place, were unable to convince them to break down their strike forces into smaller, more silent patrols. The Viet Cong usually moved and fought in the cool of the night, so the LLDB generally refused to patrol at all during darkness. The Special Forces soldiers wanted to play the guerrilla game too but had to compromise by setting up ineffective night "ambush" outposts. Some local areas south and west of Saigon were so full of pro-VC farmers, tipping off their comrades to hide or ambush, that aggressive patrolling was impossible. Other active camps, such as Tinh Bien (established by Capt. Larry Thorne's A-734 of 7th Special Forces Group in April 1964) near the Delta's Seven Mountains area, bushwhacked so many Viet Cong that it became a serious thorn to the VC lifeline into Cambodia.

At no time during the course of the Second Indochina War did Special Forces come close truly to monitoring, much less sealing, South Vietnam's border. However, the Special Forces shift to the border changed the entire complexion of the expanding conflict. While Special Forces border camps varied in border-watching effectiveness, their placement posed a worrisome threat to communist troop movement and supply routes. The very fact that Special Forces camps blocked otherwise-open routes gave MACV strategists enough reason for their employment.

2. Special Forces at War

By October 1964 there were forty-four Special Forces A-Detachments in Vietnam, of which several were staging and twenty-eight had border surveillance missions. The camps had begun to take on the unique Special Forces flavor of pioneer fortresses set out in the badlands of Vietnam. One controlling B-Detachment commander described a typical camp as:

. . . a hodge-podge of males; laborers, mechanics, contractors, soldiers, mercenaries, interpreters, officers, Montagnards, Nungs, pimps, card sharks. Some were patriots, some criminals. All were selfish. All were tough. Only the hardy survived. There were at least five languages spoken and sometimes as many as eight. There was no law except camp regulations and these were only as effective as their camp commander. Everyone in the camp had a goal and a plan as to how to achieve it. The camp had from twenty to forty women who shared the hardships. Some were related to camp members, some had come by invitation, some had no other home or friends. All were put on the payroll in some capacity. All played some role in camp defense.[3]

The Special Forces was also broadening the ethnic composition of its CIDG forces as it inherited the remainder of the CIA's paramilitary "armies" in the post-SWITCHBACK year of transition. This included sizable ethnic Cambodian groups in Vietnam's lower border stretches and the Hoa Hao and Cao Dai religious sects. These were groups that the South Vietnamese government resented, but their strong anti-Viet Cong sentiments and military proficiency blended with Special Forces designs to destroy VC influence in lower South Vietnam.

The Cao Dai was a militant Buddhist splinter group that inhabited a Viet Cong stronghold labeled War Zone C in Tay Ninh "Joyful West" Province. The symbol of the Cao Dai religion coincided with the commanding mountain in the area, Nui Ba Den (Black Virgin Mountain). The Cao Dai religious warriors were anxious to kill any Viet Cong occupying sacred pagodas atop key hills and readily died for the cause. The Hoa Hao (pronounced Wa-How), a reformist Buddhist group, was also a tough band of disciplined fighters. They had been secretly recruited by the CIA as the "Swallows" since 1961 and had already taken a high toll of Viet Cong dead and few prisoners in the southwestern Mekong Delta. Special Forces combat power was greatly enhanced by including both of these religious armies.

The scattered Special Forces camps offered lucrative targets to the Viet Cong. The crudely defended compounds were usually isolated, lacking mutual support, and deliberately placed in areas controlled by the VC or astride major VC infiltration routes. Since minefields in the predefoliation days prevented the cutting of tall grass, detachments frequently had to choose between a minefield or a field of fire. Some campsites had been placed in convenient but militarily unsound locations by Vietnamese officials. In some areas Viet Cong control was so complete that entire VC battalions were protected by the villagers from allied discovery, enabling surprise attacks to be launched at close range. Each camp was on its own during the night, as the ARVN were reluctant to move during darkness for fear of ambush. Any outside help was unlikely before daybreak.

The first Special Forces camp overrun in the Vietnam War was Hiep Hoa in the Plain of Reeds between Saigon and the Cambodian border. Since July 1963, the camp had been occupied by its second team, Capt. Doug Horne's A-21 of the 5th Special Forces Group. The local population was hostile, and camp defenses were poor. Although Hiep Hoa had a 195-man strike force and 47 recruits in training, their morale and combat proficiency were poor. The Special Forces team members, who rotated on a nightly·basis to spot-check camp security, routinely found camp defenders asleep and weapons misplaced.

Several Viet Cong had turned themselves in at Hiep Hoa in late October, claiming they were defectors, and the LLDB had kept them inside camp for rehabilitation. Colonel Morton visited Hiep Hoa early the next week and angrily ordered Captain Horne to get the VC out of the camp. His order was not carried out. He also ordered the detachment commander to conduct more border surveillance patrols. On the morning of 23 November 1963, Captain Horne led a 36-man CIDG force escorted by 7 Special Forces and 3 LLDB advisors out of camp. Lt. John Colby, the executive officer, arrived back from Saigon just as the patrol was leaving camp but was not briefed on the current situation or VC dispositions. He had 4 Special Forces, 9 LLDB, and 206 strike force personnel left inside to guard the camp in Horne's absence.

Shortly after midnight Lieutenant Colby was awakened by mortar explosions mixed with the din of rifle and machine-gun fire. The communications shack was on fire, and the blaze lighted the camp's interior. Lieutenant Colby saw that the north wall defensive positions were empty and screamed at several strike force soldiers to man their posts; his orders went unheeded. He shot one who was throwing grenades into a building. The lieutenant was wounded by the time he found the LLDB commander, who was firing a 60mm mortar. The LLDB officer refused to control the strike forces, so the lieutenant hobbled over to a 81mm mortar being fired single-handedly by a fellow Special Forces soldier.

Viet Cong sympathizers in the Hiep Hoa strike force had killed the guards and manned a machine gun position at the start of the attack. They swung this weapon around and mowed down the strike force soldiers running out of their barracks. The two other Special Forces soldiers in the camp recaptured the machine gun post and held out for a while before they were both wounded and overpowered. The Viet Cong climbed the camp walls with scaling ladders and shouting in Vietnamese, "Don't shoot! All we want is the Americans and the weapons!" They were unopposed. The lieutenant and the other team member ran after the LLDB commander and thirty CIDG soldiers exiting by the front gate. They became separated, and Lieutenant Colby evaded capture by hiding in a sugarcane field as he nursed his wounds.

The Viet Cong had completely overrun the compound, and resulting losses in equipment and personnel were heavy. The grim battle was tainted by widespread treachery. The villagers, the pro-American priest, and the Self-Defense Corps at Hiep Hoa had known of the VC attack in advance, but all had kept silent. Three camp outposts had detected the actual Viet Cong advance but made no attempt to warn the garrison. The MAAG-advised Civil Guard howitzers at the nearby sugar mill refused to fire in support. Strike force treachery inside the camp had been rampant, and the demolished compound was abandoned on 31 December 1963, despite the fact that it left the border area of Hau Nghia Province open again.[4]

Four Special Forces enlisted men had been captured at Hiep Hoa; Sfc. Isaac "Ike" Camacho and Sfc. Kenneth M. Roraback, Sgt. Claude McClure, and Sp5 George E. "Smitty" Smith. Camacho was seized in the mortar pit after he had reentered the camp to assist other possible defenders and eliminated a VC machine gun position. As Camacho surrendered, the Viet Cong grabbed the heated barrel of his carbine. This proof of his having fired enraged one of the captors, who used his rifle butt to club Camacho across the head, causing a severe gash in his skull. Camacho and the others were confined in a makeshift prison camp located on the Vietnamese border in the isolated wilderness of Tay Ninh Province's War Zone C.

The prisoners were kept in bamboo tiger cages, and chained by the ankles to bars fastened through the cages into trees. Camacho spent months carefully freeing the peg used to secure the middle beam under the thatched roof of his tiger cage. Still, escape seemed only a remote possibility as long as he remained bound by the ankle chain-and-bar combination. Finally, almost a year and a half after his capture, Camacho got the chance he was waiting for. The Viet Cong brought two captured American captains into the campsite, and took the chains off Camacho and Smith to use on the new prisoners. Camacho worked anew on freeing the tiger cage peg, which he carefully lubricated with soap for ease of removal at the right moment.

The summer monsoons had now swept over the jungle, and a violent night storm provided Camacho with his long-awaited opportunity. He prepared a dummy from extra clothing bundled on his cage cot to deceive the nightly armed guard. The storm's high winds unleashed sheets of rain across the compound and reduced visibility to a hand's length. Camacho quickly pried out the bamboo peg as the continuous thunder cracked over the noise of his labored, frantic breathing. He lifted the middle beam on the cage roof, and was almost blinded by the lightning flashing through the torrential rain. Once he had pulled the bar aside, his emaciated condition enabled him to slither out between the other two bars. Camacho replaced the bar in its socket and scurried into the underbrush in the drenching downpour.

Camacho, with the other prisoners, having been forced to provide wood-cutting details knew the familiar white sandy trail leading away from the campsite. He passed a large distinctive log and kept going into the forest, only to return full-circle to the same log an hour later. Realizing that his survival depended on correct orientation, Camacho sat down on the log in the rainstorm and tried calmly to collect his thoughts. When he set out again, he used his survival skills to follow the abundant water flow, which led to a stream and eventually emptied into a large river. Camacho floated with the river until first light, battled a boa constrictor that dropped on him from an overhanging branch, and pulled off the dozens of blood-sucking leeches that had attached to his body during his immersion. He picked up a large stick for protection and foliage smashing, and continued through the jungle.

During the next four days Camacho avoided several Viet Cong patrols. He rationed out the small amount of rice, hoarded from his cage supply, which he mixed with tropical fruits picked from banana plants and mango thickets. On July 13, 1965, Camacho crossed a rubber plantation that led him into the villge of Minh Thanh, a South Vietnamese government outpost in the midst of War Zone C. His ordeal over, Camacho became the first American serviceman to escape from the Viet Cong in the Second Indochina War. His comrades left behind shared a mixed fate. Smith and McClure were eventually released, but Roraback and the two captains were later executed.[5]

Another Special Forces escapee from Viet Cong confinement was Capt. James N. "Nick" Rowe, who had been taken prisoner on 29 October 1963, in an ambush near Tan Phu. He made his fourth escape attempt on the eve of his scheduled execution, over five years after being initially captured. Taking advantage of a sudden flight of American helicopters, Rowe struck down his guards and raced into a clearing where his frenzied waving attracted aerial observation. As one helicopter made a low-level pass, the crew noticed his bearded, non-oriental face. Rowe was whisked to safety on 31 December 1968. Still clad in black peasant clothing, he was notified that he had been promoted to Major during his long captivity. Unfortunately, instances of successful escapes such as those undertaken by Camacho and Rowe were rare, and most Special Forces troops taken prisoner either died in captivity, were released at the end of the war, or remain unaccounted for.[6]

After the fall of Hiep Hoa, the Special Forces started taking more camp security precautions. Tough mercenaries of Chinese extraction, called Nungs, were hired as bodyguards and special camp guards. The Nungs were personally loyal to the detachment commanders they served. Camp defenses were also improved and strengthened, and forward observation bases (FOB) were established. A typical FOB was a bivouac site set out at a distance from the main camp, manned by strike force companies rotating on a weekly basis to patrol and provide intelligence about VC activities. However, there were still many lessons to be learned. In July 1964 the Viet Cong assaulted two other remote border camps: Polei Krong in upper Kontum Province and Nam Dong in northern Thua Thien Province. While both battles witnessed great acts of bravery by individual Special Forces soldiers, laxity in camp defense again enabled the VC to achieve complete surprise.

Polei Krong was garrisoned by Capt. William Johnson's Detachment A-122, an LLDB team, six interpreters, and approximately seventy-four strike force soldiers when the Viet Cong struck at 2:00 in the early morning darkness of 4 July 1964. The camp was located on a river, but landside defenses were poor. There was no password, tall grass obstructed observation, and only eleven of twenty-one guard posts were manned. Two strike force companies were absent. They had been allowed to sleep overnight with their families across the river after returning from a patrol. LLDB Lieutenant Tan had not followed Johnson's advice to set up outposts at night to warn of enemy approach. The compound was full of peddlers, women, and civilian workers.

The attack started when an interpreter heard voices near the kitchen facility. A Viet Cong called out, "Where are the Americans? Take us to them." The interpreter responded by firing his entire thirty-round magazine into the VC, and the battle started. There were already a number of Viet Cong among the camp defenders. The Viet Cong opened fire with mortars and recoilless rifles, which had been dug in and sandbagged, completely undetected, only 250 yards from the camp perimeter at the edge of the airstrip. The first mortar shell hit the center of the Special Forces team house, seriously wounding Specialist 5th Class Broyles and Specialist Fourth Class Swald and slightly wounding two other sergeants.

Shortly thereafter the Viet Cong stormed the southern fenceline and exploded bangalore torpedoes to breach the wire. The camp's open machine gun nests, protected only by dilapidated sandbags, were destroyed early. The Viet Cong were able rapidly to close-assault the positions, since the crews had no grenades to cover the areas beyond the guns' turning radius or field of fire (the grenades were kept in the ammunition bunker). The Viet Cong quickly turned captured machine guns and mortars on the camp defenders.[7]

Captain Johnson ran out of the team house as VC fire poured in from three sides and mortar rounds began to hit the key compound buildings. He shot down one VC who had destroyed the generator shed and was running toward the teamhouse with another satchel charge. Sergeant Seymour also raced out to gun down swarms of Viet Cong around the ammunition bunker. More Viet Cong were fast approaching, forcing the detachment to make a last-ditch fight from its own team house parapets. The blazing supply room lighted up the compound, and the Special Forces and Nung troops were able to deliver accurate return fire with their M-79s and automatic rifles. Sergeant Walles and one Nung repulsed two VC squads encircling the east end of the team house. Sergeant Price maintained radio contact until the antenna was knocked out by mortar fire.

The Special Forces soldiers realized that the battle was already lost. The strike force had ceased to exist. While many refused to fight, others had been clubbed in their quarters or killed running to their battle stations. The Nungs fought tenaciously but were low on ammunition. There was plenty in the ammunition bunker, but it could not be reached after the start of the battle. The last resistance was the gallant performance of a Montagnard light machine gun crew on the southwest corner. They kept firing for forty minutes, piling up stacks of dead Viet Cong before their position was blasted apart by grenades and satchel charges on poles.

The Special Forces and Nung defenders retreated to the river by making a break one at a time. The withdrawal apparently became confused and disorderly. Some of the crippled and seriously wounded Americans and Nungs were not carried and had to drag themselves painfully across open ground to the riverbank. Defenders were either out of ammunition or down to their last magazine. The radio was shot up. Empty five-gallon gas cans were tucked under the wounded and floated down river. Some of the wounded were hysterical, and people were shouting they could not swim. A Nung sent to fetch a boat reported back that all the boats were mined. Fortunately, the Viet Cong never pursued them to the water's edge.[8]

At 3:15 A.M. Polei Krong was entirely in Viet Cong hands. The Viet Cong stayed in the smoldering camp for two hours caring for their wounded, searching for prisoners, and cleaning weapons. They attempted no systematic destruction and left the compound with the coming of daylight. The Americans then reentered the compound with the other two strike force companies. They found considerable quantities of unexploded VC demolition blocks and three dead Viet Cong on the barbed wire.[9]

The specter of inside VC cooperation was all too evident. One of the VC bodies had papers identifying him as a contractor employee and a complete diagram of the camp weapons and their firing patterns. Several LLDB sergeants were found assassinated along the perimeter or in their bunks with broken necks. The defeat at Polei Krong was one of the most tragic actions in Special Forces history.[10]

The Nam Dong CIDG camp was strategically situated in central northern Thua Thien Province at the junction of two mountain valleys, which served as VC infiltration routes into the lowlands around Da Nang and Phu Bai. The site also protected 5,000 Montagnards in a string of villages along the valley floor. Nam Dong was a prime VC target, and Special Forces realized that its position was too dangerous. Detachment A-726, commanded by Capt. Roger H. Donlon, was scheduled to close out the camp. Tall grass had been allowed to grow up to the very edge of the barbed-wire perimeter.

The native villagers were hostile. The district chief in Khe Tre, at the other end of the valley, had insisted that his Civil Guard instead of the camp garrison would patrol west of the airstrip. There had been fights among the 300 strike force members. On 5 July, the day after the Polei Krong disaster, a major disturbance erupted over a camp prostitute, which resulted in rock throwing and the firing of some weapons. That night the entire Nung guard force remained at their battle positions rather than sleeping in their quarters, armed and prepared for more internal trouble. Captain Donlon had 381 CIDG, 50 Nungs, 7 LLDB, 12 Special Forces, 1 Australian advisor, and 1 pathologist present in the compound.

The Viet Cong attack came swiftly and suddenly at 2:30 A.M. on 6 July 1964. The VC battalion had crossed the river and airstrip from the northeast, overran the twenty-man camp outpost, crept up through the tall grass and cut the double-apron fence. The VC achieved complete surprise. Nam Dong was smothered by a devastating mortar barrage that knocked out the Nung barracks, communications shack, and dispensary. The radio operator rolled over from his bunk and managed to tap out "under intense mortar attack" before radio contact was lost.

The first wave of screaming Viet Cong, wearing red and blue swim-trunk uniforms, charged into the camp as the rain of mortar shells ceased. Viet Cong loudspeakers blared eerily throughout the assault, urging the defenders in English and Vietnamese to lay down their weapons and surrender. The shock troops carried handcuffs for the expected prisoners.

Three circumstances (two of them by chance) prevented Nam Dong from being defeated. The camp had been originally built at a small French outpost and had then been expanded as the strike force size increased. This gave Nam Dong a second, inner, perimeter. There was plenty of ammunition at the forward fighting positions, and the Nungs were alert and manning their posts. The Viet Cong swept over the outer perimeter, but two attempts at storming the inner strongpoints were repulsed by withering machine gun fire and grenades.

Captain Donlon dashed through a hail of rifle fire and exploding grenades and killed a VC demolitions team at the main gate. Wounded in the stomach, he reached a mortar position and covered the withdrawal of the wounded Special Forces soldiers there. He carried out his team sergeant and was wounded again. He then rescued the mortar, administered first aid, and went back into action retrieving ammunition and directing final defensive positions. Wounded four times during the course of the five-hour battle, Captain Donlon's actions were largely responsible for the successful camp defense. He became the first Medal of Honor recipient in Vietnam.

Marine Colonel Merchant dispatched six Marine helicopters loaded with Special Forces and Nung troops, but heavy ground fire prevented their landing. Air Force aircraft were unable to airdrop badly needed ammunition until nine o'clock that morning, as the VC were withdrawing. The relief force was finally landed forty-five minutes later. Camp Nam Dong had been largely destroyed and was closed out by a replacement team (A-224) on 4 September 1964. Later the inner-strongpoint-perimeter concept was adapted as an inbuilt design feature for all Special Forces compounds. Under the circumstances it was a tribute to the courage and resourcefulness of the Special Forces that only three camps were actually assaulted during this period.[11]

3. The New Role of the LLDB

Besides the threat of camp attack, the Special Forces was also contending with an upheaval in LLDB organization. President Diem had been assassinated in the military coup d'état of 1 November 1963, which brought General Minh to power. Although General Minh was in turn ousted by General Nguyen Khanh two months later, the first coup was the most damaging to the Special Forces counterparts. The LLDB, which had enjoyed special status under the Diem regime, was relegated to political disfavor and integrated into the rest of the South Vietnamese armed forces on 5 January 1964.

Bad luck followed bad news. At that time Major Tat's 31st LLDB Group was still undergoing basic airborne training. During the course of qualifying jumps in the first week of February, one LLDB candidate caught his reserve parachute handle on his seat safety belt while standing up to prepare to exit the plane. The reserve parachute popped open and was sucked violently out of the aircraft, smashing the parachutist through the door and against the side of the plane. It was a messy death and was interpreted as an ominous sign by the Vietnamese.

The 31st LLDB Group moved to Camp Lam Son at Dong Ba

Thin, just south of Nha Trang, on 25 February 1964. In May the group was given responsibility for LLDB detachments in I and II Corps Tactical Zones. On 1 September 1964 it was redesignated as the 111th LLDB Group and became responsible also for the Dong Ba Thin special operations training center, assisted by Major Lewis's B-1 and A-132. The 77th LLDB Group was headquartered at Camp Hung Vuong in Saigon and was redesignated the 301st LLDB on 1 September 1964. On that date the Vietnamese LLDB had a total of 333 officers, 1,270 sergeants, and 1,066 privates assigned.[12]

A new LLDB commander, Col. Lam Son, was installed on 19 February 1964. Previously the Vietnamese military attaché to the Philippines, he had been banished from service following the November coup. After an initial spurt of activity, he languished in the job until he was relieved at American insistence. In August 1964 Maj. Gen. Doan Van Quang assumed command of the LLDB. Born at Ha Dong in North Vietnam on 16 September 1923, he had entered French Union military service as a private in 1942 and was commissioned in 1945. A paratrooper since 1948, he became the commander of ARVN ranger units in 1960 and took over a division in 1963. He brought a new sense of mission, but the LLDB was fatally handicapped by adverse political considerations and inadequate personnel.

The LLDB officers and sergeants varied widely in quality. Many inexperienced LLDB officers simply turned over all aspects of command to their Special Forces advisors. Others were military professionals who worked harmoniously with Special Forces advisors as a team. There were even exceptional LLDB leaders who skillfully used American advice and material, but stayed completely in charge. However, Special Forces found many of their LLDB counterparts to be incompetent, self-serving individuals who were uncooperative and who actively sabotaged mission accomplishment.

Relations between Vietnamese commanders and their Special Forces advisors were sensitive by their very nature. When relations became strained to the point of open animosity, CIDG training and morale suffered, camp security was imperiled, and operational effectiveness usually evaporated. Extremely poor American-Vietnamese relations existed at Plei Do Lim, a border surveillance camp located outside Pleiku. Pleiku was in the heart of Montagnard territory, and legend attributed its name to a contest that awarded the winning hamlet the symbol of supremacy: the tail of a sacrificed water buffalo. The perennial winning hamlet was called *Plei* (hamlet) *ku* (of the tail).

The Montagnards did not like the Vietnamese in the camp, and Capt. Herbert F. Hardy Jr.'s Detachment A-334 was practically squared off against camp commander Capt. Bui Van Lim and his LLDB team. The LLDB officers avoided the front and spent their time in self-enrichment at detachment expense. There were incidents over stolen rice and salt and the tossing of defensive claymore mine electrical wires into the perimeter ditches.

In mid-February 1964 Captain Hardy and two of his sergeants escorted a Montagnard strike force company into the Rapan Mountains. After seven days, on 23 February, they spotted some VC on a ridge ahead of them, but a sudden mortar shelling defeated attempts to maneuver the CIDG company into a skirmish line. S. Sgt. Dale E. Worley followed them back downhill and reorganized them. They refused to go any farther after they were hit a second time by some mortar rounds. Captain Hardy and Sfc. William E. Edge, armed only with M16 rifles, then charged the platoon-size Viet Cong training base, killing five VC and wounding twenty-five others. However, the victory was largely undone when helicopters landed the nineteen wounded tribesmen back at camp. That night, sixty-five of their dismayed comrades left their weapons and deserted.

Captain Lim put both Hardy and Edge in for the Vietnamese Cross of Gallantry. American and Vietnamese relations continued to sour, and after Hardy was killed in patrolling action on 4 March, Captain Lim withdrew recommendations for both awards. Capt. William J. Boyd took over the detachment, but camp conditions worsened. The LLDB commander was indifferent to rusting and misplaced weapons, tolerated a drunk CIDG officer, and took offense at any soldier he perceived the Americans favored. Captain Boyd retaliated by disallowing Vietnamese freedom of the inner perimeter and personally renaming the joint compound, Camp Hardy.

Finally, an inside assassination attempt was directed against the American detachment. A camp generator was set on fire on the evening of 10 May 1964, and three Special Forces sergeants responded to the alarm by hooking up the water trailer to fight the blaze. A grenade was pitched at them over the 3/4-ton truck attached to the water trailer. The resulting explosion at the door of the team house wounded Sergeant First Class Edge, Staff Sergeant Worley, and Staff

Sergeant Cade. When 1st Lt. James R. Haise arrived with half of detachment A-76 on 14 June, he discovered that the Special Forces soldiers were more distrustful of Lim than of the Viet Cong. A sizable contingent of Nung guards were brought in, which heightened Lim's hostility. The adverse American-Vietnamese relations had rendered Plei Do Lim practically combat ineffective.[13]

4. The Montagnard Uprising

Col. John H. Spears assumed command of the U.S. Army Special Forces Group Vietnam (Provisional) in August 1964. He was an infantry officer of World War II background who had no previous Special Forces experience. However, he arrived in Vietnam directly from his previous duty station with the Infantry career management branch, where he had monitored the assignment of infantry officers to Special Forces in Vietnam. He was equipped with an intimate knowledge of Army requirements and MACV desires concerning Special Forces officer material for the Vietnam conflict. He would incorporate the provisional group into the 5th Special Forces Group when it arrived that fall and command both organizations.

The American and Vietnamese military remained at odds over Montagnard utilization. Some Montagnard groups possessed soldiering potential, but Vietnamese authorities refused to permit full development of tribal resources. The Montagnard rebellion of 19 to 28 September 1964 abruptly refocused attention on the persistent minority problem in Vietnam. The Special Forces again found itself in the middle of a mess that it was powerless to prevent. MACV had an ingrained distaste for irregulars, and the Vietnamese resented the Montagnards and those who helped them. The brunt of this dual dissatisfaction fell on Special Forces shoulders. The peculiar Special Forces minority advisory role, imposed by the CIDG concept, brought high-level embarrassment and anger.

The Montagnards who revolted were all from Special Forces camps in the Ban Me Thuot area of the central highlands. Ban Me Thuot was a Vietnamese-populated city, but traditionally the Montagnard capital. Hundreds of Montagnard hamlets and their communal long houses dotted the green hills outside the town. The Special Forces camps in the region had large native CIDG contingents, whose loyalty extended only to their Montagnard leaders and Special Forces advisors.

The Vietnamese contemptuously regarded the Montagnards as inferior but dangerous and distrusted Special Forces organization of hill tribes into tactical military units. For example, many Vietnamese in Ban Me Thuot believed that a special Montagnard battalion had been formed by the United States that was armed with "two hundred small nuclear weapons." The Montagnards' attitude toward Vietnamese remained acrimonious, and continued mistreatment by Vietnamese authorities heightened their grievances. As early as July, the Special Forces personnel in several camps detected a deepening resentment in the mood of their Montagnard troops. There was also an air in the strike forces that relief was in sight; it was a shadowy feeling that the Special Forces could not nail down.

During the night of 19–20 September 1964, the Montagnard strike force components of five CIDG camps took matters into their own hands. The three companies of 414 Mnong and Rhade Montagnards at Bon Sar Pa killed eleven LLDB soldiers in the camp, held Captain Darnell and his Detachment A-311A hostage, and moved northeast on trucks to seize the Ban Me Thuot radio station and a key bridge. The radio station had been rendered inoperable when the station manager removed certain parts.

At Buon Mi Ga four companies of 614 Mnong Montagnards killed ten LLDB advisors, disarmed Captain Loa's Detachment A-121A, and motored west to Ban Me Thuot. After they left, helicopters promptly airlifted the Special Forces soldiers out of the camp. Five companies of 914 Rhade and Jarai Montagnards at Ban Don bound their LLDB advisors with rope, initially locked up Captain Terry's Detachment A-75, and moved southeast on Ban Me Thuot. Using trucks, three battalions of Montagnards had closed in on the Darlac provincial capital of Ban Me Thuot from three directions by 7:00 A.M. on 20 September.

The three companies of 462 Mnong Montagnards at Bu Prang slaughtered fifteen Vietnamese strike force leaders and another nineteen Self-Defense Corps soldiers at a nearby outpost and restricted Captain Webb's Detachment A-311B to the camp. The Bu Prang force was prevented by lack of vehicles from reaching its target, the Quang Duc provincial capital of Gia Nghia. Captain Webb had the Bu Prang strike force companies back in camp working on normal details by 21 September. Although he felt he was not completely in charge, he feared a loss of control if his Special Forces departed Bu Prang.

Capt. Vern Gillespie, commanding Detachment A-312 at Buon

Brieng, had persuaded the 715 Rhade Montagnards stationed there not to follow through with their initially rebellious intentions. As a result, the Montagnard "national" flag was not hoisted over the compound as it was at the other camps. This was later seen as the critical move that saved Ban Me Thuot from Montagnard occupation, because it left Highway 14 open from the north.

The 23d ARVN Division and Montagnard troops faced each other uneasily outside Ban Me Thuot on Sunday, 20 September. That afternoon Captain Terry convinced the Ban Don strikers to return to camp and escorted them back. There was only one clash at a Buon Mi Ga Montagnard force roadblock, which occurred at 9:00 P.M. and caused ten strike force casualties. Throughout the night leaders from both sides wrangled over Montagnard grievances, using Special Forces officers as intermediaries. The Montagnards had such a reverence for Special Forces that Colonel Freund had to dress his two signalmen in Special Forces clothing to insure their acceptance for radio communications.

Captain Loa returned to prevent a major ARVN attack on the Buon Mi Ga strike force, ironically assembled at the original CIDG "success story" complex of Buon Enao, just northeast of Ban Me Thuot. His detachment then spent several frustrating days trying to get empty trucks to move the rebel strikers back to their camp. Most were still sitting in Buon Enao without transportation at the end of the uprising seven days later.

Colonel Freund, the American II Corps advisor, and Special Forces officers remained with the highly volatile Bon Sar Pa force at their forward positions another night. The rebels were insisting on attacking Ban Me Thuot but listened to advice not to attack from their camp's Special Forces advisor, Captain Darnell, who was greatly admired and respected by the Montagnards. Finally, low-flying Vietnamese fighter-bombers convinced them to withdraw back to the Bon Sar Pa compound.

The Bon Sar Pa force was considered the most dangerous, since it had several hundred Vietnamese hostages from its takeover of a district capital on the original march toward Ban Me Thuot. Colonel Spears arrived to negotiate prisoner release. At first everything went well, but then Colonels Freund and Spears boldly cut the strands binding Lieutenant Chu (the only surviving LLDB prisoner from the Bon Sar Pa Camp) and speeded him onto a waiting helicopter. The Montagnards were infuriated and held both colonels hostage during the night of 21–22 September 1964.

Relative stability governed the other camps, and all efforts were concentrated at regaining control over Bon Sar Pa. The 47th ARVN Regiment was moved up toward the camp as the negotiations continued for the next several days. Colonel Freund finally resolved the crisis. On 28 September 1964 the Bon Sar Pa force released its prisoners and capitulated to ARVN forces outside the camp. Captain Darnell and Captain King (who arrived with another split A-Team) stayed to show the Montagnards that the American Special Forces soldiers were remaining in the camp. Captain Darnell had been instrumental in defusing tensions. The Montagnards considered his presence a sign of good faith, and he exerted a steadying influence on the Rhade tribesmen.

Although the revolt was quickly ended, the Vietnamese government was forced reluctantly to sit down and discuss Montagnard demands. An ARVN officer of Rhade descent was installed as the camp commander of Ban Don, the last camp to pull down its rebel flag. Rhade ARVN officers were also selected to command Camps Buon Brieng and Buon Mi Ga. By the middle of October, the Montagnard leaders held a congress to present their conditions. Foremost was their desire for a 50,000-man army led by Montagnards and trained exclusively by Special Forces without MAAG interference. Before the Saigon regime could respond to the long Montagnard list of demands, the central highlands was deluged by unusually heavy rainstorms during late October and early November. Communications and transportation were completely disrupted.

The Vietnamese finally instituted only a few token changes in their governing policies toward the Montagnards. The revolt had merely brought CIDG problems under sharp criticism. MACV was upset that the Montagnards devoted their loyalties to the Special Forces sponsors of the program and not to the Saigon government. This was not a fault of Special Forces, which had done its best to give all the credit to the Vietnamese. The arrogant, repressive actions of the Vietnamese officials toward the natives, however, had always betrayed the Vietnamese lack of sincerity in CIDG support.[14]

As a final postscript to the 1964 Montagnard revolt, the camps involved were all shut down within a year. Bon Sar Pa was the first to go, closed down on 1 November 1964. Ban Don was closed out on the first day of the new year, and Bu Prang followed on 15 January 1965. Buon Mi Ga was ordered abandoned on 28 April 1965. Months later the Vietnamese suddenly declared Buon Brieng to be heavily infiltrated by dissident Montagnards sympathetic to the Rhade independence movement known as FULRO, which stood for *Front Unifié Pour La Libération Des Races Opprimées* (Unified Front for the Liberation of Oppressed Peoples).

The post-SWITCHBACK transition period of provisional Special Forces, lasting from July 1963 until October 1964, had been full of internal upheavals that often took front stage. The assassination of President Diem had reshaped the LLDB, a profound development since the Special Forces priority mission was still to provide advisory assistance to the Vietnamese Special Forces. The secondary mission became the establishment of bases for the conduct of border surveillance operations, which shifted emphasis away from area development. The Montagnard rebellion had posed an uncomfortable dilemma to the Special Forces soldiers, who sympathized with the tribesmen but were sworn to defend the South Vietnamese government. However, the backdrop of sharply escalating military operations had been underlined by the major Viet Cong assaults on Hiep Hoa, Polei Krong, and Nam Dong. During October 1964, the 5th Special Forces Group (Airborne) arrived from Fort Bragg, North Carolina, to give a permanent Special Forces title to the forty-four A-Detachments fighting in Vietnam.

Notes

*Treated in section 4, this chapter.

1. MACV, *Directive* for Assumption of Operational Control of Border Surveillance Program, Directive 260815Z USMACV J3 8409. (Emphasis has been added.)

2. Charles M. Simpson III, *Inside the Green Berets*, Novato, Calif.: Presidio Press, 1983.

3. Detachment B-410, *Debriefing*, dtd 18 December 1964. The camp was in I CTZ.

4. At Hiep Hoa, 41 CIDG had been KIA and 120 WIA. Four LLDB, and 28 strike force soldiers were declared MIA. Other than the 7 bodies left behind, Viet Cong losses were unknown. MACVJ32, *Monthly Report—CIDG Program in RVN,* December 1963; U.S. Military Assistance Advisory Group III Corps Memorandum MAGTM-IIIC-3, dtd 13 January 1964; George E. Smith, *POW: Two Years with the Viet Cong,* (Berkeley, Calif., Ramparts Press: 1971).

5. Sergeant First Class Isaac Camacho's escape was documented in the 5th Special Forces Group headquarters E&E files retained at Nha Trang. In 1974, Special Forces Association Chapter IX was named in his honor.

6. James Rowe, *Five Years to Freedom,* Boston: Little Brown, 1971.

7. A 22d ARVN Division letter memorandum on the battle, which received wide dissemination in Vietnam and was copied as fact into several American publications, recites a strange story. In essence, the ARVN account states that the Viet Cong took advantage of the fact that the Montagnard construction contractor was permitted to enter and leave the camp throughout the night. When the sentry challenged a group that walked up to the main gate, a Montagnard VC simply replied, "Contractor." The sentry opened the gate and was killed. Two groups of Viet Cong rushed into the camp along the trenches, machine-gunning and grenading the strike force soldiers who were responding to an attack on the south side of the wire. In response to this report, Detachment B-330 Ltr, Subject: The Report of 22d DTA on the Attack of Polei Krong, dtd 15 August 1964, states: "It could hardly be expected that the sentry would open the gate after the attack started, yet the statement reads that the attack had already begun at the south flank. The sentry was killed in the attack; thus, the statement is pure conjecture."

8. Detachment B-330, Ltr, Subject: The Attack on Polei Krong, dated 10 August 1964.

9. Losses at Polei Krong were KIA: 46 strike force, 3 LLDB, including Lieutenant Tan; WIA; 27 strike force, 3 LLDB, 5 Special Forces, 5 Nungs, 6 interpreters. VC losses were unknown, but air strikes on retreating col-

umns led Special Forces to estimate between 105 and 175, including the few bodies found on the wire. All other VC dead had been removed.

10. The official South Vietnamese version of the battle was predictably anti-Special Forces and responsible for court-martial charges being brought against detachment members: "All Special Forces cadres, Vietnamese as well as American, when being attacked violently by enemy, ran in disorder to slip away or withdrew to hide at the river bank and did not fight out the battle to the end. . . . There was no loss of signal apparatus; even the signal shelter for direct communication to the 2d Tactical Zone was not broken into by the VC. The loss of communications right at the first gun shot is a defect of Vietnamese and American commanding levels who lost their heads and ran away . . . bunkers were piled high with sand bags, so they collapsed right away . . . alternate bunkers without covering walls with simple machine guns were destroyed right at the beginning with few expended cartridge and shell casings found at the gun positions . . . a number of soldiers were killed in their very houses inside the camp, a number were killed when running from their houses to the defense lines. Interpreting the position of the CIDG bodies, we believed they were killed and fell into the trenches; they were not fatally wounded in the standing or sitting position to fight . . . the commanding levels and CIDG cadre's irresponsible spirit and also the U.S. advisors' confidence in their weapons and their abundant ammunition were responsible for the defeat"; RVNAF II Corps, 2d Tactical Zone, 22d Tactical Area General Staff Memorandum, Subject: Lessons Learned from the Loss of a Special Forces Camp on the Night of 3–4 July 1964, No. 1661/K22CT/P3/HQ; and ARVN Tactical Zone 2, Tactical Area 22 Ltr No. 1661, Subject: Experiences After the Fall of an LLDB Camp on the Night of 3 July 1964, dtd 18 July 1964. These ARVN memorandums received wide dissemination, and portions were repeated by official U.S. Army reports.

11. Losses at Nam Dong were KIA: 58 CIDG, 2 Special Forces, 1 Australian advisor; WIA: 57 CIDG, 7 Special Forces. Viet Cong body count was 55. Headquarters, U.S. Army Special Forces Vietnam Tactical Operations Center, *After Action Report*, dtd 21 July 1964; 93d Congress, 1st Session Committee Print 15, *Medal of Honor Recipients, 1863–1973;* Capt. Robert H. Whitlow, *U.S. Marines in Vietnam: The Advisory and Combat Assistance Era*, pp. 157–8 (Washington, D.C.: U.S. Marine Corps, 1977). A good account of the battle is found in Capt. Roger Donlon, *Outpost of Freedom*, (New York: McGraw-Hill, 1965).

12. Office of the U.S. Army Advisor, 31st Special Forces Group (Airborne), Army of the Republic of Vietnam, *Report #2*, dtd 10 Feb 64; *Report #5*, dtd 29 Feb 64; *After Action Report*, dtd 16 July 1964; *Report #20*, dtd 15 Sep 64; Office of the U.S. Army Advisor, 77th Special Forces Group

(Airborne), Army of the Republic of Vietnam, *Report,* dtd 23 March 1964. The LLDB special warfare school, at Song Mao since 28 May 1962, was shut down on 20 February 1964.

13. Detachment A-321 Ltr, Subject: Summary of Acts by Camp Commander, dtd 2 Jan 1964; Detachment A-321 Ltr, Subject: Security Violations, dtd 4 April 1964; Ltr from Captain Lim to Commanding General of 2CTZVNSF, dtd 14 April 1964; Detachment A-334, *After Action Report,* Subject: Grenade Incident, dtd 11 May 1964; Detachment 76B Ltr, Subject: Suitability of Camp Commander, dtd 31 July 1964.

14. Montagnard uprising narrative was drawn primarily from Headquarters, 5th Special Forces Group, *Historical Résumé of the Montagnard Uprising;* USASFV (Prov), CIDG Monthly Report for September 1964; NMCC Operational Summaries for 21–28 September 1964 (OPSUM 141–64 et al.); and USASF S-1 File, Memorandum for Record, Subject: Revolt of 20 September 1964.

CHAPTER 6

INTO THE BREACH

1. The 5th Special Forces Group Arrives

The 5th Special Forces Group (Airborne) was formally established in South Vietnam on 1 October 1964 and absorbed the men and material of Col. John H. Spears's U.S. Army Special Forces Vietnam (Provisional). The group headquarters and headquarters company arrived in country at the end of the month, just over three years after it had been activated at Fort Bragg, North Carolina, on 21 September 1961 to provide teams into Southeast Asia. The 5th Special Forces Group presence in Vietnam enabled the 1st and 7th Special Forces Groups to concentrate once again on their respective Far East and global reserve responsibilities.[1]

Colonel Spears, who stayed on to command the 5th Special Forces Group in Vietnam, split his group headquarters in two. The tactical operations center (TOC) at Saigon, under the deputy commander, supervised operational and intelligence matters, while the administration and logistics center, under the executive officer, was located in Nha Trang along with the communications center. An entire B-Detachment had to be fragmented to provide sufficient people for this arrangement. The group commander worked in either center until the headquarters was eventually reconsolidated in Nha Trang on 10 September 1965.[2]

The Special Forces headquarters controlled its basic operating A-Detachments through a convoluted hierarchy extending down through intermediate C- and B-Detachments. Each corps tactical zone contained one C-Detachment. While these were technically command echelons, in practice they served as the principal Special Forces staff of the MACV corps senior advisors and also assisted corps LLDB officers. Seven of the ten B-Detachments, located in the provinces and ARVN division tactical zones, exercised the actual command supervision over individually encamped A-Detachments. The other three were specially modified to perform special missions at the LLDB Dong Ba Thin training center, command Project DELTA, and to provide support to MACV special operations. Complications were prevalent in the standard B-Detachment functions as well. For instance, Major Brewington's B-22 at An Khe performed road security under the operational control of the South Vietnamese Army.

The reason for transferring a stateside Special Forces group to Vietnam had more to do with Pentagon desires to effect monetary savings than to herald any long-term American military commitment there. For years, regular advisory officers had resented that Special Forces detachments from the 1st, 5th, and 7th Special Forces Groups served on a temporary-duty status in Vietnam, which entitled them to extra pay. Special Forces teams had also complained that their Vietnam preparation in Okinawa or Fort Bragg had been inadequate and that six months provided too little time for mission accomplishment overseas.

The Pentagon concluded that detachments permanently based in Vietnam, which could be continuously refilled by new personnel rotating into the combat zone on individual one-year assignment tours, would both allow continuity of service and alleviate the pay differential between Special Forces and regular Army advisors. Such a policy contradicted to Special Forces operating principles, which relied on keeping teams intact as distinct operating units. Special Forces commanders suggested that the detachments be retained as unbroken organizations, but rotated into Vietnam at one-year intervals, excluding temporary-duty pay. However, the primary patron of Special Forces, President Kennedy, was dead, and President Johnson's Joint Chiefs of Staff had little understanding or tolerance for unique Special Forces requirements separate from those of the ordinary military.

Over a six-month period, from the fall of 1964 to the spring of 1965, four C-Detachments, twelve B-Detachments, and forty-eight A-Detachments arrived on permanent change of orders to Vietnam. The temporary-duty teams were phased out as they completed their six-month duty tours. For the rest of the war, Special Forces operations would be impaired by the same disabling problems vexing the rest of the military in Vietnam: personnel turbulence and lack of unit cohesion. For an organization like Special Forces, which was premised on team integrity, the Army's individual replacement system in Vietnam was another step in the destruction of its ideal modus operandi.

The rising tempo of the Vietnam War overshadowed all Special Forces efforts. Viet Cong regiments equipped with modern automatic weapons battered ARVN forces in a succession of devastating defeats, which threatened to tear apart the country and topple Saigon's weak and coup-prone central government. This fate was avoided only by the introduction in the spring of 1965 of equally large and well-equipped American formations. In the interval, during the first crucial six months of 5th Special Forces Group existence in Vietnam, its beleaguered camps were largely on their own.

The 5th Special Forces Group manpower was extremely limited. In October 1,112 Special Forces soldiers controlled 19,260 native mercenaries. By March 1965, when the Marines landed, group strength was still roughly the same: 1,465 Americans and 19,842 tribal riflemen. Sixty-six percent of the Special Forces soldiers were assigned at the detachment level, and the valiant fighting courage of these men, scattered in various camps, prevented large areas of South Vietnam from being swept under VC military domination.

The mission of the Special Forces soldier was hard, dirty, and bloody. Far from the air-conditioned staff offices and comfortable bungalows of higher headquarters, the Special Forces advisors were crammed into dirt-walled, undergunned campsites carved out of steaming, disease-ridden swamp and jungle. There was little respite from constant danger and back-breaking labor in the dank, mist-shrouded hinterland of Vietnam. Sinewy muscles were toned and hardened by the long patrol marches over broken grassland, leg-wrenching-deep mud, and vine-choked jungle. The sweltering tropical heat baked away sweat and blistered eyelids almost shut. Foul water and malaria-infested rain forest sent burning fever and clammy chills through bodies doubled over by rucksacks of ammunition strapped under radios. Sores openly festered as lice and insects crawled across skin slashed by thorns and razor-sharp elephant grass. Deadwood and animal-trodden rice fields twisted ankles and caved in knees, while around-the-clock vigilance reddened eyes and fatigued the mind. Sudden death or crippling disfigurement threatened each measured Special Forces step.

2. Filling in the Gap: Expendable Infantry

The conventional posture of the 5th Special Forces Group, which predominated by late 1964, was caused by the desperate MACV need for frontline stiffening to bolster the flagging South Vietnamese armed forces. The Special Forces, as an unconventional warfare element, was not intended to fight as line infantry. Yet the minuscule A-Teams proved tough and scrappy, and they possessed an uncanny ability to survive the harshest combat conditions and accomplish the most difficult assignments .

The stated missions of Special Forces were readjusted in early 1965 for:

(1) Filling in the gap between commitment of U.S. combat troops and advisory influence, (2) adaptability for integration with U.S. forces, (3) prompt, flexible, and sufficient response to variable requirements, (4) intensifying appropriate aspects of counterinsurgency effort by providing staying power in hot areas, or acting as the *spearhead* of rural reconstruction, or advancing reconstruction in more pacified areas (rolling security), (5) maintaining a favorable kill ratio *if employed properly,* (6) conducting special operations, and (7) assuming command/operational control when appropriate.[3]

Most A-Detachments were on "clear, hold, and build" assignments in the jungles and swamps of Vietnam, charged with constructing and garrisoning fortified camps to hold the VC at bay in contested territory. General Westmoreland desperately threw them into the breach to fill the gap until regular Army and Marine divisions arrived. Special Forces provided highway security and convoy escort, defended airfields, cleared projected base areas for incoming Army brigades, swept critical VC avenues of infiltration, and even replaced ARVN battalions sent to other regions.

Special Forces A-Detachments were used with increasing frequency as "fire brigades." Nine A-Detachments were dispatched during the first part of 1965 to cope with deteriorating situations. Camps

Ha Thanh and Ba To were reestablished to counter VC pressure against government troops in northern I CTZ. In lower Vietnam Father Hoa's Chinese Hai Yen Camp and Phu Quoc Island were reinforced to prevent their loss. Captain Hart's Detachment A-111, on Phu Quoc Island, utilized extensive psychological operations in convincing the Khmer Kampuchea Krom (the KKK, which advocated that two Vietnamese provinces be turned over to Cambodia) to surrender to the Vietnamese. General Ky personally came to the island on 30 October 1965 to accept the KKK surrender and decorate Captain Hart for his efforts.[4] Five A-Detachments, including Major Cole's modified Detachment A-121 serving as an ad hoc B-Detachment, were inserted into coastal Binh Dinh Province to reinforce Ruff-Puff elements and prevent total collapse in that area.

Camps Buon Ea Yang (A-233) and Buon Brieng (A-232) and Detachment A-131 had to defend the Ban Me Thuot, Pleiku, and Long Van airfields, respectively. As a side note on continuing Special Forces difficulties, Camp Buon Brieng was overthrown by internal Rhade Montagnard liberation forces on 29 July 1965. The LLDB detachment was tied up, and Captain Ruggles's A-232 was disarmed. After extensive negotiations, the camp was bloodlessly returned to Vietnamese control days later, but its independent FULRO sentiments were manifest. Despite its critical strategic location in Darlac Province, Buon Brieng had to be closed out on 10 September 1965.[5]

The basic combat role of the Special Forces A-Detachments was to advise and provide operational assistance to the CIDG program. Their combat forces, the CIDG strike force companies, were just what they purported to be: civilian irregular defense groups recruited and armed to provide limited local protection for tribal villages. They were best suited for camp defense, patrolling, raids, ambushes, denial, and reaction operations. Such companies were not skilled at tactical maneuver nor equipped for routine infantry operations. They were composed of primitive and superstitious natives who could not read a compass or a map and depended on their Special Forces advisors for any sophisticated coordination, such as calling for aerial or artillery support. Special Forces doctrine never intended that strike force units become involved in extended confrontation with main force Viet Cong units.

The LLDB were nominally in charge of training the native recruits. The actual degree of Special Forces participation depended on

LLDB initiative and ability, which varied widely from camp to camp. In daily practice the Special Forces often had to train the LLDB instructors as well. The CIDG training cycles in camps ranged from two to eight weeks, but the average detachment taught a month-long course inclusive of basic soldiering, a smattering of small-unit tactics, and reaction drill. Elementary topics such as voice communications, crew-served weapons, and rudimentary first aid were considered advanced specialties to the minority groups. While adequate for CIDG purposes, this training "was not intended to train first line troops for conventional operations."[6]

The allied need to field combat forces outweighed CIDG background and limitations, and the Special Forces was ordered to combine CIDG companies and assume regular infantry missions. Unfortunately, this was a role in which they inevitably came off second best against the better organized and well-armed main force Viet Cong formations. Yet, the MACV mission statement approved for Special Forces in June 1965 was adamant:

United States Army Special Forces Vietnam resources will be employed in missions which (1) exert constant, versatile, offensive pressure against the Viet Cong in areas where the ARVN is not present in strength, (2) will interdict Viet Cong movement across international boundaries, (3) will, by quick response, prevent VC takeover of a critical area, and (4) will assist in extending GVN control.[7]

On 5 January 1965 Camps Trang Sup (A-411 under Captain Healy) and Soui Da (A-114 under Captain Ekman) mounted a six-company CIDG operation into War Zone C. After a brief encounter with the Viet Cong, the 326th Cambodian CIDG and 324th Vietnamese CIDG Companies lost heart and quit on the battlefield. Both had to be disarmed and broken up. While Phuoc Vinh (A-312 under Captain Spargo) successfully hit a VC base on the edge of War Zone D the same month, its Cambodian strike force members later refused to operate farther than one mile beyond camp. Since Phuoc Vinh defenses could be temporarily provided by its 347th Nung CIDG Company, the Cambodians "were given the choice of either putting out or getting out," and the strike force was completely overhauled.[8]

One of the saddest misutilizations of Special Forces CIDG tribesmen occurred during the first months of 1965 along Highway 19, the key artery linking the coast to the central highlands. The roadway climbed out of coastal Qui Nhon and twisted through forested gorges and mountain passes to reach the interior city of Pleiku. General Westmoreland was concerned that continued Viet Cong success there would effectively split the country in half.[9] Guarding Highway 19 was a major infantry assignment. Later that fall the entire 1st Cavalry Division would be dedicated to the task. In the meantime convoy escort and security of the passes was thrust onto the shoulders of the hapless Rhade tribesmen of the Special Forces.

Several hundred Rhade tribesmen who had participated in the Montagnard uprising and their families were forcibly uprooted and transplanted in two new camps strategically placed to cover the highway's crucial Mang Yang and An Khe passes. The Special Forces camp at An Khe (A-4 under Captain Hendricks) was manned by disciplined and loyal Rhade CIDG tribal warriors transplanted from Bu Prang. The morale among the native Rhade tribesmen at Soui Doi (A-3 under Captain Mireau), to the west of Mang Yang Pass, was much lower. They had been moved there in January from Ban Don and vehemently protested that they were being used as cannon fodder along Highway 19.[10]

Highway 19 was an old battleground. Monuments dotted the roadside midway between An Khe Pass and Mang Yang Pass, commemorating the 1954 Viet Minh ambush of French Groupement Mobile 100 during the First Indochina War. Now the Viet Cong were employing the same tactics. On 15 February 1965 a large South Vietnamese convoy was destroyed within Mang Yang Pass. In response Captain Hendricks's detachment at An Khe was ordered to secure extended portions of the highway. His camp established two forward operational bases (FOB #1 and #2) west along the roadway on 17 February 1965.

The Viet Cong assaulted both Special Forces sites three days later. While FOB #2 suffered only a light probing attack in the evening, FOB #1 situated farther up the road toward Mang Yang Pass, was overrun. Forward air control and C-123 flareship aircraft were unable to deliver needed support because clouds blanketed both bases. A Rhade response company under Captain Hendricks reached FOB #1 on the morning of 21 February after brushing past a small ambush. His force returned to An Khe with the dead and injured from the outpost, and LLDB Captain Em led a second vehicular column out of An Khe to search for the twenty CIDG still missing from FOB #1.

Captain Em's convoy was devastated by another ambush while proceeding back to An Khe at 5:30 that afternoon. The wounded captain formed a crude perimeter, which was held for two days against VC sniping and periodic assaults. Captain Hendricks's CIDG relief forces were unable to break through a strong Viet Cong roadblock to reach either Captain Em's beleaguered force or FOB #2. He was forced to retreat shortly before sunset with half his own vehicles destroyed.

Lt. Col. Lindsey W. Hale, commanding Detachment C-2 at Pleiku, had few resources to deal with the break in Highway 19. An hour before midnight he directed Captain Mireau, at Camp Soui Doi, to initiate a relief attempt heading east toward Mang Yang Pass and alerted the specially trained Rhade "eagle flight" platoon. The platoon had been created at Pleiku on 16 October 1964 for just this type of emergency reaction. He had some armed helicopters, but the A-1E Skyraider fighter-bombers also scheduled for aerial escort were diverted on another mission.

Like most CIDG companies, the 269th CIDG Company at Soui Doi was not trained to operate at night. Rhade Lieutenant Y-Lang's company was mustered for action on the morning of 22 February but they did not get rolling until after lunch. The small soldiers, their nervous faces half-buried by overlarge steel helmets and dressed in a mix of olive-drab and tiger-striped uniforms, hoisted themselves up with difficulty into the high-bodied American cargo trucks. Crowded shoulder to shoulder with 167 CIDG troops, the six trucks roared onto the highway at 12:45 P.M.

At 3:30 P.M. the motorized 269th Company rounded a curve just past the ruins of abandoned FOB #1. A civilian bus passing by in the other direction was suddenly hit by a rocket-propelled grenade and exploded in flames. The trucks braked to a stop under a hail of mortar and rifle fire. The Viet Cong assaulted the vehicles from both sides of the road as the Rhades jumped to the pavement and ran for cover. The three Special Forces advisors tried to rally the CIDG company. Withering rifle and machine gun fire broke up their counterattacks in the tall elephant grass. Sp5 Gerald B. Rose was killed leading an attempted breakout after the Rhade had faltered behind him.

In the general melee the clatter of rifle fire was mixed with the use of clubbed and edged weapons. Lieutenant Griggs was shot through the neck but gunned down five Viet Cong closing in on Sergeant Long, who was wounded in the thigh. Griggs was then hit in the chest and lost consciousness.

Individual natives attempted to surrender as they expended their ammunition but regrouped after the Viet Cong continued to kill the wounded. The CIDG used bayonets, knives, and fists to break out and escape on foot toward an outpost at Mang Yang Pass. Lieutenant Griggs had been left for dead by the Viet Cong. He regained consciousness and crawled over to a radio, overlooked by the VC, underneath his fallen radio operator. He directed firing runs by armed helicopters. Armed helicopters extracted Lieutenant Griggs and Sergeant Long after a medical evacuation helicopter was hit and force-landed at Soui Doi with pilot wounded and engine compartment on fire.

The eagle flight platoon was whirled in to the east of the ongoing battle an hour after the ambush commenced. The five Special Forces and thirty-six Rhade tribesmen dashed out as soon as the helicopter skids touched down in the churning waves of grass, the wash of the rotor blades whipping their brightly colored neck scarves. As they approached the battlefield, they were mistakenly strafed by friendly helicopters. The battered platoon continued toward the ambushed convoy, but VC snipers and machine gun nests kept stalling the drive.

The platoon was reinforced after dark at 7:30 P.M. on 22 February by the sixty-man 2d Company of the 22d ARVN Ranger Battalion from Pleiku. They established a night perimeter and moved across the smoldering 269th Company ambush zone the next morning. They later linked up with the remainder of LLDB Captain Em's shattered force and the garrison of FOB #2. The rest of the 22d Ranger Battalion was airlanded at An Khe and attempted to reach this force by marching up Highway 19 on 23 February. The advance was repulsed in a furious battle that caused heavy losses to the battalion and sent the remnants stumbling back down the road. All reserves in II CTZ had been exhausted, and a massed emergency helicopter evacuation was used to lift out the surrounded contingent from the battlefield.

Although the battle of Mang Yang Pass ended with the abandonment of the field to the Viet Cong on 24 February, the surviving 269th CIDG Company stragglers were still at large. The Rhade families at

Soui Doi wanted to put away their weapons and retrieve their dead for proper tribal burial rituals. Captain Mireau told them that the VC destruction of the civilian bus was an indication of the fate that might befall unarmed attempts to remove the bodies. He sent Staff Sergeant Scearce and Sergeant McCann to the Mang Yang Pass outpost to rally the Soui Doi ambush survivors that evening. They were sullenly received by the 112 listless Rhade troops gathered there. During Sergeant Scearce's pep talk a third of them abruptly walked away from the formation.

The two sergeants finally persuaded the Soui Doi contingent to return to the ambush zone to retrieve their fallen comrades on 27 February. The march back to Soui Doi on 1 March was filled with threats against LLDB Lieutenant Khim and the Special Forces advisors. At Soui Doi the Rhade became more lethargic and uncooperative and on 10 March refused to participate in any future combat operations. As a result, all the CIDG there were discharged and Camp Suoi Doi was turned over to the 3d Battalion, 42d ARVN Regiment, on 24 March 1965. MACV's insistence on misusing tribal strike forces far from home in a normal infantry manner had not only caused their inevitable defeat, but also cancelled a lot of difficult and patient Special Forces work to gain their loyalty and support in the first place.[11]

The Viet Cong had less success in attacks on Special Forces forts. Camp Kannack (A-231 under Captain Viau with 550 CIDG troops), situated just twelve miles north of the Highway 19 battlefield, was attacked by a Viet Cong battalion on 8 March 1965. The main assault followed an intensive preparatory mortar barrage and quickly overran two camp outposts and stormed through the outer wire barrier. Viet Cong recoilless rifles were brought up to destroy two perimeter automatic weapons bunkers, and sappers with bangalore torpedoes holed the inner wire. The superb morale of the defenders, fighting from well-prepared positions and gallantly led by Captain Viau, ultimately broke the massed attack. Two key Special Forces machine gun nests in particular, shaken repeatedly by direct recoilless rifle hits, shattered numerous charges and piled up mounds of VC dead in front of them. After daybreak, A-1E fighters strafed and bombed the withdrawing VC, followed by a Special Forces-led CIDG counterattack that regained the southern outpost where several defenders were still alive.[12]

3. Another MACV Role

Beginning in November 1964, selected 5th Special Forces Group detachments were additionally tasked as MACV sector and subsector advisory teams. This new MACV requirement was part of the larger regular advisory program, aimed at putting advisors at the province (sector) and district (subsector) level throughout Vietnam. The Special Forces was utilized because there was a shortage of MACV advisory teams, especially in the dangerous and turbulent border areas where Special Forces remained the only U.S. presence. This mission required Special Forces personnel to provide advice and direct assistance to the civil government in pacification and nation building, as well as support for the local Ruff-Puff territorial units.[13]

The first Special Forces detachment chosen for this additional task was in the Delta. Camp Tinh Bien (A-331) in Chau Doc Province was ordered to function as a dual CIDG-MACV subsector advisory outpost commencing 1 December 1964. In February 1965 MACV started giving this double mission to a large number of B- and A-Detachments. By the end of April, eleven A-Detachments had assumed district advisory duties, and seventeen more were scheduled. For the thirty-three Special Forces A-detachments that had been tapped for the advisory program by the end of the year, it meant that from 35 to 80 percent of their efforts had to be put into district rural construction and civic action. Five B-Detachments were also tasked to serve in an advisory capacity at province level.

On 7 March 1965 the 5th Special Forces Group requested civil affairs and psychological warfare personnel for detachments detailed to this kind of duty. On 10 September U.S. Army Pacific authorized a civic action-psychological operations lieutenant and staff sergeant for each A-Detachment charged with a MACV advisory mission. The addition of these two personnel boosted many team strengths to fourteen men, which hardly compensated for the extra workload. Colonel Spears stated resignedly that the additional MACV role, "adds another USSF mission and yet another master (MACV advisor) to his (detachment commander) problems."[14]

Dual CIDG infantry operations and coequal MACV subsector advisory functions became the norm for most Special Forces A-Detachments. Personnel were allocated to handle increased team responsibilities as depicted in Chart 3. The detachment commander and the executive officer often alternated so that one was in camp when the other was in the field. The muscle to handle added civil responsibilities was rendered by the promised team augmentation. This was provided by temporary-duty soldiers from the 441st Intelligence Corps Detachment, 97th Civil Affairs Group, and the Pacific Broadcasting and Visual Activity.[15]

In early 1965 all areas of Vietnam were subject to the full fury of Viet Cong onslaught. Control B-Detachments often shared the same battlefield danger as their A-Detachments. The advance party of Detachment B-34 left Kontum Province and arrived at the critical town of Song Be on 16 April 1965. Song Be was the capital of Phuoc Long Province, situated squarely astride the Viet Cong supply lifeline from Cambodia into War Zone D. There was hardly a more dangerous spot in Vietnam, and B-34's intrepid combat skill saved both town and province from being lost that spring.

Detachment B-34 was posted to the tidy, but lightly defended, compound of MACV Advisory Team 94 while the Special Forces soldiers hacked out a commanding hilltop defensive site. In the meantime Maj. Mitchell A. Sakey shrugged off adverse criticism as he installed machine guns and mortars in the transient location. His Special Forces intuition told him to fortify every campsite, no matter how temporary. His preparations were still incomplete when the Viet Cong unexpectedly attacked at 1:45 A.M. on the dark, overcast morning of 11 May 1965, but they were complete enough to enable the determined Special Forces soldiers to hold out.

The main VC assault was heralded by an intense mortar barrage, which pummeled both Song Be and the B-34 compound. The 36th ARVN Ranger Battalion positions around the town were brushed aside as the Viet Cong surged through Song Be and smashed into the American camp. Inside there were twenty-two Special Forces and fourteen other U.S. personnel. Their two billets had been blasted apart by some of the first mortar rounds. Major Sakey took over after the B-34 commander, Lt. Col. Alton E. Parks, was wounded. Sgt. Richard S. Bartlett, who had been knocked out of bed and wounded, joined Sgt. Horace M. Young on the light machine gun position covering the key southwest corner of the compound.

Sgt. Charles D. Crockett and Sp. 4th Class Amos E. Watson manned a 60mm mortar at the end of a shallow trench leading to the ammunition bunker just behind the machine gun nest. Sgt.-Maj. Robert "Mo" Frander, S. Sgt. Aldege A. Martin, and Sgt. Daniel F. Crabtree defended the other end of the trenchline a short distance away. Without flares the night was pitch black, but the machine gun crew kept the Viet Cong off the back fenceline for ten minutes before a direct mortar hit exploded on their position. Both Sergeants Young and Bartlett were badly wounded but managed to crawl back. They were carried to the medical aid station, which had been set up in the mess hall dining room.

Unable to penetrate the southwest corner, the Viet Cong ripped apart another section of the fenceline with bangalore torpedoes. Viet Cong shock troops raced through the camp, and began grenading the trenchline from the rear. Staff Sergeant Martin, crippled in the initial mortar barrage, was lying in the ditch passing mortar shells to Specialist 4th Class Watson. A grenade landed between them. With no avenue of escape, Martin turned a wooden ammunition box broadside. The detonation killed Watson instantly and badly wounded Martin.

More grenades kept tumbling into the mortar pit. Sergeant Crockett had his rifle, then his pistol, blown out of his hands and was wounded several times. A Viet Cong gunner behind the billets fired a rocket-propelled grenade directly into the trench, wounding everyone there. After expending all of his mortar shells, Crockett painfully moved back down the trench. The other sergeants pitched him grenades from the ammo bunker, and Crockett in turn heaved them at the charging VC. He could tell the difference between the grenades being tossed in his direction because the Viet Cong grenades sizzled and sparkled as they came in. The entire cratered, smoking trench was littered with dud Chinese stick grenades.

Private First Class Ward, a gasoline pumper for the 120th Aviation Company, had joined them. Sergeant Crabtree saw a Viet Cong soldier coming through another fence and told Ward to head him off. Ward raced around the billets but ran into an entire squad of Viet Cong approaching the mess hall. He fired once, then his M14 rifle jammed. Ward was quickly hit in return and blacked out.

Sgt. William D. Benning was desperately working by flashlight on the growing number of wounded in his makeshift aid station. Suddenly the VC squad stormed into the mess hall. Benning picked up a nearby pistol and shot the first Viet Cong who came through the doorway. Then he was killed, along with Lt. Henry A. Deutsch, whom he was treating for a back wound. Staff Sergeant Young, who had been evacuated there with multiple burns and wounds, had a three-inch pocket knife opened and clenched in his hands, tearing strips of cloth. He stabbed several Viet Cong intruders with the knife then dragged himself into the storeroom, where he died from loss of blood.

Sfc. Curtis Chancy from MACV Advisory Team 94, who had been wounded and deafened earlier, was in the adjoining kitchen bandaging Sgt. Shelby Green's shoulder. He used burning paper from the water heater pilot light to see what he was doing. Suddenly the refrigerator was shattered by a hail of automatic weapons fire, and he saw sparking discharges in the darkened dining room. He grabbed Green's M16 rifle and pulled the bolt back but could not get the rifle to fire. He frantically asked Green how to work the weapon, then realized he couldn't hear Green's instructions.

Both sergeants hobbled out onto the patio at the other end of the mess hall. There M. Sgt. Robert E. Gabe was defending from behind the barbecue grill. Suddenly the rear door opened, and two grenades rolled across the screened-in porch. The sergeants killed the VC grenadiers in the doorway as the grenades exploded, sending shrapnel through all of them. Gabe screamed, "Let's get out of here," and kicked out the wire screen. They crawled over to a sandbagged wall defended by several captains.

When Sp. 4th Class Johnie K. Culbreath heard grenade explosions inside the mess hall, he realized the aid station was in peril. He made a courageous individual charge toward the rear door with rifle blazing but was shot dead on the steps. U.S. Air Force Captain Lynch saw the side mess hall door open slightly. He fired his carbine through the wooden door and killed a Viet Cong who fell back inside. The rest of the VC in the mess hall were killed later in the morning trying to make a break for the fenceline.

The four Special Forces sergeants in the southwest ammunition trench held their positions throughout the battle. The Viet Cong used grenades, rocket launchers, automatic weapons, and satchel charges against them. The sergeants crouching in the three-foot-deep trench were wounded over and over, and their weapons were riddled with shell fragments. They clung to the position and prevented the southwest corner of the compound from being overrun. As Capt. Austin E. Miller later stated, "In a tactical sense the position could have been justifiably considered untenable, and men could have withdrawn without censure. They chose to remain. This sector was the key to the compound defense, and they bore the brunt of the attack."

Armed helicopters arrived overhead about two hours after the attack had been initiated, but the low clouds and smoke from the raging battle prevented them from rendering effective close support. They rocketed and strafed the ridges to the west of the town and silenced some VC artillery and recoilless rifles. Major Sakey directed the compound defense and tried to keep as many of the wounded alive as possible. His efforts were hampered by the loss of the medical supervisor and all medical supplies in the mess hall battle. Viet Cong heavy machine guns repeatedly drove off the medical evacuation helicopters, until the machine guns were silenced by airstrikes. At 8:00 A.M. sixteen wounded soldiers were lifted out.

The heroic Special Forces defense of the American compound against overwhelming odds had prevented the Viet Cong from securing the province capital. Elements of the Viet Cong *761st* and *763d Regiments* occupied the center of Song Be until noon. The 36th ARVN Ranger Battalion spent the morning assaulting the VC strongpoints in the market and temple area but became despondent after the commander, Captain Nghia, was killed. The battered Special Forces detachment kept calling in airstrikes until the 34th ARVN Ranger Battalion arrived to reoccupy the town later that evening.[16]

On 25 May 1965 Detachment A-342 was airlanded at Dong Xoai, a district capital within the same province on the northern edge of War Zone D. While the Special Forces soldiers, bolstered by a welcome team of U.S. Navy Seabees, built troop billets, communications facilities, and weapons positions, the detachment was ordered additionally to assume the MACV subsector role for Don Luan district on 1 June. The intermittent Viet Cong mortar rounds lobbed into the new camp were considered only the usual harassment, but sightings of large VC formations nearing the town increased. The horizon was blotted out by the murky night of 9 June as the Special Forces and CIDG guards walked along the outer berms of the camp.[17]

The tactical wire perimeter inclosed four separate sections of the Dong Xoai campsite: the artillery and armored car positions; the district compound, which contained eight Americans; and the CIDG compound with two CIDG companies; the LLDB detachment and twelve American Special Forces and sailors. A Cambodian CIDG company was guarding the CIDG family housing area inside the town of Dong Xoai, just across the roadway to the east. The CIDG picket teams beyond the wire perimeter were silenced by advancing Viet Cong battalions at 11:00 P.M. on 9 June. They had not been equipped with flares or radios to warn the camp, and only a few got away. The approach of the *762d* and *763d VC Regiments* remained undetected.

The opening VC mortar barrage blasted the western portions of the campsite half an hour before midnight. The camp construction had not been finished, and the Viet Cong were able to tear down sections of the tactical wire barrier that were not covered by defensive cross fire. The district compound came under heavy VC ground assault. The attackers reached the earthen berm wall several times but were beaten back by defenders using machine guns, M-79 grenade launchers, and one 3.5-inch rocket launcher firing by the light of air flares. Since ammunition storage areas had not been completed, all ammunition was fortuitously up front in the ditches. The southwestern bunker, half-buried by mud from near misses, was instrumental in defeating these initial VC charges, until it disintegrated under a direct mortar hit. The onrushing VC breached the wall at 2:30 A.M. and forced the defenders back to the district headquarters building with heavy losses.

The communications to the CIDG compound had been cut off after the radio shack was demolished by mortaring, which also burned out the phone lines. The detachment commander had been badly wounded by a mortar burst and was out of action. The fighting along the berm was violent and continuous as the Viet Cong, invisible against the blackened jungle treeline, appeared suddenly out of the nighttime gloom to rush forward in groups of six or ten men led by demolitions and flamethrower teams. One sixteen-man VC sapper element, wearing checkered cloth around their uniforms at the waist, was defeated in vicious hand-to-hand combat. At 2:00 A.M. two VC flamethrowers were able to get within range of the Vietnamese defenders and lashed them with streams of jellied fire. The CIDG defense crumbled, and the Viet Cong rushed over the compound berm. While the Cambodians managed a fighting withdrawal, the LLDB and other CIDG soldiers bolted into the town.

In the meantime the district compound had been overrun, with the exception of the allied contingent holding out inside the district command building. A quick check by the A-342 executive officer, 2d Lt. Charles Q. Williams, tallied three Americans dead, three missing, and most others wounded. He adjusted helicopter gun runs in front of their building while CIDG, sailors, and Special Forces kept up a furious volume of fire from windows, wall cracks, and doorways. Soon the yard surrounding the structure was littered with the bodies of dead Viet Cong. The battle continued unabated as daylight flooded the bloodied courtyards and debris-strewn compound.

At 9:00 A.M. a Viet Cong light machine gun, set up in a nearby schoolhouse, began taking the district headquarters under intense and accurate fire. Lieutenant Williams and a Navy Seabee grabbed a 3.5-inch bazooka, crawled outside, and demolished the school and VC machine gun with four rounds. As the pair tried to get back to the district building, the lieutenant was hit and the sailor mortally wounded by VC automatic weapons fire. By noon the VC had taken the building under direct 57mm recoilless rifle fire, and the position was taken by close assault soon after. The few American survivors were scooped up by helicopter after being chased into the howitzer pits.

The South Vietnamese relief force, composed of the 7th ARVN Parachute Battalion and 52d ARVN Ranger Battalion, had a tough battle getting to Dong Xoai. The rangers finally linked up with the few remaining Cambodians, who were making a last-ditch stand in a corner of the CIDG compound, at 7:00 A.M. on 11 June 1965. Two days later Capt. Channing M. Greene's Detachment A-311 was brought into Dong Xoai to rebuild the camp.

Serious defensive deficiencies had abounded during the battle. Not only had the camp been surprised, but there was no common defensive plan, wire and trench systems were inadequate, and no final combat line existed. The howitzers present in the camp were almost totally ineffective. The lack of mutual support between compounds doomed them to isolated battles for survival. The sheer combat fortitude of the Special Forces-led garrison had inflicted grievous Viet Cong losses, but eventual success was the result of hard-fighting relief forces and aerial support. Historically, the battle of Dong Xoai was at best only a hollow victory.[18]

4. Border Objectives

Special Forces border surveillance objectives were hurt by an insufficient native recruiting base in the rugged northern two corps tactical zones of Vietnam. The closing of unproductive camps at Ta Ko in February and A Ro in April left considerable portions of the Laotian border uncovered in I CTZ, and periodic patrols by the Da Nang reaction force hardly filled the void. In II CTZ, camps filled with transplanted Montagnards suffered lower effectiveness stemming from their lowered morale and unfamiliarity with the strange new areas. In III CTZ, where the Viet Cong maneuvered units of regimental strength, the Special Forces was forced to abandon border surveillance and turn to interdiction of interior routes and attacks on Viet Cong secret bases instead.

In the IV CTZ the flat, open stretches of marshy Delta were considered the most promising area for CIDG employment in the border surveillance role. Of the nine A-Detachments in that vast area, eight were posted along the border. Their forward outposts and patrol bases were lined up along the entire corps boundary with Cambodia. During the seven months from October through April 1965, the 4,000 CIDG troops stationed in the Delta executed the same number of patrols (4,440) and twice as many ambushes (10,154), but killed only 192 Viet Cong (not necessarily all involved in border crossing). Additionally, there was a large CIDG desertion problem in the Delta because of the difficult duty, bad living conditions, high cost of food, and low pay.[19]

One of the hardest-hit border surveillance camps was Bu Dop, northeast of Saigon on the III CTZ Cambodian front, which was occupied by A-341A (6 Special Forces under Captain Nugent), 8 LLDB, and 289 Stieng and Vietnamese CIDG troops. The rest of the split A-Detachment, A-341B (7 Special Forces under Lieutenant Olivaz), two CIDG companies, and a 130-man Nung response company was located at Camp Bu Ghia Map twenty miles to the east, where the Americans were actually expecting the attack. An hour after midnight on 20 July 1965, Camp Bu Dop was swept by a heavy volume of mortar shells and volleys of recoilless rifle fire that seriously wounded the detachment commander, damaged the camp generator, and disabled the single sideband radio.

The Viet Cong stormed forward, bridging moats and defensive wire with bamboo ladders. Viet Cong shock troops overwhelmed the northwest bunker, where the defenders died to a man at their posts, as other flamethrowers and breaching parties charged the north wall. The Viet Cong attackers raced into the camp and machine-gunned thirty CIDG manning the northern rampart from behind. The three Special Forces sergeants on the north wall were near the supply building and defended it with a light machine gun, M16 rifles, and claymore mines. Two were killed and one wounded in this action. Other Viet Cong reached the fort's inner trench, where the SF radio operator and light weapons sergeant engaged them in hand-to-hand combat at the 4.2-inch mortar pit.

In a darkness broken only by grenade explosions, VC signal pyrotechnics, and streams of tracer rounds from automatic weapons, close combat raged around the mess hall, last held trenches, and throughout the camp. The LLDB camp commander responded valiantly, shifting CIDG troops, ammunition, and weapons to critical strongpoints throughout the battle. He bolstered the southeastern corner bunker just in time to kill scores of Viet Cong trying to cut through the defensive wire and hurl demolition charges into the position.

At 2:30 A.M. aircraft arrived overhead and dropped flares, which illuminated the compound enough for aerial firepower to be used against the Viet Cong in the open and in assembly positions. The ground fighting continued in close quarters both inside the camp and along the walls. The two Special Forces men from the mortar trench led a counterattack to the east wall and linked up with the LLDB captain. During this firefight, the radio operator was hit and knocked down by a group of Viet Cong riflemen recovering bodies and equipment. A final VC attack across the airfield on the east wall was beaten back at 8:00 A.M., and the elated defenders raised a South Vietnamese flag at the east gate.

Reinforcements were helicoptered into Bu Dop at noon, most of them from Bu Ghia Map. The latter camp, which had been scheduled for eventual closeout, was already under harassing fire. The hasty evacuation of Bu Ghia Map Camp forced its deliberate destruction and abandonment the same day, an action in which all supplies and equipment that could not be immediately airlifted out were destroyed on the spot. Bu Dop was a smoking shambles. The well-executed Viet Cong assault had nearly overrun the camp before it was repulsed in violent close-in fighting, inspired by the courageous leadership of the LLDB camp commander who took over after the American detachment commander had been maimed in the opening mortar barrage.[20]

The difficult border mission consumed much Special Forces effort and was not successful in deterring large-scale Viet Cong supply and troop infiltration into South Vietnam. However, at the height of the conflict three years later, some twenty-two ARVN and American division equivalents were unable to achieve any greater success monitoring the same remote border regions. By July 1965 the first Marine division and Army brigades of this American buildup were in Vietnam alongside the 5th Special Forces Group.

From October 1964, when the 5th Special Forces Group was permanently established in Vietnam, through July 1965, Special Forces had faced its most difficult period of battlefield survival. During that period the South Vietnamese military had been rendered largely ineffective by continual defeat at the hands of the Viet Cong, and the American battalions that started arriving in March were not yet in position to provide relief to Special Forces garrisons under attack.

The escalating war had greatly expanded Special Forces operations. Most Special Forces elements, fully engaged in the CIDG program and border surveillance, were additionally tasked as MACV district advisory teams. As the Viet Cong threatened to take over large portions of the country, the Special Forces was thrown into the breach to hold key objectives. Although the Special Forces-led CIDG, untrained and ill-equipped as standard infantry, did not fare well in mobile field operations, as demonstrated by the battle of Mang Yang Pass and abortive incursions into War Zone C, they were instrumental in defending key outposts and blunting several Viet Cong offensives. The sanguinary battles of Camps Kannack, Song Be, Dong Xoai, and Bu Dop were salutary victories won by greatly outnumbered Special Forces and CIDG defenders against incredible odds.

The Special Forces units also performed a myriad of other front-line infantry assignments, from airfield and highway protection to the territorial defense of entire regions, such as eastern Binh Dinh Province and Phu Quoc Island. Without the crucial presence of a determined Special Forces organization, the Marine division and Army brigades that arrived in May would have found much more of South Vietnam under effective Viet Cong control. At the same time, by the summer of 1965, the Vietnam conflagration had outgrown any Special Forces ability to hold out alone against the North Vietnamese and Viet Cong divisions being introduced onto the battlefield.

Notes

1. The 5th Special Forces Group was officially established in South Vietnam by U.S. Army Pacific General Order 188 on 1 October 1964 but is cited in the official historical data card as arriving on 24 September 1964. The 5th Special Forces Group (Airborne), 1st Special Forces, carried the lineage of both the 1st Battalion, Third Regiment, 1st Special Service Force, and 5th Ranger Infantry Battalion of World War II fame.

2. 5th Special Forces Group, *Debriefing* of Col. John H. Spears, 15 July 1965; 5th Special Forces Group, *Synopsis of USASF Sector/Subsector Advisory Role,* dtd 1 Dec 68, Section V (Chronology).

3. 5th Special Forces Group: Capabilities of USASF Operations, *Debriefing* of Col. John H. Spears, p. 11, dtd 15 July 1965. (Emphasis in (4) is in original document and has been added in (5) by author.)

4. Headquarters, IX Corps, *History of the First Special Forces Group,* 1 January to 31 December 1965, p. 25.

5. Detachment B-23, *Memorandum for Record,* dtd 29 August 1965.

6. Army Concept Team in Vietnam, JRATA Project 1B-154, p. 29.

7. 5th Special Forces Group, *Debriefing* of Col. John H. Spears, dtd 15 July 1965, p. 11.

8. 5th Special Forces Group, *Monthly Operational Summary,* dtd 13 February 1965; Detachment C-3 Annex A to Memorandum Number 12, dtd 4 March 1965.

9. Ten years later the final conclusion of the war would be decided in this very region, as the ARVN rout down Highway 19 left the country split in two and sealed South Vietnam's ultimate defeat.

10. The Montagnards at Soui Doi actually represented a mix of tribal entities. On 1 February 1965 the 266th–269th CIDG companies stationed there were composed of 429 Rhade ("Ede"), 35 Jarai, 43 Mnong, and 5 Laotians. Detachment A-214, *Monthly Operational Summary,* dtd 1 February 1965 (at the time A-214 was also known as A-3).

11. Detachment C-2, *After Action Report,* dtd 26 March 1965.

12. 5th Special Forces Group, Memorandum for Record, dtd 11 March 1965. Losses were 34 CIDG and 3 civilians killed, 3 Special Forces, and 32 CIDG wounded; 119 Viet Cong killed by confirmed body count with estimates of additional dead much higher. Captain Viau of 1st Special Forces Group received the Distinguished Service Cross for his heroism in the battle.

13. Regional Forces and Popular Force units were the military organizations assigned to the sector and subsector commanders. Although they constituted over half the manpower in the South Vietnamese armed forces, they approximated only a lightly armed militia tied to static security duties.

14. 5th SFG Ltr to MACV J-3, Subject: Using Special Forces Commanders as Subsector advisors, dtd 13 November 1964.

15. 5th Special Forces Group, *Synopsis of the USASF Sector/Subsector Advisory Role*, dtd 1 December 1968.

16. Detachment B-34, *Action at Song Be*, dtd 18 May 1965, with 5th Special Forces Group working papers and awards recommendations.

17. Total allied forces at Dong Xoai were Detachment A-342 with 11 Special Forces soldiers; LLDB Detachment A-351 with 10 personnel under camp commander Nguyen Huy Do; 327th CIDG Company (120 Cambodian CIDG); 328th CIDG Company (147 Cambodian CIDG); 342d CIDG Company (118 Vietnamese CIDG); 111th RF/PF Company (40 men); one platoon of six armored cars; two 105mm howitzers; six light machine guns; and a 9-man U.S. Navy Seabee construction team.

18. 5th Special Forces Group, *Dong Xoai After Action Report*, dtd 7 July 1965; Republic of Vietnam Ministry of Defense 301st LLDB Group Report No. 3859/3/HQ, *Viet Cong Attack on Don Luan District Town and Camp Dong Xoai*, dtd 28 June 1965; Detachment A-311, *Monthly Operational Summary* for July 1965. Second Lt. Charles Q. Williams was awarded the Medal of Honor. Losses at Dong Xoai were 5 U.S. KIA and 16 WIA (out of 20 total); 3 LLDB KIA and 4 WIA; and 40 CIDG KIA, 124 MIA, and 54 WIA. One hundred thirty-four VC were confirmed killed in exchange, although hundreds more dead were probably carried away.

19. Army Concept Team in Vietnam, *Employment of a Special Forces Group*, JRATA Project No. 1B-154, dtd 20 April 1966; and MACV, *Monthly Evaluation Reports*, for January through April 1965.

20. Losses at Bu Dop were KIA: 2 Special Forces, 2 LLDB, 66 CIDG; WIA: 4 Special Forces, 9 LLDB, 26 CIDG; and MIA: 90 CIDG. Confirmed Viet Cong body count was set at 161. 5th Special Forces Group, *Bu Dop After Action Report*, dtd 30 August 1965; MACV Memorandum for Report, Subject: The Battle of Bu Dop; and MACV, *Monthly Evaluation Report*, July 1965.

CHAPTER 7

THE TURNING POINT

1. Special Forces and the American Buildup

The large influx of American combat and support battalions arriving in Vietnam presented Col. William A. "Bulldog" McKean, who took command of the 5th Special Forces Group on 16 July 1965, with a wealth of potential military backup and engineer support. Airmobile infantry promised quick and decisive response to CIDG patrolling opportunities or adverse camp situations. The availability of engineers assured required camp construction and defensive strengthening of existing sites. The adverse impact seemed confined to competing priorities for limited logistical and delivery assets.

In exchange the Special Forces provided support, regional intelligence, and area indoctrination for the arriving Army formations. Major Sandel's Detachment B-31 at Camp Phuoc Vinh spent the latter half of 1965 orienting the 1st Infantry Division to its area, then turned over the campsite to the division's 3d Brigade on 20 December. B-31 moved to Xuan Loc, where it assumed another sector advisory role. Major Brewington's B-22 helped the 1st Cavalry Division to settle into the An Khe area.

Several Special Forces trouble spots were cleaned up, and a rash of new camps were established in areas that had been lost to the Viet Cong. In late August a CIDG camp was reestablished at Dak To by Captain Ruhlin's Detachment A-322 in the mountains of western Kontum Province. On 17 September Detachment A-112 under Capt. C. Gregor, Jr., established Camp Mai Linh at an abandoned regional

109

force outpost in central Phu Bon "Prosperous Capital" Province, in order to regain the confidence of the reclusive Bahnar tribesmen.

The 1st Brigade of the 101st Airborne Division opened An Khe Pass along Highway 19 during September then pushed north against the Vinh Thanh Valley of interior Binh Dinh "Pacification" Province. After some sharp fighting, the area had been sufficiently cleared to allow a battalion of the 1st Cavalry Division to escort Captain Durr's Detachment A-211 into the valley during October. The 8th Engineer Battalion constructed Camp Vinh Thanh, which A-211 formally opened on 25 November 1965. The following spring, Viet Cong threats against the camp would initiate the famed 1st Cavalry Division Operation CRAZY HORSE.

Camp Duc Co, a border surveillance camp situated west of Pleiku almost to the Cambodian border, was besieged from 30 June until mid-August 1965. During the forty-eight-day siege, Capt. Richard B. Johnson's Detachment A-215 suffered heavy losses. When eight ARVN infantry, ranger, and paratrooper battalions fought their way through the surrounding Viet Cong into the camp on 17 August, they had the potential backup of two battalions of the crack 173d Airborne Brigade. This marked the first time that a large American reaction force had been earmarked to help a CIDG camp.

The American buildup did not arrive in time to prevent the loss of another Special Forces camp in Kontum Province. On 18 August 1965 the Viet Cong overwhelmed the district headquarters on the high ground overlooking Camp Dak Sut, an interim Special Forces campsite run by Captain Cook's Detachment A-218. The Viet Cong turned the full fury of their assault on Dak Sut, which was defended by 474 CIDG soldiers, a fourth of them recruits. The savage battle raged four hours, but no ARVN relief was forthcoming, and the camp was overrun before daylight. Only half the garrison, about 230 men, managed to evade back to friendly lines.[1]

The Montagnard independence movement (FULRO) flared up in the central highlands from 17 to 21 December 1965 and affected the Lac Thien, Plei Djereng, and Mai Linh CIDG camps. When the Special Forces soldiers became alerted to renewed Montagnard unrest, they moved the suspect Rhade eagle flight company (officially titled the Holloway Army Airfield Security Force) under S. Sgt. James Hayes away from Pleiku into Camp Plei Do Lim. Prompt Special Forces intervention defused a company confrontation with ARVN tanks blocking their movement down Highway 14. At Camp Lac Thien, newly opened by Detachment A-236 on 8 November, Capt. John McKinney prevented his camp's overthrow in tense 18 December negotiations with internal FULRO leaders, during which three LLDB hostages were released. Capt. Jackie Schmidt's Detachment A-213 at Camp Plei Djereng used a Nung reaction force and radio jamming to prevent his camp from being seized on 20 December. One day earlier eighty-two Montagnard rebels from the 269th and 503d Regional Forces companies sought asylum in Capt. Charles Gregor's Mai Linh Camp (A-112) after killing thirty Vietnamese soldiers at Plei Kanong. They were disarmed and turned over to government authorities.[2]

Special Forces frontline action continued at a brisk pace during the final months of the year. In the Delta, Special Forces and Viet Cong continued to contest the Cambodian border zone. Camps Cai Cai, Moc Hoa, and Tuyen Nhon struck several previously impervious Viet Cong strongholds, in one case by laboriously using poles to push plastic assault boats through miles of rice fields. The Viet Cong retaliated by assaulting seven camp outposts, wiping out three of them. Small-unit actions abounded throughout the rest of the country as well. While individual losses in the firefights were often light, their cumulative effect took an increasing toll of many old Special Forces hands. Two skirmishes are cited here as examples of the constant tempo of conflict throughout the country.

The loss of coastal Binh Dinh Province during 1965 had been largely prevented by the emergency springtime deployment of five A-Detachments into the province's eastern fringes to bolster the Ruff-Puff defenders. As part of that effort, Captain Davis's Detachment A-321 had arrived at Bong Son to advise the Hoai Nhon district on 7 May 1965. Three team members were wounded a month later on 18 June. Captain Davis had posted his 731st Regional Force Company to guard the crucial Phu Cu Pass along Highway 1. The Viet Cong overran the position in the morning darkness of 23 September 1965. Captain Davis boarded a helicopter to retrieve battle casualties at 10:45 A.M. and was joined by Staff Sgt. David A. Morgan, the demolitions sergeant serving as engineer foreman, his interpreter Mr. Dung, and Major Medaris, the senior advisor of the 41st ARVN Regiment. They were waved onto the Phu Cu Pass helipad by soldiers dressed in friendly uniforms.

As soon as the helicopter touched down, Sergeant Morgan and

the interpreter leaped out. A sudden fusillade of automatic weapons fire spun Morgan to the ground with a leg wound and riddled the aircraft, throwing the crew chief and Captain Davis to the cabin floor with serious wounds. The helicopter pulled out as bullets ripped through its fuselage, leaving Morgan and his interpreter defending the helipad against the Viet Cong. They were soon forced downhill under heavy VC fire, and Morgan was wounded again. He died as he tried to tell Mr. Dung where he had been hit. The interpreter killed several Viet Cong at close range and escaped two days later when the pass was retaken by the 41st ARVN Regiment. On 25 September Special Forces soldiers found Sergeant Morgan's body where the interpreter had reported it was.[3]

Camp Minh Thanh in III CTZ, held by Detachment A-332 under Capt. James M. Kennedy, Jr., was under two feet of floodwater during most of October, and its crumbling dirt walls were reinforced by old fifty-five-gallon fuel drums and wooden boards. On 25 October the 312th CIDG Company was ambushed in a nearby rubber plantation and thrown into a panic, which sent the soldiers blindly running into another preset VC ambush. The sudden flight left M. Sgt. Ernest Hayward and Staff Sergeant Chartier in the rear, where they stopped a Viet Cong force closing in to complete the encirclement. Sergeant Hayward was killed, but Chartier escaped with the remnants of the CIDG force. For the next several days the Special Forces battled against intense recoilless rifle and machine gun fire to reach Hayward's body. After the insertion of the III CTZ (Bien Hoa) Mike Force with plenty of air support, Hayward's remains were reached and evacuated on 27 October 1965.[4]

By the end of the year, Colonel McKean had 1,592 Special Forces personnel in seventy-eight camps, advising 28,200 CIDG and 2,300 Nungs. There were also 28,800 RF/PF troops under Special Forces control. The 5th Special Forces Group had already passed the apparent high-water mark of danger, as its remote Plei Me Camp repulsed an all-out North Vietnamese Army (NVA) assault, which in turn was swiftly punished by a massed 1st Cavalry Division airmobile counterattack.[5]

2. Plei Me: The Regular Army Steps In

The border surveillance camp of Plei Me was located thirty miles southwest of Pleiku on a small jungled ridge at the edge of the Ia

Drang Valley, along the Cambodian frontier. On 19 October 1965 Captain Moore's Detachment A-217 at the camp had a large combat patrol sweeping an area nine miles away but retained all-around security with two outposts and five squad pickets. That evening the clatter of gunfire shattered the darkness as one of the picket positions encountered advancing North Vietnamese Army troops of the *32d, 33d* and *66th Regiments*. At 10:00 P.M. the southern outpost was overwhelmed, and a fierce mortar and recoilless rifle barrage ripped through the Plei Me compound. The NVA began its assault on the 200-yard triangular camp thirty minutes after midnight.[6]

The attack was led by NVA sappers carrying satchel charges and bangalore torpedoes, followed by clustered infantry firing assault rifles from the hip. The assault pioneers rammed pipe sections filled with explosives through the barrier wire and blasted it apart in a series of detonations that rocked the camp. Streams of tracer bullets etched red lines across the blackness close to the ground as bunkered machine guns furiously pumped grazing fire into the tangle of barbed wire and struggling soldiers. The northern corner blockhouse was shaken by repeated explosions, reducing its riddled sandbags to shredded burlap. Tribal riflemen and Special Forces sergeants fired weapons so rapidly that the barrels glowed. Onrushing North Vietnamese infantry staggered and fell in writhing agony as they were pitched into the upchurned dirt. The concentrated return fire piled their bodies up in the twisted, broken wire quicker than their comrades could fill the gaps.

A flareship requested at the start of the battle arrived overhead at 2:15 A.M., and the battlefield was soon flooded in the eerie, shifting colors of discordant flarelight. The artificial candlelight wobbled underneath tiny parachutes and chased shadows across ghostly mounds of corpses and cratered earth. The North Vietnamese pressed their assault against camp fortifications and trenches with grenades and submachine guns. At 3:45 A.M. jet aircraft began screeching through the low clouds. The jungle was blasted into relief against the skyline as the horizon erupted into fireballs of yellow-white napalm.

The northwestern bunker shuddered under a direct 57mm recoilless rifle hit at 6:00 A.M., which partially destroyed the structure. Dazed and bloodied defenders, wounded by shell fragments and splinters, reinforced sagging timbers and hauled more ammunition boxes to the smoking machine guns. Two hours later NVA shock troops blew in the main gate with satchel charges, but daylight aerial fire-power forced the assailants back into the surrounding jungle. They dug emplacements around the camp within small arms range and locked it under siege.

An hour and a half later the first medical helicopter landed under intense automatic weapons fire. An armed escort helicopter flying cover for the medical evacuation was shot down. The C-3 Detachment sur-geon, Dr. Hunter, was landed to treat scores of critically burned and wounded personnel. Dr. Hunter performed emergency aid in the camp throughout the battle, although wounded three times himself. A res-cue team was sent outside of camp to reach the helicopter wreckage. The team leader, Staff Sgt. Joseph D. Bailey, was wounded in a duel with an NVA machine gun nest. The team was initially barred from returning to the camp by a heavy cross fire. Sergeant Bailey died of his wounds and Specialist Fourth Class Shea was wounded while the team was pinned down.

Plei Me's combat patrol force started its trek back to camp as soon as it was notified of the attack. The men entered the camp under scattered sniper and mortar fire in the late evening of 20 October. Two companies of the 91st ARVN Airborne Ranger Battalion at-tached to Maj. Charlie Beckwith's Project DELTA helicoptered into a landing zone four and a half miles from Plei Me the next morning. Major Beckwith led his rangers into the camp by a circuitous route that forced them to chop their way through dense jungle, but they avoided NVA ambushes. They waited outside camp through the night of 21–22 October and entered the camp under sporadic rifle fire in the morning.

Major Beckwith took over command of the camp and reorganized defenses with his additional personnel. Sgt. Jimmie L. McBynum was killed just before noon, and that afternoon three companies counter-attacked to clear the high ground. They were defeated after a bitter firefight with entrenched North Vietnamese. One crew, chained to their machine gun, had opened fire on the rear of the CIDG skirmish line after being bypassed. Losses had been heavy in the confused fighting. Capt. Thomas W. Pusser was killed, and Captain White was wounded. On 23 October Captain Moore was wounded by mortar shrapnel. Medical evacuation helicopters lifted out the critically wounded the same day.

Another counterattack by the Vietnamese airborne rangers was launched two days later to clear the north slope. The sudden charge of a solitary NVA soldier unnerved the rangers and precipitated their retreat before he was shot. Another Special Forces sergeant was wounded in the botched attack. This was the final ground action of the battle. A relief force composed of the 3d ARVN Armored Cavalry Squadron, 1st Battalion of the 42d ARVN Infantry Regiment, and the 21st ARVN Ranger Battalion arrived in Plei Me that evening. They had been severely mauled by two ambushes on 21 and 23 October, with the loss of most of their vehicles. A Nung reaction company from Camp Duc Co arrived in Plei Me without incident the day after the siege was lifted. The camp received its last mortar barrage when ten rounds killed four and wounded eight CIDG soldiers inside Plei Me at 10:45 P.M. on 29 October.

The 672 Air Force sorties had broken the NVA attack, but the low-level strafing and bombing runs were conducted under fierce machine gun fire. One helicopter and its crew were lost on 20 October along with a Martin B-57 Canberra bomber whose crew was rescued. Another B-57, hit the same day, crash-landed back at base. Another helicopter went down with its crew the next day. The pilots of both the A-1E Skyraiders, which had been shot down on 22 October, parachuted to safety and were eventually rescued by the camp defenders.

Despite the bad weather, the camp also received excellent airdrop support from the Air Force 310th Air Commando Squadron (C-123) and 92d Aviation Company (CV-2B Caribou). Over 333,000 pounds of vitally needed ammunition, food, medicines, and water had been parachuted by night into the small camp perimeter. Only 9,000 pounds had landed outside the wire. Of the nineteen C-123s hit by ground fire, seven were so badly shot up that they had to be scrapped. The two Caribou cargo planes damaged by machine gun fire were rendered unserviceable. Of the airmen wounded, one was a Special Forces sergeant who was kicking out door bundles.

Maj. Gen. Harry W.O. Kinnard's 1st Cavalry Division (Airmobile) had been moved up from An Khe into the Pleiku area as possible reinforcement for Plei Me. On 26 October 1965 General Westmoreland met with the division officers at a forward landing zone and authorized them to undertake an unlimited offense throughout the Ia Drang Valley to destroy the North Vietnamese forces responsible for the Plei Me attack.[7]

The 2d Battalion of the 8th Cavalry passed through the battered

Plei Me Special Forces Camp and retook the southern outpost (coded Objective "Cherry") on 27 October 1965. The hardened Special Forces veterans mocked the green airmobile cavalrymen retching over the putrid smell of corpses decaying in the dank jungle overgrowth, but a turning point in the war and Special Forces operations had been reached. For the first time an American formation had entered the field of battle in response to a beleaguered Special Forces CIDG camp. The division would meet its acrid test of combat valiantly during the next month's pivotal Ia Drang Valley campaign. The Special Forces were elated that the security of their remote camps might be underwritten by Army and Marine divisions. Unfortunately, such support was not always available.

3. Crises on the Northern Front

The new year of 1966 started with a blistering mortar attack on Camp Khe Sanh on 4 January. The North Vietnamese used heavy 120mm mortars for the first time in the Second Indochina War, and the bombardment thrust Khe Sanh into the forefront of the war. Khe Sanh was a quiet Special Forces border outpost tucked into the corner of Quang Tri "Great Administration" Province, near the tri-border junction of Laos and the Demilitarized Zone separating North and South Vietnam. The camp was nestled in verdant hills that once hosted rich coffee and cinnamon plantations but had since been left to return to jungle. General Westmoreland deemed the location to be of strategic significance since it overlooked Route 9, an excellent invasion route either to the west or east, depending on which army used it.

The Special Forces did not concern itself with army-level strategies. Captain Moffitt's Detachment A-101 occupancy of Khe Sanh was rapidly outclassed by the battalions of Marines which arrived during the course of the year. The 1st Battalion of the 1st Marines arrived in force on 17 April 1966, conducted Operation VIRGINIA among the Montagnards and their elephants on the Khe Sanh Plains, then marched out. General Westmoreland ordered the Marines back in September. The 1st Battalion of the 3d Marines took up positions around the camp and its airstrip as part of Operation PRAIRIE.

Navy Seabees constructed reinforced concrete bunkers for the Special Forces camp during the fall. Khe Sanh was the only hardened compound of nine Special Forces campsites in I CTZ. MACV also granted special permission for the camp to increase its CIDG strength from three companies to four. The Marines started reinforcing their Khe Sanh Combat Base in earnest, and the Special Forces detachment was soon squeezed out. On 19 December 1966 Detachment A-101 packed up and moved its Bru natives a short distance down the road, closer to the Laotian border. The new camp at Lang Vei was declared operational on 21 December 1966.[8]

Camp Tra Bong, west of Chu Lai in Quang Ngai "Great Attachment to Mankind" Province, had been one of the original CIDG mountain commando training sites from December 1962 until it was closed down in August 1963. Two years·later, on 28 August 1965, Tra Bong was reopened by a team composed of Australian and Special Forces advisors: Detachment A-107 under Australian Captain Skardon. In the first week of November, camp CIDG companies had been used as a blocking force for the 7th Marines Operation BLACK FERRET, during which newswoman Dickey Chapelle was killed by a booby trap.

The bitterest month for Tra Bong came at the beginning of 1966. The LLDB commander had claimed a loss of face in a series of conflicts with the original detachment. A new detachment of ten Americans and two Australians under Capt. John P. Fewell, Jr., arrived to mend Vietnamese–Special Forces relations on 20 January. Since the detachment was the MACV subsector advisory team for Tra Bong district, the Vietnamese district chief summoned the camp to investigate an attack on its Long Phu outpost eight days later. Captain Fewell and the LLDB camp commander, accompanied by the district chief, led a reaction force of the 144th CIDG Company. The last contact ever made with the men in this "lost patrol" was one hour before noon when they radioed, "We're going into attack, request all support you can give us." Attempts by the camp to reach the force by radio and clarify map coordinates for the support went unanswered.

Control Detachment C-1 at Da Nang sent Major Truesdale's Nung "B" Mike Reaction Group into the camp that evening. Detachment A-107 was now under 2d Lt. David B. Bussey. The lost patrol action had claimed Captain Fewell, Sfc. Elmer J. Reifschneider, Jr., S. Sgt. Earl F. Brown, and S. Sgt. Donald J. Jacobsen. The next day the Nung Mike Force found thirty-nine bodies of the lost patrol in two shattered jungle charnels, the first where they had apparently been ambushed and the other where a last stand was made. Eight bodies were never found, including Captain Fewell's.[9]

The heaviest loss for Special Forces in 1966 followed shortly in another contested region of I Corps Tactical Zone, the A Shau Valley. This isolated valley is perched on the rim of Vietnam's northwestern border in one of the most forbidding primeval stretches of tropical terrain in Southeast Asia. The Rao Lao River forks through the valley like the tongue of a serpent, spitting out of the deep Laotian rain forest. The thin silver stream glides over the rocks of the valley floor, which is wedged between 5,000-foot-high mountains. Their peaks pin rain-swollen clouds, which shroud the bottomland in overcast and create dense, rolling fogs. The winter monsoons send storms roaring through the valley that empty into sheets of hail and rain, while nocturnal strobe lightning flashes treelines into grayish focus.

Visibility was restricted and observation telescoped even in the clearing spring weather. The triple-canopied jungle slopes disappeared into fields of elephant grass twice the height of a man. In March 1966 the shabby, triangular Special Forces A Shau Camp had existed at the lower end of the valley for three years. The tin structures and muddied trenches were encompassed by rusting barbed wire, half-buried in the tall grass that had overgrown the minefields. Special Forces intelligence had detected a large North Vietnamese buildup in the area. As a result, the untenable A Loui and Ta Bat valley outposts had been razed on 8 December 1965. Camp A Shau, garrisoned by Detachment A-102 under Capt. John D. Blair IV, was the only Special Forces fort left. The A Shau Valley dominated allied strategy for the duration of the Second Indochina War, but it was swept out of Special Forces existence in less than fifty tragic hours on 9 and 10 March 1966.

Captain Blair had requested reinforcements, and one company of Nungs from the Nha Trang Mike Force under Capt. Tennis H. "Sam" Carter was sent to A Shau on 7 March 1966. The camp was too small to hold the other two Nung companies that the group had offered. His defenders numbered exactly 17 Special Forces, 6 LLDB, 143 Nungs, 210 Vietnamese CIDG, 7 interpreters, and 51 civilian laborers and post exchange girls. Among the Vietnamese were a number of convicts sent there as punishment, and the 141st CIDG Company (the camp contained the 131st, 141st, and 154th CIDG companies) was suspected of being Viet Cong.

The garrison spent the night of 8–9 March on general alert in expectation of imminent attack. They fired claymore mines and grenade launchers into the dark distance at the sounds of digging and snapping wire. At 3:50 A.M. the camp was subjected to devastating two-and-a-half-hour mortar barrage that destroyed many camp structures and temporarily severed communications. Sfc. Raymond Allen was killed by a direct hit in the center of camp and S. Sgt. Billie A. Hall, the senior medic with the Nung company, had both legs torn off. Hall was carried into the dispensary, where he calmly gave instructions for treating the numerous other wounded until he lost consciousness and died.

The North Vietnamese *95th Regiment* sent a two-company probe against the south wall at 4:30 A.M., which was quickly repulsed. A Shau was beyond friendly artillery range and depended on airstrikes for support. The low clouds and heavy morning fog prevented aircraft from spotting the camp even after daylight. Bombs were released above the clouds and the camp defenders adjusted the airstrikes by the sound of their impact. Late in the morning a light observation aircraft landed under heavy ground fire and evacuated operations M. Sgt. Robert D. Gibson. An Air Force AC-47 (Puff the Magic Dragon) ground support aircraft was hit by machine gun fire and crashed in the afternoon. Throughout the rest of the day, ammunition, supplies, and water were parachuted into the camp, but a considerable quantity landed outside the wire. Retrieval parties braved constant NVA fire to recover the precious cargo. Just prior to darkness, several helicopters landed to evacuate the seriously wounded. One Marine UH-34 was downed inside the camp.

The camp was subjected to another intensely accurate mortar shelling at 4:00 A.M. on 10 March, and most remaining buildings were battered into rubble. An hour later a massed NVA human wave assault rolled over the runway, through the tall grass, and onto the southern wall. At that point the 141st CIDG Company defected en masse to the assailants. Most crew-served weapons were blasted apart by direct hits from 57mm recoilless rifles, one of which killed Sp. Fifth Class Phillip T. Stahl. Confused and brutal fighting spread throughout the compound. The LLDB commander, Lt. Linh Van Dung, found a hiding spot and huddled in terror with his team during the battle. As an exception, LLDB operations Sergeant Yang responded heroically. After three hours of hand-to-hand combat and close-in gunfights, the Special Forces soldiers and their irregulars were forced back to the communications bunker and the north wall. Sgt. Owen F. McCann died in this fighting.

A determined North Vietnamese charge against the bunker at 8:30 A.M. was blocked by withering defensive fire. Another NVA battalion was massing across the airstrip when two B-57 Canberra bombers roared across their front and decimated the formation with cluster bomb units (CBU). The carnage and havoc caused by the two CBU explosions stopped the momentum of the NVA attack. Ammunition was redistributed among the defenders. Captain Carter, several Special Forces sergeants, and the Nungs counterattacked to regain the south wall, but casualties had been heavy, and the CIDG soldiers were demoralized. Many cowered in their holes and refused to fight.

Sergeants First Class Victor C. "Vic" Underwood, the Mike Force intelligence sergeant, and Vernon Carnahan, the detachment senior medic, had combined their small bands of surviving Nung riflemen along the camp's northern wall. The two sergeants led a handful of natives in a desperate counterattack using rifles and hand grenades. The group charged through the rubble and debris in the vicinity of the communications bunker and dispensary, where several defenders were still barricaded. The attackers were blasted apart by a torrent of automatic weapons fire from the North Vietnamese who remained firmly entrenched in their newly won positions. Both Underwood and Carnahan were severely wounded, and the counterattack was smashed. Captain Blair directed aircraft to bomb and strafe the entire camp. One A-1E Skyraider was hit and crash-landed on the airstrip, but another Skyraider immediately landed behind it and whisked the pilot to safety.

The NVA resorted to tearing down the remaining bunkers with sustained machine gun and recoilless rifle fire, and Captain Blair ordered the camp abandoned. The camp defenders formed a final line along the outside of the northern wall, which was clogged with their dead and wounded. When the first Marine rescue helicopters of HMM-163 landed at 5:20 P.M., the LLDB lieutenant triggered a stampede on the aircraft by his men and the CIDG. The hysterical rabble dropped their weapons, trampled over the injured, and struggled to get on. The wounded were left to crawl or stagger after them. Aircraft crewmen and Special Forces opened fire on the mob to prevent the helicopters from being overloaded. In the meantime the north wall defenders, unaware of the chaos at the landing zone, fired furiously to keep the NVA pinned down inside the camp.

North Vietnamese machine guns ripped into the helicopters as they took off, jammed with seventy-three camp personnel. The flight leader's helicopter had its tail rotor shot off, and it crashed. Marine Lt. Col. Charles A. House and his crew joined the rest of the defenders. Another UH-34 helicopter was also downed, and the wounded aboard perished in the flaming wreckage. Most of the other aircraft, including three Marine F-4B Phantoms and two A-4 Skyhawks flying in support, were severely damaged.

First Lt. Louis Mari and Sfc. Bennie G. Adkins carried seriously wounded S. Sgt. James Taylor through a trench, killing NVA soldiers who got in their way, and clambered through the north wall side gate. They carried Taylor down to the landing zone, only to find that all of the helicopters had left. Taylor later died of his wounds, and his body was hidden under some brush from where it was never recovered. There were still several Special Forces soldiers defending the communications bunker. They made a dash through a hail of automatic weapons fire for the north wall gate, and all were wounded. Specialist Pointon ran to the landing zone with both arms shattered and a gaping chest wound, but the helicopters had already departed. A Marine UH-1B helicopter spotted Pointon, dropped its rocket pods, and landed to take him on board. Thirteen other wounded were also crowded on, and the helicopter took off.

The remainder of the camp survivors turned into the jungle to escape during the night of 10 March. This column was spotted by rescue aircraft about noon on 11 March, but the helicopters were unable to land in the dense undergrowth. They lowered slings to lift out the personnel. The CIDG survivors mobbed the slings, and American and Nung soldiers clubbed them with rifle butts to restore order. On 12 March 1966 a final lift-out was summoned, and another panicked CIDG rush on the descending Marine helicopters ensued. This time the CIDG started shooting each other, and the mob action ceased only after a grenade tossed by a CIDG soldier exploded in the midst of his comrades. Throughout the day helicopters darted through the heavy cloud cover and picked up the last scattered bands of downed airmen and camp survivors.

There remained only one grisly footnote to the A Shau battle. Coded Operations BLUE STAR, Lt. Col. Kenneth B. Facey of Detachment C-1 flew a small body recovery party back to the camp on 18 March 1966. The North Vietnamese had quickly left the battlefield, and 200 unburied dead were scattered across the campsite. They lay undisturbed, as the Katu Valley inhabitants had not entered A Shau for fear of ghosts. Three-inch-high grass grew through compound shambles, and shell craters were almost full of muddy water. The corpses had been reduced to virtual skeletons, with pieces of flesh remaining only under rotting uniforms and boots. Osseous American remains, grasping .45-caliber pistols, with still-running watches banded about wristbones, were pulled into body bags with grappling hooks. Facey's men nervously surveyed the burned-out arms room and verified that some final hero had destroyed the safe and its classified papers with thermite grenades. There was nothing left to check, and rain showers hastened their departure. At 1:32 P.M. the BLUE STAR helicopters lifted out, and Special Forces left A Shau forever.[10]

The battle of A Shau had been a harrowing ordeal, and the defeat had much larger ramifications. The Marines initially wrote off the action as the fall of an indefensible Special Forces border surveillance camp, of no consequence to the larger war. The North Vietnamese had paid a heavy price for the camp but now had unchecked infiltration lanes through the A Shau corridor. They used the valley as a staging base for the attack on Hue two years later. Ephemeral allied efforts to regain the valley never really succeeded and culminated in the ghastly battle of Ap Bia Mountain, or "Hamburger Hill," in 1969. The fall of the A Shau Special Forces Camp indeed had a major impact on the future course of the war.

4. Special Forces Takes the Offensive

The advent of large regular Army forces in the other three tactical corps zones of Vietnam enabled many 5th Special Forces Group camps to take a bolder stance against the Viet Cong. Camp Buon Ea Yang (A-233) in Darlac Province, commanded by Capt. Ola L. Mize, a Korean War Medal of Honor recipient, was well placed with superior defenses, and soldiers there were busily employed opening Highway 21 to Ban Me Thuot. An 18 March 1966 CIDG ambush claimed a VC company commander and valuable documents that led to Camp Operation LE HAI 21.

The detachment put the operation in motion the next afternoon, and they arrived at the VC base on 20 March. Initial Special Forces–

led CIDG assaults on the stronghold were rebuffed by the entrenched Viet Cong, who then counterattacked and drove the CIDG companies into a defensive perimeter. Massive airstrikes and artillery fire saved the day, and the VC were driven from the field by nightfall. A sweep of the battleground revealed the location of another VC battalion command post ten miles away. An amalgamated Special Forces regiment was quickly put together using CIDG companies from Camps An Lac (A-234) and Lac Thien (A-236), as well as the II CTZ (Pleiku) Mike Force (A-219). An entire Viet Cong company was taken by surprise and shattered by this force and its supporting aerial firepower the following day.[11]

Sfc. Ledbetter took the 277th and 279th CIDG companies from Buon Ea Yang on another ambush the night of 30 March, accompanied by Staff Sergeants Collier and Spivey and Sergeant Blanchard. They set up along a known infiltration route and bushwhacked the leading company of a VC battalion half an hour before midnight. The VC caught in the killing zone were decimated, but the ambush positions were soon engulfed by mortar and automatic weapons return fire. The disciplined Viet Cong frontally assaulted the CIDG lines, while other VC elements temporarily flanked both companies. The main charge was disintegrated by a colossal triplex claymore mine detonation. The Special Forces sergeants took advantage of the turmoil to creep through the undergrowth, opening up with rifles and M-79 grenade fire on the VC mortar crews. This unexpected rear attack caused complete consternation, and the crewmen who were not killed fled and abandoned their weapons. The skirmish had been decided, and the VC withdrew as American aircraft arrived overhead.[12]

Camp Buon Ea Yang was a successful camp, and MACV absorbed it on 3 August 1966. The CIDG soldiers who did not convert to Regional Forces were discharged, and the Special Forces detachment moved on to set up a new camp at Buon Blech. This was the intended Special Forces operational methodology. An A-Detachment first staked out and cleared an area, then developed and secured it. Afterwards, the team would be ordered into another untamed region to tackle new combat and pacification tasks. Since 1965, MACV had optimistically forecast that all CIDG camps could be converted to Regional Force by 1 January 1967. While mopping up areas and moving on to bigger game sounded great on paper, conversion failures in the field painted a bleaker picture.

Since May 1963, all attempts at CIDG camp conversion had failed to some degree, ranging from ineffectual camp conversions at Buon Enao or Phey Srunh (13 May 1965), near total loss of assets such as at Tuc Trung (December 1963), to total loss of assets at Djirai (March 1963). In almost all camps the CIDG became accustomed to and intensely loyal to their Special Forces team. The tribesmen felt that Vietnamese care and protection were inadequate, a feeling often justified by LLDB hostility and ineptitude. The Special Forces care was undeniably superior in money, food, medical care, clothing, and other essentials. The Special Forces combat drill and wartime bonding had also instilled a pride that "CIDG was best," or at least better than the rag-tag Ruff-Puffs.

The Montagnards, who were very attached to their ancestral tribal homelands, also feared Vietnamese relocation intentions and distant RF/PF training centers where Americans would be absent. The Special Forces usually aggravated uncertainty as they closed out a camp. They hurriedly inventoried camp property and material and stripped positions of the recoilless rifles, machine guns, mortars, and radios. The CIDG was often denuded of leaders and tougher warriors, because the Special Forces took hand-picked CIDG soldiers with them, which invariably devastated the self-esteem of those remaining behind. The Special Forces also took the interpreters, nurses, and skilled workmen, leaving camp settlements to fend for themselves in the hands of occasional MACV advisors and indifferent Vietnamese officials.

Col. Francis J. "Splash" Kelly took over 5th Special Forces Group in June 1966. He was an armor officer who had been assigned to the Special Warfare Directorate in the Pentagon during the time of Operation SWITCHBACK in Vietnam. He became airborne-qualified and assumed command of the 1st Special Forces Group on Okinawa prior to taking over the 5th Special Forces Group in Vietnam.

Colonel Kelly monitored the careful pilot conversion of An Phu (A-424) in the Delta. Command scrutiny was intense, and dozens of province welfare officials and U.S. AID (Agency for International Development) personnel routinely visited with bounties of food and supplies. MACV claimed success during impressive ceremonies on 6 August, but An Phu was a scrappy Hoa Hao bandit camp capable of looking after itself. Colonel Kelly delayed further Montagnard camp conversions while he turned to another problem.[13]

Complaints and shortcomings inherent in the Special Forces assumption of the MACV sector/subsector advisory role led to an overhaul of the concept. On 4 July 1966 MACV directed changes in response to Special Forces concerns. The MACV senior advisors of each corps were instructed that Special Forces continuation in this role should be confined to the more remote areas (where MACV teams did not operate) and that such missions "must be governed by the detachment's long-term capacity to execute such a function without detracting from the CIDG program." A survey of dual capacity teams was conducted, and formal guidance was issued in the form of MACV Directive 525-15, which reaffirmed that border surveillance and infiltration interdiction was the primary Special Forces mission.

On 28 August 1966 Colonel Kelly was notified by General Westmoreland "that any detachment which can be replaced by RF/PF forces or ARVN forces, should be replaced; and any detachment improperly located to carry out the CIDG mission should be relocated." The thirty-seven detachments serving as MACV advisory teams in 1966 were sliced first to twenty-nine by the end of 1967, then to twelve by December of 1968.[14]

The Special Forces took the offensive against interior VC infiltration routes in the summer. Six miles inside War Zone C and due west of Nui Ba Den, a reaction contingent from the III CTZ Mike Force airmobiled into Trai Bi on 22 June to secure the first CIDG campsite to be planted inside a Viet Cong war zone. The next day a convoy spearheaded by the 35th ARVN Ranger Battalion brought in Captain Burroughs and his Detachment A-323, reinforced by five CIDG companies. The VC staged a welcoming pack howitzer bombardment the first night, but damage and casualties were light. Surrounded by jungle laced with Viet Cong fortifications and tunnel systems, Camp Trai Bi was steadfastly maintained.[15]

By November 1966 the Special Forces CIDG offensive was joined with the larger allied military offensive, which had been geared into action with the new brigades and divisions of the buildup. In the northern part of the country, several camps combined their irregular and regional force units for the first joint operation in I CTZ. They teamed up with U.S. and Korean Marines and ARVN forces during Operation RIO BLANCO, fought from 20 to 23 November 1966. In northwestern Tay Ninh Province, on the approaches to Saigon, 530 Chinese Nungs in three companies, led by 7 Special Forces under Capt. Thomas Myerchin of Detachment A-302, smashed deep into

War Zone C. The "China Boys" ran into a Viet Cong battalion moving toward Camp Soui Da (A-322) on 3 November as part of the first search-and-destroy mission of the war—Operation ATTLEBORO. Although losses were heavy, they had pinpointed the *272d VC Regiment*, which was instrumental in determining the commitment of larger American formations.

In tune with this heightened joint operational posture, Company B of the 5th Special Forces Group fielded a provisional CIDG battalion to screen the 4th Infantry Division's Operation PAUL REVERE IV west of Pleiku. Known as Task Force Prong, the ad hoc Special Forces contingent was composed of one CIDG company each from Duc Co (A-253) and Plei Djereng (A-251), and the 3d Mike Force Company from the II CTZ (Pleiku) Mike Force. Lt. Col. Eleazer "Lee" Parmly IV, the commander of Company B, led Task Force Prong, which consisted of 25 Special Forces, 2 LLDB, and 395 CIDG soldiers.

The 4th Infantry Division staff displayed the usual lack of knowledge about CIDG capability, and Parmly was horrified at their first battle plan to insert Task Force Prong between two divisional battalions "on an axis of advance by phase lines." He immediately requested that the CIDG be simply employed moving along the Cambodian border, so he could control them with reference to a fixed area boundary. The division relented, and Task Force Prong was airmobiled to LZ Lane on the morning of 8 November 1966, already secured by a company of the 2d Battalion, 8th Infantry.

The 4th Infantry Division swept north of Plei Djereng and west of the Nam Sathay River into the rugged tri-border highlands. The path of Task Force Prong's advance skirted the division between the river and Cambodia and took them straight into the jungled Plei Trap Valley. The 3d Mike Force Company initially surprised a mobile column of 12.7mm antiaircraft guns and captured several, but the presence of an NVA divisional AA battery spelled larger trouble. On 9 November Sgt. Carlos D. Caro's Plei Djereng CIDG company ran into NVA trenchlines across a small river and pulled back under fire to direct airstrikes and shelling against the far bank. At 10:10 A.M., as the curtain of artillery lifted, they assaulted through the stream. In the face of concentrated return fire, only a precarious toehold was established on the opposite shore. This beachhead was subjected to intense and accurate close-range fire and had to be abandoned two hours later. Two A-1E Skyraiders from the 1st Air Commando Squadron at Pleiku, commanded by Lt. Col. Eugene "Gene" Dietrich, a West Point classmate of Parmly's, covered the retreat by suppressing the NVA fortifications with napalm and 20mm cannon fire. Among the casualties, both Special Forces sergeants had been wounded, and the company called for reinforcement.

Colonel Parmly's command group escorted Sgt. James L. Lewis, Jr.'s, Duc Co company across the unknown forest, passing the carcass of an A-1E Skyraider identified only by faded letters, ZB, on the tail. They fought past a machine gun nest and linked up with the Plei Djereng company in midafternoon. The two companies then withdrew and evacuated casualties from LZ Lane. Company C of the 1st Battalion, 14th Infantry, was brought in the following morning to reattack the NVA river fortifications. While advancing back into the area, Task Force Prong was caught in a massive L-shaped ambush. The desperate fight out of the trap cost heavy losses, the wounding of five Special Forces advisors, and the death of Sp4. John E. Mitchell. The battle raged until the CIDG were able to consolidate a defensive perimeter, which was held with plenty of strafing and bombing from air support. Companies A and C of the 14th Infantry battalion linked up with Task Force Prong just after midnight, canceling the threat of annihilation.

First Lt. Robert Jacobelli's 3d Mike Force Company had been duelling snipers most of the day, and set up a perimeter three miles away in a dry lake bed that straddled the Cambodian border. Two battalions of the *88th NVA Regiment* assaulted their position at 6:00 A.M. on 11 November. Sfc. Robert "Bob" Ramsey, the company's first sergeant, and his northern outpost took the brunt of the initial attack. He decimated the lead NVA company with claymore mines as the outpost fell back across the lake bottom. Lieutenant Jacobelli requested air-strikes and radioed for assistance before he was wounded in the stomach defending the eastern edge of the perimeter. M. Sgt. Francis Quinn and Sfc. Frank Huff frantically moved up and down the battleline, cautioning the troops on fire discipline, because ammunition was running low. Supporting aircraft threw up a wall of exploding steel and dirt in the midst of the NVA assailants. During the course of the desperate morning fighting, the Mike Force company had to fall back three times to new positions.

Captain Sincere, who had returned to Pleiku with prisoners on the evening of 10 November, immediately boarded an emergency resupply helicopter (piloted by Maj. Al Cartwright) for the battlefield. First Lt. Paul J. Hess, Jr., a Special Forces quartermaster officer who had been in Vietnam only three weeks, rushed prepackaged sandbags crammed with ammunition and rations into the helicopter and jumped on. Sincere guided the pilot toward the area where he had been lifted out the day before, but the NVA had already forced the Mike Force back to the southeastern edge of the lake bed. Cartwright passed over the swirling smoke of the confused action and asked the Mike Force to pop smoke. Both the Mike Force and North Vietnamese immediately tossed out yellow smoke grenades, and as the helicopter glided toward enemy lines it was riddled by 12.7mm antiaircraft fire. Lieutenant Hess and aviation crewman Sgt. Henry T. Leonard were killed instantly, and the copilot was wounded. Major Cartwright yelled that the ship would crash unless it was lightened immediately.

Capt. Clyde Sincere jumped twelve feet as the helicopter reversed direction and wobbled into the distance. He was wounded just above the heart by grenade fragments and knocked flat. The NVA ran toward him while Sincere feigned death, but heavy Mike Force fire drove them back into the woodline. For two hours he played possum in the blazing sun. Finally, Sergeant Quinn and the company medic, Sgt. Danny Panfil, reached Sincere with a squad of riflemen. The small element raced back to the perimeter and Sincere assumed command.

By this time, four helicopters had been shot down in rapid succession, and ammunition was almost exhausted. One helicopter threw out its load of ammo-laden sandbags from 500 feet rather than get closer to the ground, forcing Sincere and Quinn to lead a charge under heavy fire to retrieve the precious cargo from the Cambodian side of the lake bed. The main Mike Force line was saved by low-flying A-1E Skyraiders, which dropped napalm and cluster bomb units into the North Vietnamese attackers, so close that defenders alike were seared and wounded. Late that afternoon helicopters managed to airland Company B of the 1st Battalion, 12th Infantry, inside the shrunken perimeter and take out the seriously wounded.

Task Force Prong continued saturation patrolling in the Plei Trap Valley through the rest of the month. CIDG companies from Camps Plei Me and Buon Blech were rotated to relieve the initial camp companies. First Lt. Larry Dring's 1st Mike Force Company took over as the reconnaissance arm of the 1st Battalion, 14th Infantry. Scattered firefights and sniper encounters persisted. On 17 November 1966 the Plei Me company was hit hard and pinned down by NVA bunkers of the *33d NVA Regiment* for two hours until 14th Infantry troops arrived.

Task Force Prong was discontinued at noon on 2 December 1966 as the North Vietnamese retreated into Cambodia. Task Force Prong verified many Special Forces truths. While the II CTZ Mike Force had performed admirably although heavily outnumbered, their weapons (except for the M16s carried by advisors) consisted of World War II–vintage arms inferior to modern NVA weapons. The camp CIDG companies, not as well trained and subject to despair under heavy fire, had again been worsted in open combat with hardened NVA units of equal size. However, the CIDG program was not intended to produce attack infantry. The natives were instead patrollers, able to navigate by the lay of the land without compasses, detect booby traps, and find the enemy. In joint operations with American line units, CIDG utility was largely negated if regular forces failed in responding promptly to such contact.[16]

Task Force Prong, Operation RIO BLANCO, and ATTLEBORO were the natural extensions of an increasingly aggressive Special Forces stance, typified by the permanent invasion of Viet Cong war zones beginning with Camp Trai Bi. The group was streamlined for combat with a diminution of dual MACV advisory tasks. The availability of large conventional forces and their supporting assets rendered Special Forces greater combat, aviation, and engineer backup. Camp survival was assured in many areas that would have otherwise been lost. At the same time, the Special Forces was still being driven from valuable border outposts, as the fall of A Shau demonstrated. While border surveillance was a dangerous and costly enterprise and success could be argued, the Special Forces was suffering outright failure in another quarter. The planned conversion of the CIDG program and the release of the trained minority soldiers to South Vietnamese government control was not working out. This boded poorly for the future, as U.S. military goals were being reoriented toward Vietnamization.

Notes

1. 5th Special Forces Group, *Command Report*, dtd 10 October 1965.
2. Detachment C-2, *Initial After Action Report (FULRO Incidents)*, dtd 23 December 1965; Detachment A-112, *Team After Action Report*, dtd 10 February 1966.
3. Detachment A-321, 1st Special Forces Group, *Final Report*, dtd 10 October 1965; and Detachment A-321, *Combat After Action Report: Battle of Phu Cu Pass*, dtd 25 September 1965.
4. Detachment A-332, *Monthly Operational Summary*, dtd 31 October 1965.
5. 5th Special Forces Group, *Command Report*, dtd 15 January 1966, Inclosure 9.
6. The combat patrol, which had departed camp on 17 October for a six-day mission, contained 85 CIDG and 2 Special Forces advisors. Each outpost had 20 men, while the pickets had 8 men each. Plei Me Camp retained 10 Special Forces, 14 LLDB, and some 250 Jarai, Rhade, and Bahnar CIDG soldiers inside the perimeter.
7. Losses inside Camp Plei Me during the battle were KIA: 3 Special Forces, 1 LLDB, 15 ARVN Rangers, 14 CIDG, 1 American news reporter; WIA: 7 Special Forces, 2 LLDB, 29 ARVN Rangers, 28 CIDG. Confirmed Viet Cong losses were 141 dead, although at least another 200 were suspected. 5th Special Forces Group, *Command Report*, dtd 10 Jan 66, Inclosure 1; 5th Special Forces Group AVSF-C Report, *Plei Me Chronology and Statistics*, dtd 17 November 1965; 5th Special Forces Group, *Monthly Operational Summary*, dtd 1 November 1965; 5th Special Forces Group Air Movements Officer Report, *Support of Plei Me;* Headquarters, 1st Cavalry Division, *Combat Operations After Action Report*, dtd 4 March 1966.
8. 5th Special Forces Group, *Command Report*, dtd 10 May 1966, 15 November 1966, 15 February 1967; Jack Shulimson, *U.S. Marines in Vietnam: An Expanding War*, Washington, D.C.: Headquarters, U.S. Marines, 1982.
9. Detachment A-107, *Monthly Operational Summary*, January 1966; Detachment C-1, *Monthly Operational Summary*, dtd 7 February 1966. At the time, Tra Bong contained the 101st, 111th, and 144th CIDG companies, which were renumbered the 116th, 117th, and 118th CIDG companies in May 1966.
10. Detachment C-1, *After Action Report*, dtd 28 March 1966; Jack Shulimson, *U.S. Marines in Vietnam: An Expanding War*, Headquarters, U.S. Marine Corps: Washington, D.C., 1982; Detachment C-1, *Combat Operations After Action Report*, dtd 23 May 1966; 5th Special Forces Group G-3 reading file and papers. Losses at A Shau were KIA: 5 Special Forces, 1 LLDB, 75 Nungs, 40 CIDG, 45 civilians, 6 interpreters; MIA: 15 Nungs, 61 CIDG; WIA: 12 Special Forces, 1 LLDB, 33 Nungs, 52 CIDG, 2 ci-

vilians, 1 interpreter. North Vietnamese losses could only be guessed at, but the Special Forces claimed 800.

11. Total losses in Operation LE HAI 21 were KIA: 1 Special Forces, 1 interpreter, and 11 CIDG; WIA: 2 Special Forces, 14 CIDG. Nine Viet Cong were captured and 142 bodies were counted on the field. 5th Special Forces Group, *Command Report,* dtd 10 May 1966, Inclosure 17; 5th Special Forces Group, *USMACV Monthly Evaluation Report,* dtd 9 April 1966.

12. Detachment A-233, *After Action Report,* dtd 1 April 1966. Losses were 2 CIDG KIA and 2 WIA. Four dead Viet Cong and 1 wounded were found the next morning, but blood trails indicated the infliction of heavy losses.

13. 5th Special Forces Group, *Résumé of the Conversion of CIDG to RF Status,* dtd 25 November 1968.

14. 5th Special Forces Group, *Synopsis of the USASF Sector/Subsector Advisory Role,* dtd 1 December 1968.

15. 5th Special Forces Group, *Command Report,* dtd 10 August 1966, Inclosure 12.

16. Losses in the battle of Plei Trap Valley for Task Force Prong were KIA: 2 Special Forces, 24 CIDG; MIA: 5 CIDG; WIA: 12 Special Forces (including Lieutenant Colonel Parmly), 1 LLDB, 71 CIDG. NVA losses were counted at 272 killed, 2 wounded, 3 captured. 5th Special Forces Group, *Command Report,* dtd 15 February 1967, Inclosure 10 with Annexes 1–5. Capt. Clyde Sincere was awarded the Distinguished Service Cross for his heroism during the battle.

Camp Trai Bi (A-323) was the first Special Forces camp established in War Zone C, being emplaced during the summer of 1966. (Author's Collection)

Captain Terry Cordell, the heroic commander of A-334 who was killed defending the Buon Enao complex on October 15, 1962, seen days earlier with Sgt. Maj. John O'Donovan greeting General Maxwell D. Taylor, the Chairman-designate of the U.S. Joint Chiefs of Staff. (U.S. Army)

Typical Montagnard CIDG soldiers on a field operation near Polei Krong in December of 1964, wearing the spotted camouflage uniforms later replaced by tiger-stripe camouflage fatigues. (U.S. Army)

Captain Roger H. C. Donlon, the first Special Forces trooper to earn the Medal of Honor, defended Camp Nam Dong with his team (A-726) on July 6, 1964. (U.S. Army)

Jarai Montagnards of Pleiku Province moving their house to a new Special Forces campsite during 1963. (Author's Collection)

Rhade Montagnard CIDG soldiers use elephant transportation at Ban Don in 1962. One of these elephants later stepped on a mine. (George C. Morton)

The smashed command bunker at Lang Vei on February 8, 1968, with destroyed NVA tank nearby. Note also the final protective barrier of gravel-filled barrels mentioned in the text. (Author's Collection)

Special Forces recon patrol passes through a village on the Cambodian frontier west of Saigon during the allied 1968 post-Tet Counteroffensive. (Army News Features)

Special Forces Civic Action—Sergeant First Class Chase of Chau Doc-based Detachment B-42 renders medical treatment to inhabitants of My Duc village. (U.S. Army)

The II CTZ (Pleiku) Mike Force assembles preparatory to parachuting over the future site of Camp Bu Prang on October 5, 1967. (Ludwig Faistenhammer)

Mortar position moved to top of bunker at flooded Camp Cai Cai in September of 1966. Note sampan used to deliver supplies. (Author's Collection)

Airboat formation of Company D uses the Mekong River near the Cambodian frontier in late 1966, as discussed in Chapter 12. (U.S. Army)

A CIDG soldier poses behind one of the North Vietnamese AA machine guns used against Mike Strike Force troops who recaptured Duc Lap's northern hill in fierce combat on August 25, 1968. (Author's Collection)

During the siege of Camp Ben Het (A-244) in the spring of 1969, the fort relied on parachuted supplies. Most remote Special Forces camps depended on aerial delivery of supplies, which were airlanded under normal circumstances. (U.S. Air Force)

Special Forces Assault troop of Task Force Ivory Coast aboard aircraft on 21 November 1970, just prior to the raid on Son Tay, North Vietnam. Courtesy Gordon Rottman Collection

Special Forces flamethrower sergeant advances up boulder-strewn Nui Coto under sniper fire during the battle of March 1969. (U.S. Army)

CHAPTER 8

ON THE OFFENSIVE

1. The Fighting Camps

By 1967 the 5th Special Forces Group had become committed primarily to fielding its 285 CIDG companies in the rugged and remote areas of South Vietnam that were not suitable for sustained allied presence. The group had eighty-two A-Detachments, twelve B-Detachments, four companies, and six special project detachments scattered in over 100 different locations. The total number of border camps that year (twenty-eight) had doubled over the fourteen border surveillance camps of 1966. The geographical pattern of Special Forces camps in Vietnam was being patterned in consonance with allied campaign plans, in contrast to the scattered, disjointed placement of earlier years.

In the northern I CTZ, the Special Forces precariously maintained a series of camps in the jungled mountains, far to the west of most allied formations occupying the coastal lowlands. In the central highlands of II CTZ, two separate lines of camps had been created. The first line ran along the eastern mountain range in Viet Cong territory near the ocean, whereas the second line was pressed up close to the Laotian and Cambodian borders. Within III CTZ the Special Forces set up a ring of camps on the Cambodian northern and western approaches to Saigon. These exerted pressure inside War Zone C, covered the northern sector of War Zone D, and were displaced to block off the shortest, western border pathway into the capital. Finally, in the broad expanse of the Delta, the Special Forces set out to back up the line of IV CTZ border camps with new sites northeast of the Mekong River and south of Long An Province to box in the Plain of Reeds.

The Special Forces camps were built and manned to provide border monitoring outposts, to gather intelligence on NVA/VC dispositions by aggressive combat patrolling, and to exert government authority in Viet Cong-dominated regions. All camps had the mission of interdicting, harassing, and destroying North Vietnamese or Viet Cong forces and their logistical lifelines. The first camp built under the new "fighting camp" program was Plei Djereng (A-251 under Captain Moore), a border surveillance camp northwest of Pleiku, which was started on 13 December 1966 by Engineer Team KB-7 of the 539th Engineer Detachment. After repeated attacks on this location, it was rebuilt on a hill overlooking the surrounding forests on 1 June 1967, using a complete fighting camp package.

Campsites were chosen according to a multitude of factors that considered terrain, weather, NVA/VC activity, proximity to secure installations, recruiting potential, and compatibility with allied operational requirements. Once the location was fixed, the ideal CIDG camp cycle was envisioned as an eighteen-month venture. It began on the day the team first occupied the campsite. The building of the camp was to be completed within thirty to forty-five days. Construction was begun simultaneously with the recruitment of young native males. Military training of the new civilian irregular defense group commenced, and within six weeks short-range patrols were fielded. As patrolling proficiency increased, the Special Forces sent its CIDG soldiers farther out on longer missions. Colonel Kelly reasoned that by the time a year and a half had elapsed, the Special Forces team would be able to turn over the camp to the Vietnamese for mission continuation. That would allow the Special Forces personnel to begin the cycle in another area.

Of course, not all camps fit into the plan. For example, the group realized that most of the camps draped along the periphery of Vietnam's western border would have to be occupied "for the foreseeable future" by Special Forces and LLDB soldiers. Some camps, such as Con Thien, set up on key real estate under the shadow of the Demilitarized Zone in January, became Marine bastions instead. Camp Con Thien was turned over to the Marines for this purpose at the end of the year. Other camps were leftovers from earlier times and were maintained for various political and strategic purposes, which precluded recycling schemes. Yet most camps fell under the "fighting camp" concept outlined in the 5th Special Forces Group 1967 CIDG camp construction program.

The Special Forces fighting camp was characterized by its speedy construction (six weeks or less), austerity, and simplicity. Designed as a miniature fortress, it emphasized mutual support, defense in depth, and use of a reserve. The camp was bounded by tactical wire, interspersed with claymore mines and barrels of fougasse flame weapons, placed to channel the attacking force into machine gun bunkers or platoon strongpoints. The Special Forces had learned not to depend on barrier wire to stop an assault force. Usually four belts of barbed wire or razor-sharp German wire were strung, and fields of fire burned off or doused with defoliants.

The camp itself was marked by a series of strongpoints, each capable of covering the other, connected by fighting trenches. In the center of the camp was the inner perimeter, or hardened core, which housed the tactical operations center, communications bunker, emergency medical bunker, ammunition bunker, and a helipad. The inner perimeter usually contained the larger crew-served weapons, such as 4.2-inch mortars and 105mm howitzers. The camp's size and number of positions were geared to a formula whereby it could be fully defended by one-quarter of the assigned camp force. The Special Forces camp was also designed to be cost-effective and to use as much native labor and materials as possible. The cost to build a standard fighting camp was $20,000 in American dollars in 1967.

Special Forces fighting camps had three principal variants. The first was called the *subsurface fighting camp,* where the soil was firm enough to place all bunkers below ground with sufficient strength to withstand direct medium mortar hits. Most camps in the mountains were of this nature. The second model was the *surface fighting camp.* This camp was put in normal Vietnam terrain, where the groundwater table was close to the surface, and there were two basic varieties. The first type had vital facilities and bunkers composed of concrete, logs, heavy timber, or reinforced steel CONEX containers. The rest of the camp structures were built out of wood. The second type used salvaged CONEX containers for all bunkers, important facilities, and even for sleeping quarters. Such a camp usually required eighty-six CONEX containers.

The final design was the *floating fighting camp,* used in the Plain of Reeds and in the lower Delta, where heavy monsoon rains annually flooded the Mekong and Bassac rivers. High water could reach depths of twelve feet above normal, which caused catastrophic inundations of the first Special Forces camps in the region. Structures were built very high, with floating floors that rose with the water level. Medical and ammunition bunkers, as well as mortar, machine gun, and recoilless rifle positions, were built on hardened platforms that also floated when secured to fifty-five gallon fuel drums. Floating helipads capable of supporting the weight of a fully loaded UH-1 Huey helicopter were installed. While the advent of renewed Army riverine operations brought development of more expensive but lighter floating materials, the Special Forces insisted on the fuel drums because of their ready availability and cost-effectiveness. Approximately 500 fifty-five-gallon drums were required per floating camp.

In mid-1967 the floating fighting camp was improved further. New bunker designs were implemented to prevent ammunition from becoming wet and malfunctioning during flood conditions. CONEX containers were put on their backs, doors up, and their interiors were waterproofed. Tarps and tin overheads kept out rain. This field expedient insured dry bunkers in six feet of water or less.

The fighting camps were constructed by various organizations, depending on the region. In the northern sector of South Vietnam, most camps were built by Navy Seabee mobile construction battalion elements. In the II and III Corps Tactical Zones, Army combat or construction engineer companies were used. ARVN engineer battalions were utilized in the Delta. The 5th Special Forces Group also made extensive country-wide use of the five-man engineer KB-Teams from the 539th Engineer Detachment (Control and Advisory), which was attached to the 1st Special Forces Group.

The 5th Special Forces Group Logistical Support Center in Nha Trang maintained a stockage level of two fighting camps. The material for each camp was stored on a structure-by-structure basis: precut, banded, palletized, and prepared for complete delivery by C-130 aircraft, either by landing or by parachute. The prestocked fighting camp packages were used both for new camps and as refurbishment of older ones, such as Mang Buk (A-246), which was rebuilt northeast of Kontum in June. The time required for complete delivery from the logistical support command to the construction site was seven days, depending on aircraft and weather. The latter was often the most critical factor, since most of Vietnam rarely had more than five months of suitable construction climate between the monsoons.[1]

The magnitude of the Special Forces camp construction and maintenance effort mandated the creation of the group staff engineer section at headquarters in December 1966. Maj. Robert Lockridge, Jr., of the Army Corps of Engineers, aligned his new section so that a professional engineer captain was dedicated to each corps tactical zone for coordination and supervisory construction purposes.

The impact of the Special Forces fighting camps in area security and population control was far out of proportion to the investment in personnel, money, and material. Although the NVA and VC had more to fear (in the sense of battlefield annihilation) from regular American units with their firepower and mobility, allied search-and-destroy missions were only transient incursions. The Special Forces–led CIDG forces, once established, stayed in their backyard. While the Special Forces could not destroy significant NVA or VC formations in open combat, they were very adept at creating general havoc and continual harassment.

The NVA/VC developed a grudging respect for the lethal, hard-driving Special Forces teams, which inevitably made conditions very uncomfortable for them as soon as they set up camp. Once the Special Forces started working an area, Viet Cong messengers began to disappear, officers fell from sniper rounds, and free movement was stifled by the threat of ambush. The NVA and VC had learned the hard way that attacking these tiny forts to rid themselves of the nuisance caused immense losses. In exchange, a successful overrun would knock over only twelve Americans and a number of half-baked native irregulars. For that reason, attacks on camps had tapered off in 1966. The fighting camps inserted deeper in VC base territory during 1967, however, forced them to challenge Special Forces expansion.

The Viet Cong were more fearful of the inroads that the Special Forces invariably made on the indigenous population surrounding a camp. The Special Forces revolutionary development program was reemphasized in 1967, after having slipped for several years as a result of the larger problems of group survival on the battlefield. Their efforts were generally effective because the group's officers and sergeants had a great deal of maturity and because they understood the culture, the nuances of the local habitat, and even the language. Many people trusted and befriended the tactful Special Forces personnel, who dispensed medicines and other welcome items with professional finesse.

While Special Forces civic action was certainly not an unqualified success that changed the "hearts and minds" of the citizenry, it was often accepted as a sincere gesture because of its sustained and diplomatic commitment. The Viet Cong had long since given up crude propaganda, which had earlier labeled Special Forces candy and medicine as poisons. By 1967 the VC resorted to warning the populace that Special Forces belied the real viciousness of the American and Saigon governments: the Special Forces had been deliberately sent in to seduce them; they would be followed by the regular henchmen. Unfortunately, the cycled replacement of Special Forces camps, combined with the sometimes-callous attitude of following units or government authorities, seemed to lend credence to this Viet Cong logic.

Col. Jonathan F. "Fred" Ladd took command of the 5th Special Forces Group on 4 June 1967. An infantry officer who served as the senior advisor to the 21st ARVN Division during the Operation SWITCHBACK period, he commanded the 1st Special Forces Group on Okinawa immediately prior to taking over the 5th.

2. Fighting Camps to the West

The 5th Special Forces Group slammed its fighting camps farther into Viet Cong territory throughout the first months of 1967. New fighting camps were opened in the midst of traditional Viet Cong base areas or border priority zones, while mobile guerrilla forces and long-range reconnaissance operations cut into NVA and VC lines of communication. The most dangerous long-term task was the creation of Camps Prek Klok and Tong Le Chon in War Zone C, the construction of Camp Bunard on the northern rim of War Zone D, and Camp Song Be on the infiltration lane from Cambodia to the latter war zone. The Viet Cong lashed back at this latest Special Forces intrusion into their home territory, and the tempo of the 1967 fighting camp battles was set.

In the third week of March 1967, the war zone penetration camps were built. Captain Fukishima's Detachment A-322 turned over its previous Soui Da campsite for use as an artillery firebase and moved into Prek Klok on 20 March 1967. The camp was set up in the northwestern border fringes of War Zone C and manned with imported Vietnamese CIDG personnel. Less than a month later, on 14 April,

Prek Klok was the first Special Forces camp to be assaulted in over a year by a large enemy force. Two Viet Cong battalions smashed into the perimeter following an intensive 82mm mortar barrage, but were stopped cold by final artillery defensive fire and camp automatic weapons. Prek Klok was closed toward the end of the year, on 9 December 1967, and its assets transferred to a new camp at Katum, closer to War Zone C's Cambodian border, which was opened on 21 February 1968.

The next war zone camp was established at Tong Le Chon in Binh Long "Peaceful Dragon" Province. Detachment A-334 opened this border surveillance camp along a bend of the Saigon River, deep in the jungled recesses of War Zone C on 24 March 1967. There was no local populace in its remote area, and the CIDG garrison lived in tents on the outer perimeter. Tong Le Chon had a dismal record of high desertion rates and poor morale, primarily a consequence of its isolation, lack of adequate living quarters and facilities, and camp constuction requirements. Interpreters and skilled laborers were obtained only by offering premium wages, and most quit their jobs after a few days. Discipline was practically nonexistent. By the first week of August, the camp strike force had dwindled to 51 Montagnards and Cambodians in two platoons. The other 142 CIDG soldiers on site at the time were from Camps Loc Ninh and Minh Thanh, posted to Tong Le Chon on a twenty-day rotating company basis.

Camp defenses reflected the poor state of affairs at Tong Le Chon. The wire barrier surrounding Tong Le Chon had not been checked for four days prior to the attack of 7 August. Later it was determined that the outer wire may have been cut or marked prior to commencement of the main NVA assault. About half of the emplaced claymore mines failed to detonate because their explosive compound had been removed by CIDG personnel and used for cooking fires. The Special Forces personnel had to physically check CIDG patrols that were sent outside the gate to insure that they actually departed the camp. On the evening of the attack, such confirmation was lacking. None of the scheduled listening posts and ambush security patrols were actually posted, and without its pickets Tong Le Chon was devoid of any local warning protection. Defensive complacency was highlighted by lack of concern over the presence of the *165th NVA Regiment*, known to be in the immediate vicinity. The Special Forces team believed that certain towns along Route 13 were targeted by the North Vietnamese for attack instead of their camp.

The night of 6–7 August was clear and the temperature was a tropically humid 78 degrees Fahrenheit. In addition to Captain Berg's 10-man Detachment A-334, Tong Le Chon contained 3 Special Forces personnel from Detachment A-302, the III CTZ (Bien Hoa) Mike Force with 326 men, and 4 Special Forces personnel with 247 Mike Force troops from the Nha Trang Mike Force. Just after midnight, the southeastern portion of the camp was hit by mortar fire that steadily increased in volume. Counter-mortar and artillery fire was called in, and helicopters and fire support gunships arrived overhead. At 1:22 A.M. the North Vietnamese mortar rounds began falling on the camp's inner perimeter, and the command bunker took a direct hit. The supply tent was set on fire, and the smoke forced abandonment of the adjacent communications bunker. The night was also lighted by the furious blaze in the fuel and oil storage area.

Half an hour later the North Vietnamese *165th Regiment* masscharged the southeastern perimeter, where the wire was cut with large American wire cutters and lanes were marked with white rags. The attacking infantry stormed into the perimeter behind sappers armed with satchel charges, B-40 rocket launchers, and bangalore torpedoes. Some twenty men of the Minh Thanh company surrendered on the outer wall, and the North Vietnamese raced into the camp. The attack might have succeeded in overrunning the compound were it not for the fortuitous detonation of the camp's mortar ammunition dump, which exploded in the midst of the North Vietnamese assailants. The tremendous blast instantly dismembered the lead element and stunned and dazed the rest of the infantry. A prompt Special Forces–led Mike Force counterattack expelled the North Vietnamese infantrymen in close combat.

A slackening in mortar and direct fire against the camp followed until 3:11 A.M., when another mass charge was thrown against the south and east walls. Several effective airstrikes and automatic weapons fire stopped the attack. One hour later the NVA again tackled the badly damaged southeast wall. One NVA rifle squad captured a perimeter CONEX machine gun bunker, but they were mopped up shortly before dawn.

At daybreak helicopters brought in both Army and Air Force medical personnel and began evacuating the wounded. This process was marred by the cowardice of many CIDG and Mike Force soldiers who used bloody wrappings to feign wounds and tried to sneak aboard outgoing helicopters. The medics had to rip off all dressings to prevent desertion by lightly wounded or uninjured soldiers. Several malingerers had to be forcibly taken off the medical evacuation helicopters. That afternoon the 1st Battalion of the 2d Infantry, 1st Infantry Division, arrived in Tong Le Chon and ended any threat to the camp's continued survival.[2]

In direct contrast to the Tong Le Chon experience, the battle of Loc Ninh resulted in a total Special Forces victory. The Loc Ninh Camp had been set up as a border surveillance camp in the same province by Detachment A-331 on 10 December 1966. In September 1967 a large buildup of *9th VC Division* elements was detected in the Loc Ninh sector. An attack was expected, and the only surprise was the actual duration and extent of the onslaught. The Viet Cong battered the camp from 29 October through 4 November 1967 in a series of heavy barrages and mass human wave assaults.

The defensive posture of Camp Loc Ninh was extremely good, and morale was high among the Vietnamese, Montagnard, and Chinese Nung garrison. The perimeter was roughly diamond shaped, and a CIDG company was billeted along each of the defensive walls. The weather during the battle was cool and the wind calm. The moon was in its last quarter, and, except for the normal early morning haze, visibility was excellent.

An hour after midnight on 29 October, a nearby Ruff-Puff compound was assaulted by the Viet Cong, while mortar suppressive fire was leveled against Loc Ninh Camp. A battalion of the *273d VC Regiment* moved closer to the camp boundary and blasted it with close-in fire from rocket-propelled grenades and machine guns for the rest of the night. Medium and heavy mortars of the *84th VC Artillery Regiment* contributed heavily to this bombardment. Nevertheless, the Loc Ninh garrison managed a relief expedition into the RF/PF post at daybreak and expelled the Viet Cong, rescuing the American advisor and Vietnamese district chief located there.

The initial Viet Cong assault on Loc Ninh Camp itself was launched just after midnight on 31 October. A full battalion stormed out of the rubber trees across open ground and the airstrip, converging on the camp from two directions. At the same time the camp was subjected to a withering direct-fire and mortar barrage. The VC attack was bloodily repulsed in front of the wire barriers by bunkered automatic weapons and tactical airstrikes. Many Viet Cong were pinned down in the bomb-cratered fields by the intensity of the defensive fire and were repeatedly strafed and rocketed by helicopter gunships. Except for a short but intensive mortar barrage, fired to assist VC body recovery effects, contact diminished to sporadic gunfire by the next day.

The Viet Cong staged another mass attack thirty minutes after midnight on 2 November, but it, too, was annihilated by a concentrated hailstorm of bullets, claymore mines, and low-level aircraft strafing and rocketing runs. After the final airstrike, the Viet Cong were seen dropping weapons and fleeing from the field in complete disorganization.

The Loc Ninh defenders had severely trounced all VC assault forces. The predictable Viet Cong tactics of following mortar barrages with charges at approximately midnight reaped a grim punishment. At least three full-scale battalion attacks had been made during the heaviest fighting. Over 1,000 Viet Cong bodies had been left across the smoking earth, compared to the incredibly light casualties suffered by the Loc Ninh defenders. Four Special Forces personnel had been lightly wounded, and only 6 CIDG were killed (another 39 had been wounded). The 1st Infantry Division arrived to commence pursuit operations soon afterwards.[3]

Camp Bunard, along the Song Be River in Phuoc Long "Happy Dragon" Province, was chosen to deny VC access to both local VC rice fields and War Zone D to the south. The camp also served as another link in a chain of outposts along Highway 14 from Chon Thanh to Ban Me Thuot. The future campsite was taken by the first mass Special Forces–led CIDG parachute jump of the war in Operation HARVEST MOON on 2 April 1967. The cloudless sky was dotted with more than 300 parachutes as Captain Wilson's Detachment A-503 Mike Force warriors spilled out of C-130 aircraft to secure a landing zone in dense foliage ten to fifty feet high.

The paratroopers were followed by Capt. Ambrose W. Brennan's Detachment A-344 (redesignated from A-342 at Dong Xoai) with 700 CIDG troops helicoptered behind them. Lack of water and sand was finally resolved by having CH-47 Chinooks sling-load water trailers and sandbags in rope nets to the campsite. Despite Special Forces fear of strong VC reaction, only scattered sniping and patrol brushes materialized during the rest of the year.[4]

Throughout the year the Special Forces border camp of Bu Dop (A-341), just northwest of Song Be, was continually subjected to pressure by the North Vietnamese Army. In one battle, 27 to 29 November, a search-and-destroy mission out of Bu Dop, reinforced by a company from Dong Xoai (A-342) and Duc Phong (A-343), was outmaneuvered and split up by North Vietnamese forces. Special Forces suffered considerable casualties, including one advisor killed, another missing in action, and three more wounded. Bu Dop was rocketed and mortared from 2 to 8 December 1967, resulting in numerous losses (eleven Special Forces members wounded) and severe destruction within the compound.

The first Special Forces camp planted in War Zone C, Trai Bi, was phased out by Capt. Louis Lopez, Jr.'s, Detachment A-323 from 8 to 22 December 1967 in a grueling operation under fire. The Viet Cong unexpectedly defended the selected location of the new campsite, another war zone area at Thien Ngon. A rough battle ensued at the campsite, culminating in a 200-round mortar barrage and a VC battalion ground attack. During that time, the road convoys were delayed and the trucks were ravaged by CIDG pilferers. The lack of water created dire problems until a VC well was found near a road junction. All but fourteen CIDG had deserted from Camp Trai Bi by the second night. The new fighting camp at Thien Ngon, built by the 588th Engineer Battalion, experienced considerable shelling through the end of the year.[5]

Fighting camps were also being arranged to mask certain border regions of the central highlands within II Corps Tactical Zone. To permit this realignment of Special Forces resources within the country, other camps had to be closed out. Two CIDG camps, at Plei Mrong in Pleiku Province and Vinh Gia in the Delta, were turned over to LLDB control on 1 May and 27 June, respectively. Although the United States boasted that the transfer resulted from heightened confidence in the Vietnamese, the action had been mandated to conserve Special Forces manpower and to facilitate the opening of new fighting camps elsewhere. Camp Lac Thien of Darlac Province was converted to Regional Forces control on 1 October 1967. Its team and assets were used to open a new fighting camp at Bu Prang, forty-five miles southwest of Ban Me Thuot, four days later.

The opening of Bu Prang, in the extreme western border reaches of Quang Duc "Great Virtue" Province, was heralded by a spectacular Special Forces–CIDG mass parachute jump on 5 October 1967. Maj. Chumley Waldrop parachuted with his 11 Special Forces and 37 Vietnamese pathfinders to establish the drop zone on the cigar-shaped landing zone, an elongated patch of grassy hills interspersed with dense foliage. The cloud ceiling was only 750 feet, and it was raining. Achieving complete surprise, Lt. Col. Ludwig "The Blue Max" Faistenhammer, commanding Company B, led 50 Special Forces and 275 LLDB and Montagnard troops of the II CTZ (Pleiku) Mike Force in the main parachute assault.

Capt. Spencer A. Folsom's Detachment A-236 and two CIDG companies from the recently closed Lac Thien Camp arrived by helicopter behind the air assault and began constructing the new fighting camp. A trench system and outer wire were quickly erected, while the two Mike Force companies extensively patrolled the area. The first convoy arrived at Bu Prang on 26 November after only one ambush, opening Highway 14 from Ban Me Thuot to the Cambodian border. After initial problems with CIDG rebellion, Camp Bu Prang ultimately became very successful in hindering VC area infiltration routes.

Some of the hardest fighting of 1967 transpired in the mountain wilderness near the isolated Dak To (A-244) border surveillance camp. In May a series of camp patrols from Capt. Larry S. Gossett's detachment encountered dug-in NVA positions along the twisted trails and ridges around the camp. As a result of one skirmish, a Dak Seang (A-245) CIDG company reinforced the Dak To force in a body recovery operation on 16 May. The task force made good progress, since there was no opposition, and retrieved four CIDG killed the previous day.

The two companies linked up under Captain Gossett's command and passed through several unoccupied NVA trenches. Shortly after crossing a jungle stream, they were suddenly engulfed in heavy automatic weapons fire from bunkers hidden in the thick vegetation. They had run into a well-camouflaged *24th NVA Regiment* way station and supply area. The CIDG immediately fell back under the intense fire. M. Sgt. Gerald V. Parmentier of A-245 and Sp. 5th Class Samuel R. Allen of A-244 were killed, and 1st Lt. Walter L. Penn and Sfc. Raymond H. Fahling were wounded trying to rally their CIDG troops in the thick underbrush. The CIDG frantically cut out a landing zone and called in airstrikes. Parmentier's body was finally recovered the next day by another company that was sweeping the battlefield.

On 14 June 1967 a Dak To CIDG unit broke and fled from its night positions when attacked by an NVA company, leaving two Special Forces and eight CIDG missing. Later the same morning a company from the II CTZ (Pleiku) Mike Force with four Special Forces personnel were inserted to recover the missing personnel. A reinforced North Vietnamese company had established a horseshoe-shaped ambush at the initial battlefield, realizing that a recovery attempt was probable. Their well-planned ambush disintegrated the Mike Force unit. When the bombing strike was delivered in response, the North Vietnamese rushed the defensive perimeter. This sudden assault allowed the NVA to escape the bombing and overrun the frail defensive line, leaving two more Special Forces troopers killed and the other two missing. The surviving native soldiers evaded NVA pursuers in the thick jungle and staggered into Dak To on 16 June.

The next day Dak To Camp was plastered by heavy mortars, resulting in the death of the LLDB camp commander, Lt. Le Quang Nghia, and the wounding of three Special Forces and two Air Force personnel. As a consequence of this increased activity, the camp was occupied by elements of the 173d Airborne Brigade from July until mid-October. On 28 October the 1st Brigade of the 4th Infantry Division moved into the compound. Three North Vietnamese regiments were located in the immediate vicinity, and heavy fighting erupted to the southwest of Dak To commencing on 5 November 1967.

Although the resulting campaign in the Dak To area was decided by line battalions, culminating in the battle of Hill 875 (which was taken Thanksgiving Day), Detachment A-244 was heavily involved. Capt. Jimmy L. Braddock, who took over the detachment in late October, conducted six company-size operations with the camp garrison. One savage firefight resulted when a CIDG platoon, attached to a company of the 1st Battalion, 503d Infantry (Airborne), was struck by NVA on the night of 8 November. In the meantime the camp itself was continually pummeled by mortar rounds. On 15 November Dak To was practically leveled by a catastrophic fire in the 4th Infantry Division ammunition dump. By the end of the month, the crisis had passed and the North Vietnamese slipped back across the Laotian-

Cambodian border. Reconstruction of Dak To commenced on 26 November 1967.[6]

The belt of border camps in II CTZ was given renewed emphasis after MACV's difficult November campaign in the highlands, which had consumed the 4th Infantry Division and 173d Airborne Brigade. Previously, many camps of II CTZ were scheduled for closure and their assets projected for northward insertion into I CTZ. The chain of surveillance camps included launch sites for long-range MACV-SOG teams in the rugged tri-border region. Ben Het was already being built for such purposes in the northern Plei Trap Valley. Complementing this Plei Trap–Bu Prang highland border camp line was Tieu Atar, opened on 20 December 1967. Opened two months ahead of schedule and constructed by the 299th Engineer Battalion, it was the last fighting camp constructed during the year.[7]

3. Fighting Camps to the North and South

The 5th Special Forces Group also concentrated on establishing more fighting camps to the south of Saigon in the Delta marshes. Additionally, two new border surveillance camps were picketed at opposite ends of the country in February. Con Thien was built in the far north only two miles south of the DMZ. Camp To Chau was constructed in the extreme southwestern tip of Vietnam next to the Gulf of Thailand along the Cambodian border. New campsites in the Delta were occupied at My Phuoc Tay and My An in the Plain of Reeds. A string of Special Forces waterway interdiction forts was implanted almost directly west of Saigon toward the Cambodian border, which during the course of the year included Duc Hoa, (new) Hiep Hoa, Tra Cu, Luong Hoa, and Duc Hue.

The third camp in this line and the first one built in 1967, was Tra Cu. The campsite was opened on the morning of 10 January, in Special Forces Operation CHECKMATE. Capt. Eldon L. Perdew's Detachment A-352 was airmobiled into the future site, escorted by the 38th ARVN Ranger Battalion. They fought off persistent Viet Cong probing attacks as the compound was built at the junction of the Song Vam Co Dong River and Kinh Gay Canal, a main VC infiltration route.

The controlling headquarters for this line was Detachment B-35, which opened Camp Duc Hoa for this purpose in December 1966. The initial camp in line had been (new) Hiep Hoa, established by

Capt. Jack T. Stewart's A-351 on 25 May 1966 and moved to the town sugar mill. The location was not far from the old Hiep Hoa campsite, which had been the first Special Forces compound lost in the war, during late 1963. Hiep Hoa Camp was cycled out on 30 December 1967 after a newer fighting camp at Duc Hue was implanted about twenty miles northwest of Duc Hoa, only two miles from the Cambodian border. Duc Hue was opened on 15 November 1967 and built by the 30th ARVN Engineer Battalion. It was occupied by Detachment A-351A, the redesignated half of the Luong Hoa Special Forces team.

Camp Luong Hoa had been established in Operation VICTORY TRAIL on 26 May 1967 by Capt. George M. Massey's Detachment A-353 as the southern anchor of this line. Luong Hoa was located at the junction of the Song Vam Co Dong River and the Kinh Xang Canal, part of a major canal network that provided access to Saigon. There was no significant contact with the Viet Cong, but plenty of casualties still resulted from booby traps and mines. Luong Hoa was turned over to the 51st ARVN Ranger Battalion on 22 October, and Capt. John C. Johnson's CIDG troops were helilifted to Tra Cu while his team went on to a new assignment at Duc Hue at the northern end of this fortress line.

Two new fighting camps were put in the Plain of Reeds. Captain Haralson's Detachment A-424 took over the ARVN firebase at My Phuoc Tay. The compound already contained two 155mm howitzers, and was revamped along Special Forces fighting camp guidelines commencing 10 February 1967. The opening of the other camp posted to the grassland, My An (Detachment A-426), was accompanied by heavy fighting between CIDG and ARVN troops against a Viet Cong battalion. This lasted through the on-site planning and initial construction phases in late February and March 1967.[8]

In upper northern I CTZ, within sight of North Vietnamese ridgelines, Camp Con Thien was established by Captain Chamberlain's Detachment A-110 on 20 February 1967 at Hill 158 and completed by Navy Mobile Construction Battalion 4. However, Con Thien was secretly slated as a critical strongpoint along Defense Secretary Robert S. McNamara's Project PRACTICE NINE "electric fence" antiinfiltration barrier system projected to parallel the DMZ. Already heavy Army 175mm guns stationed there were pounding North Vietnamese territory, and four days later the campsite was lashed by heavy return shelling. North Vietnamese pressure mounted as the camp suffered a series of six heavy mortar attacks in March and another three bombardments in April. Elements of the 1st Battalion of the 4th Marines moved in to insure adequate security.

On the thirteenth anniversary of the communist victory at Dien Bien Phu, 8 May 1967, two *812th NVA Regiment* battalions tried to overrun Con Thien. The brunt of the assault fell on the weakest section of the camp, where Marine defenses tied into CIDG trenches. The North Vietnamese assault riflemen stormed into the perimeter at two points using rockets, flamethrowers, grenades, and satchel charges. They broke through the 146th CIDG Company defensive lines at 2:45 A.M. Captain Chamberlain and two Special Forces sergeants held the sandbagged command bunker in an exchange of grenades and rifle fire during the confused fighting. After several repeated direct hits by B-40 rockets, a North Vietnamese flamethrower shot a stream of liquid fuel through the bunker aperture. For some reason, the ignition of the fuel was not complete. When the bunker occupants witnessed the flash and roar, they immediately abandoned the position.

The North Vietnamese also concentrated on the communications bunker and team houses, but fighting was heaviest in the Marine sector. The Special Forces retreated to the Navy Seabee positions, where a cohesive defense line was established. Difficult fighting continued, but by 6:30 A.M., as early morning light flooded the battlefield, it became apparent that the North Vietnamese had waited too long to effect an orderly withdrawal. An hour later all action had been terminated except for small pockets of resistance. These were swiftly eradicated by the Marines.[9]

Con Thien suffered massive artillery and rocketing bombardments through the month. Over 1,500 rounds were received, and on one occasion 250 landed in just four minutes. The attention paid Con Thien was directly relative to its greater significance. Con Thien was part of the big-unit war and national strategy, and the Special Forces was soon brushed off to make room for more artillery and Marines. The camp was turned over to the 1st Battalion, 9th Marines, on 25 July 1967.

Capt. John J. Duffy's Detachment A-101 at Lang Vei was the most endangered Special Forces camp in South Vietnam. It was located in the northwestern corner of the country along Route 9 almost to the Laotian border. The camp had been set up at Lang Vei since the Marines had taken over its former Khe Sanh location. The post contained 320 Bru tribal CIDG personnel, and from 2,300 to 2,800 Bru natives lived in the nearby village.

At five minutes before seven o'clock on the evening of 7 March, two Air Force jet fighters came in low from the southwest. The lead plane dipped both wings once on the first pass before releasing its napalm ordnance on the center of the village. The planes made three repeated passes parallel to the highway. For twenty minutes they dropped napalm and bombs, which spewed exploding fire over the camp, landing zone, minefield, and village. Secondary explosions from camp ammunition and mines added to the raging fire, which quickly consumed most of the village. Personnel seeking shelter in underground bunkers died from suffocation and heat. Many of the wounded were horribly burned and disfigured.

The disaster was one of the worst tragedies to befall the Special Forces CIDG program during the war. Although the Special Forces personnel quickly organized rescue parties, distributed all the blankets and clothing on hand, and called in medical evacuation helicopters, their capabilities were overwhelmed by the magnitude of the carnage. The hearty Bru natives, who in 1963 had welcomed Special Forces with open arms, were now paying the terrible consequences of being caught in the midst of a major war.[10]

The next untoward incident to befall Lang Vei occurred on 4 May 1967. The Special Forces camp was penetrated by a reinforced company that followed behind a blistering mortar barrage. The combination caused heavy damage and plenty of casualties. The attack on Lang Vei was staged at 3:15 A.M., right on Viet Cong nighttime schedule, and was assisted by several VC infiltrators posing as recruits. They killed the guards and led the attackers—who breached the wire with bangalore torpedoes—through the minefields and toward key positions in the heart of the compound. By 1967 this was a tired scenario, but it was still happening. The Special Forces command group, all in one bunker, were wiped out at the same time. The detachment commander and his executive officer were killed, and the team sergeant was seriously wounded. The Marines at Khe Sanh Combat Base, six miles to the northeast, responded with artillery support, but the Viet Cong got away after taking only light casualties.

The incidents at Lang Vei were part of the incipient struggle for domination of northwestern South Vietnam. The 4 May Lang Vei assault was a prelude to the larger siege of Khe Sanh. The battles for these locations would become vital milestones of the Second Indochina War during the next year, a year that would also pitch Special Forces back into conventional frontline fighting during Tet-68.

Notes

1. 5th Special Forces Group, AVGB-EN Ltr, Subject: Calendar Year Planning, dtd 25 April 1967; 5th Special Forces Group, *Command Report,* dtd 15 February 1967.

2. Losses in the Tong Le Chon battle were KIA: 25 CIDG, 1 LLDB; MIA: 14 CIDG; WIA: 7 Special Forces, 1 LLDB, 89 CIDG. NVA losses were 152 killed, 2 captured, of whom 1 died of wounds the next day. 5th Special Forces Group, *Command Report,* dtd 15 November 1967, Inclosure 10.

3. 5th Special Forces Group, *Command Report,* dtd 15 February 1968, Inclosure 8.

4. 5th Special Forces Group, *Command Report,* dtd 15 May 1967, Inclosure 15; Detachment A-344 Don Luan district [Camp Bunard Data Summary], circa Dec 67; Phuoc Long sector, Song Be Detachment B-34, *After Action Report,* dtd 12 June 1967.

5. Detachment A-323, *After Action Report,* dtd 10 January 1968.

6. Detachment A-244, *Operations After Action Report,* dtd 22 May 1967; and *Monthly Summaries,* dtd 30 June and 30 November 1967.

7. Company B, 5th Special Forces Group, AVSFB-CO Ltr, Subject: Employment of Civilian Irregular Defense Group, Mike Force, Mobile Guerrilla Force, and Long Range Reconnaissance Projects for CY 68, dtd 29 May 1967.

8. 5th Special Forces Group, *Command Report,* dtd 15 May 1967, Inclosures 13 and 14.

9. Casualties during the Con Thien battle were KIA: 44 Marines, 14 CIDG; WIA: 110 Marines, 4 Special Forces, 5 Navy Seabees, 16 CIDG. Two-hundred and twelve NVA were confirmed killed in the attack. 5th Special Forces Group, *Command Report,* dtd 15 August 1967, Inclosure 11; Detachment C-1, *Draft History,* undtd; Maj. Gary L. Telfer and Lt. Col. Lane Rogers, *U.S. Marines in Vietnam: The War of Attrition, 1967,* (Washington, D.C.: U.S. Marine Corps, 1967).

10. Losses in the accidental bombing were KIA: 10 CIDG, 1 LLDB, 125 civilians (estimated); WIA: 12 CIDG, 1 LLDB, approximately 200 civilians. Detachment A-101, *After Action Report,* dtd 7 March 1967.

CHAPTER 9

TIME OF DECISION

1. The Battles of Tet-68

The NVA/VC Tet-68 offensive, which commenced 30–31 January 1968, achieved initial success because of the tactical surprise and confusion resulting from hundreds of country-wide attacks. Some of those battles were of considerable magnitude. The coming of the expected Tet truce had created a gradual reduction in Special Forces military operations. Many camps were practically idled by large numbers of CIDG personnel who had authorized passes for the holidays and of those who were absent without leave at the same Tet celebrations. Many of these soldiers became stranded after the Viet Cong struck the towns and cities, so many camp companies were well below strength in the battles that followed.[1]

In II CTZ Special Forces elements were involved in several pitched battles. At Ban Me Thuot Special Forces Detachment B-23 was involved in extended action from 30 January through 6 February 1968. The 23d and 24th Mobile Strike Force companies joined other allied units at Pleiku in a fierce block-by-block struggle to root the Viet Cong out of the downtown sector during 30 January to 4 February. The 26th Mobile Strike Force Company was dispatched to Phan Thiet on the morning of 3 February and assisted the 3d Battalion of the 506th Infantry by dislodging VC elements from concrete bunkers and buildings. The mobile strike force was not released until 20 February.

The considerable allied combat power stationed in Kontum was divided into separate compounds, each with its own defensive sector and area of responsibility, and doomed to wage an individual battle of survival. Detachment B-24 fought in defense of its own compound from 30 January to 4 February assisted by a CIDG company from Dak Pek (A-242) and two platoons of the 7th Squadron, 17th Cavalry. The numerous rocket and mortar attacks were interspersed with ground probes. In several instances, the VC penetrated the detachment's perimeter but were repulsed by supporting helicopter gunships. In the absence of any controlling headquarters, general havoc marred the battle. When howitzer shells from artillery of the 24th Special Tactical Zone compound slammed into the Special Forces B-24 compound on 31 January, the Vietnamese commander denied firing any tubes. Special Forces personnel were monitoring the gun reports. After more rounds hit B-24 positions, the Special Forces threatened to retaliate with their own heavy mortars. The errant shelling promptly ceased.[2]

The garden city of Dalat was nestled in the pine-forested highlands of II CTZ, and its beauty had escaped the war's destruction. Tet-68 brought ten days of difficult street fighting after Viet Cong elements occupied sections of the town. As Special Forces camp companies from Trang Phuc (A-233) and Nhon Co (A-235) were flown in to help clear the "honeymoon haven" on 5 February, they saw vacation villas surrounded by barbed wire and flowered fences embraced by sandbags.

The Nhon Co CIDG company was led by 1st Lt. Thomas K. Richie and Sfc. Frederick Schiller. The weather was cold and windy as they combined with other CIDG soldiers, Ruff-Puffs, ARVN Rangers, and cadets from the Vietnamese National Military Academy. Company morale and responsiveness to commands remained good, despite heavy casualties, until the seventh day. At that time the Nhon Co soldiers threatened to desert en masse because they were not relieved and replaced along with two other CIDG companies. This crisis was resolved by the timely arrival of a gratuity bonus from the provincial government. During the remaining days of combat, fatigue and continual fighting caused the Nhon Co soldiers to become sluggish. Typically, the Special Forces soldiers were constantly at the front, directing the CIDG company commanders and calling in aerial and artillery support, while most LLDB counterparts stayed in the rear.

The battle of Qui Nhon was typical of Special Forces participation in the II CTZ engagements. There was no advance indication of infiltration into Qui Nhon by Viet Cong forces, yet the *D-10 Sapper Company* and *K-2B Battalion* seized the radio station, railroad yard, and military security services headquarters before dawn on 30 January 1968. Lt. Col. Robert N. Longfellow of Detachment B-22 garnered two CIDG companies from Phu Tuc (A-224) and Cung Son (A-221) and shoved them into the maze of houses and alleys that morning. The weather was clear and warm as the two companies sallied into the Qui Nhon railway complex. A 106mm recoilless rifle crew under M. Sgt. Victor G. Franco from Ha Tay (A-227) positioned its weapon on the roof of a hotel. As Sgt. Michael R. Deed's Cung Son company advanced toward the engine shed, the VC opened fire from the lubrication pits beneath the locomotives.

The Cung Son company took considerable losses in a vain effort to reach the entrance of the engine shed. Both companies withdrew as Franco's gun blasted the locomotive works with direct fire. The CIDG force surged forward before the smoke had dissipated and cleared the pits in sharp combat. The companies spent the next day searching and detaining all military-age males in the hovels southwest of the rail yard. They rounded up 500 youths despite considerable sniper fire. On 1 February the Cung Son company cleared the Phu Tai ammunition dump as the Phu Tuc company retook the radio station. These Special Forces elements fought in Qui Nhon until 5 February.

Since the CIDG had no previous experience in urban warfare, they displayed extreme reluctance to move forward unless led by example. Consequently, most of the Special Forces participants were killed or wounded. The CIDG had borne the main brunt of the Qui Nhon fighting, and the lack of over-all allied control led to several unfortunate firefights between other contingents. Of these, the Vietnamese national and combat police proved the most troublesome: "While there was shooting, none of them could be found, but once the shooting stopped they were out parading around."[3]

Detachment B-22 continued to clear the rich, flat rice paddies in the coastal plain north of Qui Nhon for the remainder of the month. Three camp companies from Cung Son (A-221), Dong Tre (A-222), and Vinh Thanh (LLDB A-120) took on several entrenched village strongpoints and fortified treelines. The Cung Son company, under M. Sgt. Johnnie B. Miller, made repeated attempts to take Loc Ha #2. A medical evacuation helicopter, landing to remove some wounded CIDG soldiers, was raked by heavy automatic weapons fire. The crew chief, gunner, and the three Special Forces advisors from A-221 were all wounded. The Dong Tre company reinforced, but the LLDB contingent was stopped by another bunker-studded village. After the village was abandoned during the night, the LLDB-led force entered and removed one CIDG body that could not be recovered earlier.

The LLDB refused to search the village any further, despite continued prodding from the Special Forces advisors present. While the CIDG forces were aggressive and responsive to commands, the LLDB constantly held them back:

Many times the United States Army Special Forces personnel attempted to move the troops forward, but the CIDG said they couldn't do it because the VNSF would not give the order to move. Attempts to persuade the VNSF to move were met with negative results. For the most part the VNSF could not be found. . . . In addition, an extension for clearance of airstrikes from 1600 until 2400 had been granted to Special Forces so that the attack could be pressed forward. However, when a set of fighters arrived on station and the FAC (Forward Air Controller) started to put in the fighters, it was halted and the FAC stated that he did not have clearance to put in the fighters. The USASF in the field stated that the clearance extension was approved and that the FAC could put in the airstrike. An investigation was conducted and it was learned that the C.O. Detachment B-11 VNSF (the overall LLDB commander) would not give approval for the airstrike because he wanted to break contact and bring all of his troops home.[4]

Far to the south, in the marshy Delta flatland of IV CTZ, the Special Forces was also involved in heavy Tet-68 fighting. Since the VC were striving to get into populated areas, many outlying camps were bypassed—although they were still mortared and several of their outposts were overrun. For example, the Viet Cong isolated Detachment A-411 at My Phuoc Tay by overrunning the majority of Ruff-Puff positions along the land and water avenues to the camp.

Wherever Special Forces fortresses coincided with towns or cities, they became directly involved. At 4:15 A.M. on 2 February 1968, two Viet Cong companies made a determined attempt to take Moc Hoa. The compound of Detachment A-414 located there never came under direct assault, but it was severely rocketed and mortared. Most rounds landed either in the barrier wire or in the moat on the east side of the camp.

On the morning of 31 January 1968, the Viet Cong tackled the provincial capital of Chau Doc near the Cambodian border. Small VC groups infiltrated the town and took possession of numerous buildings throughout the city. The sector headquarters at Chau Doc was Special Forces Detachment B-42, reinforced by nine Navy river patrol boats, a tough Provincial Reconnaissance Unit (PRU) of Project PHOENIX, and a portion of Navy SEAL Team 2. While the Navy craft lent direct fire support from the Bassac River, B-42 formed small but well-armed fire teams from the Special Forces, SEAL, and PRU personnel. Although 1,239 homes were gutted and a large portion of the city was destroyed by fire, the Viet Cong were routed after a day and a half of savage combat. They withdrew using civilians as shields, which accounted in part for the large number of town inhabitants killed in the fighting.

Special Forces Company D was located at the Can Tho Airbase, a focal point in the battle of Can Tho, which commenced on 29 January 1968. The Special Forces headquarters compound suffered severe blast and fire damage. Two Viet Cong assaults on the western perimeter were repulsed with the aid of Cobra helicopter gunships. Special Forces personnel were also involved in the larger contest for the city and university area. The fighting lasted until the Viet Cong were pushed from Can Tho's outer edges on 5 February.

Detachment B-43, located at Cao Lanh, was cut off by an extended Viet Cong siege during most of February. The city's outposts were either eliminated or abandoned during the first few days of the engagement, although several VC assaults on the town itself were defeated. The Viet Cong were dug into earthen bunkers reinforced with banana tree logs, and defied numerous mobile strike force and Vietnamese army attempts to clear the nearby fields. Throughout this time, Detachment B-43, normally a control and sector headquarters, was in reality reduced to the status of an isolated A-Detachment.

The Tet-68 offensive impacted very unevenly on Special Forces components throughout the country. While II and IV CTZ Special Forces camps were engulfed in Tet-68 combat, the campaign had only a peripheral effect on Special Forces camps in the northern portion of the country (I CTZ). In III CTZ no camp was directly threatened, and the most significant result was the temporary Viet Cong interdiction of overland supply lines from subordinate A-Detachments to Company A headquarters in Bien Hoa. This was caused by the heavy fighting in the Saigon-Long Binh-Bien Hoa area.

Perhaps the most interesting Tet-68 encounter in I CTZ was reported by Camp Ba To (A-106). On 1 February 1968 the Ba To district headquarters was attacked by 700 Viet Cong, half of whom carried spears and knives. The bizzare assault cracked the perimeter, and sappers disposed of the district building and several bunkers with plastic explosives. They were driven off by mortar fire. Another similarly armed VC company, pushing Montagnards in front of them, was broken up by Special Forces-led camp troops on the airstrip. Six Viet Cong were captured, along with twenty spears, thirty-five knives, and one carbine.

Many Special Forces headquarters units added to the Tet-68 confusion by neglecting their administrative and logistical functions whenever they found themselves part of the battle zone. The Special Forces headquarters personnel either disregarded all routine duties and observed the fighting or avoided their normal assignments and became involved in the fighting. As a result, a gradual paralysis hampered the field detachments. As Company A recorded:

> Even with bombs dropping, machine gun and rifle fire heard nearby . . . headquarters personnel must follow routine duties to accomplish their assigned mission. A headquarters is not a personnel volunteer pool. A non-functioning headquarters is the same as an overrun headquarters, for all practical purposes.[5]

The primary effect of the NVA/VC Tet-68 offensive on Special Forces was the reestablishment of camp CIDG forces as regular line infantry in conventional engagements. Whenever possible, the Viet Cong had concentrated against populated areas, using local and main force units as the initial entry elements. Sizable North Vietnamese units served in reinforcing and blocking roles or simply did not engage in offensive activity. While actual activity around Special Forces camps was minimal, many camp strike forces saw extended combat in city-clearing operations. The CIDG personnel were unsophisticated jungle warriors and were not trained in house-to-house fighting. Their performance as quick-reaction infantry in urban warfare varied, but under the circumstances MACV mustered all available manpower. CIDG limitations quickly surfaced if employed in extended operations without stiffening and plenty of support. Many camp strike force soldiers became dismayed when their comrades were buried in cities distant from tribal homelands.[6]

2. Defeat at Lang Vei

Several North Vietnamese Army divisions had encircled the Marine combat base at Khe Sanh by January 1968, placing the nearby, more westerly, Lang Vei Special Forces frontier surveillance camp in imminent danger. Detachment A-101, commanded by Capt. Frank C. Willoughby, occupied the dog-bone-shaped compound. It was located astride Route 9 only a mile and a half from the Laotian border.

The presence of North Vietnamese armor was verified on 24 January 1968 as the Kha tribal 33d Laotian Volunteer Battalion and their dependents streamed into Lang Vei after being overrun by NVA tanks across the border. They arrived as Captain Willoughby's team was still rebuilding Lang Vei according to fighting camp specifications. Although the task was 80 percent complete, antitank mines and other sophisticated defense measures were still not in place. In response to the possibility of armored attack, Willoughby had received 100 light antitank weapons (LAWs). Training was limited to his team and ten selected CIDG soldiers, leaving seventy-five of the weapons on hand. However, the Americans discounted any actual tank assault on the camp. North Vietnamese armored participation, although possible, was expected to be limited to a fire support role firing tank cannon from the jungle.

Much of the camp routine was disrupted by the arrival of the Laotians, even though they were quartered in the old Lang Vei campsite. The Laotian battalion commander refused to take orders from the American captain, forcing the commander of Company C, Lt. Col. Daniel F. Schungel, to fly into Lang Vei on 6 February to provide an officer of equal rank.[7] First Lt. Paul R. Longgrear's Hre tribal 12th Mobile Strike Force Company also arrived to shore up defensive firepower. That evening the camp was pounded by mortars in conjunction with a heavy shelling of the Marine Khe Sanh base, which prevented any effective artillery support for Lang Vei.

A combined NVA infantry-tank assault drove into Lang Vei shortly after midnight on 7 February 1968. Two North Vietnamese PT-76 amphibian tanks lumbered toward the outer perimeter, their headlights sweeping the tangle of barrier wire as infantry rushed behind them. Sfc. James W. Holt destroyed both tanks with well-aimed shots from his 106mm recoilless rifle. The hulks burned fiercely as more tanks roared around the wreckage and began to roll over the 104th CIDG Company's defensive positions. S. Sgt. Peter Tiroch, the assistant intelligence sergeant, ran over to Holt's position and loaded projectiles into the weapon. Before Sergeant Holt could fire at another target, the flare illumination died out, but seconds later another flare lighted up the landscape. Holt quickly lined up a third tank in his sights and destroyed it with a direct hit. They chambered the last antitank round, fired it off at the same tank to make sure it was destroyed, and raced from the weapons pit just before it was demolished by return cannon fire. Tiroch watched Holt run over to the ammunition bunker to look for some hand-held LAWs; it was the last time Holt was ever seen.

Colonel Schungel, Lieutenant Longgrear, S. Sgt. Arthur Brooks, Sgt. Nikolas Fragos, Sp. 4th Class William G. McMurray, Jr., and LLDB Lieutenant Quy desperately tried to stop the tanks with LAWs and grenades. They even climbed on the plated engine decks, trying to pry open hatches to blast out the crews. North Vietnamese infantrymen followed closely behind the vehicles, dusting their sides with automatic rifle fire. One tank was stopped by five direct hits, and the crew members were gunned down as they tried to abandon the vehicle. First Lt. Miles R. Wilkins, the detachment executive officer, left the mortar pit with several LAWs and fought a running engagement with one tank beside the team house without much success. Often either the LAWs malfunctioned or their rockets bounced off tank hulls without exploding.[8]

NVA sappers armed with satchel charges, tear gas grenades, and flamethrowers fought through the 101st, 102d, and 103d CIDG perimeter trenches and captured both ends of the "dog bone" by 2:30 A.M. Spearheaded by tanks, they stormed the inner compound. Colonel Schungel and his tank-killer personnel moved back to the command bunker for more LAWs. They were pinned behind a row of dirt- and rock-filled fifty-five-gallon drums by a tank that had just destroyed one of the mortar pits. A LAW was fired against the tank with no effect. The cannon swung around and blasted the barrels in front of the bunker entrance. The explosion temporarily blinded

McMurray and mangled his hands, pitched a heavy drum on top of Lieutenant Wilkins, and knocked Schungel flat. Lieutenant Quy managed to escape to another section of the camp, but Schungel and Wilkins were unable to follow because of the approach of yet another tank.

Schungel pitched two grenades under the tank, which was shooting at the camp observation tower. At the same time, someone destroyed the tank with a LAW. Schungel helped Wilkins over to the team house, where he left both doors ajar and watched for approaching NVA soldiers. Wilkins was incapacitated and weaponless, and Schungel had only two grenades and two magazines of ammunition left. He used one magazine to kill a closely huddled five-man sapper squad coming toward the building. He fed his last magazine into his rifle as the team house was rocked with explosions and bullets. They limped over to the dispensary, which was occupied by NVA soldiers, and hid underneath it, behind a wall of sandbags.

Several personnel, including Captain Willoughby and Lieutenant Quan, the LLDB camp commander, were trapped in the underground level of the command bunker. After the tank had fired point-blank into the barreled barricade, Lieutenant Longgrear had retreated through the bunker entrance and reported Schungel killed. Willoughby guessed that his men in the bunker were the only Americans left alive. His communications had been silenced after the outside radio antennas were cut down. Satchel charges, thermite grenades, and gas grenades were shoved down the bunker air vents, and breathing became extremely difficult. Some soldiers had gas masks, but others had only handkerchiefs or gauze from their first aid packets. Vomit and rubble covered the floor of the smoke-filled bunker.

The LLDB personnel inside surrendered when the North Vietnamese announced they were going to blow up the bunker, walked up the stairs, and were summarily executed. The last sapper attempt to destroy the bunker was made at dawn. Two large charges were put down the vent shaft and detonated, partially demolishing the north wall and creating a large hole through which grenades were pitched. The beleaguered defenders used upturned furniture and debris to shield themselves. Willoughby was badly wounded by grenade fragments despite his flak jacket and passed out at 8:30 A.M. Incredibly, the battle was still going on in other parts of the camp.

Aircraft had been strafing the ravines and road since 1:00 A.M., although coordination was difficult. One bomb landed in the midst of the Laotian battalion, positioned at the old Lang Vei campsite, but fortunately the dud failed to detonate. Throughout the battle the Laotians refused to participate, claiming that they would attack at first light. Sfc. Eugene Ashley, Jr., the intelligence sergeant, led two assistant medical specialists, Sgt. Richard H. Allen and Sp. 4th Class Joel Johnson as they mustered sixty of the Laotian soldiers and counterattacked into Lang Vei. The Laotians bolted when a North Vietnamese machine gun crew opened fire on them, forcing the three Americans to withdraw.

Team Sfc. William T. Craig and S. Sgt. Tiroch had chased tanks throughout the night with everything from M-79 grenade launchers to a .50-caliber machine gun. After it had become apparent that the camp was overrun, they escaped outside the wire and took temporary refuge in a creek bed. After daylight, they saw Ashley's counterattack force and joined him. The Special Forces sergeants persuaded more defenders fleeing down Route 9 to assist them and tried a second assault. After it met similar results, third and fourth counterattacks were tried. Between each assault, Ashley directed airstrikes on the NVA defensive line, while the other Special Forces soldiers cajoled and gathered tribal warriors for another attempt. On the fifth counterattack, Ashley was mortally wounded only thirty yards from the command bunker.

Captain Willoughby had regained consciousness in the shattered bunker about 10:00 A.M. and established radio contact with the counterattacking Americans. The continual American airstrikes had forced the North Vietnamese to begin withdrawing from the smoldering compound. Colonel Schungel and Lieutenant Wilkins emerged from beneath the dispensary after it was vacated by the North Vietnamese. They hobbled past two tanks gutted by bombs and walked out of the camp.

The Special Forces personnel in the bunker also departed in response to orders calling for the immediate evacuation of the camp. They carried out Sgt. John D. Early, who had been badly wounded by shrapnel while manning the tower, but were forced to leave Sp. 4th Class James L. Moreland inside the bunker. Moreland, the medic for the mobile strike force, had been wounded when the sappers first breached the north wall and became delirious after receiving a head injury in the final bunker explosion. First Lt. Thomas D. Todd, a

Special Forces engineer officer in charge of upgrading Lang Vei's airstrip, held out in the medical bunker throughout the battle. That afternoon he was the last American to pass through the ruined command bunker. He saw Moreland, who appeared to be dead, covered with debris.

Major George Quamo gathered a few dozen Special Forces commando volunteers within the MACV-SOG base at Khe Sanh (FOB #3), and led a heroic reinforcing mission into Lang Vei. His arrival enabled the Lang Vei defenders to successfully evacuate the area, and Colonel Schungel related that "the Americans who survived Lang Vei owe their lives to Major Quamo and his airmobile force." Although many soldiers and the seriously wounded were evacuated by Marine helicopters at 5:17 P.M., most of the Bru and Laotians were forced to retreat to Khe Sanh on foot.

Casualties in the Lang Vei battle had been extremely heavy. Among the Special Forces, ten were missing and presumed dead while thirteen others were wounded. Although their fates were unknown at the time, three of the missing were prisoners. Sp. William McMurry, Jr., the junior radio operator, was captured outside the bunker. Sfc. Harvey G. Brande, a platoon leader of the mobile strike force company, was captured after being wounded by mortar fragments and having tried to destroy an advancing tank with his M72 LAW. Sfc. Dennis L. Thompson, a radio operator supervisor, was taken prisoner as well. All three were released five years later, in 1973.[9]

3. Disaster at Kham Duc

After the fall of Lang Vei, Kham Duc (A-105) remained the only border camp in I CTZ. Kham Duc was located on the extreme western fringe of Quang Tin "Great Faith" Province close to Laos. The 23d Infantry Division (Americal), headquartered on the opposite, coastal side of the province at Chu Lai, had backup responsibility for the camp. Kham Duc was initially established at the wish of President Diem, who enjoyed hunting in the area. He had planned to build a summer palace and sporting lodge at the site and once stationed the entire 6th ARVN Regiment there. The first Special Forces detachment (A-727B) arrived at Kham Duc in September 1963 and found the outpost to be an ideal border surveillance site with an all-weather, macadam-surfaced airfield already in place.

Kham Duc was located on a narrow, grassy plain encompassed

by rugged, virtually uninhabited jungle. The only village in the area, located across the airstrip, was occupied by post dependents, camp followers, and merchants. The camp and its airstrip were hedged in by the Ngok Peng Bum ridge to the west, and the high Ngok Pe Xar mountain, which loomed over Kham Duc to the east. Steep-banked streams full of rapids and waterfalls cut through the tropical wilderness. The Dak Mi River flowed past the camp over a mile distant, under the shadow of the Ngok Pe Xar.

Five miles downriver was the small, forward operating base of Ngok Tavak, built around an old French fort. Ngok Tavak was defended by the 113-man 11th Mobile Strike Force Company with its 8 Special Forces and 3 Australian advisors. Since Ngok Tavak was outside friendly artillery range, 33 Marine artillerymen of Battery D, 2d Battalion, 13th Marines, with two 105 mm howitzers, were located at the outpost.

Capt. Christopher J. Silva, the commander of Detachment A-105, helicoptered into Ngok Tavak on 9 May 1968 in response to growing signs of NVA presence in the area. Foul weather prevented his scheduled evening departure. A Kham Duc CIDG platoon fleeing a local ambush also arrived and was posted to the outer perimeter. Later it was discovered that the CIDG force contained Viet Cong infiltrators.

Ngok Tavak was attacked by an NVA infantry battalion at 3:15 A.M. on 10 May shortly after moonset. The base was pounded by mortars and direct rocket fire. Simultaneously with the main frontal assault, the Kham Duc CIDG soldiers moved toward the Marines in the fort yelling, "Don't shoot, don't shoot! Friendly, friendly!" Suddenly they lobbed grenades into the Marine howitzer positions and ran into the fort, where they shot several Marines with carbines. They also sliced claymore mine and communication wires.

The defenders suffered heavy casualties but stopped the main assault and killed the infiltrators. The North Vietnamese dug in along the hill slopes and grenaded the fighting trenches, where the mobile strike force soldiers were pinned by concentrated machine gun and rocket fire. An NVA flamethrower set the ammunition ablaze, banishing the murky flare-lighted darkness for the remainder of the night. Sfc. Harold M. Swicegood and the Marine platoon leader, Lieutenant Adams, were both badly wounded and moved into the command bunker. Medical Specialist Fourth Class Blomgren frantically reported that the CIDG mortar crews had abandoned their weapons. Captain Silva tried to operate the main 4.2-inch mortar but was wounded in both arm and abdomen. Sgt. Glenn E. Miller was shot through the head as he ran over to join the Marine howitzer crews.

The North Vietnamese advanced across the eastern side of Ngok Tavak and brought forward more automatic weapons and rocket-propelled grenade launchers. In desperation, the defenders called upon the Air Force AC-47 (Spooky) gunship to strafe the perimeter and the howitzers, despite the possible presence of friendly wounded in the gun pits. The North Vietnamese countered with tear gas, but the wind kept drifting the gas across their own lines. After three attempts, they stopped. A grenade fight between the two forces lasted until dawn.

At daybreak Australian Warrant Officers Cameron and Lucas, joined by Blomgren, led a CIDG counterattack to clear the old French fort. The North Vietnamese pulled back under covering fire, and the howitzers were retaken. The Marines fired the last nine shells and spiked the tubes. Later that morning medical evacuation helicopters supported by covering airstrikes took out the seriously wounded, including Silva and Swicegood. Two CH-46s were able to land forty-five replacements from the 12th Mobile Strike Force Company, but one helicopter was hit in the fuel line and forced down. Another helicopter was hit by a rocket and burst into flames, wrecking the small helipad. The remaining wounded were placed aboard a hovering helicopter. As it lifted off, two Mike Force soldiers and one of the stranded aviation crewman grabbed the helicopter skids. All three fell to their deaths after the helicopter had reached an altitude of several hundred feet.

The mobile strike force soldiers were exhausted and nervous. Water and ammunition were nearly exhausted, and Ngok Tavak was still being pounded by sporadic mortar fire. They requested permission to evacuate their positions, but were told to "hold on" as "reinforcements were on the way." By noon the defenders decided that either aerial reinforcement or evacuation was increasingly unlikely, and nightfall would bring certain destruction. One hour later they abandoned Ngok Tavak.

All the weapons, equipment, and munitions that could not be carried were hastily piled in the command bunker and set afire. A LAW was used to destroy the intact helicopter that had been grounded with a ruptured fuel line. Sergeant Miller's body was abandoned. Sgt. Thomas H. Perry was later discovered to be missing. He had last been seen alive on the perimeter when he was told to join the escape column. The survivors evaded through dense jungle to a helicopter pickup point midway to Kham Duc. Their extraction was completed shortly before 7:00 P.M. on the evening of 10 May 1968.[10]

In concert with the initial Ngok Tavak assault, the main Kham Duc camp was blasted by a heavy mortar and recoilless rifle attack at 2:45 A.M. that same morning. Periodic mortar barrages ripped into Kham Duc throughout the rest of the day, while the American Division airmobiled a reinforced battalion of the 196th Infantry Brigade into the compound. Lieutenant Colonel Schungel and a Special Forces command party also landed, but the situation deteriorated too rapidly for their presence to have positive effect.

The mortar attack on fog-shrouded Kham Duc resumed on the morning of 11 May. The bombardment caused heavy losses among the frightened CIDG soldiers, who fled from their trenches across open ground, seeking shelter in the bunkers. The LLDB commander remained hidden. S. Sgt. Richard B. Gill stated laconically, "control of the CIDG was sorry as hell." His own CIDG soldiers refused orders to check the rear of the camp for possible North Vietnamese intruders. That evening the 11th and 12th Mobile Strike Force companies were airlifted to Da Nang, and half of the 137th CIDG Company from Camp Ha Thanh was airlanded in exchange.

The *1st VC Regiment, 2d NVA Division,* began closing the ring around Kham Duc during the early morning darkness of 12 May. Outpost #7 was assaulted and fell within a few minutes. Outposts #5, #1, and #3 had been reinforced by American troops but were in North Vietnamese hands by 9:30 A.M. Most of the American soldiers later counted as missing at Kham Duc were lost in that harrowing, futile outpost defense. Company-size NVA assaults followed half an hour later against three sides of the main perimeter. Although the attacks were repulsed, the American Division called it quits. The North Vietnamese occupied the high ground and registered intensely accurate fire against aircraft on the shell-pocked airstrip. At noon a massive NVA attack was launched against the main compound. The charge was stopped by planes hurling napalm, cluster bomb units, and 750-pound bombs into the final wire barriers. The American Division officers frantically called for immediate extraction.

The aerial evacuation was disorderly and, at times, on the verge of complete panic. One of the first extraction helicopters to land was exploded by enemy fire, blocking the airstrip. Engineers of Company A, 70th Engineer Battalion, frantically reassembled one of their dozers (previously torn apart to prevent capture) and pushed the wreckage off the runway. Eight more aircraft were blown out of the sky. The American artillerymen (Battery A, 3d Battalion, 82d Artillery) quickly destroyed their five howitzers. Intense antiaircraft fire from the captured outposts caused grave problems. Control over the indigenous forces was extremely difficult. Lieutenant Bernhardt kept a horde of CIDG soldiers in the trenches at riflepoint to prevent them from mobbing the runway.

The Americal Division upset the scant hopes for orderly evacuation. Vietnamese dependents were shoved out of the way by soldiers from Company A of the 1st Battalion, 46th Infantry, who insisted on getting aboard the departing aircraft first. Finally, as more Americal infantry tried to clamber into the outbound planes, the outraged Special Forces staff convinced the Air Force to start loading civilians. The women and children were squeezed between elements of the 2d Battalion, 1st Infantry. S. Sgt. Richard F. Campbell watched as some 200 unruly refugees shoved their way onto a C-130 aircraft, trampling over weaker adults and children on the ramp. As the plane took off, it was shot down and crashed in flames on the north end of the runway.

By the time Air Force Lt. Col. Joe M. Jackson landed his C-123 aircraft to pick up the three-man Air Force combat control team at Kham Duc, the NVA had overrun much of the camp. North Vietnamese machine guns were set up on the airstrip. The camp was engulfed in flames, ammunition dumps were continuously exploding and littering the runway with debris, and the entire area was being raked by NVA automatic weapons and recoilless rifle fire. The usable portion of the airstrip was dangerously reduced by demolished aircraft and burning equipment. Jackson rescued the team and took off under a heavy cross fire.

The Special Forces command group was the last organized group out of the camp. As their helicopter soared into the lowering clouds, Kham Duc was abandoned to advancing NVA infantry at 4:33 P.M. on 12 May 1968. The battle had resulted in a total North Vietnamese victory. The last Special Forces border surveillance camp on the northwestern frontier of South Vietnam had been destroyed.[11]

4. Spring Reconstruction

Although Special Forces border surveillance had suffered severe setbacks with the destruction of Camps Lang Vei and Kham Duc, these losses only confirmed that the level of conflict had surpassed the ability of Special Forces outposts to influence South Vietnamese territorial integrity. Established to police Viet Cong infiltration routes before the advent of foreign armies onto the battlefield, the Special Forces campsites were neither designed nor rationally expected to prevent regular divisions from crossing the frontier. The Second Indochina War had become a full-scale conventional contest.

The Special Forces continued to develop fighting camps in other areas. The personnel from Kham Duc were used to open a new camp at Nong Son on 24 June 1968. Detachment A-101 was rebuilt and officially occupied a new campsite at Mai Loc the same day. The assets of Prek Klok were transferred into Katum, established by A-322 on 21 February, and the resources at Moc Hoa were redeployed to Thanh Tri (A-414) on 15 March 1968.

The major North Vietnamese road network, which had been extended out of the tri-border area as far east as Camp Polei Kleng and as far south as the lower Plei Trap Valley, was challenged by the construction of Ben Het. From early February until mid-March, Ben Het was continually mortared and rocketed, but the Special Forces fortress was completed regardless. Ben Het soon assumed strategic significance as a vital launching site for MACV Studies and Observation Group (MACV-SOG) special operations reconnaissance teams.

Other new camps, built at Duc Hue (A-351) and Thien Ngon (A-323), were also continually harassed by mortaring and ambushing of engineer components. Thien Ngon had been established near two major VC infiltration lanes from Cambodia using the personnel and assets from Trai Bi. The construction of the camp proved a dangerous assignment for the 588th Engineer Battalion. Several road clearing and security elements were ambushed with heavy losses. The initial construction phase of the camp ended on 22 February when Thien Ngon was formally opened.[12]

After the experiences at Lang Vei, the Special Forces took tanks seriously. When NVA armor was reported just across the Cambodian border near Camp Ben Soi, Detachment A-321 dispatched a hunter-killer company into the area. On 26 February 1968 the lead combat reconnaissance platoon spotted a VC company and three tanks in bivouac. The Viet Cong were standing around camp fires; the tanks were parked with their motors off. The two recon platoons advanced on line and took up firing positions about 150 yards from the nearest tank. The Special Forces senior advisor initiated action by firing the first shot, and an M72 LAW round hit the PT-76 tank at the base of the turret and caused a large explosion, followed by the glow of multicolored tracer rounds bursting from turret hatches. The engines of the remaining two tanks were quickly started, and the tanks roared west into Cambodia.

On 21 April 1968 the loss of Camp Tra Cu (A-352, Capt. Allan W. Keener) was narrowly averted. At 3:00 A.M. the camp was hit by hand-held rockets, recoilless rifles, and mortars fired from the west across open ground, from the north across the Vam Co Dong River, and from the east across the Binh Gay Canal. Thirty minutes later a ground assault was launched, and one squad reached the camp's inner compound perimeter berm. First Lieutenant Pharoah, Sergeant First Class Formyduval, and Specialist 4th Class Funderburk performed heroic service steadying the CIDG riflemen. Several CIDG braved intense hostile fire to recover lost weapons from the VC and remained in almost untenable positions in order to defend the camp. The LLDB commander, although severely wounded, displayed calm courage in directing and inspiring his men.

The Viet Cong were finally repulsed, despite several ugly incidents. In one case a CIDG soldier refused to fire on the attackers and attempted to swing his .30-caliber machine gun against the Special Forces compound. He was apprehended before he could complete his act. Later investigation revealed that a large VC infrastructure existed within the camp. Among the penetration agents were several assistant platoon leaders or squad leaders. They were supposed to guide the VC into the camp after having breached the defenses from the inside. All the claymore mine wires on the northern perimeter had already been cut. The Viet Cong attack was unsuccessful because assistance from inside elements was largely foiled, and flareships and Air Force AC-47 "Spooky" aircraft promptly arrived overhead.[13]

5. The Status of Special Forces

The global Army Special Forces personnel situation had become quite serious by mid-1967. Shortages of experienced personnel in the operations, intelligence, medical, signal, and engineer basic skill areas were particularly acute. In response, during August and September of that year, the Department of the Army asked the 5th Special Forces Group to substitute non-Special Forces qualified individuals wherever possible. The situation was so serious that on 26 December 1967 General Johnson, the Army Chief of Staff, was personally briefed on the matter.

Recruiting shortfalls and a declining retention rate were the main culprits. While almost 80 percent of all Special Forces enlisted men worldwide had served in Vietnam, only 30 percent of the Special Forces soldiers reporting into Nha Trang were volunteers for Vietnam duty. Declining volunteer rates and assignment restrictions gravely hampered attempts to keep the 5th Special Forces Group up to strength. Already authorized were grade substitutions up to three levels and the direct in-country recruitment of non-Special Forces arrivals at the 22d and 90th Replacement Battalions. While intended as a stop-gap measure, the policy became permanent.

Personnel support requirements for the 5th Special Forces Group were mathematically precise. With involuntary second tours and the maintenance of current between-tour time, the Army could support 1,830 Special Forces enlisted spaces in Vietnam. By coupling involuntary second tours with cuts in between-tour time and trimming Special Forces stateside "training base" cadre, the Army could increase the support level to 2,685 sergeants in the combat zone. The Army had only a marginal capability to support Special Forces in Vietnam, even at present levels.

Some of the problems stemmed from the requirement for 5th Special Forces Group to maintain MACV special operations units at 100 percent strength, a directive reconfirmed by the Pentagon on 27 and 31 December 1967. The group was so overtaxed that on 7 March 1968 Colonel Ladd informed MACV that the provision of all requested personnel to such projects would force the closure of some camps or the unacceptable reduction of all A-Detachment strengths.[14]

Beginning on 3 February 1968, the 5th Special Forces Group had been additionally levied for personnel outside the Provincial Reconnaissance Unit (PRU) Project PHOENIX program. Most were needed as USARV Ruff-Puff advisors, but sergeants were also taken to bolster the 3d Brigade of the 82d Airborne Division. While the total personnel taken amounted to eight officers and seventy-three sergeants, the group could hardly spare any of them.

Looming over all projected personnel planning was the terrible factor of battlefield casualties. Teams defending isolated campsites in Viet Cong countryside and sweeping NVA infiltration routes suffered high cumulative losses. Even routine patrolling inevitably cost a life or limb periodically, and entire teams could be decimated within twelve months' time. Most Special Forces veterans boasted at least one Purple Heart. The band of pre-Vietnam Special Forces warriors dwindled with each embattled camp and missing patrol, and only luck or promotion into the higher staff ranks was keeping a nucleus of the old 77th Group assignees alive.

In the wake of high officer losses, most junior officers reporting for combat duty with 5th Special Forces Group were now 2d lieutenants whose total military experience consisted of Officer Candidate School, jump school, and the thirteen-week Special Forces officer crash course at Fort Bragg, North Carolina. The group considered them immature and unqualified ersatz leaders. Maj. Daniel A. Smith, the Company D operations officer wrote on 8 July 1968, "One cannot expect a twenty-year-old lieutenant with one year in the Army to advise successfully a thirty-year-old Vietnamese captain with ten years' combat time."[15]

The A-Detachments, the heart of Special Forces in the field, were universally understrength or underpowered. Team captains and executive officers normally had less than two years' service, and some teams were commanded by lieutenants. Only two or three master sergeants and sergeants first class were usually present in any team, although some teams had no master sergeants. The remaining enlisted men were on their first tour of Army duty. Typically, teams operated with only one qualified medical specialist and one radio operator. While the new Special Forces trooper possessed excellent potential, being extremely motivated, intelligent, and physically fit, his dependability and professional competence were only as developed as experience permitted.

By mid-1968 only 10 percent of the replacements reporting for duty with the 5th Special Forces Group had battlefield experience. Another 10 percent were not parachutists, and almost 25 percent were not even Special Forces-qualified. Many of the "shake and bake" sergeants (some of whom were awarded staff sergeant rank in stateside training mills) and some junior officers had no idea even how to read a military map. On 8 April 1968 the 5th Special Forces Group was forced to institute a twelve-day combat orientation course in Vietnam conducted by the MACV Recondo School for all replacement personnel, except sergeant-majors and field grade officers. Bewildered senior sergeants and officers could hardly believe that the Special Forces had been so ravaged by incessant Vietnam warfare.[16]

Notes

1. The majority of material for this section came from 5th Special Forces Group, *Operational Reports*, dtd 15 February and 15 May 1968, and from specific Tet after action reports of the detachments involved.

2. Detachment B-24, *Combat Operation After Action Report*, dtd 14 February 1968. The 24th STZ Commander was relieved on 10 February because of his incompetence.

3. Detachment B-22, *After Action Report for Tet Offensive*, dtd 24 February 1968.

4. Detachment B-22, *After Action Report*, dtd 9 March 1968.

5. Company A, 5th Special Forces Group, AVGB-SFA Ltr, dtd 4 March 1968.

6. On the burial problems, one A-Team reported, "This problem is [caused by the] failure to return CSF [camp strike force] KIA's to their assigned camps. Of the seven CSF killed in Dalat only two have been returned to this location. One CSF was buried in Dalat at the request of his family. This detachment was informed that the remaining four were buried at Nha Trang by the direction of LLDB high command. At the present time there is a certain amount of resentment toward the USASF and the VNSF by the dependents living in this area because of this, and also a feeling of insecurity by a number of the CSF who would like to know if they are killed that they would be returned to An Lac for burial." Detachment A-234 Ltr to Commanding Officer, 5th SFG, dtd 29 February 1968.

7. Camp Lang Vei strength on 6 February 1968 totalled 24 Special Forces, 14 LLDB, 161 mobile strike force, 282 CIDG (mixed Bru and Vietnamese), 6 interpreters, and 520 Laotian tribal soldiers, not including civilians. Lieutenant Colonel Schungel was on his first Special Forces assignment, although he had served a previous Vietnam tour as an advisor to an ARVN unit in I CTZ. Colonel Ladd had appointed Schungel commander of Company C upon his arrival in Vietnam. Schungel, who was already an airborne infantry officer, performed brilliantly and was promoted to Deputy Commander of 5th Special Forces Group on 6 July 1968.

8. Following the battle of Lang Vei, eighteen M72 LAWs were test-fired by Detachment A-109 at Thuong Duc. Six failed to fire: "Three of these six failures were due to malfunctions within the firing mechanism. A second check of all firing pins and safeties was conducted, after which a second attempt was made to fire the weapon. They again failed to fire. The tube was collapsed and extended back to the firing position, and a third attempt was made to fire the weapon with negative results. The remaining three M72 LAWs ignited, but the rocket failed to leave the launcher tube. Of the twelve rockets that did fire properly, one failed to detonate upon impact." Headquarters, 21st Military History Detachment, 5th Special Forces Group, AVGB-MH Ltr dtd 22 March 1968, p. 9.

9. Losses at Lang Vei were (less Laotians who were unrecorded) KIA or MIA: 10 Special Forces, 5 LLDB, 165 CIDG, 34 mobile strike force, 5 interpreters; WIA: 13 Special Forces, 3 LLDB, 29 CIDG, 32 mobile strike force. Seven NVA tanks were confirmed destroyed and another two counted as probably destroyed. NVA casualties were unknown and not estimated. Sergeant First Class Ashley was posthumously awarded the Medal of Honor. 5th Special Forces Group, *Combat After Action Interview Report*, dtd 22 March 1968; Company C, *After Action Report*, dtd 22 February 1968.

10. 5th Special Forces Group Mobile Strike Force Company C, *After Action Report Ngok Tavak FOB*, dtd 16 May 1968, and related papers including statement of Capt. Euge E. Makowski, who landed with the elements of the 12th Mobile Strike Force Company.

11. Losses at Kham Duc and Ngok Tavak were KIA: 12 Army, 12 Marines; MIA: 26 Army (including 3 Special Forces), 1 interpreter, 1 nurse, 677 CIDG and civilians; WIA: 112 Army (including 5 Special Forces), 21 Marines, 29 CIDG. NVA losses were estimated at 345 total. A total of ten aircraft were shot down. Seven 105mm howitzers, fifteen 81mm mortars, fifteen trucks, and a score of miscellaneous vehicles were also lost. Air Force Lieutenant Colonel Jackson received the Medal of Honor for his heroism. 5th Special Forces Group, Company C, *After Action Report*, dtd 31 May 1968, with Annexes A–E; Department of the Army Memorandum for Secretary of the General Staff, dtd 3 February 1970 (Peers inquiry on mistreatment of civilians by Americal Division).

12. Detachment A-323, *Camp Opening Report*, dtd 9 March 1968.

13. Detachment A-352, *After Action Report*, dtd 9 May 1968. Camp CIDG strength consisted of 318 Vietnamese and 84 Cambodians at the time of the attack. Losses were KIA: 6 CIDG, 1 civilian; MIA: 1 CIDG; WIA: 5 LLDB, 13 CIDG, 3 civilians. Viet Cong losses were 64 body count and 1 wounded and captured.

14. On 7 March 1968 the 5th Special Forces Group had 527 officers, 21 warrant officers, and 2,241 enlisted men assigned (a total of 2,789). MACV-SOG had an assigned Special Forces strength of 60 officers and 424 enlisted men, not counting Project DANIEL BOONE with 18 officers and 122 enlisted men, and Detachment B-53 with 5 officers and 28 enlisted men. The aggregate Special Forces strength in Vietnam was 3,386 troops.

15. Company D, *Field Grade Debriefing*, dtd 8 July 1968.

16. The majority of sources used in this section was derived from the adjutant files of 5th Special Forces Group, 1967–68; 5th Special Forces Group, *Operational Report*, dtd 15 August 1968; and the remarks in reports of the Field Grade Officer Debriefing and Sergeant Major Debriefing Programs instituted in compliance with 5th Special Forces Group Regulations 1-2, dtd 5 January 1968, and 1-2, dtd 17 July 1969, respectively.

CHAPTER 10

SPECIAL FORCES IN CRISES

1. New Directions

Col. Harold "Hank" Robert Aaron, previously commander of the 1st Special Forces Group and a World War II veteran of the 65th Infantry Division, took over the 5th Special Forces Group on 4 June 1968. That same month General Westmoreland left Vietnam and turned over the reins of MACV command to Gen. Creighton W. Abrams, a well-respected but very conventional leader. That fall General Abrams instituted changes geared at placing the primary burden of fighting the war back on the South Vietnamese, along with less direct American combat participation.

Under General Abrams's new campaign plans, Colonel Aaron's 5th Special Forces Group was charged with (1) exercising command of subordinate Special Forces detachments; (2) advising and assisting the LLDB; (3) subsector advisory roles in I and IV CTZs; (4) providing intelligence to the MACV commander; (5) conducting special operations; (6) running the MACV Recondo School, which trained long-range patrol personnel for major combat units; (7) providing logistical support to the CIDG program; and (8) organizing, training, equipping, and commanding the Mobile Strike Force (MSF) commands.[1]

In actuality General Abrams was moving to fold Special Forces down in harmony with his "One War" campaign plans. By mid-November 1968 it was evident that a phasedown of the CIDG force levels would be forthcoming. Along with it General Abrams was planning a sizable reduction in Special Forces personnel, with the ultimate objective of dispensing with the group. The peak 5th Special Forces Group strength of 3,542 was reached on 30 September 1968. Thereafter it was continually trimmed by a series of cutbacks that followed hasty CIDG camp conversions.

Since U.S. policy now dictated that the South Vietnamese would defend themselves, General Abrams ordered the CIDG camps converted to Regional Force status or turned over to the exclusive control of the LLDB as soon as possible. The remaining years of formal Special Forces presence in Vietnam were marked by the headlong rush to rapidly turn over Special Forces installations to the Vietnamese government, regardless of their readiness or the consequences.

The premature conversion of Camp Ben Soi (A-321) to complete LLDB control on 2 July 1968 was an early example of Vietnamese inability to take over full CIDG responsibility. Apparently, a large factor in making the turnover was the excellent English proficiency and assurances of the local LLDB camp commander. Once the transition was made, padded CIDG strengths became rampant, intelligence and operational reliability dwindled, and camp defenses deteriorated. Finally, the II Field Force Vietnam commander was forced to reestablish the Special Forces A-Detachment in the camp.[2]

One of the worst Ben Soi episodes had occurred on 31 July 1968, when a combined operation with Trang Sup (A-301) encountered a fortified Viet Cong bunkerline. As the forward Trang Sup company pulled back to a bomb crater to call in airstrikes, a volley of automatic weapons fire killed the LLDB lieutenant. The CIDG, seeing this, began a disorganized withdrawal. Two Special Forces advisors were wounded trying to find the other LLDB leader, who had run away. When the CIDG witnessed the Americans getting hit, they bolted from the field, leaving all casualties behind. The Ben Soi element mistakenly fired into the retreating Trang Sup company, producing complete panic. The Viet Cong counterattacked, forcing 1st Lt. Ronald L. De Paolo to hold the landing zone with the forty-seven Cambodians he convinced to stay with him.[3]

The Vietnamese government considered the LLDB an unwanted stepchild, a legacy of the Diem regime kept in existence to appease the U.S. Army. This adverse policy naturally curtailed the improvement of LLDB military attributes. The lack of progress was evidenced in camps such as Thien Ngon (A-323), which covered a critical slice of Viet Cong infiltration territory near Cambodia. The LLDB commander limited camp operations to predictable three-day sojourns, which netted very few contacts and fewer VC casualties. The NVA/VC knew exactly how far the camp forces traveled in a day and a half before starting their return to Thien Ngon and operated at will outside that operational radius.

After considerable Special Forces prodding, two Thien Ngon CIDG companies conducted an air assault seven miles northwest of the camp on 9 November 1968. They were escorted by four LLDB and four Special Forces advisors. Half an hour before noon, a VC platoon attacked one element, and the entire company immediately broke and ran, led by the LLDB commanders. Ten Cambodian soldiers were left behind. The pair of Special Forces advisors with the unit made several futile attempts to slow down the retreat. The commander of Detachment B-32, Lt. Col. Harry S. Hilling, Jr., and his esteemed LLDB counterpart, Maj. Le Van Hanh, arrived overhead in a command helicopter. Hanh ordered his LLDB to return to the battlefield and retrieve the missing men, but he was ignored.

Major Hanh diverted the other camp company to the contact area. The unit retrieved four bodies and six Cambodians still fighting at the scene. The company, led by S. Sgt. Charles Cooper, performed admirably during the firefight, which lasted the rest of the day and throughout the night. The two other heliborne operations conducted by Thien Ngon forces, one in April and one in June 1969, were terminated early by the LLDB officers in charge. In one case the excuse given was that the troops were cold and wet, and on the other occasion, that they were out of water.[4]

Counterpart relations between the LLDB and Special Forces were generally poor and varied from friendly indifference to active hostility. Inner camp compound protective arrangements kept their tactical operations centers and team houses separate. Any story of a missing patrol or a wounded advisor abandoned during a firefight spread through the A-Detachments like wildfire. There was little resulting confidence in LLDB loyalty, and many Special Forces soldiers firmly believed that they would be deserted in adverse combat. Although some teams worked together harmoniously in an atmosphere of mutual respect, the animosity that prevailed between most LLDB and Special Forces detachments prevented the group from really meeting its major goal of "advising and assisting the LLDB."

In the meantime General Abrams perceived Special Forces merely as an economy of force arrangement, whereby pressure could be maintained against the NVA/VC at minimal cost in American lives. CIDG soldiers were cheap and cost-effective. While the price of initial issue for a CIDG soldier was about 71 percent that of a regular American soldier, his daily subsistence and pay were only 16 percent of the U.S. soldier's cost.[5]

The CIDG was broken down into two distinct elements: the camp strike forces and the mobile strike forces (formerly designated as Mike Forces). The camp strike forces, numbering roughly 42,000, consisted of locally recruited members, usually from nearby hill tribes, which served the camps on a contract basis. While technically under LLDB control, these people were keenly aware that they were paid, clothed, supplied, and fed by the American Special Forces. Inherent in the nature of the CIDG program was its vulnerability to infiltration by Viet Cong or VC sympathizers, draft evaders, and deserters.

The mobile strike forces, some 10,000 strong, were recruited to fight for extended periods of time anywhere in South Vietnam. In theory they were jointly commanded by the LLDB and Special Forces, but in actuality the latter exercised complete authority. These forces provided the primary means at Special Forces disposal for reinforcement of threatened camps and were constituted into ready reserve reaction commands within each corps tactical zone.

While the CIDG forces represented the equivalent manpower of four ARVN divisions, and defended some 13,351 square miles of the countryside, the CIDG remained a paramilitary organization composed of civilians hired as soldiers. Their only official military standing was simply the fact that personnel on active CIDG duty were exempted from the draft. Their lack of fundamental military prowess was sometimes shocking. On some operations lowland Vietnamese CIDG contingents carried blaring transistor radios. When one Special Forces team sergeant was asked why operations were not planned in a particular sector outside Gia Vuc (A-103), he bluntly told his company commander, "The VC up there are too tough and our CIDG too sorry."

In many camps Special Forces distrusted either the CIDG or LLDB to the point that they carried personal weapons whenever they left the team house. Colonel Schungel spotted one team house full of holes at Camp Gia Vuc and found out the building had been machine-gunned by a vengeful CIDG after one of his comrades lost a drunken "quick draw" contest to an American. The Special Forces member had been whisked out, and the incident pretty well covered up.[6]

After the passage of stringent Vietnamese draft laws on 19 June 1968, the CIDG card, which allowed deferment from regular military service, suddenly became a prized object. Discharged CIDG soldiers, fired from the camp strike force, could find themselves in the South Vietnamese Army in a matter of hours. This gave Special Forces the leverage to bring many CIDG companies under control. On the opposite side of the coin, the Special Forces lost almost complete control over its interpreters, who were put in CIDG support platoons to keep them out of the draft. The LLDB, resentful over the interpreters' high pay rates and American camaraderie, began harassing and fining them.

The Special Forces also used its network of contacts throughout the country to meet many CIDG program needs. For instance, the Ethnic Minority Affairs officer in Ambassador Robert W. Komer's important Civil Operations and Revolutionary Development Support (CORDS) program was Al Roman. He was a retired Special Forces master sergeant who had served in both highlands and Delta during the early period of Special Forces involvement. Mr. Roman visited the camps and interested his superiors in their well-being. In this manner Special Forces acquired the services of a host of agricultural and other technicians, as well as favored commodity support.

2. Autumn and Winter Battles

The next round of Special Forces battles erupted in August and September 1968 and locked several critical camps in pitched battles. In I CTZ the earlier loss of the northern outpost Camps Lang Vei and Kham Duc enabled the North Vietnamese to concentrate against two interior camps within the region. During early August, elements of the *3d NVA Division* escalated rocket attacks and skirmishing around Ha Thanh (A-104), which guarded the western gateway to Quang Ngai city.

One of Ha Thanh's outposts was seized on 23 August 1968, but a Special Forces-led CIDG counterattack regained the position in a bitter, three-hour struggle. The North Vietnamese continued their buildup, and the next day Ha Thanh was reinforced by elements of the Da Nang 1st Mobile Strike Force and Americal Division. On the night of 25 August, the camp was severely bombarded and assaulted by two NVA companies, but the attack was promptly repulsed. During the same night, AC-130 gunships and airstrikes were employed to discourage the approach of vehicles, possibly tanks, sighted moving toward the camp from the southwest. The arrival of additional mobile strike force personnel the following day enabled the Special Forces to begin aggressively sweeping the jungle around the camp. Continuous firefights and mortar or rocket attacks pummeled the camp and surrounding villages until 28 September, when the NVA withdrew.

The camp at Thuong Duc (A-109), located on the main western approaches to Da Nang, was also threatened. Throughout September NVA forces entrenched themselves in the mountains that surrounded the campsite on three sides. Just after 2:00 A.M. on 28 September 1968, elements of the *21st NVA Regiment* overran Outposts Alpha and Bravo located about 600 yards southwest of the main camp. Later that day camp forces recaptured both of these positions in hard combat.

During the next few days, NVA forces occupied several villages around the camp and drove out their inhabitants. Radio transmissions, monitored on a captured communist Chinese radio by Special Forces personnel, indicated that the North Vietnamese were taking high losses because of the incessant aerial and artillery pounding and were in desperate need of replacements and medical supplies. The radio interceptions enabled camp forces to shatter a resupply unit that was caught in the open fields northwest of the camp on 2 October, causing over a hundred casualties.

North Vietnamese probes against Thuong Duc positions, supplemented by numerous rocket and mortar barrages, continued throughout early October. It was also apparent, however, that the North Vietnamese had given up any thought of assaulting the camp or pressing their drive closer to Da Nang. The safety of Thuong Duc was assured after several Marine and ARVN battalions moved to clear the area in Operation MAUI PEAK, which commenced on 6 October 1968.[7]

On the evening of 22 February 1969, the NVA/VC launched their Post-Tet offensive, a small but coordinated campaign of widespread barrages and ground probes on military installations throughout South Vietnam. Camp Tien Phuoc (A-102, Capt. John E. Cleckner), set up to protect the approaches to Tam Ky and the industrial An Hoa area, was bombarded just before midnight. At 2:00 A.M. on 23 February, a camp outpost was overrun by a Viet Cong unit partially composed of female personnel. The outpost was quickly recaptured by CIDG troops supported by camp artillery at daybreak. Although wounded in the leg, LLDB camp commander Captain Diep personally led the assault against three machine gun bunkers. Still, Tien Phuoc remained closely besieged until contacts diminished during late March.[8]

In III CTZ, north of Saigon, the border camp of Loc Ninh (A-331, Capt. Harry L. Zimmermann) had always been endangered by the NVA/VC, as it hindered infiltration into War Zone D. Beginning on 9 August 1968, intelligence reports indicated that North Vietnamese units were building up along the Cambodian frontier north and west of the camp. One hour after midnight on 18 August a composite battalion of the *7th NVA Division* bombarded the compound with mortars, recoilless rifles, and rockets. Poor weather hampered air support the following night when a reinforced company lunged into the perimeter wire and tried to take Loc Ninh's northwestern corner. The assault was driven back, although contact continued until 22 August. Elements of the 11th Armored Cavalry and 1st Infantry Division assisted in mopping up the area and safeguarding the camp.[9]

Several camps that formed a protective ring in western III CTZ for the key provincial capital of Tay Ninh were also hit in August. The border camp of Katum (A-322, 1st Lt. Donald L. Giddens) was rocketed then assaulted by the *5th VC Sapper Battalion* on 18 August 1968. The Viet Cong, dressed in black shorts and camouflaged tunics, used automatic rifles, hand-held rocket launchers, and gas grenades as they penetrated the outer berm. The VC were forced to retreat by overwhelming defensive firepower; they regrouped and surged forward again. The battle raged for ten hours before the Viet Cong were defeated.

Camp Katum was pounded by 82mm mortar shelling and 122mm rockets throughout the following week. During one ten-minute period, over 150 mortar rounds pelted the compound. The camp was initially reinforced by a camp strike force company from Trang Sup then bolstered by the 1st Battalion of the 3d Mobile Strike Force. During the latter part of August and all through September, the camp was subjected to constant artillery and rocket bombardment in an attempt to wear down the defenders and destroy morale.

Just before 3:00 A.M. on 25 September 1968, the camp was blistered by a savage rocket and mortar barrage, with over a hundred rocket-propelled grenades fired into identified CIDG defensive positions. Half an hour later the *5th VC Sapper Battalion* made another determined bid to overrun the star-shaped perimeter. Within fifteen minutes the northwestern star point fell as Viet Cong flamethrowers and satchel charges were used to tear down bunkers. However, the camp's 105mm howitzers fired cannister charges at point-blank range into the VC swarming over the fallen strongpoint. A prompt CIDG counterattack routed the remaining Viet Cong, and the threat to Katum was ended.[10]

Barely forty-eight hours later two battalions of the *9th VC Division* tried to overwhelm Thien Ngon (A-323, Capt. Jerry R. Winchester), a camp protecting the southeastern approaches to Tay Ninh as well as routes leading into Saigon. The detachment enjoyed excellent rapport with the LLDB, and the CIDG morale was high because most positions had been hardened to withstand all medium-caliber shelling. On the night of 27 September 1968, the camp began receiving sporadic rocket and mortar fire, which increased until 10:00 P.M. Between midnight and dawn three mass assaults were hurled against the camp's ramparts. Each was heralded by brief but intensive mortar and rocket barrages and spearheaded by sapper squads that tried to blow lanes through the barrier wire with bangalore torpedoes. The presence of abundant armed airpower mauled the VC attackers and prevented them from reaching the camp's defensive lines. This proved to be the last major attempt to take a Special Forces camp during 1968. The successful defenses of Katum and Thien Ngon had ended the threat on Tay Ninh.[11]

3. Highland Battles

The first major NVA/VC attack on a Special Forces camp within II CTZ in over a hundred days was launched on 18 August 1968 against Dak Seang (A-245). The camp protected the northern approach to Kontum city, and the *101D NVA Regiment* took advantage of the darkness and bad weather to attempt a quick victory. They shelled the compound with mortars and B-40 rockets at 3:30 A.M., followed by a three-company assault against the western perimeter while a reinforced company hit the eastern wire. After twenty minutes of gunfire, the two-pronged assault was broken up at the barriers. Later attacks at 4:25 A.M., however, breached the perimeter wire. Air support was hindered by the foul weather, which consisted of lowering clouds, fog, driving rain, and strong wind. Nevertheless, the ground assault was beaten back with artillery shelling and defensive fires. The battle of Dak Seang was a splendid example of the ability of a fortified A-Detachment to defeat a determined attack with a minimum of outside assistance.

One of the hardest-fought Special Forces battles of the war transpired at Duc Lap (A-239, 1st Lt. William J. Harp). The camp had been established during November 1966 near the old site of Bon Sar Pa, which had been closed because of FULRO troubles. Duc Lap was situated on two hills overlooking a broad, fertile plateau nine miles from the border, and its strategic location covered the southwestern approaches toward Ban Me Thuot. The CIDG Rhade and Mnong tribal warriors lived with their families in hillside bunkers and caves just behind the fighting trenches.[12]

The *95C NVA Regiment* initiated a ground probe of the compound, supported by intensive mortar and rocket fire, at 1:30 A.M. on 23 August 1968. Two battalions of the *320th NVA Regiment* assaulted the government district headquarters four miles away. By dawn Duc Lap was surrounded by well-equipped, crack North Vietnamese infantry. Antiaircraft fire brought down an Air Force F-100 fighter that morning. The pilot was saved by Special Forces personnel who sped out of the camp in a jeep and 3/4-ton truck and effected a daring mobile rescue. Two 2d Mobile Strike Force companies from Pleiku were airmobiled to the north of the camp but were driven back by entrenched NVA on the nearby heights.

That night the North Vietnamese infantry stormed the smaller, northern hill of the camp. No Americans or LLDB had been posted there, and in the absence of Special Forces leadership, the 563d and 564th CIDG companies were overrun after half-hearted resistance. The CIDG defenders were armed with carbines and averaged only four weeks of military training. They simply pulled back into their bunkers and waited for help, neglecting even to fire the claymore mines. The NVA reduced each bunker in turn, hampered only by shelling from the main camp positions across the saddle. Soon after gaining possession of the hill, North Vietnamese gunners used captured weapons and stocks of ammunition to renew concentrated fire on the remaining hill.

Three 2d Mobile Strike Force (MSF) companies tried to break the siege on 24 August 1968. The relief force was decimated in a fierce battle on the camp's airfield runway, but the 202d Company, led by wounded Australian Capt. David G. Savage, reached the barricaded front gate. Australian Warrant Officer Lawrence Jackson recalled seeing the "Welcome to Duc Lap" sign at the gate, in the midst of barbed wire rolls, scattered weapons, and mangled NVA sapper bodies. "Some welcome," he muttered as the ragged force struggled into the compound and reinforced the defense.

Shortly after the company's arrival, Maj. Roland Greenwood, who was in the camp as the executive officer of Detachment B-23, held a coordination meeting outside the tactical operations center. A B-40 rocket explosion shattered the group of key personnel, killing S. Sgt. Harold F. Kline and a Montagnard howitzer gunner and seriously wounding Greenwood, LLDB Capt. Hoang Kim Bao (the camp commander), Sfc. Harry Umeda, and Lieutenant Vinh of the 202d MSF Company. Medical helicopters were unable to fly through the curtain of fire until twenty-four hours later to evacuate the casualties.

The North Vietnamese made another major effort to smash the camp just before dawn on 25 August. The ground assault was timed to take advantage of the temporary break in air cover between the nighttime Air Force AC-130 "Spectre" gunship and the arrival of daylight F-100 fighters. The NVA attack from the north hill swept into the saddle and seized four bunkers just outside the inner trench of the main hill. Another NVA company approached from the southwest. Sappers pierced the outer wire and crawled forward through the tall weeds. The middle wire was breached by bangalore torpedoes, and the North Vietnamese infantry charged through a hail of defensive machine gun fire and artillery shelling to reach the inner wire. The assault was checked within grenade range of the trenchworks. During this fighting, the radio operator S. Sgt. Michael B. Tooley, a popular cartoonist and hero of the earlier pilot rescue, was killed by a sniper.

Meanwhile, airstrikes were directed against the captured bunkers, but napalm was dropped almost on top of the 561st CIDG Company positions. The Montagnards began streaming from their positions in complete panic. The tribesmen grabbed their wives, children, bundles of clothing, and other possessions and started running toward the Special Forces inner compound on the main hilltop. Sgt. James Alward suddenly saw the first three terrified, weaponless CIDG soldiers coming up the hill. He shouted, "What the hell's going on here?" as team M. Sgt. Thomas T. Boody yelled, "Get those people back in position!"

Sergeant Alward recalled:

We threatened, and pushed them. I grabbed this one guy, he had been in the second 81 [mm mortar position]. He could get along in broken English. I said, "You get those damn people back into those trenches or we're dead." I pushed him toward them. Then I walked toward clusters of CIDG, threw out my arms, and said, "Get back, get back, into those positions." It seemed we were being overrun by the CIDG. They brought all their families with them. There's nothing you can do when a Montagnard's with his family. That's his one concern. So we decided to let them get their families into the bunkers and pits. Then we hustled their asses out. All of us Americans were out there, physically pushing them, grabbing them, shaking our rifles in their noses, making them go back to their positions. They finally did, not as well as before, but at least we had a real tight perimeter at the top of the hill. At that time this was the only position that the friendlies had. We just sat tight then. That's all we could do. We went back to our mortar pits and constantly watched that these people didn't break again.[13]

Sp. 4th Class John S. Wast, a platoon leader in the 202d MSF Company, fired his M16 rifle over their heads, grabbed as many people as he could, and spun them around as he paddled them on the behind and pointed downhill, all the while wondering how the stateside newspapers would describe the episode. The Australians were less polite. They had pushed the 202d into camp at great cost, and when the company started to break as well, they furiously rushed forward, grabbing and hitting and shoving them back on the line. By 9:30 that morning order was finally restored and the trenches were manned again.

The situation in Duc Lap was grim. The Special Forces soldiers were planning how to evacuate the camp and were passing out thermite grenades for destruction of vital documents and equipment. Greenwood and Umeda were incapacitated and propped up in a corner of the bunker. Greenwood had his M16 weapon pointed at the door, and Umeda held his .45-caliber pistol across his chest, determined not to be taken alive. The low point of the battle had been reached.

At 10:00 A.M. Sp. 5th Class Donald Childs, accompanied by LLDB medical Sgt. Le Van Lai, grenaded and destroyed several of the captured bunkers on their own volition. Childs was finally driven off by NVA automatic weapons fire that killed his Vietnamese comrade. The unauthorized counterattack infuriated the team sergeant, Boody, who had clashed with Childs at an earlier camp, "I just knew he was going to get killed. He only had a few days to go, and I didn't want him to take any more chances." However, their gallantry had restored the fighting spirit of the camp. Childs left Vietnam six days later with a Silver Star and Boody's acknowledgment: "They did a spectacular job."

Ammunition pallets and supplies were parachuted to the beleaguered garrison by low-flying C-7A Caribou aircraft. The 513th and 522d MSF companies under Capt. Joseph F. Trimble from the 5th Mobile Strike Force at Nha Trang had airlanded at Ban Me Thuot the day before. The two companies were helicoptered to the west of Duc Lap during the morning and marched toward the camp through open fields and overgrown farmland. The soldiers passed decomposing bodies and broken pipe bombs under a blistering noon sun as they used NVA-breached wire lanes to enter Duc Lap. Minutes later Pleiku's 201st and 203d MSF companies arrived through the western gate.

All thoughts of a last stand vanished, and a hasty counterattack scheme was put into action. Sfc. Rudolph Nunez's Nung 513th MSF Company charged forward at 2:30 P.M., hitting the rest of the bunkers between the hills. At the same time, S. Sgt. Manuel Gonzales, Jr.'s, 522d MSF Company, composed of Rhade, Raglai, and Jarai Montagnards, counterattacked directly up the NVA-occupied northern hill. The newly arrived Pleiku companies clambered out of the trenches with them as 1st Lt. Norman E. Baldwin yelled, "Let's go! Over the top!"

Thick black smoke clung to the hill and dusted the charging soldiers with a fine grainy powder. The hill itself was a smoldering heap of upturned earth and wreckage, pockmarked by bomb craters, and littered with a tangle of twisted metal, wrecked sandbags, coiled barbed wire, unexploded ordnance, and milky plastic globs from napalm explosions clinging to the scorched earth.

The line wavered as the mixed companies came under machine gun fire, but Nunez kept his Nungs moving forward. Lieutenant Baldwin led his 201st Company through the middle gate and up the hillside. S. Sgt. Leslie L. Brucker, Jr., a medic in the same unit, rushed forward firing and yelling for people to follow him. He was closely followed by the others as they scrambled for the peak. Suddenly the North Vietnamese opened up from the rear, and Baldwin was hit in the shoulder by a round that exited low in his back. He kneeled over to Sfc. Philbert B. Arellano and muttered, "Arellano, I'm dying. I've had it." Arellano dragged him over the ridge away from the direction of fire and shouted for medical assistance.

S. Sgt. Brucker was near the body of Sp. 5th Class Forestal A. Stevens, a platoon leader in the 522d MSF Company who had been the first man killed on the hill when he had rushed a bunker. Brucker raced through a fusillade of automatic weapons fire and helped Arellano carry the wounded lieutenant to safer ground. Brucker checked S. Sgt. Robert A. Skinner, the medic of 513th MSF Company, who had been seriously wounded trying to help Arellano on the fire-swept slope, and ran back for morphine. Brucker was killed as he started back uphill. Arellano desperately broke open his albumin can and tried to insert the needle into Baldwin's veins, but they had already collapsed. There was no pulse; he realized the lieutenant had died.

After two hours of hard fighting, the four companies had become hopelessly intermingled as they pressed forward against bitter resistance. Moreover, several elements had become isolated as Captain Trimble led his men around the base of the hill to clear out the lower bunkers. Several more Special Forces leaders had been seriously wounded, including Sergeant First Class Nunez. Sfc. Denver G. Minton, a platoon leader of the 201st MSF Company, managed to lead a small group of Montagnards up the western side of the northern hill. From there they initiated flanking fire down the NVA-held trenchline and bunker complexes on the eastern slope, although Minton was wounded directing his troops.

The 522d Montagnard commander, Y-Gaul Nie, yelled at his men to move up. Running forward along the top of the trenchline, he fired his M16 at the fleeing North Vietnamese until he was killed by a grenade heaved back in his direction. Later the Special Forces found out that the gallant Montagnard officer, the son of an assistant province chief in Ban Me Thuot, was a high-ranking FULRO official.

Meanwhile, Captain Trimble and the 522d MSF Company, spearheaded by Staff Sergeants Gonzales and Arnulfo Estrada, had pushed two-thirds of the way around the base of the hill and held positions that cut off all North Vietnamese escape from the camp. M. Sgt. Donald E. Beebe of the 203d MSF Company reached Minton's position with more Montagnards and sent for reinforcements. Sp. 4th Class Edward L. Woody and Sfc. James C. Cooper led the 513th

MSF Company in a frenzied downslope charge that spilled into some of the last NVA-held trenches. Woody had leaped out of a crater on the main slope and thought he was being closely followed by Chinese Nungs. He reached a bunker only to find himself alone facing several North Vietnamese infantrymen. Before the startled defenders could open fire, he killed them with one blast of the shotgun he always carried as a medic (to "keep people's heads down when I work on somebody").

S. Sgt. John L. Maketa, a platoon leader in the 522d Company, joined up with remnants of the 201st Company under Sergeant First Class Minton and made the final charge down the eastern slope on top of the remaining defenses. Sp. 5th Class Paul R. Severson, another medic of the 201st, reached the trenchworks slightly ahead of the others and was killed in hand-to-hand combat with a squad of North Vietnamese. Sgt. Walter M. Hetzler, the medic of the 522d, furiously fired into the NVA around Severson's body, killing all of them. The battle sputtered out as the North Vietnamese fell back in disorder and scrambled to get out through the eastern wire. The retreating NVA were mowed down by concentrated Special Forces weapons fire directed from the newly gained hilltop.

By late evening the North Vietnamese had either been pushed out of the camp or killed, after five bloody hours contesting the northern hill. No prisoners were taken. The CIDG, nervous over several early encounters with bypassed snipers, simply shot any wounded as they advanced. Duc Lap had been a salutary Special Forces victory, achieved entirely by internal Special Forces mobile strike force response without outside assistance.[14]

4. Trouble in Special Forces

Many senior Army commanders were adamantly opposed to Special Forces, primarily because they did not understand its purposes or functions. In fact, Special Forces leaders throughout the Army were continually called upon to justify their very existence. General Abrams's dissatisfaction with Special Forces was probably grounded in a distaste for all unconventional military operations. This displeasure was aggravated in Vietnam by perceived laxity in Special Forces discipline and appearance.

A-Detachment troops were used to working hard and took considerable liberties in playing hard. Many Special Forces personnel in remote forts felt abandoned by higher headquarters, a feeling intensified by haphazard mail delivery, nondelivery of movies or recreational gear, and a slow and sometimes unresponsive decorations system. They ignored reveille and PT (physical training) schedules, wore whatever uniforms they chose, and displayed a marked absence of military courtesy toward staff officers and visiting officials.

Although the Special Forces trooper was considerably older and more mature than the average soldier, his lifestyle often added to the negative impression at MACV level. MACV staff officers carped constantly about Special Forces excessive drinking, overt living arrangements with local women, avoidance of military formations, and other practices not tolerated in conventional Army units. Perhaps most discomfiting to these staid Army fundamentalists were the "outlandish uniforms": tiger-striped fatigues minus nametags and rank insignias, replete with scarves, Montagnard beads, and other native trappings. While some of these distinctive items were actually required for battlefield identification among CIDG components, the combination was practically guaranteed to irritate the most placid conventional line officer.

Col. Robert B. "Bob" Rheault assumed command of the 5th Special Forces Group on 29 May 1969. A 1946 graduate of the U.S. Military Academy, he had been assigned to the 10th Special Forces Group at Bad Tölz, Germany, in 1958–59. Rheault proved himself one of the most dynamic, well-respected Special Forces officers ever fielded. He completed the Special Warfare School in 1961 and commanded the 1st Special Forces Group on Okinawa immediately prior to his present duty. His tenure of command in Vietnam would be cut short by one of the most troubling incidents to rock both the Army and Special Forces establishments during the war.

In order to fulfill one of the major Special Forces missions in Vietnam, providing intelligence to MACV, a myriad of special operations had been established by the 5th Special Forces. One of the most secret was Project GAMMA, a unilateral, clandestine intelligence-collection operation targeted against NVA/VC base areas in Cambodia and the Cambodian government's complicity with NVA/VC forces. On 28 February 1968 Special Forces Detachment B-57 was relocated from Saigon to Nha Trang and on 1 April was officially designated as Project GAMMA headquarters.

The intelligence-collection personnel were integrated in the A-Detachments, using the cover of augmentation of civil affairs and psychological operations offices. Project GAMMA was authorized five collection teams, but in order to expand operations for better coverage of the border, the teams had been reduced to two men at some locations. This enabled Project GAMMA to establish four additional operational sites (for a total of nine). These personnel operated from Duc Co and Duc Lap in II CTZ; Bu Dop, Loc Ninh, Thien Ngon, and Duc Hue in III CTZ; and Moc Hoa and Chau Doc in IV CTZ.

Soon Project GAMMA was producing 65 percent of the information on NVA location and strengths in Cambodia and a full 75 percent of the information on NVA installations. On 27 October 1968 the BLACKBEARD collection plan was officially implemented. While Project GAMMA produced only 6 percent of the input to the BLACKBEARD program, that small contribution provided more than half of the total usable reports and valid information. Colonel Aaron had increased Project GAMMA levels from thirteen nets with fifty-two coded agents to seventeen nets and ninety-eight coded agents. On 11 December the principal MACV intelligence officer, Maj. Gen. Phillip B. Davidson, Jr., congratulated Colonel Aaron on the fact that GAMMA covered a full 90 percent of the BLACKBEARD border target areas and submitted a very high percentage of the intelligence assessments received by his staff.[15]

By early 1969 Maj. David E. Crew's Detachment B-57 Project GAMMA had developed into the finest and most productive intelligence-collection operation the United States had in Southeast Asia. Much of the success resulted from the fact that its indigenous agents served an intelligence-gathering network that operated without South Vietnamese awareness. At the time, some of B-57's most important informational sources began to disappear, and it was obvious that the intelligence net had been compromised. The B-57 operations officer, Capt. Budge E. Williams, was very concerned about the jeopardy that threatened the entire GAMMA program.

Capt. Leland L. Brumley was the Special Forces chief of counterintelligence and reported directly to Maj. Thomas C. Middleton, the 5th Special Forces Group intelligence officer. Captain Brumley coordinated with B-57, but his main job was uncovering suspected double-dealing by the LLDB. Brumley's assistant was Chief Warrant Officer Edward M. Boyle. Although serious graft and corruption were almost hallmarks of the LLDB command, they were finding grimmer evidence. The highest levels of the LLDB were involved in active weapons and medical supply sales to the North Vietnamese Army and were murdering their own troops if threatened with exposure. About the time Brumley was fitting all the pieces together, his contacts also began drying up. He joined the search for the obvious leak.[16]

In the spring of 1969, a reconnaissance unit, operating in classified territory, discovered a roll of film and other documents in a base area. The roll of film contained a photograph of agent Thai Khac Chuyen meeting with several North Vietnamese intelligence officers. Sgt. Alvin L. Smith, Jr., who used this agent, first identified Mr. Chuyen in the picture. Sergeant Smith's team leader was Capt. Robert F. Marasco. Mr. Chuyen was returned from the field, arrested, and flown to Nha Trang for interrogation. Polygraph tests indicated that Mr. Chuyen was lying when he denied that he had compromised any security matters, also when he denied that he was working for the Viet Cong.

Various means of dealing with Mr. Chuyen were discussed, including the possibility of killing him. The 5th Special Forces Group executive officer, Lt. Col. Kenneth B. Facey, strongly opposed this option. No final decision was made, but the B-57 commander, Major Crew, and his operations officer Williams, went to CIA headquarters in Saigon. The officers returned and reported that the CIA official had told them that "elimination" of Mr. Chuyen "might be the best course of action."[17]

In the meanwhile Mr. Chuyen had undergone ten days of interrogation and solitary confinement. According to Captain Marasco, Chuyen was drugged with morphine and rendered unconscious on 20 June 1969. He was carried to an outboard motorboat, which sailed into Nha Trang Bay, where Chuyen was struck on the head to draw blood, shot twice in the head, weighted with chains and tire rims, and dumped into shark-infested waters. In spite of intensive dredging by the Navy coastal minesweeper USS *Woodpecker* (MSC-209), no body was ever found. A cover story was developed and received approval from Colonel Rheault. The cover story basically related that Chuyen had been sent on a "one-way mission" to "test his loyalty."

The cover story began to unravel when Sergeant Smith, concerned that he knew too much and was in personal danger, sought sanctuary with the Central Intelligence Agency in the Nha Trang CIA office. There he related that Mr. Chuyen had been executed; Smith successfully passed a lie detector test. General Abrams, a staunch opponent of Special Forces, was enraged that Rheault had given him the same cover story; he ordered Rheault, Smith, and six officers (Crew, Middleton, Marasco, Brumley, Williams, and Boyle) arrested after a brief investigation. All were charged with premeditated murder in the summary execution of a Vietnamese national and jailed immediately, although the charges against Boyle and Smith were held in abeyance pending the disposition of the charges against the remaining defendants.

The case received widespread publicity and caused a public furor in defense of the accused Special Forces personnel. Most Americans were keenly aware of the exemplary reputation of the Special Forces as an elite fighting force, and many citizens believed Rheault and his men were being victimized in the understandable disposal of a double agent. The resulting uproar swept through the political community and military establishment and boomeranged directly against General Abrams.

On 29 September 1969 Secretary of the Army Stanley Resor announced in a brief statement that the CIA, "though not directly involved in the alleged incident," had refused to make any of its personnel available as witnesses ("in the interest of national security"), thereby making a fair trial impossible, and that all charges had been dropped. Colonel Rheault immediately requested and received retirement. Rheault stated, "The charges should have been dropped because to conduct the trial would have been dangerous and damaging. It would also have been a travesty of justice to try dedicated soldiers for doing their job, carrying out their mission, and protecting the lives of men entrusted to them in a wartime situation."[18]

The incident affected Army Special Forces units worldwide. The 63d U.S. Army Reserve Command in Los Angeles, California, reported:

Men of our Special Forces (Green Berets) had a difficult time following the disclosure of the sacking of the commanding Beret colonel in Viet Nam following an incident which saw his alleged complicity in the murder of a Vietnamese. Local press tried to interview our men, but they were told to state each time "no comment" as they obviously had no knowledge of the affair.[19]

In addition to the Article 32 investigation, General Abrams had taken another step aimed at destroying Special Forces effectiveness.

On 21 July 1969 he had appointed Col. Alexander Lemberes, a non-parachutist and non-Special Forces officer, as the commander of the 5th Special Forces Group. When Cmd. Sgt.-Maj. Myron J. Bowser saw Lemberes don the green beret, Bowser angrily told Lemberes to take it off until he became qualified. Colonel Lemberes attempted to skirt actual American airborne training requirements by going to the LLDB training center at Dong Ba Thin and making three jumps from a helicopter. He suffered a broken leg on the third jump in an accident that many suspected had been deliberately rigged by Special Forces personnel.

Colonel Lemberes fraudulently awarded himself the parachute badge, but by this time even General Westmoreland, now the Army Chief of Staff, had had enough of Abrams's anti-Special Forces vendetta. Since Lemberes's injury temporarily prohibited field command, he was ordered replaced. On 31 August 1969 Col. Michael "Iron Mike" Daniel Healy, an outstanding infantry officer with a solid Special Forces background, assumed command of the 5th Special Forces Group. The Special Forces had weathered a severe crisis of confidence, and Colonel Healy's inspired leadership was desperately needed to rekindle group morale.[20]

Notes

1. MACV Directive 10-11 and MACV/JGS Combined Campaign Plan AB-144.

2. Company A, 5th Special Forces Group, *Field Grade Officers End of Tour After Action Report*, Lt. Col. Robert M. Campbell, dtd 25 June 1969.

3. Casualties in the 31 July 1968 contact were KIA: 1 LLDB, 33 CIDG, 1 interpreter; MIA: 4 CIDG; WIA: 2 Special Forces, 34 CIDG. Viet Cong losses were posted as 5 killed. Company A, 5th Special Forces Group, Ltr, Subject: Analysis of the Ben Soi-Trang Sup contact of 31 July 1968, dtd 6 August 1968.

4. Detachment B-32, *Field Grade Officer Debriefing Report*, Lt. Col. Harry S. Hilling, Jr., 13 August 1969.

5. Actual costs in 1968 were as follows: initial issue equipment, U.S. $81.67, CIDG $22.67; M16 rifle, U.S. $124.00, CIDG $124.00; daily base pay, U.S. $4.59, CIDG $.55; daily parachute pay (if applicable), U.S. $1.83, CIDG $.29; daily combat pay, U.S. $2.16, CIDG $.29; daily cost of living, U.S. $.30 (foreign duty pay), CIDG $.38; patrol ration, U.S. $3.90, CIDG $1.30.

6. 5th Special Forces Group AVGB-DCO, *After Action Report*, 1969 (report by Lt. Col. Daniel F. Schungel).

7. Thuong Duc casualties from 28 September to 19 October 1968 were KIA: 21 CIDG, 8 RF/PF; WIA: 9 Special Forces, 32 CIDG, 6 RF/PF. NVA losses in direct camp attacks were counted at 68 dead. Detachment A-109, *After Action Report*, dtd 20 October 1968.

8. Casualties at Tien Phuoc from 23 February to 24 March 1969 were KIA: 1 Special Forces, 54 CIDG, 1 ARVN, 30 civilians; MIA: 1 CIDG; WIA: 12 Special Forces, 3 LLDB, 1 U.S. Navy, 136 CIDG, 13 ARVN, 60 civilians. Detachment A-102, *After Action Report*, dtd 21 April 1969.

9. Loc Ninh casualties were KIA: 4 CIDG; WIA: 1 Special Forces, 1 LLDB, 24 CIDG. NVA losses were reported as 61 confirmed dead. Detachment A-331, *After Action Report*, dtd 1 September 1968.

10. Casualties in the September Katum attack were KIA: 14 CIDG, 1 civilian; WIA: 17 CIDG. NVA losses were 61 confirmed dead and 10 prisoners, 6 of whom were wounded. Detachment A-322, *Penetration After Action Report*, dtd 10 October 1968.

11. Casualties in the Thien Ngon attack were KIA: 5 CIDG; WIA: 4 Special Forces, 8 CIDG. The NVA losses were 140 dead and 3 captured. Detachment A-323, *After Action Report*, dtd 12 October 1968.

12. On 31 July 1968 Duc Lap contained 10 Special Forces, 11 LLDB, and 635 CIDG soldiers in the 561st–564th CIDG companies. Weapons included

two 105mm howitzers, four 81mm mortars, one 4.2-inch mortar, and two 106mm recoilless rifles.

13. Duc Lap after action interview of Sgt. James Alward, Tape V, Side B, point 61.

14. Casualties in the Duc Lap battle were KIA: 6 Special Forces, 1 LLDB, 37 CIDG, 20 civilians; MIA: 9 CIDG; WIA: 13 Special Forces, 7 LLDB, 80 CIDG. NVA losses were 303 by body count, and probably much higher. 5th. Special Forces Group, *Combat After Action Interview Report*, dtd 27 November 1968.

15. DA Form 638, Recommendation for Award for Meritorious Achievement and related papers, dtd 7 April 1969, concerning the Distinguished Service Medal for Colonel Aaron, and MACJ212-1 Ltr, dtd 11 December 1968.

16. John S. Berry, *Those Gallant Men*, (Novato, Calif.: Presidio Press, 1984), p. 102.

17. The CIA official was later approached by Army Criminal Investigation Division (CID) officers who asked him for a signed statement verifying that he had given such advice, but the official, after checking with his superiors, told them that he could not sign the statement. Later, however, when the official was asked by a CID agent in the presence of the CIA chief in Saigon and a representative from the staff of the MACV commander, General Abrams, if he indeed offered such advice, he responded affirmatively. Homer Bigart, "How Beret Affair Unfolded," *The New York Times*, 6 October 1969.

18. *The New York Times*, 10 November 1969.

19. 63d U.S. Army Reserve Command, *Annual Historical Supplement*, dtd 31 December 1969.

20. Col. Michael D. Healy had entered the Army in June 1945 as an enlisted man and was commissioned on 9 December 1946. He served with the 4th Ranger Infantry Company and the 187th Airborne Infantry Regiment in the Korean War. In 1953 he volunteered for the newly formed 77th Special Forces Group where he served as operational detachment commander, operations officer, and instructor in guerrilla warfare. He attended the U.S. Marine Corps school at Quantico, Virginia, and was assigned to the European-based 10th Special Forces Group in January 1957. He was assigned to U.S. Army Special Forces (Provisional) as senior advisor to the 77th LLDB Group and performed with distinction in Saigon during the 1 November 1963 coup d'état. In June 1966 he returned to Vietnam and commanded the 4th Battalion, 503d Infantry, of the 173d Airborne Brigade, for thirty consecutive months. He was in Vietnam on his third voluntary tour and had just returned the 1st Brigade of the 9th Infantry Division to Hawaii when recalled to take over the 5th Special Forces Group. In Vietnam, Col. Healy was also known as "Blind Mike" in reference to his glasses.

CHAPTER 11

SPECIAL RECONNAISSANCE

1. Project DELTA

While most A-Detachments were committed to manning static defenses and training natives in local defense, the Special Forces also sought ways to strike deep into uncontrolled territory to seek out Viet Cong formations and their sources of supply. On 15 May 1964 a select number of Vietnamese and CIDG warriors under Special Forces leadership began classified long-range patrolling under the codeword LEAPING LENA. This project provided the groundwork for the formation of a combined American–South Vietnamese special reconnaissance unit capable of conducting the most hazardous and critical missions inside the country as required by MACV and the Vietnamese Joint General Staff. Organized as Project DELTA in October 1964, Detachment B-52 was created to provide a control headquarters during June 1965.

During the war, Detachment B-52 ranged throughout South Vietnam. The unit conducted secret, long-range reconnaissance into VC sanctuaries, collected intelligence for tactical or strategic exploitation, planned and directed airstrikes on normally inaccessible targets, made bomb assessment surveys in enemy-controlled areas, used reconnaissance-in-force missions against concealed NVA/VC positions, executed hunter-killer missions at night by employing airborne and starlite sniperscopes, recovered allied prisoners, captured NVA or VC personnel for intelligence purposes, rescued downed aircraft crews, employed wiretap methods on NVA/VC communications lines, mined transportation routes, misled enemy counterintelligence with decep-

194

tion missions or dummy infiltrations, channeled NVA/VC personnel into targeted zones with the assistance of harassing gas and smoke agents, performed psychological warfare operations, flew airborne personnel detector missions, and conducted extensive photo reconnaissance, which included the processing, printing, interpretation, and production of imagery intelligence reports.

In September 1965 Detachment B-52 began a training program for its own replacements in patrol techniques. A year later, on 15 September 1966, Detachment B-52 established the MACV Recondo School based on this program, after General Westmoreland directed the 5th Special Forces Group to train personnel for Army long-range reconnaissance patrol (LRRP) units. The school instructed selected allied personnel throughout the war.

By 1965 Project DELTA fielded only six combined Reconnaissance/Hunter-Killer teams, each containing eight carefully selected LLDB and two Special Forces members. These were backed up by the three-company South Vietnamese 91st Airborne Ranger Battalion, activated during November 1964 under LLDB auspices, using CIDG recruits at Nha Trang. However, some early teams were entirely American or South Vietnamese. Project DELTA was even used as a camp reinforcement unit, exemplified by Major Beckwith's valiant relief expedition to Camp Plei Me in October, a function later performed by Mike Forces.

Project DELTA was radically altered and expanded in the next two years. Designed to gather operational intelligence, the majority of Project DELTA's information was collected by its own reconnaissance teams and roadrunners, organized into two distinct platoons. The Strike Recondo Platoon was organized into sixteen six-man reconnaissance teams, each composed of three Special Forces and three LLDB members. These reconnaissance teams were infiltrated into areas to collect information, capture prisoners, direct artillery and airstrikes, or lead Mike Forces to targets of opportunity. Mission accomplishment was expected within five days, after which teams were exfiltrated at preselected points, debriefed, and the information submitted to the supported command.

The Roadrunner Platoon, with eight teams of four indigenous personnel, differed from reconnaissance teams in many ways. The roadrunner teams adopted the dress, equipment, and documentation of the NVA or VC forces present in the area. Cover stories were adopted to conform to the current NVA/VC situation. Since they deliberately and openly traveled along trails and through way stations and base areas, they were called "roadrunners." Continuous radio communication was maintained through the use of indigenous personnel in the same radio relay aircraft supporting the reconnaissance teams.

The recondo and roadrunner platoons were supported by intrinsic Project DELTA reaction and reinforcing units, which were held ready for swift deployment to destroy lucrative targets detected by the reconnaissance or roadrunner teams, conduct strengthened reconnaissance in force, or assist in emergency situations. The six-company Vietnamese 81st Airborne Ranger Battalion served as DELTA's largest reaction force. The battalion had been renumbered from the 91st after the Saigon regime had "purified" it entirely with ethnic Vietnamese. Normally, four of the battalion's light infantry companies were fielded with DELTA missions, while the other two remained in garrison under direct control of the LLDB high command.

Other specialized support was rendered by the CIDG mortar platoon, the crack Nung security element, and the Bomb Damage Assessment (BDA) Platoon that doubled as the project's Immediate Reaction Element. Since Project DELTA was mission oriented, it was usually placed under the operational control of a specific allied division for the duration of a given operation. If a battle absorbed all DELTA contingents, regular infantry battalions were sent from the headquarters exercising operational control of the mission.

Project DELTA maintained a permanent compound in Nha Trang at the same time that it manned a forward operating base on a combat operation. This required Detachment B-52 to have a large labor force of nearly 200 civilians, ranging from electricians and carpenters to attractive female clerks and nurses. Skilled workers were taken from the rear base labor force to the FOB because of the lack of craftsmen in forward locations.[1]

Project DELTA recon and roadrunner troops were usually inserted at twilight by four UH-1D helicopters escorted by two gunships. The command helicopter led the formation, followed by one insertion helicopter, two recovery helicopters, and two attack helicopters. While the latter maintained close station over the infiltration site, the command pilot kept the recovery helicopters and his own aircraft at a higher altitude.

The command pilot directed the insertion aircraft to the exact location as clarified by the accompanying recon platoon leader. In dense jungle the ground party often used ladders or they rappelled from the helicopter. The recovery helicopters were prepared to extract soldiers and aircrew in case the insertion helicopter accidentally crashed or was destroyed by hostile fire. Forward air control aircraft also orbited the area in case airstrikes were needed. The entire formation conducted deceptive landings either before or after the actual insertion.

Extraction procedures paralleled insertion, depending on the weather and combat situation. The forward air control aircraft arrived over the area first to locate the team's recognition panel. After the command helicopter made positive team identification by using predesignated codes, the ground personnel were lifted out.

The first intelligence-gathering missions were costly, since these tasks placed a premium on mastering difficult techniques, with little chance for error deep in Viet Cong territory. During Operation MASHER in the first month of 1966, the 1st Cavalry Division requested Project DELTA reconnaissance assistance in the jungled An Lao Valley of Binh Dinh Province. Major Charlie Beckwith's Detachment B-52 left Nha Trang in C-123 aircraft and landed at Bong Son on 26 January 1966. The schedule provided insufficient preparation prior to the commitment of the recondo teams. They were inserted into the operational area the very next evening, despite marginal weather. Operation 2-66 in the An Lao Valley was one of the worst disasters to befall Project DELTA in the Vietnam War.

Sfc. Henry A. Keating's Team Eskimo was composed of five Special Forces sergeants. In a skirmish with Viet Cong on the morning of 28 January, Staff Sergeant Dupuis suffered a head wound from grenade shrapnel. The team climbed a ridgeline overlooking the valley and radioed for extraction. The helicopter spent two hours unsuccessfully searching for the team in the drizzling rain. The aircraft returned after refueling, spotted Keating's panel, and dropped rope ladders to them in the high elephant grass.

Team Capitol, a six-man American team under Sfc. Frank R. Webber, Jr., scouted several trails on 28 January but was spotted by woodcutters. Webber led his men to higher ground where they spent the night. Heavy fog and rain hampered their difficult trek through the tropical underbrush, which became so thick at the base of a rock cliff that they were forced to crawl on their hands and knees. At noon on 29 January, the team reached a small clearing, assumed defensive positions, and prepared to discuss its next move. Suddenly, Viet Cong automatic rifle fire ripped through the foliage. Sfc. Jesse L. Hancock was killed instantly and S. Sgt. George A. Hoagland III collapsed on his back, mortally wounded. Both Webber and Sfc. Marlin C. Cook were also wounded in this initial volley of fire.

The surrounding jungle was so dense that no one knew where the firing was coming from. Cook had been hit in the stomach and back. Although paralyzed from the waist down, he returned fire into the shrubbery. Webber's lower arm was shattered, but he also fired into the foliage as S. Sgt. Charles F. Hiner ran over to Cook's position, took the radio from his backpack, and frantically called for assistance. S. Sgt. Donald L. Dotson was shot through the chest and killed while trying to move across the clearing.

Hiner managed to contact an aircraft, and the team emergency was relayed to the forward air controller. After spotting Hiner's red smoke grenade, the control aircraft departed to guide two helicopter gunships to the team position. After some initial confusion in relocating the shattered team, the helicopters were overhead and responded to Hiner's desperate pleas to make gun-runs on his own perimeter. Hiner was wounded, but the VC fire became sporadic. Webber crawled back from the edge of the clearing and dragged Cook with him to the rock where Hiner was. Minutes later Cook was killed by helicopters strafing through the middle of the clearing.

Hiner and Webber were the only team members still alive, and they were both faint from loss of blood. Hiner kept passing out over the radio, but he regained consciousness in time to hear that Lieutenant Holland's reaction team was working its way to them and needed signal smoke. Ten minutes later the rescue group reached them. Rope ladders were used to lift the two wounded sergeants and four bodies out of the jungle.

The third team, Roadrunner, was led by Sfc. Marcus Huston. They exchanged gunfire with Viet Cong near a stream and were evading uphill on 28 January, when they came under fire for the second time. Staff Sgt. Frank N. Badolati was hit in the upper left arm with such force that the arm was nearly severed. Sfc. Cecil J. Hodgson's rifle was blasted out of his hands. The other sergeants opened fire and provided covering fire as the team ran from the area. Badolati begged the team to leave him and save themselves. A tourniquet was applied to his arm and morphine was administered four times during the retreat. The team paused to radio a distress call near a rock ledge and was inadvertently split up by renewed fighting.

Huston and Staff Sergeant McKeith took Badolati with them, although he protested, encouraging them to continue without him. Badolati realized that his comrades would stop if he did, so he kept moving through sheer willpower. Finally, his wounds forced him to halt, and he told Huston, "Save yourselves." Huston and McKeith placed Badolati among the boulders near a mountain stream, where they prepared for a final stand. Badolati died during the next two hours. They put his body at a fork in the stream and continued moving until dark. The next morning, Huston and McKeith's panel was sighted by an L-19 aircraft, and the forward air controller diverted an extraction helicopter to them.

The other element under M. Sgt. Wiley W. Gray was involved in another firefight before they could reach the emergency pickup point. Gray heard S. Sgt. Ronald T. Terry yell that he had been hit and turned around to see him holding his side with both hands. Within seconds Terry was shot again and killed. Gray could not find Hodgson (later declared missing in action). Suddenly helicopter gunships appeared overhead, strafing the area as part of the Huston-McKeith extraction. The confusion enabled Gray to escape, and later that afternoon he was able to signal rescue helicopters with his flare pistol.[2]

Major Beckwith was wounded in his helicopter during the extractions and replaced. After Operation 2-66, Project DELTA was overhauled and conducted multiple reconnaissance missions across the Central Highlands throughout I and II CTZ. The next combat fatality did not occur until Operation 10-66 (9 August to 5 September 1966) while DELTA was under the operational control of the 196th Infantry Brigade in War Zone C. In that operation DELTA teams that had infiltrated from Song Be and Tay Ninh reconnoitered extensive trail networks entering the area from Cambodia. The Viet Cong were reluctant to engage the Special Forces, possibly from fear of airstrikes, but on the afternoon of 27 August, contact was lost with Team #2.

Maj. Robert E. Luttrell, commanding Detachment B-52, was aloft with the air relay pilot and spotted a red panel, smoke, and a signal mirror being flashed at them. Helicopters were dispatched to the scene, and medical Sgt. Timothy O'Connor dashed out under heavy fire to place seriously wounded patrol advisor Sgt. Johnny Varner in the pickup aircraft. O'Connor was wounded in the leg trying to reach Sgt. Eugene Moreau, who already appeared dead. An LLDB team member crawled into the helicopter from the other side, and they lifted off as automatic weapons fire cut across the landing zone. Shortly thereafter, another LLDB team member was spotted in the forest and taken out by McGuire rig. The 4th Company, 91st Airborne Ranger Battalion, arrived on the battlefield after dark and retrieved the bodies of Moreau and LLDB Corporal Mo. Although Operation 10-66 resulted in one Special Forces soldier killed and another four wounded, extensive DELTA-directed airstrike damage was inflicted on Viet Cong installations.[3]

Project DELTA returned to War Zone C in Operation 12-66 during late September, after vainly searching for a downed F4 Phantom crew near Cam Ranh Bay. Airstrikes were used to silence several VC base facilities. On 15 October the unit was dispatched to Khe Sanh in Operation 13-66 and found an extensive storage area just south of the DMZ near the Laotian border. Aerial bombing caused large secondary explosions and intense munitions fires. During the second phase of the operation, a patrol was destroyed by the North Vietnamese on 2 December 1966. Sgt. Irby Dyer III was killed, and the LLDB survivors last saw S. Sgt. Russell P. Bott attending to the wounded patrol leader, Sfc. Willie E. Stark, whom he refused to abandon even though they were surrounded and outnumbered.[4]

The next three operations (1-67 through 3-67) were cancelled by intensive training in Nha Trang. Project DELTA reentered the An Lao Valley under the 1st Cavalry Division in Operation 4-67. Commencing 4 March 1967, fifty-two reconnaissance missions verified slight Viet Cong presence, since bivouac and way stations had fallen into disuse and trail activity was light.

Project DELTA entered the A Shau Valley west of Hue on 10 April 1967 during Operation 5-67. Forty-eight patrols gained vast intelligence value at the cost of five wounded Special Forces members. The sweeps proved that the NVA were using the valley as a major infiltration corridor, had linked Route 922 from Laos to other roads, and were using vehicular convoys at night. DELTA elements directed hundreds of airstrikes into the area and substantially reduced the North Vietnamese traffic.

The A Shau intrusion was also harrowing. On the afternoon of 14 May, Staff Sergeant Gleason's Reconnaissance Team #1 was being landed when the helicopter was blasted by automatic weapons fire, causing it to lose all oil pressure. The pilot crash-landed, and everyone formed a defensive circle around the downed aircraft. One NVA machine gun was silenced, and after dark another helicopter lifted out the crewmen and three LLDB soldiers. Staff Sergeants Gleason and Brierley remained with an LLDB soldier and were joined by a DELTA sergeant who had voluntarily left the recovery aircraft to make room for those taken out. A second helicopter trying to reach them struck the trees with its rotor and crashed only twenty yards away. The crew and another Special Forces sergeant joined the first group. All personnel were extracted under flarelight at 9:30 P.M., without further incident.[5]

Operations SAMURAI I to III extended Maj. Charles "Chuck" A. Allen's DELTA searches from the northern stretches to the A Shau Valley into Happy Valley, west of Da Nang, where further infiltration was discovered from 10 July through the end of October 1967. Elements overran an NVA aid station, capturing numerous documents and prisoners. In the Happy Valley area DELTA ranger, roadrunner, and recon forces fought a series of firefights with the *368B NVA Rocket Regiment,* which had been bombarding the Da Nang area.

From 27 November 1967 to 28 January 1968, Major Allen moved his unit into the Plei Trap Valley along the Laotian border of II CTZ for Operations SULTAN I and II. His teams confirmed that the *32d NVA Regiment* had moved into the area following the battle of Dak To. Project DELTA moved north again into the A Shau Valley for Operations SAMURAI IV and V, which lasted from 3 March until 20 May 1968. General Westmoreland ordered the unit to help interdict infiltration routes leading into Hue. Despite unfavorable weather and the first real jump in casualties, the Special Forces and LLDB rangers engaged the North Vietnamese in a series of deliberate confrontations.[6]

Operation ALAMO was conducted next in the III CTZ Song Be River area near Cambodia. Project DELTA was under control of the 5th ARVN Division. The lack of helicopters necessitated reducing the usual twelve reconnaissance teams operating at any one time to only six. Twenty-seven missions were conducted during a month of September patrolling that uncovered a large number of base sites, hospitals, ammunition stocks, and food caches. Project DELTA was responsible for the discovery of a number of high speed, bamboo-matted infiltration trails.

Project DELTA was displaced north on Operation WAR BON-
NET in the An Hoa vicinity but returned south to Binh Long Province
in III CTZ during Operation ARES on 16 November 1968. Eighty-
five missions identified a major rear service and supply area there.
On 29 March 1969 the unit was flown back into I CTZ and placed
under the control of the 101st Airborne Division (Airmobile). During
Operations CASS PARK I and II, followed by TROJAN HORSE I
and II, reconnaissance teams scoured the Vuong River Valley, An
Hoa basin, and northwestern fringes of the country. Captured documents enabled the 3d Marine Division to gain additional appraisals
of several regiments and battalions operating in its area.

During Operation CASS PARK II, Roadrunner Team #103 was
infiltrated southwest of An Hoa on 17 June 1969. Two days later they
spotted thirty NVA walking along a trail, followed by one 37mm
antiaircraft gun that was being pulled by two water buffaloes. Reconnaissance Team #1A had spotted something much prettier the day
before. Their final report stated:

181515H Vic[inity] coord[inates] Z0085002, tm [team] obsrd
[observed] a group of 12 VC moving NE, all were walking and
dressed the same as en[emy] mentioned before, all had wpns
[weapons] but no packs nor web gear. Approx[imately] in the
center of this group tm obsrd a Caucasian female. The Caucasian
female was dressed in white shirt, dark pants, with her shirt tucked
in her pants. She was without head gear. Her clothes were clean
and neat. Hair was strawberry blond, roughly shoulder length.
Smooth light skin. Weight approx 140 to 145 lbs, height 5'6",
large bust, female was not carrying anything. She was not under
duress. She seemed well fed and in good health.[7]

Project DELTA stayed in the north until 9 November 1969. During the last three weeks of December, Operation YELLOW RIBBON
verified lack of major NVA activity west of Pleiku within the previous
six months. Project DELTA undertook Operation SABER AND SPURS
on 11 February 1970 and was attached to another Special Forces unit
for the first time in detachment history. Working under Company A
at Bien Hoa, sixty-three missions confirmed that certain NVA rear
service units were still using northern portions of III CTZ but fled at

the sight of patrols. The same task was continued in Operation CAV-ALRY GLORY.

On 10 May 1970 Project DELTA commenced its last two operations in Vietnam, DELTA DAGGER I and II. Operationally controlled by the 101st Airborne Division (Airmobile), the unit swept through southwestern Quang Tri Province and adjacent Laotian border regions. There were no significant contacts or sightings after the end of May, and on 30 June Maj. George F. Aiken's Project DELTA ceased all tactical operations and returned to the rear base at Nha Trang. The personnel were reassigned and Detachment B-52 was deactivated on 31 July 1970.

Project DELTA was a very successful Special Forces long-range reconnaissance operation. The intelligence provided the identities of more than seventy NVA/VC units and enabled the capture of numerous supply caches, documents, and prisoners. It rendered vital information on enemy troop concentrations, infiltration networks, extent of fortifications, and lack of activity in areas planned for extensive allied search operations. The data were often gained in remote and largely inaccessible areas of the country, and were produced with minimal casualties.[8]

2. Projects OMEGA, SIGMA, and RAPID FIRE

Whereas Project DELTA operated country-wide under the direction of the MACV commander, as approved by the South Vietnamese Joint General Staff, other Special Forces reconnaissance projects were tailored for regional employment by the field force commanders. After General Westmoreland placed priority on DELTA utilization in the northern portion of South Vietnam, Projects OMEGA (Detachment B-50) and SIGMA (Detachment B-56) were created to give I and II Field Force Vietnam, respectively, a long-range patrol capability in remote areas of their corps tactical zones.

Organization of projects OMEGA and SIGMA was similar to that of Project DELTA, except for the composition of the reaction and reinforcing components. A regular ARVN ranger battalion was planned as attachment to each project, but Special Forces wanted nothing to do with the regular South Vietnamese military establishment. As a result, three Mike Force companies were assigned instead to each project to provide reinforcing capability.

The reconnaissance teams were identical to those of Project

DELTA, but there were only eight of them. Likewise, the four road-runner teams were composed of CIDG personnel infiltrated into Viet Cong–held territory, using members dressed in regional NVA/VC uniforms, armed with appropriate weapons, and carrying proper paperwork. The reinforcing Mike Force companies were composed of highly trained, airborne-qualified CIDG soldiers capable of operating anywhere in South Vietnam for limited periods. This was a marked departure from the standard CIDG forces, which were limited to "native environment" effectiveness within tribal homelands.[9]

Project OMEGA, located at Ban Me Thuot under I Field Force Vietnam, was authorized 9 Special Forces officers and 65 enlisted men, as well as 660 CIDG Sedang, Jeh, and Rhade Montagnard personnel. The unit was committed to combat on 11 September 1966 and was engaged in nine operations during its existence. Although Project OMEGA patrolled a rough area, total Special Forces casualties were six wounded in action (five on the first two operations). After Operations MARCH I and II in the Plei Trap Valley along the Cambodian border during the period from 8 July to 30 October 1967, Lt. Col. Mearlen G. La Mar's Detachment B-50 assets were transferred to MACV-SOG.

Project SIGMA was located at Camp Ho Ngoc Tao near Tu Duc, along Highway 1 between Saigon and Long Binh. Chinese were used for the 168-man camp defense company and one of the commando companies, while Cambodians were used for the roadrunner and reconnaissance elements and the other two commando companies. Detachment B-56 was under the operational control of II Field Force Vietnam and was first sent into combat during Operation GOLF on 11 September 1966. Project SIGMA performed fifteen operations in War Zones C and D before its assets were transferred to Project DANIEL BOONE on 1 November 1967.[10]

Sergeants Boyd W. Anderson and Michael R. Newbern were the first Detachment B-56 Special Forces members killed in action. The unfortunate action transpired when Team #5 was participating in Operation FONDULAC (12 to 25 October 1966). Survivors Thach Sa Van Dinh and Son-Nghinh related the incident. The team's presence in the area had been detected the evening before, but the two sergeants made the decision to elude the Viet Cong during the night. No situation report or request for extraction because of compromise was sent to the FOB. The team was ambushed on the morning of 22 October 1966 and quickly overwhelmed. Sergeant Anderson was hit in the leg and tried to crawl to the side. Staff Sergeant Newbern was wounded but sent out a distress call on the radio before he died. Anderson reached for the handset next but was killed before he could broadcast. Lt. Col. Richard D. Reish, B-56 commander, analyzed the episode as a fatal case of American overconfidence.[11]

On 1 November 1967 Projects OMEGA and SIGMA were transferred to MACV-SOG. Project RAPID FIRE (Provisional Detachment B-36) had been organized by Maj. James G. Gritz on 1 August 1967 to fill the gap in the strategic and tactical reconnaissance capabilities of II and III CTZ that would be created by the impending transfer. Detachments A-303 (Mobile Guerrilla Force 957) and A-304 (Mobile Guerrilla Force 966) were assigned under Gritz's command.[12]

Detachment B-36 (Provisional) was located at Long Hai with redesignated Detachments A-361 and A-362, an augmentation of twenty Army long-range patrol personnel, two Cambodian Mike Force companies, and one camp security company. Project RAPID FIRE initially contained ten reconnaissance teams and the two reaction companies. The special task force was committed to combat in War Zone C on 5 September 1967 in Operation RAPID FIRE I. The last operation, RAPID FIRE IX, conducted in Hau Nghia Province, ended on 23 May 1968, when Detachment B-36 was released from provisional status and officially activated to command the 3d Mobile Strike Force Command.[13]

3. Strategic Projects and Missions

The Military Assistance Command Vietnam Studies and Observation Group (MACV-SOG) executed special operations and missions under the guise of a MACV staff agency charged with the preparation of various Vietnam studies. In actuality, MACV-SOG was a joint service high command unconventional warfare task force engaged in highly classified operations throughout Southeast Asia. MACV-SOG's area of responsibility included Burma, Cambodia, Laos, North and South Vietnam, and the provinces of Yunnan, Kwangsi, Kwangtung, and Hainan Island in China. Activated on 24 January 1964, the organization was a MACV subordinate command and not a Special Forces unit. The 5th Special Forces Group funneled required personnel into MACV-SOG through the group Special Operations Augmentation, making it appear that the men were assigned to the group when, in fact, they were under secret orders posting them to MACV-SOG.[14]

Cross-border reconnaissance and intelligence operations into Laos were commenced by mixed Special Forces and LLDB teams under Project SHINING BRASS in September 1965. As U.S. combat commitment to Vietnam increased, participating elements upgraded the intensity of operations by emplacing antipersonnel devices, engaging NVA or Pathet Lao personnel in open combat, performing B-52 bomb damage assessment, and controlling airstrikes. The project, aimed at countering North Vietnamese infiltration through Laos into South Vietnam, became the largest and most important Special Forces strategic reconnaissance and interdiction campaign in Southeast Asia. SHINING BRASS was renamed PRAIRIE FIRE in 1968, and finally PHU DUNG on 8 April 1971.[15]

On 26 January 1967 General Westmoreland advanced a plan for further expansion of Special Forces PRAIRIE FIRE operations to include deep penetrations of long duration in Laos for the purpose of developing a resistance movement within certain ethnic groups. Ambassador Henry Cabot Lodge replied that a clear assessment of political implications could not be made but agreed to further study. In May, Lodge was succeeded by Ellsworth Bunker, and action on the expanded plan for PRAIRIE FIRE "stalled out." While PRAIRIE FIRE operations continued until the end of the Second Indochina War, Special Forces was prohibited by the Congressional Cooper-Church Amendment from crossing into Laos on such missions after April 1971.[16]

As early as 1963, Special Forces identified Cambodia as a likely Viet Cong sanctuary and source of supply, and reported that the South Vietnamese border controls were ineffective in stopping such VC use. Since the Joint Chiefs of Staff had put tight restrictions against employment of American personnel in Cambodia, the Special Forces began building camps along the frontier. Throughout the Second Indochina War, nearly all Special Forces border surveillance efforts were directed against Cambodia, and only half a dozen camps faced Laos. On 3 May 1965 Cambodia severed diplomatic relations with the United States, and battlefield events later in the year verified active North Vietnamese military use of the country.

The Joint Chiefs of Staff authorized General Westmoreland to develop a cross-border reconnaissance capability using Special Forces on 27 June 1966, and the undertaking was coded Project DANIEL BOONE. Permission was not granted to use these teams until May 1967, and then only for the small section of the Cambodian tri-border area above the Se San River. The DANIEL BOONE operations were expanded in October 1967 to cover Cambodia's border facing Vietnam to a depth of twenty, and later thirty, kilometers, which was divided into two zones. Zone Alpha stretched approximately from Snuol north to Laos, Zone Bravo from Snuol to the Gulf of Thailand. However, missions in the latter zone required Presidential approval on a case-by-case basis.[17]

In many cases vital MACV-SOG information was simply not acted upon. Throughout latter 1967 the Special Forces DANIEL BOONE teams detected a menacing North Vietnamese and Viet Cong buildup in such areas as the "Fish Hook." These later proved to be key NVA/VC staging bases for the Tet-68 offensive, but General Westmoreland's urgent requests to launch spoiling attacks into the detected bastions had been denied. The success of this strategic reconnaissance effort was not capitalized upon.

Project DANIEL BOONE was renamed SALEM HOUSE, and in December 1968 mission restrictions were finally relaxed. The Cambodian border region was divided into three zones as Zone Bravo was split in two. The new zone, Charlie, or Central Salem House, extended from Snuol to the town of Prey Veng, while Bravo, or Southern Salem House, now extended from there to the Gulf of Thailand. Special Forces received permission to scour Zones Alpha, or Northern Salem House (nicknamed the "Wasteland"), which extended as far west as Kratie and Stung Treng, and Charlie, without prior Washington approval. Zone Bravo excursions required Presidential approval, which Nixon readily granted. Although the Air Interdiction Zone (AIZ), nicknamed FREEDOM DEAL, later gave Special Forces maneuver area behind Alpha as far as Kompong Thom city, helicopter range limited such missions. Project SALEM HOUSE was renamed THOT NOT on 8 April 1971.[18]

In addition to Projects SALEM HOUSE and PRAIRIE FIRE, the Special Forces sent teams north of the international demarcation line inside the western DMZ as part of Project NICKEL STEEL. Formerly, the Special Forces spike teams that were sent into the DMZ under III Marine Amphibious Force authority were called DOUBLE CROSS operations. There were also other projects throughout MACV-

SOG jurisdictional regions that required Special Forces assistance, such as BRIGHT LIGHT teams. These teams performed specific prisoner and evader and/or escapee-recovery missions.

Although most MACV-SOG launch sites were emplaced in existing Special Forces camps along the South Vietnamese border, other sites were also used in Special Forces operations. For example, the launch site at Nakhon Phanom, Thailand, was used as an alternate PRAIRIE FIRE jumping-off point after September 1967. The training centers at Kham Duc and Long Thanh (Detachment B-53) trained selected Special Forces and indigenous personnel in commando tactics. While natives were chosen for their absolute loyalty and excellent jungle-fighting abilities, several security and reaction companies were simply hired from the CIDG Mike Forces.

The eight operational commands within MACV-SOG were known as studies groups to maintain their cover on organizational charts. Most Special Forces personnel served in the Ground Studies Group (SOG 35), Airborne Studies Group (SOG 36), or Training Studies Group (SOG 38). Some were assigned to other elements, such as the Recovery Studies Division (SOG 80), which was established to implement Joint Recovery Task Force requirements searching for crashed aircraft and missing personnel.

The Ground Studies Group was part of the Command and Control Detachment, located at Da Nang. The detachment controlled the Kham Duc Training Center and four forward operating bases. FOB-1 at Phu Bai was specifically oriented toward PRAIRIE FIRE, while FOB-2 at Kontum handled both PRAIRIE FIRE and DANIEL BOONE missions. Each base had fifteen Reconnaissance Teams (known as Spike Teams) and contained a reaction force, an exploitation battalion of four SLAM (Search-Location-Annihilation-Monitors) companies composed of Hatchet Force (later Hornet Force) platoons. Multiplatoon forces short of SLAM company size were known as Havoc Forces. FOB-3 at Khe Sanh and FOB-4 at Da Nang provided another seventeen Spike Teams each for all MACV-SOG missions and projects.[19]

On 1 November 1967 MACV-SOG absorbed Projects OMEGA and SIGMA and reorganized. In lieu of the four FOBs, the Ground Studies Group (SOG 35) now included Command and Control North at Da Nang for NICKEL STEEL and PRAIRIE FIRE areas of operation, Command and Control Central at Kontum for PRAIRIE FIRE and Zone Alpha DANIEL BOONE, and Command and Control South at Ban Me Thuot primarily for Zone Bravo and Charlie DANIEL BOONE missions.

MACV-SOG Special Forces reconnaissance team missions normally included linear, area, point, and route reconnaissance; road, trail, and river watch; route mining, interdiction, and ambush; capture of prisoners; bomb damage assessment; ground photography; wiretap; direction of artillery and airstrikes against targets of opportunity; limited direct ground combat as part of a mission; crash site inspection; and allied prisoner recovery. Each team contained three Special Forces and nine indigenous special commandos and was generally supported by four helicopters, four helicopter gunships, one A-1E aircraft (as required), and one forward air controller aircraft.

MACV-SOG Special Forces exploitation, or hatchet, forces were capable of rapid engagement of reconnaissance-team-produced targets by direct ground combat. Tailored elements ranging from one to three platoons could perform reconnaissance-in-force, route interdiction, ambushes and raids, security of temporary patrol bases to support reconnaissance teams, short-term area denial, cache destruction, and allied prisoner recovery.

The Airborne Studies Group (SOG 36) was responsible for agent operations that complemented other cross-border intelligence and psychological warfare programs. These included the "Earth Angels," teams dressed in NVA uniforms composed of North Vietnamese ralliers; "Strata" teams, which translated into short-term roadwatch and target acquisition teams; "Pike Hill" Cambodian intelligence collection teams dressed in Khmer Rouge uniforms; "Oodles" clandestine notional agents in North Vietnam; "Borden" diversionary NVA agents; "Cedar Walk" Cambodian unconventional warfare teams; and "Singleton" single agents.

Special Forces missions in MACV-SOG were unusually hazardous. For example, a number of night HALO (High-Altitude, Low-Opening) parachute jumps were made into remote areas. Sometimes missions were too successful. In one program, teams inserted faulty and rigged ammunition into the North Vietnamese munitions system on a selected basis throughout Cambodia, Laos, and Vietnam. The program, labeled ELDEST SON, ITALIAN GREEN, and, later, POLE BEAN, was a tremendous success. The contaminated ammunition exploded firing rifles, killed mortar crews, jammed machine guns, and was beginning to affect North Vietnamese morale and to cause them to lose faith in their bullets and shells. On 23 February 1970 the Joint Chiefs of Staff decided that the program should be stopped and ordered MACV-SOG to cease the operations.

The MACV-SOG missions remained highly dangerous. On the morning of 24 April 1969 a Command and Control South hatchet platoon led by Capt. Paul R. Cahill was air assaulted into Cambodia by four helicopters. The platoon contained three Special Forces members and twenty-five Montagnard special commandos. Immediately after leaving the landing zone, the platoon was hit by concentrated automatic weapons fire while approaching its initial rallying point. Sfc. Jerry M. "Mad Dog" Shriver led several commandos in a charge on the machine gun bunkers in the woodline, which were protected by entrenched NVA soldiers.

Captain Cahill and the platoon medical aidman, Sgt. Ernest C. Jamison, were forced to take cover in a bomb crater. Cahill maintained radio contact with Shriver after he entered the forest until transmissions ceased; Shriver was never seen again. Jamison jumped out to retrieve one of the wounded Montagnards who had fallen in the charge. The medic reached the soldier but was almost torn apart by concentrated machine gun fire. At that moment Cahill was wounded in the right eye, which resulted in his total blindness for the next thirty minutes. The platoon radioman, Y-Sum Nie, desperately radioed for immediate extraction.

Maj. Benjamin T. Kapp, Jr., was in the command helicopter and could see the platoon pinned down across the broken ground and rims of bomb craters. North Vietnamese machine guns were periodically firing into the bodies in front of their position and covering the open ground with grazing fire. The assistant platoon leader, 1st Lt. Gregory M. Harrigan, reported within minutes that half the platoon was killed or wounded. Harrigan himself was killed forty-five minutes later.

Helicopter gunships and A-1E aircraft constantly bombed and rocketed the NVA defenses. The heavy ground fire peppered the aircraft in return, wounding one door gunner during low-level strafing. Ten airstrikes and over 1,500 helicopter rockets were used in an effort to force the NVA to break contact. Several attempts to lift out survivors had to be aborted. First Lt. Walter L. Marcantel, the third in command, tried to disengage from the bunkerline. He called for napalm only ten yards from his frontline, and both he and his nine remaining commandos were burned by splashing napalm from the explosions.

After seven hours of continuous fighting, three helicopters dashed in and pulled out fifteen wounded troops. As the aircraft lifted off, several crewmen saw a panel being waved from a bomb crater. A fourth helicopter set down, and Lt. Daniel Hall twice raced over to the bomb hole. On the first trip he recovered the badly wounded radio operator, and on the second trip he dragged Harrigan's body back to the helicopter. The aircraft was being buffeted by shellfire and took off immediately afterwards. No further MACV-SOG insertions were made into the NVA stronghold. Jamison was declared dead and Shriver missing in action by later Army board proceedings.[20]

The dangers inherent in MACV-SOG's cross-border raids matched the high stakes involved. For every insertion like Cahill's that was detected and stopped, dozens of other commando teams safely slipped past NVA lines to strike a wide range of targets and collect vital information. The number of MACV-SOG missions conducted with Special Forces reconnaissance teams into Laos and Cambodia increased from 117 in 1966 to 258 in 1967, 327 in 1968, and 452 in 1969. Demolished convoys, blazing ammunition depots, slain guards, and kidnapped personnel highlighted the most sustained American campaign of raiding, sabotage, and intelligence-gathering waged on foreign soil in U.S. military history. By 1970, when 441 recon missions included commando forces up to company strength, MACV-SOG's legacy of success had already earned it a global reputation as one of the most combat effective deep-penetration forces ever raised.

However, as Colonel Roger M. Pezzelle aptly points out,

The fact that full-scale unconventional warfare was not conducted throughout the history of MACSOG-V (that is, between 1964 and 1972) raises some difficult issues. The short tour of duty, with its inevitable effect on unconventional warfare, was undoubtedly a major reason for the lack of special operations in Vietnam. On MACSOG-V's behalf, it must be said that the missions it performed—strategic reconnaissance and other covert operations not yet declassified—it did well.

MACV-SOG service was the first major application of Special Forces in a strategic ground reconnaissance and exploitation role. Special Forces success in this mode was combined with foreign internal defense programs, like the CIDG concept, to expand SF scope far beyond its limited prewar major mission of guerrilla warfare.

Notes

1. Project DELTA became stabilized at 11 Special Forces officers and 82 enlisted men, alongside 34 LLDB officers and 87 enlisted men, although actual field strength varied. Increases placed the Nung Security Company at 105 men, and the CIDG Roadrunner Company at 123 men. The BDA and Mortar Platoons had 36 men each. The LLDB airborne ranger battalion was finally fixed at 43 officers and 763 enlisted men. Civilian hire was set at 198 persons. 5th SFGA Form 252-R, B-52, *Monthly Operational Summary*, dtd 28 February 1970; Detachment B-52, *Unit History SOA*, dtd 18 July 1970. The number of teams and compositions given in the text are representative because the composition of Projects DELTA, OMEGA, and SIGMA varied from year to year. However, Col. Francis J. Kelly, in *Vietnam Studies: U.S. Army Special Forces, 1961–1971*, (Washington, D.C.: Department of the Army, 1973), gives a tentative organization for these elements on pages 138 and 139. His samples are actually the 5th Special Forces optimum submissions to MACV extracted from proposed organizational tables, which were not adopted in their entirety.

2. Detachment B-52, *After Action Report*, dtd 9 February 1966.

3. Detachment B-52, *After Action Report*, dtd 7 September 1966.

4. Detachment B-52, *After Action Report*, dtd 8 October 1966.

5. Detachment B-52, *After Action Report*, dtd 16 June 1967; Detachment B-52, *Debriefing Report, Team #1*, dtd 15 May 1967.

6. Detachment B-52, *After Action Reports*, dtd 7 April 1968 and 11 June 1968.

7. Detachment B-52, *After Action Report*, dtd 25 July 1969, Appendix I, X(16). (Bracketed clarifications added by author.)

8. Material for this section derived primarily from Detachment B-52, *Unit History*, dtd 18 July 1970; and 5th Special Forces Group, *Case Study— Project DELTA*, dtd 5 January 1965.

9. 5th Special Forces Group, *Fact Sheet*, Subject: 5th Special Forces Group Long Range Reconnaissance Projects, dtd 22 April 1968.

10. Project FLAMING ARROW, which was to be conducted by 5th Special Forces Group within the confines of South Vietnam, raised the teams and other assets but were absorbed by DANIEL BOONE. The latter was the code word for cross-border operations into Cambodia.

11. Detachment B-526, *After Action Report*, dtd 28 October 1966.

12. 5th Special Forces Group, *Development of the CIDG Program, 1964– 1968*, dtd 22 April 1968; Company A, 5th Special Forces Group, Ltr, Subject: Long Ranger Special Reconnaissance, dtd 24 July 1967.

13. Detachment B-36 (Provisional), *Historical Summary*, dtd 6 December

1967; and 5th Special Forces Group, *Operational Report*, dtd 15 August 1968.

14. Shelby L. Stanton, *Vietnam Order of Battle*, Washington, D.C.: U.S. News, 1981.

15. PHU DUNG (pronounced Foo Young) was the name of the illusion appearing to opium smokers.

16. CINCPAC, *Command Histories*, 1967, Vol. II, and 1970, Vol. II.

17. JCS Messages 271912Z Jun 66 and 202247Z Oct 67; CINCPAC Message 262246Z May 67.

18. COMUSMACV Message 300937Z Jan 68, and JCS Messages 192348Z Feb 68 and 141806Z Dec 68. THOT NOT (pronounced Tot Note) was named after an abundant mangrove species in Cambodia.

19. In early 1967 Special Forces strength in Command and Control was 102 officers and 465 enlisted men. Headquarters contained 24 officers and 83 enlisted, FOB-1 and 2 had 7 officers and 70 enlisted and 135 indigenous each, while FOB-3 and 4 had 6 officers and 73 enlisted and 153 indigenous each. The reaction battalion had 18 officers and 28 enlisted, while each company had 4 officers and 2 enlisted men, not including indigenous troops. 5th Special Forces Group, command briefing chart folder and MACV-SOG glossary.

20. Command and Control Detachment South, AVGB-CCS Ltr, Subject: MIA Board Proceedings and Recommendation, dtd 2 May 1969.

CHAPTER 12

THE GREEN BERET NAVY

1. Assault Boats and Sampans

The Army Special Forces was engaged in bitter swamp forest warfare in the rice marshes and canals of Vietnam's lower Delta region. To maintain offensive striking power against Viet Cong support bases and strongholds, the Special Forces developed its own small navy. This unique Special Forces fleet initially existed as individual Delta camp collections of sampans and small engineer assault boats. Prototype airboats were tested during the 1965 rainy season, but Colonel Kelly was the real driving force behind airboat procurement and employment in the 5th Special Forces Group. Airboat sections and platoons would bring a new dimension to waterborne Special Forces operations, but they did not become readily available until October 1966.

The Mekong Delta south of Saigon was a vast flatland of winding rivers and interconnecting canals, mixed with rice paddies, bogs, and trackless marsh and forest. Larger rivers featured floating rice, with stems twelve feet long. Paddy land, flooded enough for fields to boast two rice transplantings a year, was typically broken by waste areas of sedge marsh and palm swamp. Extensive and poorly drained, these marshy plains had reeds up to seven feet high, and the grass often dried out in the winter. The lower regions were further divided by sluggish tidal streams and channels fringed with dense mangrove and bottomless mud flats. With the exception of the Seven Mountains area along the western Cambodian border, the level plain was broken only by stream and canal banks, paddy dikes, and raised roadbeds. Vast areas of the Delta were inundated by the rainy season and remained waterlogged for months. Dense forest swamps, such as the Nam Can Forest on Ca Mau Peninsula, also existed.

The wet season in the Delta lasted from mid-May through early October, as the southwest monsoon drenched the lowlands with rain accumulated from its passage over thousands of miles of ocean. Unleashing a torrent of savage thunderstorms in May, the weather would then lapse into a monotonous pattern of daily afternoon showers. This rainfall and cloudiness reached a peak in July and August, when heavy downpours often washed out the horizon and reduced visibility to zero. The fall transition period lasted barely a month, followed by the northeast monsoon season, which brought cool, dry weather from early November until March. The abrupt change from southwest to northeast monsoon periods could bring about severe wind gusts and thunderstorms, some hail, and unexpected flooding. During the dry winter period, scattered clouds drifted across the sky, and dense morning fog and haze clung to riverbanks and marshlands.

The Delta's tropical climate and terrain hindered responsive military maneuver against the Viet Cong, who struck suddenly, then swiftly faded into the backcountry. Even with conventional boats, Special Forces mobility was limited. Meadows of sea grass were dense enough to cause prop-fouling at low tide. Mangrove swamps blocked boat movement with sixty-foot trees and mazes of gnarled roots. Soldiers attempting to use the network of mangrove roots as ledges found them slippery and surrounded by quicksand and soft, deep mud. The freshwater swamps were filled with towering cajaput trees, which formed an unbroken jungle canopy. Small streams and canals hampered off-road movement. Many of the narrow, shallow waterways could be traveled only by sampans. Although rice-field dikes were generally low, tiny clusters of houses and Nypa palms provided good opportunities for ambush. The deep ditches around vegetable gardens offered excellent trenches and escape routes. Grassy marshes could be set ablaze in the dry season, creating confusion and smokescreens.[1]

The primitive watercraft initially available at camp level afforded a flimsy method of transportation, easily subject to ambush. On 26 April 1966 Detachment A-425 sent an assault boat from its new campsite under construction at Thuong Thoi, in Kien Phong Province, to Tan Chau to obtain parts for a bulldozer. The boat carried Sgt. Brent J. Baumert, interpreter Chau Men, and Filipino Technical Representative Gaodencio Deliguin. On the return trip the boat was suddenly taken under fire, sending its three occupants into the water. The boat went in circles until a VC sampan darted out and captured it. The Viet Cong were also observed dragging a person from the river. A Khmer Kampuchea Krom reaction force from A-430 was stopped by a minefield, which wounded one American and a Cambodian striker, who had part of his foot blown off and later died.[2] Capt. Ronald D. McCoy, the commander of A-425, arrived with his camp force to scour the area, but nothing was found. Although the technician's body was later recovered, the Special Forces sergeant and his interpreter had to be listed as missing in action. Camp Thuong Thoi had been moved from An Long in order to monitor more closely the Cambodian border. In 1967 airboats operating from this post would be involved in one of the most savage actions of the Green Beret navy.[3]

Lt. Col. Joseph Fernandez's Detachment B-41 was colocated with its subordinate A-414 at Moc Hoa, an old Special Forces camp, first established in November 1963 to overwatch the northwestern portion of the Delta and the adjacent Cambodian border. Located on the flat Plain of Reeds in Kien Tuong "Clarity of View" Province, Moc Hoa had been transformed into a key staging fortress for other detachments sent farther afield. In the fall of 1966, the entire area was in the throes of a massive flood. Moc Hoa was crowded with refugees, and the rising water had breached portions of the sandbagged perimeter. Craft simply floated over the wire barriers and entered the compound. Throughout the province most camp walls had collapsed, forward operational bases and runways were submerged, and all artillery had been evacuated. The same floodwaters had also forced the main force Viet Cong out of traditional safe havens and fortified cache sites into open ground, boats, or trees, where they were visibly vulnerable.

When the rising waters first reached flood stage on 17 September, each of B-41's six camps had roughly fifty sampans, between five and ten plastic assault boats, and four to six sampan motors. None of the camps had any adequate outboard engines. Capt. William G. Baughn's Dan An Camp boat units at Binh Thanh Thon (A-413) were typical. Each underpowered, six-horsepower motorized assault boat had to either tow or tie two sampans alongside. Thirty assault boats were soon rushed to Moc Hoa, accompanied by mechanics who brought along fifty-one outboard motors. They were parceled out to the various camps. Mortars were placed in aluminum engineer assault boats and each A-Detachment was soon capable of floating two companies.

However, the ad hoc mortar platforms were only marginally effective, and inexperience with boat handling and maintenance stymied CIDG operations.[4]

Three floating helipads were towed into Moc Hoa by barge, enabling armed helicopters to fly in support of operations. On 14 October helicopters were sent aloft in response to a contact east of Tuyen Nhon and intercepted the rear echelon of a Viet Cong formation equipped with sampans and captured U.S. assault boats. During the height of the flood in the first part of October, eight Navy river patrol boats arrived to reinforce the sector. Little camp fleets, a mixture of plastic and wooden boats, paddled and puttered into the Delta seas, escorted by Navy patrol boats that loomed over them like battleships. The Navy's heavy .50-caliber machine guns counterpunched VC emplacements in Cambodia and hammered bunkers challenging the CIDG armada. Although able to reach most areas of the province, the Navy vessels were still hampered by debris and grass that fouled propulsion pumps.[5]

Special Forces advisors found that waterborne operations were often hamstrung by LLDB ineffectiveness. On 12 October 1966 the Special Forces advised fleet of twenty sampans and nine assault boats at Kinh Quan II (A-416) was sent under LLDB 2d Lt. Pham Ba Tuoc to search for Viet Cong. Just days earlier an RF/PF outpost outside the former camp had been overrun, and high water along the LeGrange Canal had forced remaining Ruff-Puff units to sit exposed atop their bunkers and houses. The fields were immersed in three to twelve feet of water, interlaced with tramtree woodlines and high bamboo thickets. Early that morning the Kinh Quan II flotilla linked up with a waterborne Special Forces–advised Regional Force platoon led by district chief Captain Chanh from Ap Bac. Only at that juncture did the Vietnamese attempt last-minute coordination, and the Special Forces advisors insisted that Captain Chanh be given a radio so both Vietnamese commanders would have communications.

First Lt. John R. Gentry sat in the LLDB command boat along with Lieutenant Tuoc, Special Forces Staff Sergeant Menefee, and five Vietnamese CIDG soldiers. The boats entered a known VC stronghold long designated as a free-bombing zone and began passing numerous camouflaged sampans and empty thatch houses. Water buffaloes, chickens, ducks, and pigs were seen everywhere. Finally,

Lieutenant Gentry asked Lieutenant Tuoc to begin a systematic search and destroy of all Viet Cong property.

"No VC, these my friends," Lieutenant Tuoc replied. Gentry repeated the request more forcefully, but again Tuoc vigorously refused. Infuriated, Gentry called Captain Chanh on the radio and effected a rendezvous at noon to discuss the situation. The district chief stated, "All houses in area are guerrilla," and "Lieutenant Tuoc must destroy everything in sight." Gentry then got both officers to agree that the captain was in charge of the mission. The assault boats guarded the sampans as they proceeded south to set fire to the abandoned VC dwellings.

Two of the regional force assault boats, powered by forty-horsepower outboard motors, ventured away from the main fleet. At 12:45 P.M. a 57mm recoilless rifle suddenly opened fire and blew one boat to pieces. The other boat sped back to the rest of Captain Chanh's force, who immediately dispatched the remaining eight assault boats to the contact point. Slowly probing forward, they were peppered by small arms fire around 1:30 P.M. The boats began to make a left flank turn against the dense treeline.

At that critical juncture Lieutenant Tuoc immediately ordered the Kinh Quan II element to stop and refused to commit his boats. Gentry demanded that he immediately move forward and come on line. Lieutenant Tuoc hesitated again, and Gentry angrily ordered the boat driver to get into action. As they sped into the firefight, the other boats followed. Suddenly the LLDB command boat was raked with machine gun fire. Sgt. Gene A. Menefee was hit in the head and mortally wounded. Two CIDG soldiers were also severely wounded. Lieutenant Tuoc cowered in the bottom of the boat. Throughout the firefight he made no attempt to fire his weapon or bandage the wounded men.

Lieutenant Tuoc's indecision had delayed assembly of the boats into one formation, allowing the Viet Cong fire to concentrate on individual craft. The automatic weapons fire was very intense. Four boats were hit in quick succession and rendered inoperable. Gentry saw the CIDG occupants of two boats jumping over the side to escape the fusillade of bullets. After a desperate forty-five-minute exchange of gunfire, helicopters arrived overhead to strafe the VC positions. This allowed the boats enough reprieve to break contact and retreat north.[6]

Three days later A-414 at Moc Hoa dispatched a Cambodian CIDG boat company to Kinh Quan II, reinforced by two more platoons and Captain Luce from B-41 headquarters. They combined assets with Kinh Quang II for an operation on 15 October, guarded by five river patrol boats of Navy Task Force 116 and a platoon of helicopter gunships. The aerial scouts spotted seventy VC sampans ahead in the flooded terrain, and the usual problems plagued the operation. Loose weeds slowed propellers and clogged pumps, and Vietnamese cooperation was lacking. At the time of the helicopter sighting, harassing rifle fire had scattered the Special Forces craft, and one hour was lost gathering all the boats together. Eager for pursuit, they moved out without finalizing coordination. After another hour, the LLDB lieutenant was in a good position, but he exercised no control and allowed his forces to drift apart. The Viet Cong boats that survived the helicopter attacks were able to slip away. Finally, prior to the official termination of the operation, he returned to Kinh Quan II, leaving the Special Forces advisors from both Moc Hoa and his own camp alone in VC territory.[7]

Booby traps and maintenance problems compounded the dangers. One Kinh Quan II boat crew had three killed and six others wounded on 3 November by a booby trap set along a dense thicket of tramtrees in five feet of water. The boat tripped a wire on the surface of the water, which pivoted a bamboo pole into the air and exploded a grenade tied to the end. Engine or petrol difficulties were most hazardous in the midst of combat. Fuel drums that were dropped from helicopters split open upon impact with the water, even at low level. Volunteer maintenance personnel carrying premixed fuel had to be helicoptered into firefights to get outboard motors restarted under fire. In one instance B-41 had to airlift a civilian technical representative into a raging battle, where he frantically managed to fix three inoperable engines.[8]

Border incidents continued unabated. Captain Baughn's Binh Thanh Thon Detachment A-413 was responsible for border surveillance along the Rach Cai Co Canal. Every patrol along the boundary had been ambushed for months, and the job was nearly impossible. On 8 October 1966 a 114-man camp force and half of the A-Team departed on patrol in ten motorized assault boats with eighteen sampans, escorted by six Navy river patrol boats. The task force reached a recently abandoned borderline village just before noon, found numerous VC weapons, and began burning the hootches. Viet Cong machine guns hidden in the palms on the Cambodian side of the canal opened fire, wounding one American and one CIDG soldier. Caught in the ambush killing zone, the camp watercraft desperately maneuvered to break contact. Navy Capt. Howard G. Fox of PBR-101 reversed course and returned fire to cover the smaller craft. Geysers of water rocked his boat, which took one hit on the forward armored plating. PO Stuart E. Taylor, the skipper of PBR-116, raked the treeline with machine gun and grenade fire. One of his crew was wounded when a .50-caliber shell exploded in his weapon.[9]

On 2 November 1966 the detachment was again on the Rach Cai Co Canal, using the camp's 482d and 484th CIDG companies with 120 men under Captain Seybold. At 1:20 P.M. the three lead boats were blasted by a sudden hail of machine gun, recoilless rifle, and mortar fire from the Cambodian shoreline. One of the plastic assault boats took a direct hit from a 60mm mortar round, burst into flames, and sank. Another assault boat was abandoned, but the command helicopter immediately strafed and destroyed it. The helicopter took two hits and force-landed on the Vietnamese side of the canal. Several of the two-man sampans had been cut loose and were riddled with bullets. VC claymore mines were discharged into the stream. The rest of the fleet grouped at a mound of dry ground and returned fire. No attack on the Viet Cong ambush position was feasible, since VC automatic weapons dominated the 500 yards of open water separating the two forces. During this action, the camp's best CIDG company commander and several other troops were killed, and morale at Binh Thanh Thon was shattered for months. Captain Baughn suspended the border patrols.[10]

2. Combat Airboats

The Special Forces believed that modified versions of the "swamp buggy," then popular in the Florida Everglades, could add a flexible dimension to the increasingly dangerous maritime operations in the Delta. The Hurricane Company's seventeen-foot *Aircat* was finally selected as the Special Forces combat airboat. Each weighed approximately 1,150 pounds, was powered by a 180-horsepower Lycoming aircraft engine, and mounted a .30-caliber A-6 machine gun on the bow. Capable of thirty-eight miles per hour while carrying 300 pounds, they could skim over aquatic grasses and leap rice-paddy dikes, requiring only an inch of water under their fiberglass and Styrofoam hulls. The use of airboats in combat was a relatively new development, but their versatility soon included patrolling, blocking escape avenues, reconnoitering, transporting reserves or supplies, and providing medical evacuation. Elaborate tactics were devised for racing over water and marsh in pairs, or in massed formations to raid enemy strongpoints. Even ambush seemed feasible if crews let them drift or if they silently paddled into position, opened fire, then dashed into motorized pursuit.[11]

The most serious problem was the deafening noise of the airboat's engine propeller. Radio communications were impossible unless the engine was idling or shut down. Special Forces signal experts experimented with various devices. They inserted receivers into earmuff headsets designed for workers near jet engines and installed microphones in Air Force oxygen masks. Airboat crews finally adopted a system of arm and hand signals. Although the noise canceled surprise, the high speed and unexpected mobility of the craft were counted on to stun and outwit the Viet Cong, and early expectations even relied on other noises, from overhead helicopters or other nearby airboats, to mask detection.[12]

Because of maintenance and training considerations, airboat control was generally retained at B-Detachment level. A-Detachments having a need for airboat services formed special platoons from their camp soldiers and relied on their command B-Detachment headquarters to provide the needed boats and support. The first groups of airboat trainees arrived at Can Tho, Company D headquarters, on 2 October, and the first seventeen airboats arrived aboard a Navy Landing Ship Tank (LST) eleven days later. The boats were flown by C-130 aircraft directly to the outlying camps.

Camps scheduled for priority on airboat deployment (six airboats each) were, in order, A-414 at Moc Hoa, A-415 at Tuyen Nhon, A-412 at Cai Cai, A-413 at Binh Thanh Thon, A-425 at Thuong Thoi, A-351 at Duc Hue, A-352 at Tra Cu, A-422 at Vinh Gia, and A-416 at Kinh Quan II. The first two trained airboat platoons arrived at Moc Hoa under Detachment B-41 responsibility on 27 October, followed by another airboat platoon sent to Cai Cai on 9 November. Advanced and unit training was completed at those sites. The actual combat employment of airboats, however, had to be learned by Special Forces on a trial-and-error basis.[13]

Moc Hoa was a major airboat base. Capt. Thomas G. Hendrick's

A-414, technically a subsector advisory team accountable to the senior American advisor of the 7th ARVN Division, was temporarily transformed into B-41's primary airboat unit. The team's 491st to 495th CIDG companies were composed of either Cambodian or Cham personnel. Sfc. David S. Boyd became the first commander of the airboats. On 2 November 1966 six airboats were committed as flank security for four CIDG companies of A-414 and A-415 sweeping the Vam Co Tay River from Moc Hoa to Tuyen Nhon. Airboat riverine limitations quickly became apparent. Lack of adequate communications, reduced speed in deep water, and dense vegetation along the riverbanks prevented their cutting off a Viet Cong withdrawal.

On 14 November 1966 the area north of Tuyen Nhon on the Cambodian frontier was tackled by one CIDG company led by A-414 operations Sfc. Lyle L. Kimball, in eight assault boats and twelve sampans, accompanied by an airboat platoon under Sergeant First Class Boyd. Kimball's group moved up the Vam Co Tay River then entered a small channel leading north into the objective area. The stream was clear of debris but too narrow for the boats to turn around. Thick growth covered the stream's edges. The airboats were supposed to serve as flank security, but under the circumstances Boyd decided to move them across the marsh ahead of the main force and attempt to trigger possible Viet Cong ambushes by shooting blindly into suspected hiding places. His airboats made disjointed, individual strafing runs in close proximity to their chosen targets.

At 8:50 A.M. this tactic triggered a hornet's nest of VC return fire. The opening burst of Viet Cong automatic weapons from the treeline killed Sergeant Boyd, the airboat commander, and threw the formation into panic. Control was not regained for ten minutes. During that time, the airboats milled in disorder and sustained numerous hits. The three other Special Forces airboat advisors that Boyd had brought along, all of them specialists fourth class, could not get the CIDG to respond to them. Specialist Nelson was wounded as his airboat pulled out, and he dropped his M16 over the side. Another airboat was dead in the water with an engine failure. After three tactical airstrikes, the others were able to retreat. In view of the calamity and high number of losses, Sergeant Kimball realized the men in his company would have to retrieve the stranded airboat by themselves.

Both sides were trying to recover the airboat, and the CIDG recovery party assaulted into locked combat. Their own assault boat machine guns rendered supporting fire, while orbiting helicopters strafed the charging Viet Cong. Kimball had already lost one of his assault boats and two sampans. The airboat was finally reached and moved back a safe distance. At ten o'clock the CIDG formed an assault line, waited until aircraft smothered the woods, then advanced toward the VC positions with M-79s and automatic weapons blazing. They were initially thrown back but got into the treeline on the second try, only to be hit by intense, well-aimed fire all along their front. Specialist John Mayo was killed instantly, and the CIDG soldiers retreated. Both Sergeant Kimball and his ARVN boat driver were wounded. Their boat, the last out, was buffeted by concentrated fire until it was finally out of range.[14]

By mid-November the floodwaters had receded to a point that still precluded foot operations but made assault boat travel impossible. Airboats and Navy Patrol Air Cushion Vehicles (PACV) dominated the Delta during this period, which lasted until 12 December. Three giant U.S. Navy air cushion craft and eighteen sailors were quartered at Moc Hoa during the last weeks of November and the first week of December. On 21 November the first of ten combined Navy PACV–Special Forces operations throughout Kien Tuong Province was launched. Each air cushion vehicle carried eight members of the Special Forces–advised Provincial Intelligence Platoon. The PACV craft moved over both dry and flooded terrain, restricted only by treelines, and high reeds, which caused them to stall.[15]

These highly effective, agile strike craft ranged across the countryside. One of the most successful actions occurred on 22 November 1966, when A-414 engaged a full company of Viet Cong regulars. The PACV and airboat teams were called into the battle. Their presence routed the Viet Cong, who attempted to flee into Cambodia. This movement was quickly blocked by six helicopters that airlanded a CIDG company to seal off any escape. All forces converged on the trapped unit. After a fierce two-hour struggle, the entire VC company was annihilated, and only one CIDG soldier was wounded in exchange. Over fifty sampans were destroyed, and an outboard motor lost during the 14 November battle was recovered.[16]

3. Defeats and Victories

During the winter dry season, the Delta camps were improved or rebuilt to withstand future flooding, while their garrisons trained toward improving sampan patrols during the next high-water season. Despite this preparation, the employment of airboats during the year in the Delta would be practically limited to Kien Phong Province. There were still only a limited number of Special Forces personnel and technicians familiar with airboat operations and logistics.

Detachment B-43 was deployed to Cao Lanh in Kien Phong "Wind of Knowledge" Province during the dry season in February 1967. An airboat facility was finished in May. The shop was designed to provide full service, from replacing a fiberglass hull to complete engine overhaul. As a result of the 1966 campaign, the Viet Cong realized the tactical potential of airboats in flooded areas and attempted to eliminate them before the monsoons arrived. The facility was the main target of a devastating VC mortar and rocket attack on 3–4 July, which caused extensive damage. The maintenance shed was completely destroyed, causing the loss of one airboat and six airboat engines, as well as all the spare parts and special tools needed for boat repair.[17]

Capt. Jeffery Fletcher's Thuong Thoi Detachment A-432 had been redesignated from A-425 on the first day of June. With the onset of the floods on 9 September, two airboat sections were attached to his command under Capt. Thomas D. Culp and Sfc. Robert A. Anspach from A-401's Mike Force at Don Phuc. They began operating out of the camp in the open marshlands along the Hong Ngu River near the Cambodian border. Fletcher was worried about his 454th CIDG Company manning a border outpost on the Mekong River and the increase in leaking that threatened the main camp berm. His camp was about to witness one of the most crippling defeats that Special Forces airboats would suffer.

At 8:30 on the morning of 11 September 1967, the six airboats departed on a reconnaissance mission. Each boat carried four men, and the force included three Special Forces advisors, one interpreter, one LLDB noncommissioned officer, and ten Chinese and eight Cambodian Mike Force soldiers. Sfc. Robert A. Anspach headed the formation in Boat 1, accompanied by LLDB Sergeant Binh, one Chinese soldier, and interpreter Chau Van Sang, who doubled as driver. Capt. Thomas D. Culp went in middle Boat 3, and the A-425 team sergeant, M. Sgt. James W. Lewis, occupied the last one, Boat 6. The operation was to sweep north to within a mile of the Cambodian border then west to the Mekong River.

For an undetermined reason, possibly the change in appearance of the landscape because of flood conditions, the airboats passed their intended turning point and proceeded in line down a stream to the river that formed the international boundary. The rice paddies were under six to ten feet of water, and the dry banks of the river were covered with trees and heavy brush. As the first four airboats left the stream and entered the Vietnamese portion of the river about five miles northwest of the camp, Viet Cong bunkers on both sides of the channel caught them in a lethal cross fire.

Concentrated machine gun fire riddled all six airboats in the first burst, killing Sfc. Robert A. Anspach immediately. This resulted in fatal confusion. Instead of trying to break out of the area immediately, the column circled and doubled back into the killing zone. The lead boats in the river were hit repeatedly. LLDB Sergeant Binh screamed at Sang to turn back. Sang could not hear him over the din of the racing engine, but he did not need any prodding. Sang desperately drove Boat 1 back toward the mouth of the stream, as the Chinese soldier returned fire with the machine gun. The water was splashing with near misses as the airboat rocked from additional hits. Just before the airboat reached the west bank, it went dead in the water. Sang jumped out and swam ashore. The airboat, containing Anspach's body, was later observed from the air being pushed and pulled across the border by the Viet Cong.

Boats 2, 3, and 4 tried to execute a clockwise circle in the river, but the maneuver was ripped apart by the intensity of fire directed at them. The impact of multiple shells cut into the shrill whine of the motors. Boat 2 plowed into the riverbank, gashed its hull, and sank. Captain Culp in Boat 3 was shot in the left arm, crouched in the boat, and returned fire at treeline with his M-79 grenade launcher. Airboat driver Than Ky Diep roared the airboat back downstream, but the craft took several more rounds, and Captain Culp was killed. The driver of Boat 4, Ly Phoi Sang, was wounded in the right shoulder, and the airboat was hit in the crankcase. He managed to get the airboat back into the stream, where it lost power.

The crewmen of Boat 5 were killed and wounded in the first few seconds. Their boat drifted to the south bank of the river, where it was captured. Master Sergeant Lewis had been wounded in Boat 6 but kept radio contact until he lost consciousness. The driver, Hoang Van Sinh, steered his airboat out of the maelstrom, but the engine was shot to pieces. The badly damaged airboat drifted to the stream bank.

The firing had lasted two minutes. One boat had sunk, two were in VC hands, and two others were immobilized. Only Boat 3 was still running. The remaining airboat section raced out of Thuong Thoi under Staff Sergeant Jackson of A-401 and Sergeant First Class Pollock of A-432. Aircraft guided these five airboats to the battle site, where they linked up with Boat 3 and collected the survivors huddled on the shorelines. Pollock reached Boat 4 and towed it back to camp. Boat 2 was later evacuated by Chinook helicopter. Airstrikes were called in to destroy Boat 6 and the bunkers on the near side of the river.[18]

Farther north in III Corps Tactical Zone, B-35 began posting its detachments along the major river and canal network providing access to the capital of Saigon during 1967. The Vam Co Dong River and Kinh Xang Canal had long been used by the Viet Cong as a troop movement and resupply route from Cambodia. Tra Cu (A-352) was moved to the river and canal intersection on 10 January, Luong Ha (A-353) was opened on the canal 26 May, and Hiep Hoa (A-351) had relocated from the original village outskirts to the Sugar Mill by the river. During the rainy season beginning in September, plastic assault boats and fiberglass airboats of B-35 moved through the local waterways, flooded rice paddies, and sugarcane fields, which abounded in the area.[19]

Wearing unzipped flak jackets, closed with only one snap for easy discard if necessary, the Special Forces boat crews checked the identification papers of Vietnamese and passed ropes underneath water craft to detect hidden supplies. Viet Cong detainees were yanked out of their sampans, bound hand and foot, and put in the bottom of the small assault boats, while captured sampans were tied alongside. Concussion grenades were pitched into the water around empty sampans, forcing up submerged VC swimmers who were killed with rifles and pistols. To flush out VC ambushes, supporting aircraft would pretend to fly off and crewmen on boats coming under fire would toss out red smoke grenades. The boats then dashed out at full throttle, and the aircraft returned to strafe targets near the surface scum that had been emitted by the smoke pots hitting the water.

The Viet Cong retaliated with mines and underwater stakes that ripped the bottoms out of conventional boats, and an array of non-delay fused trip grenades that disabled airboats. A lot of ambushing was possible since the airboats left telltale pathways, even in the open Plain of Reeds, and they were prone to travel known channels or previously used routes because of their speed, routine, and restricted visibility. The persistent Special Forces airboats continued to gain the upper hand, and their ability to reach normally inaccessible areas was becoming decisive in taming large swaths of former VC territory.[20]

4. Years of Success

In February 1968 the commander of Company D, Lt. Col. Ludwig "The Blue Max" Faistenhammer, Jr., began reorganizing the 4th Mobile Strike Force Command. This Delta-wide response unit was tagged to include three crack Mobile Strike Force battalions, along with a 184-man mobile strike airboat company with its own maintenance section. As a result, Detachment A-441 was moved from Moc Hoa on 15 June and redesignated A-404 as the airboat company control headquarters at Cao Lanh. The airboats were soon adorned with skull-and-crossbones insignias and took the call sign "Jolly Roger." They were soon to become famous throughout Vietnam. Airboat sections were also stationed at Moc Hoa and Cao Lanh, and the Airboat Training Center was kept at Don Phuc. In the fall of 1968 Company D established a mission support site at an old deserted school house at Tram Chim. Airboat operations were staged out of Cao Lanh (A-404), Cai Cai (A-431), and Thuong Thoi (A-432). Company D's Green Beret navy contained 61 airboats and 103 plastic assault boats when the high water arrived in September 1968.[21]

The mobile strike airboat company was formalized with its own table of organization and equipment on 1 November 1968. Airboats saw excellent service as firing platforms for 106mm recoilless rifles. To gain more firepower, Special Forces began replacing the .30-caliber machine guns with heavier .50-caliber ones on two airboats in each six-boat section. Airboat CIDG crews usually consisted of three men: one driver, one gunner wielding an M-60 or .50-caliber machine gun, and an M-79 grenadier who doubled as an assistant machine gunner. Patrols carried a medic and an airboat mechanic. During the 1968 flood period, airboats performed excellent service in reconnaissance and surveillance, water convoy cover, and the interdiction of VC water traffic through raids and ambushes. In positioning airboats as blocking forces, the Special Forces had learned that airboats did not have the capability of conducting the attack themselves and avoided undue losses. According to Lt. Col. Carl J. Nagle, the Deputy Commander of Company D, "Operations this season [1968] have proven the versatility of the airboat. It is a formidable support weapon for Special Forces operations."[22]

During the spring of 1969, the Special Forces airboat company and the U.S. Navy began planning for joint cordon-and-search operations and integrated patrols. There were setbacks, such as the ambush of a Navy gunboat–Special Forces A-404 airboat force in the southern coastal U-Minh Forest on 5 May 1969. However, the airboat had become a formidable weapon that the VC had learned to fear. Small Viet Cong motor craft that attempted to outrun or outfight the machines were inevitably caught and destroyed by 1st Lt. Dan McKinney's airboats, which streaked across rice paddies and high-jumped dikes with machine guns blazing.

In response to pleas from the Kien Tuong provincial VC commander, the Viet Cong *Ca Mau Battalion, 2d U Minh Regiment,* underwent specialized mobile antiairboat training inside Cambodia. The unit reentered Vietnam and ambushed an airboat from Tra Cu Camp (A-326) on 29 July 1969 near the end of French Canal. One Special Forces airboat rider was killed and two wounded. Navy and camp reaction forces were summoned into battle, rescued the survivors, and engaged the VC unit in an intense firefight that eventually included elements of the 3d Brigade, 25th Infantry Division.[23]

As the water level rose in the late fall, airboat action intensified. On 6 October S. Sgt. Raymond R. Ross's airboat section attached to Camp Thuong Thoi (A-432) was alerted by WO Thomas R. Maehrlein, flying an L-19 airplane, that seventy-five armed sampans were trying to head down the Mekong River just inside Vietnam. Maehrlein swooped down to rocket and strafe the VC force. The airboats sped after the remaining two dozen sampans fleeing toward a border island in the river. The swiftness of the airboat arrival prevented the Viet Cong from getting back across the boundary. Recoilless rifle and machine gun fire erupted from both the island and east riverbank. Cobra gunships supported the airboats as they closed the island, but the airboats took hits. Two were damaged and Specialist 4th Class Davis, on the last airboat, was wounded in the arm.

Capt. James E. Palmer airmobiled CIDG ground reaction troops from Chi Lang into the battle under S. Sgt. James R. Kerns of A-432, along with an LLDB officer. Once on the ground, the LLDB commander insisted on breaking contact because of "the proximity of the Cambodian border." The first lift was safely extracted, but a helicopter went down near the river when its rear rotor blade struck the water on the second lift-out. The airboats returned to secure the crashed helicopter until a Chinook helicopter could sling-load it out. Twenty CIDG soldiers had to be taken out by the airboats, all of which reached Thuong Thoi safely.

Tra Cu (A-326) lost its executive officer of the B-36 Mobile Strike Force airboat contingent, Sfc. Marshall T. Markham, when his lead airboat detonated a *Ca Mau Battalion* bomb device 16 October near the Industrial Canal. The blast demolished the airboat, killed Markham and his interpreter, and wounded the other two Mike Force soldiers on board. On 23 October A-404 airboats engaged 100 Viet Cong sampans in a running skirmish northwest of Vinh Gia, destroying 16 of them with no losses in return.[24]

The last year of actual airboat warfare was 1969. The 5th Special Forces Group had ninety airboats in 1970, all concentrated in the Delta within Company D. In September the Green Beret navy began phasing down as supply officers arrived from MACV to start turning the airboats over to the Vietnamese. The Cao Lanh–based "Jolly Roger" Detachment A-404 (airboat) had been preparing for closeout since 1 August. Capt. Joseph Duster, the last Special Forces airboat commander, backhauled all airboats and equipment to Company D headquarters at Can Tho. On 14 November 1970 he signed over the final property papers, and the 4th ARVN Ranger Support Company occupied the A-404 compound at Cao Lanh.[25]

During the war, the Special Forces had many problems with airboats. The engine noise, maintenance, and lack of shielded weapons were the most obvious. Airboats also required an extensive logistical tail and gobbled up exorbitant amounts of fuel, oil, ammunition, and spare parts. Trigger-happy airboat crews compounded the problem by firing on practically every cluster of weeds, bushes, and trees within range of their weapons. Aircraft coverage that provided navigational and firepower assistance was later found essential.[26]

In the final analysis, however, the airboats were quite successful in extending Special Forces operational capability to cover otherwise secure Viet Cong channels and bases. Also, the unique Green Beret navy was a colorful example of Special Forces flexibility in militarily overcoming the terrain obstacles of the Delta and the waterways of lower Vietnam.

Notes

1. Advanced Research Projects Agency, *Project Agile*, Report No. BAT-171-45, dtd 16 May 1966.

2. The Khmer Kampuchea Krom, or KKK, was an underground Cambodian political faction. The loyalty and participation of its members in the CIDG program wavered, and the KKK was not held in high esteem by Special Forces.

3. Detachmment A-425, *After Action Report*, dtd 28 April 1966, supplemented by Company D Ltr, Subject: Incident at Det A-425 on 26 April 1966, dtd 28 April 1966.

4. Detachment B-41 Ltr AVSFD-B-41, Subject: Flood After Action Report, dtd 27 November 1966; and A-413, *Monthly Operational Summary*, dtd 30 September 1966.

5. Detachment B-41, *Operational Summary*, dtd 28 October 1966.

6. Detachment A-416, *After Action Report*, dtd 13 October 1966.

7. A-414, *Operation After Action Report*, dtd 19 October 1966.

8. A-416, *After Action Report*, dtd 5 November 1966; and B-41, *Monthly Operational Summary*, dtd 28 October 1966.

9. Advisory Team 85, *Informal Investigation of Border Violation*, dtd 12 October 1966.

10. Detachment A-413, *After Action Report*, dtd 3 November 1966, and *Monthly Operational Summary for Month of 1–30 Nov 66*.

11. 5th Special Forces Group, "Airboat Program," Inclosure 15 to *Operational Report*, dtd 15 February 1967; and Brown, Don, Sp5, "Terrors of the Delta," *The Green Beret*, Vol. IV, Number 9, p. 12–13.

12. 5th Special Forces Group, *Operational Report*, dtd 15 August 1967, p. 29.

13. 5th Special Forces Group, "Air Boat Operations," Inclosure 14 to *Operational Report*, dtd 15 February 1967. Initially six airboats constituted one platoon. During 1967, with the availability of more airboats, a platoon consisted of twelve airboats, divided into two sections of six airboats each.

14. Detachment A-414, *After Action Report*, dtd 16 November 1966.

15. Detachment A-414, *Monthly Operational Summary*, dtd 24 November 1966, and *After Action Report*, dtd 23 November 1966; Detachment B-41, *Monthly Operational Report*, dtd 30 December 1966.

16. Detachment B-41, *Monthly Operational Summary*, dtd 30 November 1966.

17. 5th Special Forces Group, *Operational Report*, dtd 15 May 1967, pp. 11, 40, and *Operational Report*, dtd 15 August 1967, pp. 2, 13.

18. Detachment A-432, *After Action Report—Airboat Operation*, dtd 13 September 1967, and *Monthly Operational Summary*, dtd 26 September 1967;

5th Special Forces Group, *Monthly Operational Summary*, dtd 12 October 1967, Inclosure 4.

19. 5th Special Forces Group, *Historical Summaries of USASF A-Detachments*, compiled in November 1967.

20. 5th Special Forces Group, *Operational Report*, dtd 15 November 1967, pp. 36, 37.

21. 5th Special Forces Group, *Operational Report*, dtd 15 August 1968; Company D, *Debriefing by LTC Ludwig Faistenhammer, Jr.*, dtd 16 May 1968. In a special boat report dtd 28 September 1968, Company D had its watercraft disposed of as follows: airboats: 61 at Cao Lanh; plastic assault boats: 12 at My Phuoc Tay (A-411), 12 at Kinh Quan II (A-412), 16 at Binh Thanh Thon (A-413), 14 at Tuyen Nhon (A-415), 3 at My Dien II (A-416), 7 at Vinh Gia (LLDB A-149), 13 at Cai Cai (A-431), 17 at Thuong Thoi (A-432), and 9 at My Da (A-433).

22. Company D, *Field Grade Debriefing* of Carl J. Nagle, dtd 23 January 1969; 5th SFGA TOE CIDG/MS-4, dtd 1 Nov 68; Airboat Training Command paper, *Airboat Section Capabilities*, updated; Gruschow, Sp4 Jim, "Guardians of the Delta," *Green Beret*, Vol. V, Number 9, pp. 8, 9.

23. Detachment A-415, *After Action Report*, dtd 1 August 1960.

24. 5th Special Forces Group, *Operational Report*, dtd 14 November 1969; and Detachment A-326, *After Action Report*, dtd 16 October 1969.

25. Company D, *After Action Report: A-404 Closing*, dtd 24 December 1970.

26. Detachment B-43, *Field Grade Officer Debriefing* of Maj. William C. Hazen, dtd 1 November 1967. The report cites typical airboat fuel and ammunition expenditures for a one-month period within B-43.

CHAPTER 13

MOBILE GUERRILLA AND STRIKE FORCES

1. The Mike Forces

The most significant change in the organization of the Civilian Irregular Defense Group program occurred during the summer of 1965, when the Mike Force was established. The Mike Force was a direct outgrowth of the "Eagle Flight" Detachment formed at Pleiku on 16 October 1964 to react to emergency combat situations at the small Special Forces camps within the western highlands. This "eagle flight" consisted of five 1st Special Forces Group personnel of Detachment A-334B and thirty-six Rhade tribesmen. These Montagnards were trained in various Special Forces skills and underwent parachute training. The eagle flight troops were rewarded with higher ranks, a special pay scale, and hazardous duty allowances of 1,000 piasters per month. They were armed with M2 carbines and directly supported by six transport helicopters and three helicopter gunships from Camp Holloway outside Pleiku. The "eagle flight" was used for reconnaissance, search and seizure, and camp reaction missions; and Captain Lockridge moved the contingent to Ban Me Thuot in January 1965.[1]

As a result of the continued success of this mobile "eagle flight," each C-Detachment within 5th Special Forces Group dedicated an A-Detachment to raise and train reaction forces for its own corps tactical zone, commencing in the fall of 1965. These were known as Mike Forces, supposedly because the *M* in mobile was spelled phonetically as "Mike." In the north A-113 initiated the I CTZ (Da Nang) Mike Force using Chinese Nungs and Rhades, while A-219 resorted to Rhade and Jarai Montagnard employment in the II CTZ (Pleiku) Mike Force.

The III CTZ (Bien Hoa) Mike Force under A-302 was composed of Vietnamese, Cambodians, and Chinese Nungs. The country-wide Nha Trang Mike Force and IV CTZ (Don Phuc) Mike Force were not formed until February 1966. The former was organized as a battalion of 594 Rhade, Cham, and Chinese troops by Detachment A-503; and the latter used Chinese and Cambodians under Detachment A-430, created at Don Phuc with Special Forces cadre selected throughout the Detachment C-4 area.[2]

The experiences of Detachment A-219 were typical of early recruiting efforts. Local recruiters in Pleiku bagged a large number of volunteers with promises of unreasonably high pay, leadership positions, and palace guard working conditions. On 15 September 1965 the detachment arrived at Camp Duc Co in C-123 aircraft with 109 Nungs to begin combat training. On 20 September a training patrol led by S. Sgts. John H. Thompson and Nathaniel Jackson made the unit's first contact with the Viet Cong, and four days later a platoon led by S. Sgt. Joseph Sharp and Sgt. James Brewer drew first blood in a firefight outside Plei M'nou village. Once the real nature of the duty became obvious, the resentment over the unauthorized promises, coupled with a misunderstanding in the subsistence allowance paid, led to the refusal of 146 Nungs to continue in Mike Force service. The force was reconstituted with Rhade personnel.[3]

The Mike Forces were intended as multipurpose reaction units, but instead they were initially utilized primarily as interior guards for the C-Detachments and the group headquarters compound. The value of these troops in large part resulted from the fact that they represented the only combatant formations exclusively under Special Forces command. Authority over other CIDG resources was either shared with the LLDB or technically under LLDB control. With the hiring of more Nung camp security elements and bodyguards, the Mike Forces were freed for a wide range of field duties.

The 184-man Mike Force companies became the reserves of Special Forces, each containing a thirty-four-man eagle flight reconnaissance platoon. The Mike Forces differed from the camp strike forces in many respects. Mike Forces were specifically designed for employment under short reaction time conditions and were not restricted by camp defense responsibilities. The Mike Forces were conventionally organized with crew-served weapons, such as medium mortars and a range of recoilless rifles, which allowed them to deliver much of their own supporting fire. Because of the higher wages and more strenuous training, the Mike Force troops were better-than-average CIDG soldiers. They were also theoretically airborne-qualified, although personnel turbulence and continual combat requirements kept many companies from achieving that status (as late as 1970, for example, only two of the twelve companies in the 4th Mobile Strike Force Command were actually airborne.)

The Mike Forces also had limitations. As mobile response forces, they usually lacked intimate knowledge, which the local camp CIDG possessed, of the terrain and inhabitants in an operational area. In some cases language and ethnic differences created friction with camp strike forces. Logistically, Mike Force operations were expensive and largely reliant on aerial delivery. The Mike Forces were also subject to the same loss of motivation in extended field operations away from their home bases that plagued the whole CIDG program. Finally, after intense Vietnamese pressure, they were brought under joint Special Forces–LLDB control in December 1966.[4]

The main Mike Force utilization was threefold: reinforcement of camps under construction or attack, performing raids and patrols, and conducting small-scale conventional combat operations. During 1966, the Mike Forces became an effective and critical factor on the Special Forces battlefield. In accord with their increased importance, the number of companies was expanded within each C-Detachment jurisdiction. During the course of the year, a second wave of A-Detachments was formed to command increased Mike Force assets. The I CTZ (Da Nang) Mike Force created Detachment A-100, the II CTZ (Pleiku) Mike Force added Detachments A-217 and A-218, and the III CTZ (Bien Hoa) Mike Force organized Detachments A-303 and A-304. However, these second wave A-Detachments were committed to the Mobile Guerrilla Force concept that fall.

The Nung Security Platoon, which initially guarded the headquarters of 5th Special Forces Group at Nha Trang, had been recruited in 1964. By 1965 the force had grown to three full companies, and most of their operations throughout the year were spent in the Dong Bo area outside Nha Trang, where they guarded the approaches to the city. The Nung security force was designated as a Mike Force during that time, and in March 1966 it was used to reinforce Camp A Shau. After incurring heavy losses there, the Nungs were sent to Detachment B-50 for reorganization, additional recruiting, and training. Capt. Lee Wilson assumed command of the newly created Detachment A-503 and began recruiting Montagnards, his six companies coming under the operational control of Project OMEGA (Detachment B-50).

The Nha Trang Mike Force was given the two-fold mission of serving as a country-wide reaction force to support besieged camps and deploying into any Special Forces tactical area of responsibility as required. The remaining original Nungs were formed into the headquarters and service company and a heavy weapons, security, and two special platoons. This would allow three of the Mike Force companies to deploy with Project OMEGA's reconnaissance teams as a reaction force and forward base security. The remaining three companies stayed in Da Nang, where they began airborne and airmobile training.

During 1966, the Nha Trang Mike Force intervened in two other battles, at Thuong Duc and Tra Bong. Late in the year two combat reconnaissance eagle flight platoons were formed in the headquarters. Capt. Robert A. Costa assumed command of Detachment A-503 in 1967, and two LLDB officers and four LLDB sergeants were assigned as liaison for the LLDB High Command. In 1967 the Nha Trang Mike Force was placed under Company E (Provisional) and participated in the battles at Tan Rai, Phu Nhon, and Buon Blech. That September, Project OMEGA deployed to Ban Me Thuot and permanently absorbed its three Nha Trang companies. The 4th, 5th, and 6th Mobile Strike Force companies were left under Detachment A-503, which recruited two others (7th and 8th) under the new commander, Capt. Lawrence O'Neil. His Nha Trang Mike Force participated heroically in the battle of Nha Trang during Tet-68, although O'Neil was severely wounded in the engagement and was replaced by Maj. Richard A. Clark.

Typical of the Nha Trang Mike Force missions was the employment of the 5th and 6th Mobile Strike Force companies in support of Tong Le Chon, just after an attack had been made on the fort in August 1967. Captain Costa's two companies, together comprising 247 Vietnamese CIDG with 7 Special Forces personnel, arrived at Quan Loi on the morning of 7 August. They were flown to Camp Tong Le Chon by CH-47 helicopter in five lifts. There Costa's men were given the mission to conduct combat operations and assist Detachment A-334 in defending and rebuilding the camp.

Just after noon on the day of their arrival at Tong Le Chon, the two companies advanced on line into an area between the Saigon River and the camp defensive perimeter. As the Mike Force troops entered the hilly ground covered with thick underbrush, they came under fire from foxholes, trenches, and bunkers. The companies engaged in a close firefight then pulled back to allow an airstrike and artillery to work over the area. Led by two Special Forces armed with flame-throwers, the companies assaulted the NVA earthworks again at 3:00 P.M. and fought until nightfall, when they returned to the Tong Le Chon compound.

The next day the 6th Mike Force Company reentered the battle-ground to recover weapons, equipment, and documents from the dead North Vietnamese. On 9 August the same company ventured south-west of the camp to track NVA withdrawal routes. They located a well-traveled trail, complete with four-foot-high stakes topped with white directional arrows. For the next two nights, the Mike Force companies maintained listening posts and platoon ambush sites but made no contact. As the immediate threat to the camp was obviously over, Captain Costa's companies were pulled out on 12 August 1967. Casualties had been light (four Special Forces and eleven Mike Force wounded), but fifty-one North Vietnamese were killed in skirmishing adjacent to the camp. This type of reinforcement mission was the standard Mike Force assignment.

A further maturity of the Mike Force concept was realized during Operation BATH (12 March to 3 April 1968) in the central highlands. The reconnaissance operation saturated the area south of An Khe in an effort to locate and harass the *95B NVA Regiment*. The entire op-eration was under II CTZ (Pleiku) Mike Force headquarters command and used the 22d, 26th, and 27th Mobile Strike Force companies to provide quick reaction forces for Company E, 20th Infantry (Long Range Patrol), which had been placed under Special Forces control in January.

Operation BATH combined the lethal recon teams of Company E, 20th Infantry, with the native prowess of the Mike Force to fuse a highly successful combination. Joint American-CIDG teams were helicoptered from An Khe and infiltrated into the rolling hills, where they reconnoitered trails, base areas, and NVA positions for periods up to seven days at a time. Mike Force companies using eagle flight techniques pounced on targets and assisted with reconnaissance-in-force sweeps.[5]

Unfortunately, one of the most embarrassing Mike Force episodes of the war occurred just days later on Operation DEVERALL with the 4th Infantry Division. A series of events culminated in the refusal of two mobile strike force companies to conduct a bomb damage assessment in an area where fellow Mike Force troops had recently undergone intense combat with the North Vietnamese.

Both companies had excellent combat reputations, and one had been awarded the Order of the Green Scarf by LLDB commander Major General Quang for its outstanding combat performance in Pleiku city during Tet-68. However, since the Tet-68 offensive, I Field Force Vietnam changed Mike Force employment from thirty-day, single-company missions to open-ended multicompany operations. The level of combat demanded continuous employment with little or no rest for either the Montagnards or Special Forces personnel.

Operation DEVERALL was originally a II CTZ (Pleiku) Mike Force sweep to find elements of the *2d NVA Division* reported north of Dak Pek. On 16 April 1968 the 22d and 26th Mobile Strike Force companies started searching for the North Vietnamese, whom they found entrenched on high ground on 24 April. Both Mike Force units were scattered after suffering a sharp reverse. On the following afternoon after combat had subsided, two more companies (the 24th and 25th) were airlifted onto the battlefield. At that time the 4th Infantry Division assumed operational control of the Special Forces units and ordered a withdrawal.

The Special Forces soldiers requested that they be allowed to stay in the area and that the 4th Infantry Division insert battalions to exploit the situation in accordance with the original plan of operations wherein the division would maneuver against the NVA once they were located by the Mike Force. The request was denied, and on 26 April the Mike Forces were withdrawn while B-52 bombers pounded the area for three days. During those three days, the fresh companies intermingled with the two companies that had experienced the hard fighting. Stories and rumors of NVA strength quickly developed.

On 30 April the 24th and 25th Mobile Force companies, which had reinforced, were informed that they were going to conduct a heliborne assault the next day into the same battlefield and conduct a bombing assessment. The area was still outside of artillery range, and on the scheduled day of attack, the 4th Infantry Division was unable to provide the helicopters. The two companies were then ordered to proceed on foot, and they refused to go.

The II CTZ (Pleiku) Mike Force disarmed both companies and released them from further Special Forces duty. The misadventure was another instance of lack of understanding by U.S. conventional units over CIDG employment. The basic lesson was that even Mike Forces were civilian paramilitary units. They possessed strong family ties, and their effectiveness and morale had been sharply diminished by the continuous field duty ordered by I Field Force Vietnam in the wake of the Tet-68 offensive. CIDG troops were simply not capable of prolonged field maneuvering in excess of four weeks, especially without rest between operations. Apparently the Mike Force troopers had also been told that DEVERALL was a twenty-day operation. When a promise was made to CIDG personnel, it had to be fulfilled; otherwise, mission failure became a definite possibility.[6]

2. Blackjack

The 5th Special Forces Group realized that the Viet Cong had numerous secret bases and complete freedom of movement throughout certain areas of South Vietnam. The Special Forces decided to stab at the elusive VC network by using small bands of Special Forces–led CIDG troops operating as mobile guerrilla forces. The Mobile Guerrilla Force was the brainchild of Colonel Kelly, who dubbed its operations with his favorite call sign, "Blackjack." In fact, Blackjack operations became so famous that Colonel Kelly's code word became his nom de guerre, and his other nickname, "Splash" (gained by avoiding the coral drop zones on Okinawa), faded from use. Colonel Kelly's mobile guerrilla task forces were a refinement and amplification of the mobile strike concept.

Each mobile guerrilla force consisted of an A-Detachment that controlled one 150-man Mike Force company trained in extended patrolling and a 34-man combat reconnaissance eagle flight platoon. The mobile guerrilla task forces were theoretically intended to operate independently for as long as thirty to sixty days in remote regions of South Vietnam. The roving mobile guerrilla forces were to be resupplied by aerial means, such as modified napalm bomb canisters filled with foodstuffs and ammunition, dropped by A-1E Skyraiders. The mobile guerrilla forces employed conventional ranger tactics to locate, watch, and harass Viet Cong safe havens through ambush, destruction of storage areas, and airstrike direction.

The pilot mobile guerrilla mission was BLACKJACK 21. After five weeks of training and planning, the month-long combat sweep was conducted through the mountains and valleys of the Plei Trap Valley in southwestern Kontum Province. Led by the assistant group operations officer, Capt. James A. Fenlon, Task Force 777 was composed of 15 Special Forces and 249 Montagnard Mike Force troops and was devoid of LLDB participation. Although Colonel Kelly appointed Fenlon to be in charge of BLACKJACK 21, in actuality the Montagnards responded only to their own Mike Force leader, 1st Lt. Gilbert K. "Joe" Jenkins. Commencing on 13 October, the task force entered its mission area, where it waded the seasonably low waters of countless streams; trudged through the bamboo, black palm, and jungle along the ridgelines; and struggled across the dense vine tangle of untended rice fields.

The task force initiated a number of small ambushes. In the morning darkness of 5 November, one ambush team killed three North Vietnamese soldiers who were transporting tin boxes full of grenades and walking bicycles down a trail. As the team left the vicinity, they rigged plastic explosives and claymore mines to the bikes, which were left on the pathway. Later that afternoon explosions were heard from the site. The stay-behind ambush group was moving forward to rejoin the main task force, when they suddenly came under fire from an NVA company. The first two Montagnards in the column were killed, and the remainder of the team was pinned down by heavy automatic weapons fire. Sfc. Robert F. Head heard noises of digging and chopping all around their position, while the North Vietnamese signaled each other by using animal calls.

The combat reconnaissance platoon and a rifle platoon were dispatched to the isolated element, but they were making slow progress in the thick vegetation. Sergeant First Class Head decided to disengage at once. He quickly tossed three fragmentation grenades and a tear gas grenade, fired several rapid bursts from his M16 rifle at the nearest NVA machine gun nest, and ordered the team to get out. The team made a mad dash for the Dak Hodrai River more than 100 yards away, where Sergeant Head and his men linked up with the recon troops. An airstrike was called in as the task force crossed the river. Sfc. Ben W. Hancock, the platoon medic, spotted more North Vietnamese crossing the water from another direction, and Sfc. William Roderick and Sfc. Alvin H. Young moved upstream, using telescopic sights to kill several of the NVA soldiers. On 9 November, after platoon-size ambush positions along the river failed to make further contact, Task Force 777 was extracted from the valley.

BLACKJACK 21, like the other mobile guerrilla expeditions, was not a true "guerrilla" enterprise, since it employed troops not native to the targeted region. Likewise, the conventional search-and-destroy theme of Task Force 777 was underlined by the fact that it was looking for North Vietnamese Army regulars, not Viet Cong partisans. Intelligence value was limited. They captured one prisoner who claimed to be a member of an infiltration group but who refused to give his unit identification and "died in captivity."

Task Force 777 was still a successful test of the basic mobile guerrilla doctrine. For an entire month Special Forces and Montagnard troops had remained deep in NVA/VC territory where reinforcement and even medical evacuation were prohibited. A surgeon, Capt. Homer G. House, and four medical sergeants escorted the task force and treated wounded, sick, and injured CIDG personnel on ponchos spread out over the ground. The Mike Force troops had been expecting the same medical helicopters they had in training and were openly disgruntled by the "hard-core" Special Forces medical practices. One trooper suffering a neck wound was denied a litter and told to walk; another, with a fractured arm, was given only an ace bandage and required to continue carrying his weapon, pack, and rocket launcher, since "the bone had good alignment." However, this dismay passed after these two proved capable of keeping pace, and the Montagnards realized Dr. House was a true doctor, able to gauge severity of injury.[7]

BLACKJACK 22 began on 10 December 1966 in the Boun Me Ga area of western II CTZ. Task Force 768 comprised 12 Special Forces, 6 interpreters, and 173 Montagnards under Capt. Robert Orms, again using 1st Lieutenant Jenkins's proven Mike Force company from Detachment A-219. At 4:30 P.M. on 9 January, the Viet Cong attacked the patrol base. Although the VC had the upper hand, their poor markmanship enabled the Special Forces troops to hold their ground and rally their Mike Force natives. However, after Captain Orms was wounded in the face and arm, recon platoon leader Sgt. Jackie L. Waymire was mortally wounded in the head, and two Montagnards were hit in the leg, the mobile guerrilla force was forced to break radio silence and request a medical evacuation mission.

Lieutenant Jenkins took over the task force, and after a cross-jungle trek of an hour and thirty minutes, they reached a landing zone suitable for lifting out the casualties. As the evacuation helicopter started to descend, it came under machine gun fire. Platoon leader Sfc. Lloyd L. Millner and radioman Sgt. Donald C. Ferrell ran into the clearing and fired at the North Vietnamese position, so that it could be suppressed by helicopter gunships. The casualties were boarded on the medical aircraft.

Within the next few days the mobile guerrilla force determined that it was in the middle of a Viet Cong stronghold with more forces massing against it. On 12 January the remainder of Task Force 768 was extracted under the cover of A-1E airstrikes, which kept the Viet Cong at a distance until the mobile guerrilla force was aloft in helicopters. BLACKJACK 22 had been successful in confirming the presence of a large VC safe haven, but the mission had been compromised after the first firefight two days before the patrol base was attacked. After the patrol base skirmish, Special Forces direction was dictated in response to Viet Cong maneuver.[8]

BLACKJACK 31, undertaken from 8 January to 7 February 1967, was one of the most successful Special Forces mobile guerrilla operations. Task Force 957, commanded by Capt. James G. "Bo" Gritz, was composed of a 105-man Mike Force company and 8 interpreters under Detachment A-303. Captain Gritz's men ranged through War Zone D, raiding fixed bases, emplacing mines and boobytraps, and using seventy-seven airstrikes against a wide variety of targets at the cost of only 1 CIDG soldier killed.[9]

Task Force 489 initiated the first mobile guerrilla operation in the Delta, labeled BLACKJACK 41 RED. Capt. George Maracek led a Khmer Kampuchea Krom (KKK) Mike Force from Detachment A-430 at Don Phuc into the Seven Mountains area of Chau Doc Province on 19 January 1967. There he linked up with local Khmer Kampuchea Krom Viet Cong leaders and convinced them to join the Special Forces as a permanent guerrilla force in that locale. After numerous contacts using female agents, the Don Phuc Mike Force was posted to Nui Cam to flush out noncooperative VC and to assist negotiations. BLACKJACK 41 WHITE continued the same operation, although the task force was redesignated 399 and primarily battled for control of

Nui Giai. Heavy fighting in the Seven Mountains region continued throughout most of year as BLACKJACK 41 BLUE followed.[10]

The BLACKJACK operations conducted during the spring and summer of 1967 represented the peak of the mobile guerrilla force campaign and encompassed most isolated regions of Vietnam. For instance, the II CTZ (Pleiku) Mike Force was active in other areas of the central highlands outside the western frontier. Detachment A-218 formed Task Force 876, which penetrated the Soui Kon River valley of Binh Dinh area on BLACKJACK 23 from 5 March to 3 April 1967. Led by Capt. Clyde J. Sincere, Jr., the mobile guerrilla force confirmed the use of the area as a NVA/VC headquarters and supply area. Unfortunately, a bombing run on 9 March 1967 mistakenly hit the mobile guerrilla force positions, killing Sfc. Frank C. Huff and two CIDG, as well as wounding two more Special Forces sergeants and nine CIDG members.[11]

The III CTZ (Bien Hoa) Mike Force also remained active. Task Force 966, led by Capt. Thomas G. Johnson, and containing 126 Cambodians under Detachment A-304, moved into eastern Phuoc Tuy Province during BLACKJACK 32 on 15 March 1967. The force used stealth and bold action to surprise and interdict several Viet Cong pathways, but VC trackers led larger forces to the mobile guerrilla force by the afternoon of 3 April. Surrounded in a perimeter on the edge of a large clearing, the task force smothered the advancing Viet Cong with airstrikes before being lifted out.[12]

In the northern sector of the country, Task Force 768, under Capt. Jules J. Bonavolonta of Detachment A-100, performed BLACKJACK 12 (also known as Operation OCONEE), a reconnaissance-in-force mission that entered Quang Nam and southern Thua Thien provinces at the end of March. By 19 April, North Vietnamese forces had converged on the mobile guerrilla force and were flanking it in a bitter firefight. The unit was extracted under fire, which caused numerous casualties and several blasted helicopters.

Mobile guerrilla forces used increasingly sophisticated methodology as the BLACKJACK series continued. BLACKJACK 42 in June marked the first mobile guerrilla force amphibious infiltration, when Task Force 399 struck the Viet Cong Long Toan Secret Zone in southeastern portion of the Delta's Vinh Binh "Permanent Peace" Province. Backup for BLACKJACK 41 WHITE was provided when three companies of the Nha Trang Mike Force parachuted south of Nui Giai (appropriately, on Drop Zone "Blackjack") at dawn on 13 May 1967 as part of the assault on that mountain fortress. During BLACKJACK 33 in May, mobile guerrilla forces were used for the first time in conjunction with 5th Special Forces Group strategic reconnaissance when Project SIGMA used Mike Force resources.

Mobile guerrilla forces differed in many ways from Special Forces strategic reconnaissance and could not replace Projects OMEGA and SIGMA when the latter organizations became part of MACV-SOG in November. The mobile guerrilla forces entered hostile areas after intensive preparation with company-size, independent units for sustained periods of time. They were not capable of saturating a large area with short-term patrols and lacked roadrunners and heliborne reconnaissance teams. Moreover, the mobile guerrilla force was primarily designed to harass and disrupt targets with conventional ranger tactics, while strategic reconnaissance was primarily concerned with gathering intelligence by observing and reporting without open confrontation. Even the qualifications and skills required of the CIDG troops were different. Long-range patrol members were trained in special infiltration and extraction techniques that are largely unknown to mobile guerrilla force troops.

Mobile guerrilla forces had other drawbacks as well. The entire concept of secretly fielding a company-size CIDG unit in any NVA/VC-held area in excess of one or two weeks, much less thirty days, without medical evacuation or overt supply, was unrealistic and was never really achieved. The North Vietnamese and Viet Cong were quick to detect the unit soon after insertion. In most cases the detected mobile guerrilla force was unable successfully to evade and had to be extracted under pressure or in the midst of combat. Almost every BLACKJACK mission was complicated by serious command, personnel, and resupply problems.

While the BLACKJACK operations were extremely beneficial search-and-destroy operations, Special Forces never could employ them as intended because of two overriding factors: (1) the inherent limitations of the CIDG troops, and (2) the simple fact that by 1967 most Viet Cong guerrilla sanctuaries were actually North Vietnamese regular army staging camps. Finally even the term *mobile guerrilla force* was a misnomer, since the Mike Forces were not indigenous to the Blackjack operational areas. The Special Forces personnel were not partisan leaders but commanders of combat companies and platoons temporarily conducting search operations in NVA/VC-controlled territory. On 23 May 1968 the mobile guerrilla forces were merged with the Mike Forces into new structures properly designated as Mobile Strike Force Commands.

3. The Mobile Strike Force Commands

In March 1968 the Nha Trang Mike Force was expanded as a Special Forces light infantry brigade capable of serving throughout South Vietnam. On 23 May 1968 Detachment B-55 was formed to command the 55th Mobile Strike Force Command. The detachment contained Detachments A-503 and A-551(later redesignated A-504), each of which controlled one mobile strike force battalion. The battalion companies were given distinctively colored scarves for battlefield identification and esprit.[13]

Detachments B-16 at Da Nang, B-20 at Pleiku, B-36 at Long Hai, and B-40 at Can Tho were officially activated to command the 16th, 20th, 36th, and 40th Mobile Strike Force Commands in their respective corps tactical zones. Effective 29 June 1968, the 5th Special Forces Group standardized the internal structure of these commands. Each command was authorized a 135-man reconnaissance and a 224-man headquarters and service company, except the 55th MSFC, which had no reconnaissance company but a larger, 336-man headquarters and service company. The number of battalions (each of three 184-man rifle companies) varied. The 16th Mobile Strike Force Command had a single battalion, the 55th initially had two, and the other commands had three battalions. The 40th Mobile Strike Force Command also contained a 184-man airboat company. In the fall of 1968, the mobile strike force commands were renumbered to conform to their numerical corps designations and dropped the second digit, so that the 16th MSFC became the 1st MSFC, and so on.[14]

The 2d Mobile Strike Force Command practically doubled during 1968, as it contained three battalions at Pleiku and also satellited separate battalions under Detachment B-22 at Qui Nhon, B-23 at Ban Me Thuot, and B-24 at Kontum. On 1 April 1969 the mobile strike force companies in II CTZ were reconsolidated at Pleiku and trimmed down to a total of six. By that date every other mobile strike force command had one battalion, except for the 5th, which was at full brigade strength with three battalions.

Some of the hardest Special Forces combat during 1969 and 1970 occurred in the Delta. For twenty years the Viet Cong had turned the rocky crags of the Seven Mountains in Chau Doc Province into virtually invincible bastions. The principal peak was a sinister slab of boulder-strewn granite known as Nui Coto. Locally, the mountain was called "Superstition Mountain" since the populace firmly believed that any Viet Cong there were protected from death. Since July 1968, numerous attempts by the 4th Mobile Strike Force Command and other allied units to clear Nui Coto had been repulsed with heavy losses. Artillery, airstrikes, and even massed B-52 bombing had failed to reduce the labyrinth of underground passages and boulder-protected bunkers.

During February 1969, intensive meetings were held between representatives of the Special Forces, IV Corps Tactical Zone, and the Vietnamese 44th Special Tactical Zone. Everyone agreed that the mountain had to be taken from the *510th VC Battalion*. The only question was which unit would be assigned the almost suicidal mission of assaulting it. Maj. John E. Borgman's 5th Mobile Strike Force Command was selected. His three battalions were moved from their Nha Trang base to positions west of the mountain by 15 March 1969. In order to standardize ammunition supply requirements and adequately arm the command, the mobile strike troops were issued M16 rifles. Unfortunately, they were given many obsolete weapons, without the forward assists, forcing them to fight with inferior rifles.[15]

Before dawn on 16 March 1969, an artillery barrage pounded the hill, and at 5:30 A.M. the mobile strike force companies stepped across the line of departure and advanced across the dry rice fields at the base of the mountain. Hidden deep within the cave-studded rocky mountainside, the VC gunners waited. The face of Nui Coto was actually a jumbled mass of huge boulders, some the size of two-story houses. Wedged into those formidable obstacles were expert Viet Cong sniper teams. Machine guns were thrust from the natural bunkers at cavern entrances. An hour later, as the Special Forces–led strike troops began to climb the jagged stones, VC automatic weapons fire and grenades swept the slope.

Nearly 20 percent of one company became casualties in two minutes as the hail of bullets ripped through the lead assault wave. Effective return fire was impossible because the defenders remained unseen in the extensive cave complexes and in cracks between gigantic rocks. Yet the mobile strike troops pushed farther upslope, clambering over huge boulders, clawing their way up treacherously steep paths, dodging automatic weapons fire and grenades that were showered upon them. Their objective was a height on Nui Coto called Tuk Chup Knoll, but christened "Million-Dollar Knoll" after the amount of costly ordnance used against it.

The lead shock troops reached the summit of Tuk Chup Knoll at 8:05 A.M., then the real battle began. Previous allied attempts to take the knoll had used various techniques in vain, ranging from frontal assaults upslope to heliborne landings on top of the peak, followed by attacks downhill. Major Borgman had a solid line of men extending up the west side of Tuk Chup Knoll, from its base to the summit, and he planned slowly to move this line around the mountainside, destroying each defensive strongpoint in turn. The 1st Battalion had responsibility for the lower portion of Tuk Chup and was linked into the 2d Battalion, which would tackle the upper half. The rest of 16 and 17 March was spent in preparation for the attack. During the lull, both battalions were subjected to continual B-40 rocket, M-79 grenade, and rifle fire. S. Sgt. Benedict M. Davan was killed leading his company in an assault against one of the VC firing positions, which launched a devastating B-40 rocket barrage.

The Special Forces got a good break on the day before the general advance. Their incessant, blaring loudspeakers, appealing for surrender, had finally unnerved nine Viet Cong defenders. The soldiers warily entered the battalion lines with arms upstretched and were immediately treated to candy and beer. The grateful VC prisoners gave detailed information on gun locations and the extent of ammunition stocks.

On 18 March the two battalions began their sweep around Tuk Chup Knoll. The battalions were arranged to advance in depth with several lines of troops. Thus, Viet Cong who appeared out of crevices and split caves to shoot at the back of the front wave would be encountered by another line of soldiers. Early in the afternoon Sfc. Stanley H. McKee's company of the 1st Battalion was attacked by the Viet Cong who crawled into the rocks among them. When the Vietnamese ran to the rear, the incident threatened the whole advance. Sergeant McKee hit so many fleeing people that he severely bruised his knuckles, but nothing could stop the panicked troops from throwing off their packs and running away. Finally, napalm had to be brought in almost on top of McKee's position to allow him to bring out the wounded who had been left behind.

The reserve company was rushed into the breach, and the entire line began moving forward again. Methodically, the troops searched every cave for hiding Viet Cong. Boulders were carefully cleared one by one. Progress was slow and tedious, interrupted by the crack of sniper rifles and the clatter of sudden machine gun bursts reverberating through the rocks. Throughout 19 March the steady advance continued as casualties mounted. Hardly any results were witnessed against the unseen Viet Cong.

While the LLDB personnel were performing with extraordinary valor, and the Rhade and Koho Montagnard mobile strike companies behaved aggressively with high morale, the Special Forces were having trouble with the 511th Vietnamese and 513th Cholon Chinese companies. The Cholon Chinese were nearly all draft evaders and frightened by the operation. As usual on combat assaults, they wore their names on red cloths pinned over their hearts and wrapped burning joss sticks with red cloth to their rifle muzzles to insure Buddhist protection. Sfc. Agostino Chiarello commanded the lead company of the 1st Battalion, which was advancing under the pall of burning incense, and had to herd his dejected Chinese forward by throwing grenades at them.

Sgt. Kenneth L. Rayburn tried to seize some high ground with his platoon before dark. Suddenly a torrent of Viet Cong grenades began tumbling down on them, and Rayburn was blown off a rock trying to keep the Chinese moving. He insisted that he was only lightly wounded and stayed on the mountain. Rayburn was forced to halt his advance at that spot, not realizing that underneath their overnight position there was a VC tunnel leading to the higher ground. The next morning the Viet Cong came out of the tunnel holes and gunned down several men. Two days later Rayburn was seriously wounded by an AK-47 bullet which punctured his lung, while fighting in the tunnels near the same location.

At midnight on 20 March, Major Borgman declared a ceasefire that lasted until dawn. Loudspeakers blasted the hillside, calling for immediate surrender, while village vendors peddled beer, soda, and new joss sticks among the frontline troops. The advance continued at 7:30 A.M., after a thundering barrage of artillery and airstrikes pounded the remaining segments of the hill. During the next two days, numerous caves and natural blockhouses were taken by riflemen and Special Forces volunteers armed with flamethrowers. On 22 March an immense cavern was uncovered with numerous tunnel networks. The following day a hospital complex was discovered, protected by a field of boobytraps.

Shortly before 8:00 A.M. on March 23, a platoon of the 1st Battalion encountered a sniper element, and the firefight quickly developed into scattered fighting along the entire front. Sfc. Albert G. Belisle directed his platoons to maneuver against the sniper team, and Sgt. John M. Greene's platoon used fire and movement to advance closer to the position. Suddenly, a B-40 rocket explosion wounded three mobile strike soldiers. Sergeant Greene called for smoke grenades to screen him as he scrambled forward to the fallen men. The smoke only partially masked his dashes to the wounded soldiers, but he managed to pull two men behind a boulder. Greene returned to retrieve the last Montagnard, who was so badly wounded that immediate bandaging was required before movement was attempted. As he was applying that emergency aid, a sniper fatally shot Sergeant Greene through the head.

That evening a three-man indigenous patrol, composed of Ha Lys, Mang So, and Ha Non, returned to the frontline after one of the most daring escapades of the battle. The trio of mobile strike troopers had traveled more than 300 yards underground and forward of the general advance. They found several huge caverns and ammunition rooms filled with weapons. They watched as 100 male and female Viet Cong made final preparations to abandon Nui Coto. During the expedition, the patrol killed seven female sentries and rearmed itself with AK-47 assault rifles. The trio was later challenged by Viet Cong guards at a cave entrance. The patrol members quickly raised the captured weapons as a signal of identification and were able to bluff their way past the guards.

Above ground, the battalions continued to battle their way forward. More caves and gun positions were cleared on 24 and 25 March. Intelligence gained by the few prisoners and three-man patrol indicated that the 5th Mobile Strike Force Command was approaching the main VC complex of caves where the legendary VC leader, Chau Kem, was rumored to have his headquarters. The two battalions located the main cave on 26 March, but most of the Viet Cong had already slipped away. The Special Forces uncovered hundreds of weapons and thousands of documents, films, and records. This marked the last organized resistance on Tuk Chup Knoll, although skirmishing continued until 8 April, as subsidiary caves and rock enclaves were explored. The 5th Mobile Strike Force Command had secured one of the most vaunted VC strongpoints in South Vietnam.[16]

The Seven Mountains had not been totally subdued, however, and another bastion at Nui Khet remained to be dealt with. On 13 March 1970 Colonel Healy alerted Lt. Col. Charles S. Black, Jr., the new commander of the 5th Mobile Strike Force Command, that another battalion would be needed for Operation INTREPID, the code word for the storming of Nui Khet. Capt. James W. Ficken's 1st Battalion, composed of the 511th, 512th, and 513th companies and reinforced by the 2d Combat Reconnaissance Platoon and other elements of headquarters company was slated for the mission. They arrived at Chi Lang from Nha Trang a week later.

On the evening of 20 March 1970, the battalion began clearing the Nha Bang woods to the east of Nui Khet mountain. After three days of difficult combat, the 511th and 512th companies refused to continue moving forward because of a misunderstanding between them and their LLDB personnel. The battalion returned to its forward positions northeast of Chi Lang, where the dissension among the troops was quelled. Thirty-eight mobile strike force troops resigned, but the incident was far costlier than anyone knew at the time. The failure to clear VC mortar positions in the woods later caused high casualties on the mountain.

The battalion was moved to Camp Vinh Gia (LLDB Detachment A-129) and cleared the Tram forest from 26 March until 2 April 1970 to confirm combat prowess. Then the three companies were moved up for the actual assault on Nui Khet. Several O-2 "loudmouth" and "litterbug" aircraft heralded the Special Forces appearance by dropping thousands of leaflets and using loudspeakers. Unfortunately, the leaflet drop was off target and the winds "carried the propaganda effort several kilometers west of Nui Khet." The 3d Battalion of the 4th Mobile Strike Force Command was moved into the adjacent Nha Bang woods to provide flank security and blocking positions. However, this supporting battalion was decimated by a volley of errant South Vietnamese 155mm shells, and it had to be pulled from the area. The 513th Company was used as the new flank security.

The 5th Mobile Strike Force's 1st Battalion was ordered to storm the mountain fortress as scheduled. After an intensive bombardment, the 511th and 512th companies started to scale the southwest side of Nui Khet at 3:30 P.M. on 3 April 1970. They were engaged in heavy fighting just below the military crest. Despite exploding B-40 rockets and withering machine gun fire, several troops of the 2d Combat Reconnaissance Platoon intermixed with some 511th men gained a foothold on the top of the mountain. They were pushed back by concentrated, interlocking fire from a cluster of twelve reinforced concrete bunkers built on the mountain peak. Viet Cong mortar tubes in the jungle below began bombarding the battalion's forward lines, and the mobile strike troops tried to find shelter in the boulders.

The 513th Company brought ammunition and water to the forward companies that evening as Special Forces mortars and Cobra helicopter gunships of the 7th Squadron, 1st Cavalry, rocketed and strafed the VC strongpoints. At dawn on 4 April, the depleted battalion reattacked. A rock ledge on the southern side of the mountain summit was cleared after savage combat. Staff Sergeant Brady was seriously wounded in the chest by hand grenade and B-40 rocket fragments. The forward momentum of the assault was then brought to a stop by concentrated Viet Cong fire. The mobile strike force pulled back and directed airstrikes into the VC positions. After being repulsed a second time, the battalion established night defensive lines just below the military crest.

Sgt. Brian L. Buker, a platoon leader in the 513th Company, volunteered to lead two platoons up the fire-swept mountainside of Nui Khet to bring critically needed water and ammunition to the forward companies that were dug in near the summit. Approximately halfway up the mountain, his overloaded men were ambushed and began to receive concentrated mortar fire. Sergeant Buker immediately led a successful counterattack into the VC ambush positions, rallied his troops, and traversed his way to the elements near the top of the mountain. After linking up with the lead battalion elements, the eastern perimeter was probed by the Viet Cong. Sergeant Buker spurred his exhausted force into the thick of combat and personally led the flanking charge through intense rifle and B-40 rocket fire.

On the morning of 5 April, the 513th Company was ordered to replace the 511th and the shattered recon platoon on the west side of the mountain. At 9:00 A.M. the new company spearheaded the final assault on Nui Khet. The troops cleared several VC bunkers by close fighting at point-blank ranges in the narrow passes between the rocks. Light antitank weapons and hand grenades were used to neutralize several positions and gain the mountaintop. The 512th and 513th companies linked up on the summit just after noon and began flushing out the Viet Cong from the numerous caves and tunnel systems. One bunker complex was not cleared because of its mortar support from the Nha Bang woods. Sergeant Strode was wounded in the face by mortar shrapnel just before noon. Sergeant First Class Parker was wounded in the right arm half an hour later; it was his third wound of the battle. Throughout the day and evening the fighting troops were resupplied by water and ammo parties from the rear company, which returned downslope with litters of dead and wounded.

The battalion continued routing Viet Cong defenders from Nui Khet throughout the next day as isolated pockets of resistance were subdued in sharp combat. The last bunker complex still held out. Captured Viet Cong were brought forward to urge surrender, using loudspeakers, but all efforts to persuade the occupants to give up failed. After four Cobra rocket attacks and forty rounds of direct 106mm recoilless rifle fire, Sergeant Buker braved VC machine gun and rocket fire to lead his mobile strike troops closer to gain better firing positions against the bunkers.

After Buker had moved his men forward, another concrete bunker was spotted. Buker realized that the route of advance was channelized because of the rocky terrain and that VC flanking fire from the newly discovered machine gun bunker would expose any withdrawal attempt to devastating crossfire. He charged into a hail of bullets and pitched four grenades into the newly found bunker to destroy it. Buker miraculously survived but was seriously wounded by a B-40 rocket blast while regrouping his men. Bleeding profusely, he crawled forward to another Viet Cong position in the rocky wall and eliminated it with a grenade. Sergeant Buker was killed shortly afterwards by a mortar round. The last VC bunker was taken at 5:45 P.M., after a final pitched battle. Operations on the mountain top were constantly mortared by Viet Cong mortar fire from the unsecured jungle below, but Nui Khet was in Special Forces hands.

The Battle of Nui Khet was one of the last major mobile strike force command actions of the Second Indochina War. Another savage battle was fought at Nui Ek mountain by the 2d Battalion of the 5th Mobile Strike Force Command two miles north of Camp Dak Seang from 28 April to 15 June 1970. These engagements were full-fledged, direct-assault, mountain-warfare operations. Although the various mobile strike force commands were active in many actions throughout Vietnam, the 5th Mobile Strike Force Command battles represented the final transition of Mike Force evolution from small Rhade eagle flight emergency reaction detachments to conventional shock battalions capable of tackling hardened NVA/VC fortresses. Intrinsic mobile strike forces enabled the 5th Special Forces Group to clear threatened camp tactical areas of responsibility with only a minimum of ARVN and regular Army assistance.[17]

Notes

1. 5th Special Forces Group, *Monthly Operational Summary*, dtd 13 February 1965; 5th Special Forces Group, *Development of the CIDG Program, 1964–1968*, dtd 22 April 1968. Before 1965 the Special Forces was prohibited from actually parachuting the Rhades, so the first eagle flight troops completed only the jump-tower phase of airborne instruction.

2. 5th Special Forces Group, *Operational Reports*, dtd 10 May 1966 and 15 February 1967. Detachment A-430 was redesignated A-401 on 1 June 1967.

3. Detachment A-219, *Monthly Operational Summary*, dtd 1 October 1965. CIDG financing is outlined in Appendix D.

4. 5th Special Forces Group, *Operational Report*, dtd 15 May 1967, Inclosure 9; 5th Special Forces Group, *Employment of Civilian Irregular Defense Group and Long Range Reconnaissance Projects*, dtd 21 July 1968.

5. II Corps Mike Force, *After Action Report*, dtd 18 April 1968; 5th Special Forces Group Assistant ALO, *After Action Report*, dtd 29 April 1968; 5th Special Forces Group, *Operational Report*, dtd 15 February 1968.

6. Company B, *Lessons Learned Concerning Employment of CIDG Troops During Operational DEVERALL*, undtd. During the battle, the companies were also referred to as the 202d, 204th, 205th, and 206th MSF companies.

7. 5th Special Forces Group, *Combat Operation After Action Report*, dtd 18 November 1966, with taped interviews.

8. Detachment A-219, *After Action Report*, dtd 27 January 1967. The operation is also discussed in the "marathon patrol" chapter of S. L. A. Marshall, *Ambush* (New York: Cowles Book Company, 1969), and differences in his version were resolved in favor of the after action report. Although the enemy is identified as Viet Cong, there were strong indications that they were actually North Vietnamese.

9. Detachment A-303, *After Action Report—Operation BLACKJACK 31*, undated.

10. Company D, *BLACKJACK 41*, dtd 27 February 1967; 5th Special Forces Group, *Operational Report*, dtd 15 May 1967; Detachment 401, *After Action Report*, dtd 21 May 1967.

11. Detachment A-218, *After Action Report*, dtd 12 April 1967.

12. Detachment A-304, *After Action Report*, dtd 9 April 1967.

13. The scarf colors were as follows: 1st Battalion, 5th MSFC, 511th Co., red; 512th Co., black; 513th Co., forest green; 2d Battalion, 5th MSFC, 521st Co., yellow; 522d Co., navy blue; 523d Co., light blue. The combat reconnaissance platoons had camouflage scarves cut from T-7 camouflage parachute canopies.

14. 5th Special Forces Group, *Operational Report*, dtd 15 August 1968.

The authorized strengths were first established at: 16th MSFC (911), 20th and 36th MSFC (2,015), 40th MSFC (2,199), and the 55th MSFC (1,430). This book utilizes the final MSFC designations (1st–5th) in the text, unless otherwise stated, as a matter of clarity.

15. Detachment B-55, *Field Grade Officer's Debriefing Report*, dtd 16 April 1969.

16. 5th Special Forces Group, AVGB Ltr, dtd 26 July 1969, Inclosures 8 and 9. Casualties in the 1969 Nui Coto battle were KIA: 34; WIA: 137; 29 Viet Cong killed and counted and 17 captured. Sergeant Greene was awarded the Silver Star, and Staff Sergeants Rayburn and Davan received the Distinguished Service Cross. The Detachment B-55 compound at Nha Trang was renamed in memory of Davan. Each of the three volunteers in the cave patrol received an American Bronze Star for Valor.

17. Casualties at Nui Khet were KIA: 1 Special Forces, 1 LLDB, 20 CIDG; WIA: 17 Special Forces, 1 LLDB, 115 CIDG. Thirty-eight NVA bodies were counted although actual losses were doubtless much higher. Detachment B-55, *5th MSFC After Action Report B-4-A*, dtd 14 June 1970.

CHAPTER 14

THE SECONDARY FRONT

1. The Final Border Campaign

When Col. Michael Healy took over the 5th Special Forces Group, he commanded twelve line B-Detachments, five special B-Detachments, the Nha Trang Installation Command, the MACV Recondo School, and sixty-three A-Detachments, of which forty-eight were in a border surveillance mode (twelve in II CTZ, nine each in I and III CTZ, and eight in IV CTZ). On the day he assumed command, 31 August, group strength stood at 3,413 Special Forces, 29,848 camp strike force, and 8,793 mobile strike force soldiers. The group also employed 2,968 civilians in jobs ranging from parachute riggers to camp nurses, although a moratorium on civilian hire had been declared on 11 June 1969.

Throughout the final years of 5th Special Forces Group presence in Vietnam, the campaign waged along South Vietnam's frontier at the border camps would dominate combat activity. This bitter struggle was considered a secondary front by MACV compared to the large divisional expeditions against A Shau Valley and Cambodia. However, there were several reasons why the Special Forces stubbornly retained possession of these threatened fortified outposts, despite the high casualties and the high cost of defending them.

Special Forces border camps remained essential to MACV attempts to impede NVA/VC infiltration. They served as ideal bases from which offensive ground operations could be launched and supported by artillery. South Vietnamese and American troops rarely operated beyond cannon or howitzer range, since artillery provided them with considerable firepower advantage over the North Vietnamese. Allied campaign plans increasingly charged the ARVN with conducting sweeps of the clearing zones to prevent NVA/VC incursions farther into the countryside. Since the network of Special Forces border camps was never completed, the NVA simply shifted major infiltration routes outside the artillery support of the established camps and moved through the gaps between them. The South Vietnamese Army was then being directed to patrol those gaps. Any relocation of existing bases would have resulted in ARVN reluctance to enter such dangerous frontier areas.

Most border camps were barraged by highly mobile NVA rockets, mortars, and recoilless rifles and not by fixed artillery. Displacement to areas more distant from the border would not reduce camp vulnerability to this type of attack. It would only result in a corresponding de facto eastward relocation of the Special Forces front line, since the NVA/VC would quickly fill any void created by removing the camps from the frontier.

Relocation of the camps away from the international border and closer to populated areas, in order to decrease vulnerability and to better safeguard farmland and cities, was not a viable solution either. Such a move actually would have decreased population security by thinning MACV's protective shield and by reducing allied ability to detect and react to North Vietnamese approach marches. Instead of battling NVA infiltration zones along the border, the major actions that typified the last Special Forces years would have been fought near population centers in South Vietnam's consolidation zones.

In the IV CTZ Delta region the situation was different. Except in the Plain of Reeds, the border area was heavily populated. There were many major cities near the Cambodian boundary that would have been left unsecured by any Special Forces withdrawal. Since the magnitude of the population precluded their resettlement, closing the IV CTZ border camps was considered impractical.

The political impact of relocating the border camps was even more potentially detrimental than the military consequences. Even if the South Vietnamese government agreed to such a scheme, the Thieu regime would have been accused of abandoning control of national borders and regressing to the territorial influence that had existed in 1964–1965. Additionally, the abandonment of well-established camps might have caused speculation that the United States lacked confidence in South Vietnamese ability to defend them. General Abrams considered these possible interpretations unacceptably damaging to the progress of Vietnamization. President Richard M. Nixon feared any adverse moves that provided fuel for unfavorable public opinion in the United States.[1]

As a result of these considerations, the Special Forces was committed to a difficult campaign along the border throughout the latter period of American presence in Vietnam, long after levels of combat had dropped elsewhere. The situation was resented by many professional Special Forces soldiers, who realized the futility of maintaining remote garrisons that couldn't be supplied once the Americans left. The more isolated camps relied on complete aerial delivery of supplies. The South Vietnamese Air Force was unable logistically to support twelve of the camps, and it was projected to have extreme difficulty supporting eight others.

The MACV staff hoped that upon the departure of Special Forces the Vietnamese Air Force could support the air-dependent camps if regular land routes could be maintained to the others. Roadways might be cleared to camps such as Bu Dop and Katum. In the Delta, potential water and overland routes permitted access to all camps except Cai Cai, which was completely air dependent. Knowledgeable Special Forces and LLDB officers were less optimistic about the chances of overland security.

2. The Last Highland Battles

The Special Forces retained six camps along the rugged border in South Vietnam's western highlands. These were Ben Het, Bu Prang, Duc Co, Duc Lap, Dak Pek, and Dak Seang. All of them were violently besieged during the final years of Special Forces presence in Vietnam.

Camp Ben Het (A-244, Capt. Louis P. Kingsley) was located seven miles east of the tri-border junction of Vietnam, Laos, and Cambodia and monitored several major NVA infiltration routes. The North Vietnamese made little attempt to hide their buildup around the camp, and the Special Forces prepared for the inevitable attack. Antitank mines were sewn along a key road to counter the possible employment of NVA armor.

From 23 February to 3 March 1969, Ben Het was bombarded and subjected to ground probes. On the night of 3 March, the camp received 639 rounds of mixed artillery and mortar fire. A battalion from the *66th NVA Regiment*, supported by ten PT-76 tanks, launched an attack on the west hill of Ben Het. The hill was held by a CIDG company, reinforced by several American M-48 tanks, under detachment executive officer 1st Lt. Michael D. Linnane, heavy weapons Sfc. Richard V. Grier, and medical S. Sgt. Robert F. Umphlett. Two reinforcing CIDG companies, from Dak Pek (A-242) and Mang Buk (A-246), were also present.

The tanks drove straight up the road into the minefield, where two of them were disabled. Tank cannon, artillery, and airstrikes were used to defeat the advancing armor. One American tank situated on the west hill was hit and disabled in exchange. The 1st Battalion of the 2d Mobile Strike Force, standing by at Kontum, was subsequently inserted into the area to relieve pressure on the camp. The only unfavorable incident occurred on 10 March, when the Dak Pek and Mang Buk companies quit and started to walk home, but their Special Forces advisors convinced them to remain until transport arrived.[2]

Both camps at Ben Het and Dak To were besieged by the *28th* and *66th NVA Regiments* from 5 May until 29 June 1969 during rainy southwest monsoon weather. Mountaintops were frequently obscured by low clouds and thunderstorms, making helicopter navigation difficult. The terrain around Ben Het was rugged and covered by triple-canopy jungle, bamboo, and brushwood. The summer campaign became a test of South Vietnamese ability to safeguard a threatened Special Forces border camp, backed only by American artillery and airpower.

Small sapper units hit the two camps on 11 May and succeeded in penetrating the perimeter wire at Dak To before being repulsed. While the 42d ARVN Regiment operating in the vicinity took the brunt of battlefield activity, Ben Het was continuously rocketed and mortared throughout the period. By the end of June, the camp was in shambles, and every building and vehicle on the main hill had been severely damaged. Roads leading into the camp were effectively cut off by repeated ambush, and in the latter part of June the North Vietnamese moved into dug-in positions around the airstrip in an effort to block all resupply.

Aircraft were forced to run a gauntlet of heavy ground fire, while movement inside the camp was hindered by accurate sniper fire. The North Vietnamese advanced trenches and tunnels out of the jungle through Ben Het's outer wire. CIDG soldiers discovered two tunnel complexes under North Hill on 27–28 June. The tunnels went under all three wire systems into the hillside perimeter and included cache bunkers. North Hill was abandoned and bulldozed down to practically half its original height. The siege was lifted in July, after ARVN operations confirmed that the North Vietnamese had withdrawn into Cambodia.[3]

Maintaining Ben Het after the siege also proved a difficult proposition. The 20th Engineer Battalion completely rebuilt and reinforced all fighting bunkers and repaired the runway. The reconstruction was finished 15 November 1969, but the hard work required of the CIDG garrison caused a high desertion rate. New CIDG recruits were attracted with generous pay offers, but they had little or no training. The Special Forces was angry at the lack of CIDG manpower and complained that the garrison was being filled with Cambodians who were "incompetent, filthy, and thoroughly unreliable."[4]

While a succession of Special Forces detachments enjoyed good relations with LLDB camp commanders Captain (later Major) Tuoc and Major Lich, relations between other team members and their LLDB counterparts were less cordial and often taxed by the long hours and back-breaking labor. Supply arrival was uncertain, and there were acute shortages of ammunition and illumination rounds. Costly mobile strike force operations were required to keep the North Vietnamese away from the camp.

Camp Ben Het was powerless to prevent major infiltration into the highlands despite its strategic position along a main branch of the Ho Chi Minh trail. The NVA were able to fix the CIDG within the confines of the camp by siege or threat of attack, sometimes using only a token force, while North Vietnamese soldiers moved around it. While these circumstances canceled much of its military significance, the political value of Ben Het was quite high. The camp had withstood sieges and repeated attacks, even where NVA tanks had been used. For that reason the Special Forces kept Ben Het in existence.[5]

Camps Bu Prang (A-236) and Duc Lap (A-239) were threatened next, when the same North Vietnamese regiments moved south from the Ben Het vicinity into adjacent Cambodian territory during the latter part of August 1969. The camps watched over the trackless jungled hills between them, where tropical forests offered excellent concealment to large concentrations of NVA troops. Both were besieged during the cool, dry weather from 28 October to 27 December 1969.

The LLDB and Special Forces enjoyed good relations at Camp Bu Prang. The detachment commander, Capt. William L. Palmer, had 336 mostly Rhade and Cambodian CIDG defenders. As the NVA buildup was heightened around the camp, mobile strike force troops started maneuvering in the area. American artillery was emplaced on three nearby, mutually supporting fire support bases: KATE, ANNIE, and SUSAN.

The 5th Battalion of the 22d Artillery posted three howitzers at Fire Support Base KATE to the east of Bu Prang. The Special Forces provided security for the firebase, with CIDG personnel rotated on a periodic basis. Sgt. Daniel Pierelli, the A-233 weapons sergeant, was sent to FSB KATE on 27 October 1969 with the Trang Phuc (Ban Don) company. Capt. William L. Albracht, the A-236 exective officer at Bu Prang, arrived the day after to take charge of all CIDG security at FSB KATE.

Commencing on 29 October, the hilltop fire support base was subjected to steady recoilless rifle, medium mortar, and B-40 rocket fire. During the evening, the An Lac (234) CIDG company started to helicopter onto the hill, but intensive ground fire prevented the helicopters from landing more than 40 men. With those reinforcements, FSB KATE contained 2 Special Forces and 2 LLDB leaders, 196 CIDG soldiers, and a platoon of Army artillerymen.

The North Vietnamese concentrated more troops against the base. On 30 October a helicopter gunship was hit by gunfire; it broke in half and crashed in flames, killing all aboard. The fire support base was desperately low on water and bullets. The latter problem was compounded by the need for two different kinds of ammunition. Pierelli's Trang Phuc soldiers had M2 carbines, but the Bu Prang and An Lac men had M16 rifles. The two 155mm howitzers had been knocked out, and the 105mm howitzer was severely damaged. On the evening of 31 October the firebase was ordered abandoned.

Captain Albracht assembled all the FSB KATE personnel on the northern edge of the hill. Equipment that could not be carried was destroyed with thermite grenades. Suddenly, the North Vietnamese fired parachute flares into the night and mortared the hilltop. The defenders began running through the perimeter wire, and as the mob raced downslope, one CIDG soldier accidentally tripped a flare.

Everyone dropped to the ground as the entire hillside was brilliantly illuminated. Captain Albracht was certain that the North Vietnamese would begin firing, but the night was silent. As soon as the flare died out, he formed the troops into an orderly column. The CIDG point-man headed the unit in a different direction than planned, but Captain Albracht realized that the natives had an intuitive grasp of the land. The diversion skirted NVA machine guns, but the column became disorganized after entering the darkened tropical forest.

Shortly afterwards the first CIDG soldiers were fired upon as they entered a clearing. When the clatter of machine guns started, the CIDG panicked and fled through the jungle. Albracht and Pierelli tried in vain to stop them. The captain counted their remaining intact band of twenty CIDG and was assured the American artillerymen were all present (actually two were later discovered missing in action). Albracht linked up with the 252d and 253d MSF companies of the 5th Mobile Strike Force Command as planned, and the group proceeded safely to Bu Prang. Since Fire Support Base KATE had been abandoned to the North Vietnamese, both ANNIE and SUSAN were evacuated on 2 November 1969, which left only the artillery inside the Bu Prang compound for camp defense.[6]

The reinforced 23d ARVN Division exercised operational control over all CIDG units during the campaign. The commander of the division had authorized that correspondents have access to the battlefield, but the commander of Detachment B-23 revoked clearance for correspondents to enter Camp Bu Prang on 2 November. The press raised an uproar and demanded to know who was in charge of the operation, the United States or South Vietnam. Although Colonel Healy quickly countermanded the B-23 order, General Abrams was infuriated.[7]

Abrams angrily denounced Special Forces performance in the ongoing battle during a staff meeting held in Saigon three days later. He maintained that the Vietnamese Joint General Staff chief, General Vien, and the II CTZ commander, Lieutenant General Luan, had both told him that the CIDG troops were not fully responsive to the commander of the 23d ARVN Division. General Abrams endorsed this excuse as the South Vietnamese rationale for not coming to the support of CIDG forces at Fire Support Base KATE. General Abrams continued to rage that "the only way we could reverse this attitude was to accelerate U.S. Army Special Forces disengagement from the CIDG program."[8]

Heavy shellings and ground probes against allied elements throughout the Bu Prang and Duc Lap areas increased in intensity. On 16–17 November 1969 Bu Prang endured the heaviest barrage of the siege. Bombardments and sapper attacks continued for the rest of the month but tapered off after 5 December when camp CIDG forces began venturing beyond the camp perimeter. After the first week in December, all North Vietnamese activity decreased significantly, and only occasional mortaring and ground contacts were being reported.[9]

The Bu Prang–Duc Lap campaign had been largely decided by American airpower. A total of 1,309 U.S. tactical fighter sorties were flown in support of the operation over the sixty-day period. Additionally, eighty-seven B-52 bombing raids had pounded the surrounding jungle. After the siege, Bu Prang was razed to the ground and relocated eleven miles to the southeast, in an area of lesser risk.

The new campsite was constructed by the 19th Engineer Battalion starting on 28 January 1970. Monsoon mud slowed work past April, and the new fortress was not totally finished until November. All materials were flown to the site, since Highway 14 leading to the camp was unsecured. However, when completed, new Bu Prang was the ultimate Special Forces fighting camp, situated on a commanding hill and built completely underground.

Camp Dak Seang (A-245) was located in the northwestern fringes of Kontum Province, six miles from the Laotian border, in the Dak Poko Valley amidst towering, heavily forested mountain ranges. During February and March, the *28th NVA Regiment* had moved into the valley completely undetected, felled trees with power saws and established sophisticated earthworks as close as a mile from the camp perimeter.

The siege of Dak Seang commenced at daybreak on 1 April 1970, when NVA mortars and recoilless rifle fire flattened three buildings, knocked down the camp communications antennas, and caused numerous casualties. A CIDG company from Plateau Gi (A-111) was air assaulted outside the camp perimeter, spent the night surrounded by NVA, and moved into the compound in the morning. Elements of the 42d ARVN Regiment also joined the defense. A wall of air-dropped napalm discouraged North Vietnamese sappers during most the the day.

At 4:45 P.M. on April 2, the North Vietnamese stormed the camp but were promptly defeated with the assistance of tactical air support.

The NVA attacked again at 7:00 P.M. and reached the wire on the western wall before being repulsed by helicopter gunships. Two more attempts were made to breach the perimeter after midnight. Two helicopters were shot down during the morning. The 1st and 4th MSF battalions of the 2d Mobile Strike Force Command were airmobiled into landing zones in close proximity to Dak Seang.

The North Vietnamese tried to rush the camp lines in the early hours of 4 April, starting from dug-in positions only thirty yards from the outer wire. The attempt was crushed by withering defensive fire. Although Dak Seang was continually bombarded, communications to neighboring detachments was restored on 5 April. Emergency airdrops resupplied the camp with ammunition, generators, and radio equipment. Renewed confidence was marred by an accidental bombing of the compound during the afternoon, followed by misguided helicopter strafing of the forward trenches. Throughout the day the camp was probed six times by sapper squads.

The North Vietnamese began to react to ARVN and mobile strike forces advancing through the valley on 6 April, which eased direct pressure on Dak Seang. The camp was still subjected to constant barrages and received an exceptionally heavy bombardment two days later. Most aboveground camp structures were destroyed by that time. Although the siege lasted until 8 May, the major focus of combat shifted to South Vietnamese units fighting to relieve the camp.[10]

Because of the activity at Dak Seang, the MACV did not expect a major North Vietnamese drive against the border camp at Dak Pek (A-242), located in the northern portion of the Dak Poko Valley. The Dak Pek camp complex occupied seven hills and was established overlooking a major NVA infiltration route from Laos along the boundary of I and II CTZ into both Quang Ngai and Binh Dinh provinces. However, the siege began in the morning darkness of 12 April 1970; the camp was suddenly pounded by mortars and rockets, followed by a sapper attack on the Special Forces hill.

The surprise attack was conducted by a sapper company supported by two infantry companies and internal camp Viet Cong sympathizers. The North Vietnamese swiftly carried the hill and practically wiped out the 203d CIDG Company that was defending the MACV-SOG launch site at the camp. The latter hill was captured so quickly and NVA weapons set up so fast that the Special Forces initially radioed headquarters that the CIDG company had turned on them by firing into the main compound. A third hill also fell to the NVA onslaught, enabling them to gain both 105mm howitzers and hold more than half the area of the camp.

A company from Plei Mrong and the 1st MSF Reconnaissance Company were airlifted inside the camp perimeter. After aircraft blistered the NVA-held portions of Dak Pek with napalm, three Special Forces assaults were made against the MACV-SOG hilltop. All the attacks were repulsed in the lower wire by direct NVA recoilless rifle fire. The key position was finally recaptured on 14 April as the hard-fighting mobile strike force recondo troops scaled the summit. North Vietnamese infantry staged another major assault the next day but were defeated.

The North Vietnamese began abandoning their newly won positions rather than endure further airstrikes. Although the siege of Dak Pek lasted until 9 May 1970, the level of combat consisted of mortar and rocket barrages. Dak Pek was practically destroyed, but Special Forces had again successfully defended an isolated frontier camp against overwhelming odds.[11]

3. The CIDG Program Closes Down

The successful conversion of the CIDG program to Vietnamese control, once Special Forces assistance was no longer required, had always been the ultimate goal of the 5th Special Forces Group in Vietnam. However, when General Abrams ordered execution of the CIDG program phasedown on 27 August 1969, many camps were incapable of independent effectiveness. MACV attached only minor importance to the sustained ability of such camps to fulfill their operational requirements or even to survive once Special Forces was pulled out. Great political pressure now attended having the Vietnamese immediately conduct the war effort with lessened U.S. assistance, regardless of the consequences.

A concerted effort was made by Special Forces to raise the combat readiness of each CIDG camp during the conversion cycle. The Special Forces teams were confronted with an awesome task. They had to motivate and indoctrinate CIDG personnel, especially the Montagnards, to become assimilated into the regular South Vietnamese armed forces. There were CIDG administrative and medical processing, transfer of property and equipment, preparation of MACV advisory teams, and CIDG reorganization into regular South Vietnamese rank and unit structure. The first CIDG camps were converted under these phasedown directives on 31 January 1970.

The transition process was complicated during the entire period by ongoing combat in many locales. Battles erupted throughout South Vietnam for control of the camps and were not limited to border regions. One of the most savage NVA/VC attacks during this stage of the war was directed against Camp Ba Xoai (A-421) in the Delta's Seven Mountains area near Cambodia. The camp's defenses consisted of one cattle fence and occasional concertina wire, and fighting positions with no overhead cover except for the concrete and palm-log bunkers.

In the early morning of 14 January 1970, sappers approached through heavy vegetation to within ten feet of the inner perimeter, where they launched B-40 rockets and tossed hand grenades. Mortar and rocket bombardment quickly destroyed Ba Xoai's primary generator bunker, mortar pits, searchlight and communications bunkers, and the Special Forces team house area. The alternate communications bunker was wrecked by either sapper activity or sabotage (a few VC infiltrators were identified in the 487th CIDG Company).

Two companies of infantry charged toward the camp. The excellent defense rendered by the Cambodian Khmer Kampuchea Krom (KKK) CIDG under LLDB supervision, aided by prompt helicopter gunship response, defeated the assault by dawn. The CIDG machine gunners stayed atop their bunkers throughout the attack, where they had excellent fields of fire, and refused Capt. Brian G. MacDonald's urging to move under cover. Individual riflemen jumped on top of the berm in order to gain better aim at the advancing North Vietnamese. One CIDG soldier voluntarily started firing an 81mm mortar after the crew had been killed. He expertly brought the shellfire within the wire and impacted the rounds throughout the sector to break up an attack. The soldier was later discovered to be an ex-ARVN mortar crewman.[12]

The spirited CIDG defense of Ba Xoai encouraged MACV optimism that Special Forces had been unduly concerned about the continued proficiency of the camps. High expectations were reinforced by defeats of further NVA attacks in the Seven Mountains area on Ba Xoai and Chi Lang (B-43) on 30 March 1970. Unfortunately, not all CIDG troops were as good, and camp efficiency varied accordingly. The next month Camp Mai Loc would be challenged.

Camp Mai Loc (A-101) was the only border camp in I CTZ within five miles of the Demilitarized Zone. The camp had been established on 24 June 1968 by the detachment that had been overrun at Lang Vei. Mai Loc was located on the western edge of the coastal plain on the fringes of a populated, fertile area.

Mai Loc was an unhappy camp from the start. Although 6,000 Bru Montagnards had been resettled in the vicinity at the same time and were used to garrison Mai Loc, they were unwelcome in the area by the Vietnamese. Large bonus payments had to be instituted to retain CIDG personnel, because of Mai Loc's dangerous position near the DMZ. The Special Forces constantly recommended closure of the camp because CIDG performance was below acceptable standards, recruitment was poor, and the camp was located so close to American firebases that CIDG operations had been canceled. MACV replied that the camp was well located and politically important.

Late in the evening of 9 April 1970, well-trained sappers from the *24th NVA Sapper Company* began slipping through the high grass and penetrating the perimeter wire from several directions. In one instance the sappers used a hole in the wire that the LLDB had created as a shortcut for themselves and had refused to repair on the rationale that "the CIDG would desert if they could not travel in and out as they desired." One squad, moving into the southern wire, was detected about midnight and taken under fire. Although some members were wounded, they remained motionless and silent until the firing ceased and the camp resumed normal alert status. The sappers then continued cutting wire and emplacing bangalore torpedoes. At 2:20 A.M., with some sappers already inside the inner Mai Loc compound and CIDG perimeter, the signal was given to launch the attack.

Extremely accurate mortar fire smothered critical American positions while B-40 rockets were used to demolish other targets. The team sergeant, M. Sgt. Gale Stopher, Jr., was in his bunker when the first mortar rounds descended on the camp. He dashed over to the CIDG area and organized their defense; then he went over to check on a "Duster" antiaircraft tank position. Finding two wounded Americans there, he radioed the tactical operations center and informed them that he was bringing them to that location. As Stopher approached his own bunker, he was fatally wounded by a mortar shell.

Individual sappers heaved satchel charges into key bunkers and were soon in control of the inner perimeter. Sergeant First Class Bailey started out of the medical bunker in response to a call for assistance in treating a wounded American when he heard a satchel charge being thrown in. He rushed back downstairs and was able to reach the air shaft when the charge went off. Five seconds later a second explosion rocked the structure. Bailey heard voices and people coming down the steps, followed by a third satchel charge and another detonation.

The tactical operations center in the command bunker was also under close attack. After one explosion immediately outside, all power was lost. The LLDB personnel were engaged in a firefight with several approaching groups of sappers and infantry. First Lieutenant Wolfgramm arrived, and the LLDB went inside. Four minutes later Wolfgramm spotted a large group of North Vietnamese charging toward the bunker. He fired off a magazine and ran down the stairs. Satchel charges were dropped into the stairway behind him.

After an hour of fighting, tanks from the 3d Squadron, 5th Cavalry, crashed into the camp and secured the inner perimeter. Mai Loc was closed on 27 August 1970 because of the persistent danger of North Vietnamese attack, poor CIDG performance, and probability of loss without retention of U.S. presence in the area. Detachment A-101 was then inactivated.[13]

Thuong Duc (A-109) was subjected to siege from late April through early June 1970, but the rush to shut down the CIDG program continued despite adverse tactical situations. On 26 June General Abrams sent a message to Colonel Healy telling him to publish the final CIDG plans. Four days later the group published OPORD 3-70, which directed the complete conversion of the CIDG program to ARVN Ranger status, and the subsequent phasedown of 5th Special Forces Group. This order required conversion of the thirty-eight remaining A-Detachment camps to ARVN ranger battalions by the end of the year, with Special Forces strength in support of the CIDG program reduced to zero by 31 March 1971.

As the camps in the four military regions of South Vietnam converted to the ARVN ranger program, the respective Special Forces B-Detachments and company headquarters terminated operations and closed down. The continued NVA menace to Thuong Duc required a delay in its conversion, but the Special Forces team was withdrawn on 15 November. With that turnover, the last CIDG camp in the northern Military Region 1 had been phased out. Already there had been trouble in the absence of Special Forces advisors. A week after the redesignation of the CIDG at Tra Bong as the 61st ARVN Ranger Battalion on 31 August 1970, the camp had suffered a devastating sapper attack because of the lack of communications with higher headquarters and the inability of the new MACV advisors to provide immediate support. Most of Tra Bong was destroyed, and Special Forces personnel were distraught at the prospects that this would happen at many other camps.

The dizzy phaseout of the CIDG program continued, as MACV policy was rigidly fixed in spite of North Vietnamese activity, mass Montagnard desertions, uncontrolled LLDB looting, and Special Forces protests. Thus, all CIDG camps in South Vietnam were converted to ARVN ranger status by the end of December. On 31 December 1970 the CIDG program officially terminated.

The strength of 5th Special Forces Group was steadily eroded during the last months by a series of personnel reductions in support of MACV redeployment. Standing proud and erect in the drizzling rain on 28 February 1971, Colonel Healy presided over the last 5th Special Forces Group formation in Vietnam. U.S. Ambassador Ellsworth Bunker and the MACV commander, General Abrams, had been invited to the final parade at Nha Trang headquarters but refused to attend. Colonel Healy's fiercely independent Special Forces troopers took this latest high command insult in stride. The close-knit, dedicated Special Forces men had survived hundreds of isolated, imperiled camps and fought some of the most savage battles of the Second Indochina War.

Colonel Healy pinned the Distinguished Service Cross on Sfc. Antonio J. Coelho, a stocky man of few words who had twice led helicopter teams through gunfire to save American and Vietnamese soldiers. The medal was the last of thousands of decorations for valor presented to Special Forces soldiers by the group in Vietnam. Then the men quietly gathered underneath a camouflaged cargo parachute canopy to exchange drinks and farewells. The next day a small honor guard boarded aircraft at Nha Trang Air Base to bring the colors back to Fort Bragg. The Department of the Army officially closed 5th Special Forces Group out of South Vietnam effective 3 March 1971.

The Special Forces could justly take pride in the fact that the Civilian Irregular Defense Group program, for all its faults and problems, was a great military accomplishment. The Special Forces had undertaken a vast and dangerous mission, which lasted a decade. They had mobilized the tribal groups and oppressed minorities of South Vietnam residing in remote areas and had organized them into dozens of the camp forces fighting for the allies. These had protected the small villages most vulnerable to armed attack, patrolled the highly dangerous North Vietnamese infiltration routes and Viet Cong base areas, monitored the borders, and served as conventional infantry in open battles. This difficult task was achieved despite the reluctance of the Saigon regime and the open hostility of a MACV commander. While the LLDB had been technically in charge, the Special Forces had commanded the CIDG forces in practice, and 5th Special Forces Group colonels commanded more troops than any American divisional major general.

Colonel Healy summed up the progress of the CIDG program from its beginnings to the final conversion into ARVN rangers when he replied to a reporter's question, "We took them out of loincloths and put them into uniforms, and now they are elite forces."[14]

Notes

1. MACJ3-032, *MACV Position on Relocation of Border Camps*, dtd 20 March 1970.
2. Detachment B-24, *After Action Report*, dtd 20 March 1969; Detachment A-244, *Detachment Highlights*, March 1969. Ben Het contained the 291st–293d CIDG companies (497 mostly Sedang Montagnard CIDG), four 175mm guns of Battery B, 1st Battalion, 14th Artillery, and a platoon of tanks from Company B, 1st Battalion, 69th Armor. Losses sustained within the camp 1–25 March 1969 were KIA: 6 U.S., 2 CIDG, 2 civilians; WIA: 15 U.S., 15 CIDG, 3 civilians.
3. Casualties in the Ben Het siege were KIA: 1 Special Forces, 1 LLDB, 15 U.S. artillerymen, 15 ARVN, 52 CIDG, 23 civilians; MIA: 4 CIDG; WIA: 16 Special Forces, 7 LLDB, 138 U.S. artillerymen, 70 ARVN, 141 CIDG, 11 civilians. Confirmed NVA dead totaled 98 bodies. Detachment B-24, *Defense of Camp Ben Het After Action Report*, dtd 21 September 1969.
4. Detachment A-244, *Monthly Operations Summary*, for January 1970.
5. 5th Special Forces Group, *Evaluation of Ben Het's Effectiveness*, dtd 13 January 1970.
6. 21st Military History Detachment, *Combat After Action Interview Report*, dtd 28 March 1970.
7. I Field Force Vietnam, *I FFORCEV Forward Mobile Staff After Action Report*, dtd 15 March 1970.
8. 5th Special Forces Group, *Memorandum for Record*, Subject: Briefing of COMUSMACV on U.S. Army Special Forces Disengagement from the CIDG Program, dtd 6 November 1969.
9. CIDG casualties from 28 October to 16 December 1969 were KIA: 1 Special Forces, 25 CIDG, 1 LLDB; WIA: 18 Special Forces, 2 LLDB, 148 CIDG, 2 Australians with MSF units. NVA casualties were recorded as 165 killed. 5th Special Forces Group, *Situation Updates*, in Bu Prang files; 5th Special Forces Group, *Operational Report*, dtd 13 January 1970.
10. Detachment B-24, *After Action Report*, dtd 22 May 1970. Casualties at Dak Seang were KIA: 2 LLDB, 44 CIDG, 6 civilians; WIA: 14 Special Forces, 4 LLDB, 80 CIDG, and 11 civilians, not including losses in the MSF battalions. While total NVA losses were unknown, 222 bodies were counted in the camp wire.
11. Detachment B-24, *After Action Report*, dtd 22 May 1970. Casualties at Dak Pek were KIA: 34 CIDG, 4 civilians; MIA: 7 CIDG; WIA: 22 Special Forces, 1 LLDB, 98 CIDG, 9 civilians. The Special Forces claimed 420 NVA were killed in the battle.
12. Casualties at Ba Xoai were KIA: 2 Special Forces, 10 CIDG, 1 civilian;

WIA: 16 CIDG. 11 NVA bodies had been left in the wire, but total losses were much higher. Detachment B-43, *Attack on Camp Ba Xoai*, dtd 24 February 1970.

13. Mai Loc casualties on 10 April 1970 were KIA: 1 Special Forces, 5 other U.S., 22 CIDG, 2 civilians; MIA: 7 CIDG; WIA: 1 Special Forces, 12 other U.S., 16 CIDG, 1 civilian. 17 NVA were killed in exchange. Company C, 5th Special Forces Group, *After Action Report*, dtd 30 April 1970.

14. 5th Special Forces Group, *Keystone Robin After Action Report*, dtd 28 February 1971; George McArthur, *Chicago Sun-Times*, 28 February 1971.

CHAPTER 15

FAR EAST MISSIONS

1. Special Missions

One of the most spectacular Special Forces missions of the Second Indochina War was the raid on Son Tay Prison, twenty-three miles west of Hanoi in North Vietnam, by Colonel Arthur D. "Bull" Simons's Task Force Ivory Coast, on 21 November 1970. The task force contained fifty-six Special Forces troops gathered from the 6th and 7th Special Forces Groups and the U.S. Army special warfare center at Fort Bragg, North Carolina, as well as from the infantry ranger school at Fort Benning, Georgia. Officially activated on 8 August as Joint Contingency Task Force Ivory Coast, the planning for the raid had been conducted by Brig. Gen. Donald D. Blackburn, the Special Assistant for Counterinsurgency Activities (SACSA) for the Joint Chiefs of Staff, who had initially conceived the idea for the raid and proceeded with the classified study group. The task force landed at Takhli, Thailand, on 18 November, after six months of planning and three months of intensive rehearsals. The secret commando raid was aimed at rescuing over one hundred American prisoners of war from the North Vietnamese Son Tay prison compound in a daring, thirty-minute surprise attack.

The task force boarded Air Force HH-53 helicopters at Udorn airbase in Thailand and flew over Laos into Son Tay, while other Air Force and Navy aircraft staged diversionary attacks and sealed the area from NVA reinforcements with concentrated aerial firepower. At precisely 2:18 A.M., 21 November, Air Force Lt. Col. Herbert E. Zehnder crash-landed his craft containing Capt. Richard J. "Dick"

Meadows' assault group directly into the Son Tay prison courtyard. Although they had planned to crash, the helicopter hit a clothesline and smashed into a tree during the descent, causing an unexpectedly hard landing.

Air Force Lt. Col. John A. Allison landed his helicopter containing Lt. Col. Elliott P. "Bud" Sydnor's command group (security) element just outside the prison wall exactly according to plan. Sydnor's demolitions expert, M. Sgt. Herman Spencer, used explosives to breach the seven-foot wall. They joined the assault group, which was fighting its way through the compound and searching the buildings. Sfc. Tyrone J. Adderly, the command group ground guide, eliminated one particularly dangerous automatic weapons position with his M79 grenade launcher.

In the meantime, Air Force Lt. Col. Warner A. Britton fortuitously landed Col. Arthur D. Simons and his 21-man support group in the wrong camp at the nearby secondary school compound. There Simons and his men were quickly engaged in a furious firefight with hundreds of Russian and Chinese troops whom they mowed down until Britton returned to lift out the team. By destroying this previously unknown force, Simons and his troops had eliminated the main external threat to the rest of the task force only four hundred yards from the prison itself.

Within the Son Tay prison, the troops under Meadows and Sydnor had killed over fifty guards, thoroughly searched all structures, and checked for possible tunnels, but they had not found any prisoners. The Special Forces commandos were extracted after spending twenty-seven minutes on the ground; the last act being Captain Meadows' destruction of the wrecked helicopter before leaving. Later it was discovered that the prisoners had been relocated from Son Tay in July, due to flooding in the region. Despite this incredible lack of intelligence transmission at higher government levels, the raid was not entirely futile. Realizing America's serious concern over the safety of its prisoners, the North Vietnamese government began better treatment and instituted other reforms.[1]

The Special Forces units that remained in South Vietnam after the departure of the 5th Special Forces Group were masked by cover designations, and their missions were shrouded in secrecy. Since the task of defending fortified camps had ended with the liquidation of the

CIDG program, the Special Forces could devote all its resources to special mission and unconventional warfare training assignments.

The LLDB was dissolved, since the CIDG camps were converted to ARVN border ranger posts. The Special Forces combed the LLDB ranks for the best personnel to form the nucleus of the Vietnamese Special Mission Service. The remaining LLDB members were transferred into the regular South Vietnamese Army. The former commander of MACV-SOG Command and Control North, Lt. Col. David P. Cole, was directed to Nha Trang to form the Special Mission Advisory Group (SMAG). Cole staffed the new unit with selected residual 5th Special Forces Group personnel and began retraining the former LLDB troops in unconventional warfare techniques on 1 February 1971. At the end of the month, the Nha Trang compound was formally transferred to his jurisdiction.

The Special Mission Service was trained for an entire year and became operational in January 1972. The unit was then given cross-border raiding and reconnaissance responsibilities and was relocated to Da Nang and Kontum in February. The Special Missions Advisory Group was deactivated on 1 April since its training purposes were over. The SMAG Special Forces troops were directly integrated into the Special Mission Service.

The Special Mission Service was part of the Vietnamese Strategic Technical Directorate, which was the counterpart organization of MACV-SOG and which maintained a Liaison Service with it. In March 1971 MACV-SOG's Command and Control North, Central, and South were redesignated as Task Force Advisory Elements 1, 2, and 3, respectively. These titular changes reflected their subordinate "advisory" status to the Strategic Technical Directorate Liaison Service and were politically imposed alterations that had little initial impact on actual activities. Each task force was composed of 244 Special Forces and 780 indigenous commandos, and their reconnaissance teams remained actively engaged in cross-border intelligence collection and interdiction operations. A further change occurred when the Airborne Studies Group (SOG 36) was absorbed by the Ground Studies Group on 1 October 1971. Airborne Detachment A became the Special Operations Detachment at Long Thanh, advising the "earth angel" and "Pike Hill" teams of Strategic Technical Directorate Group 68; and Airborne Detachment B retained its title at Da Nang, assisting parachute commando missions of Group 11.

Task Force 1 Advisory Element was forced from the Hickory Hill radio relay site in early June 1971. The Hickory post had existed on strategic Hill 953, in northwest Quang Tri Province at the edge of the Demilitarized Zone, since June 1968. On 3 June 1971 heavy North Vietnamese artillery began battering the bunkered Hickory defenses. On 4 June five wounded Special Forces and ten indigenous commandos were medically evacuated, leaving S. Sgt. Jon R. Cavaiani and Sgt. John R. Jones with twenty-three commandos defending the mountaintop. An NVA battalion stormed the summit and captured Hickory Hill on 5 June 1971. Cavaiani led a spirited defense but was captured as the last positions fell, while Jones was declared missing in action. That left MACV-SOG with only the Leghorn radio relay position located in the tri-border area of Laos.[2]

The MACV-SOG site at Nakhon Phanom in Thailand, which existed as a separate element to provide launch capability during adverse weather conditions in Laos, was disbanded on 30 March 1972. A month later, on 30 April Colonel Sadler's MACV-SOG was discontinued and replaced immediately with Strategic Technical Directorate Assistance Team 158 under Colonel Presson. This new organization was responsible for the proficiency of the Vietnamese Technical Directorate and all its elements: the Special Mission Service, the Liaison Service, and the Coastal Security Service. While Special Forces served the first two services, the Navy SEALS were incorporated into the latter. The former MACV-SOG Ground Studies Group (SOG 35) was absorbed into the Liaison Service. The SOG-35 combatant arms, Task Force Advisory Elements 1, 2, and 3, continued their missions exactly as before, except that the special commando exploitation companies were disbanded.

The addition of the Special Mission Service enabled the Strategic Technical Directorate and its assistance team to divide the former MACV-SOG jurisdictions between the Liaison and Special Missions Services. The latter teams became responsible for wiretaps, prisoner snatches, road watch, trail mining, and other tasks in North Vietnam and Laos. The Liaison Service and Task Force 1 (Long Thanh), Task Force 2 (Kontum), and Task Force 3 (Ban Me Thuot) performed similar operations in Cambodia and South Vietnam. The Special Forces–commanded Golf-5 Commando Security Company, a reaction force for the Leghorn radio relay site as well as the Liaison Service's general strike force, was stationed at Kontum.

This commando company was composed of 21 Special Forces troops in charge of 150 carefully selected Rhade, Sedang, and Jarai Montagnards. Many of the hand-picked Montagnards had had six years' combat service with Special Forces. The company also contained its own guard platoon of 54 Nungs. One of the company's most important missions was performed after a highly secret C-46 China Airlines aircraft crashed near Pleiku on 5 June 1972. Ten key Special Forces personnel of Team 158 had been killed in the crash, as well as Lieutenant Colonel Mendoza of the Military Equipment Delivery Team, Cambodia. The commandos were rappelled into the deep jungle, and all bodies were recovered, despite unfavorable weather.[3]

The special commando company was then diverted to the crash site of a Cathay Pacific Airlines passenger jet that had been downed in another region of the central highlands. On 16 June 1972 they took out sixty-five bodies but were forced to abandon the mission two days later when North Vietnamese Army troops began reaching the area.

On 23 April 1972 the North Vietnamese initiated a general offensive in the western highlands that pushed rapidly toward Kontum. By 10 May the *320th NVA Division* was on the outskirts of the city, forcing Task Force 2 and the commando company to relocate to Ban Me Thuot. The commando company was again moved to Pleiku, where it was redesignated as the Special Mission Force on 11 July 1972. In view of its successful China and Cathay Pacific aircraft expeditions, the Special Mission Force was reoriented specifically toward BRIGHT LIGHT prisoner/evadee recovery and crash-site missions. Special Mission Service Group 75 was assigned as the reaction unit for the Leghorn radio relay site.

The campaign for the western highlands was bitter and prolonged. In the drenching June monsoons John Paul Vann, the legendary commander of Military Region 2, personally directed the successful defense of Kontum. He goaded ARVN commanders on the battleline into action and shuttled almost daily, night and day, to threatened sectors of the field. On one of his flights into Kontum on the critical night before the 23d ARVN Division counterattacked, his helicopter crashed and Vann was killed. He was replaced by Brig. Gen. Michael D. Healy, who became chief of the Second Regional Assistance Command.

Healy was keenly aware of the potential of the Special Forces existing within the Liaison Service and requested that the reconnaissance teams be employed to assist the South Vietnamese drive to recover Duc Co. That September the entire Liaison Service was directed to perform forward ranger assignments for the 22d and 23d ARVN divisions, which pushed through the jungles southwest of Pleiku to regain Duc Co. The Special Forces teams performed with extraordinary valor in heavy frontline fighting and were responsible for directing many of the critical B-52 bombing raids that proved the key to final South Vietnamese success at Duc Co.

After elements of the *320th NVA Division* overran the Plei Djereng forward launch site on 4 September 1972, even the Special Mission Force had to be committed into the Pleiku Province battles. The Liaison Service reconnaissance teams were used for ranger purposes until the end of October. A great need for effective ranger reconnaissance units still existed in the western highlands, and in response Strategic Technical Directorate Assistance Team 158 formed the Special Training Team to instruct the South Vietnamese army long-range patrols in such tactics.

Only two Liaison Service operations were staged into Cambodia while the drive on Duc Co consumed the teams as ranger infantry. On one of the two Cambodian ventures, three teams were parachuted into the Parrot's Beak area of Cambodia on 2 September 1972. Despite the loss of several Special Forces patrol members, either killed or missing, the teams reconnoitered the area for ten days before being extracted. Thirty-five B-52 bombing runs were used to destroy the numerous NVA logistics bases that were detected. The Liaison Service resumed cross-border operations in December and continued the raids until the cease-fire of 28 January 1973.

Instead of task forces, the Special Mission Service had control over five groups of the Strategic Technical Directorate. Group 71 at Hue, Group 72 at Da Nang, and Group 75 at Kontum contained nine reconnaissance teams each. Groups 11 and 68 contained the Special Forces–led short-term reconnaissance and target acquisition (strata) teams, stationed in Da Nang and Saigon, respectively. Additionally, Group 68 employed the "earth angel" and "Pike Hill" teams, which were billeted and trained at Camp Yen The in the vicinity of Long Thanh, Vietnam.

While the Special Forces in this unit were initially responsible only for cross-border operations, the North Vietnamese spring 1972 Nguyen Hue offensive forced many teams into a ranger combat role in an attempt to save the northern provinces of South Vietnam. The entire Special Mission Service was placed under the operational control of Vietnamese Military Region 1. The teams fought as advance ranger and reconnaissance infantry in front of the South Vietnamese Airborne and Marine divisions during the counterattack toward Quang Tri through July and August. This mission was discontinued after the South Vietnamese Marines recaptured the Quang Tri citadel on 15 September 1972. On 9 October the Special Mission Service assumed responsibility for the 81st ARVN Airborne Battalion tactical frontage midway between Hue and the Laotian border. Just over a month later, on 15 November, the Special Mission Service was disbanded.

Strategic Technical Directorate Assistance Team 158 was deactivated on 12 March 1973 as part of the last U. S. military phasedown in Vietnam. The team's operating elements represented some of the most crucial but unsung Special Forces efforts of the Second Indochina War. While the cross-border exploits of the Special Forces teams were spectacular, the NVA Nguyen Hue offensive of 1972 pitched the same teams into a much more critical role. The Special Mission and Liaison Service reconnaissance teams served as emergency ranger infantry. They were in large part responsible for blocking the North Vietnamese onslaught and enabling the South Vietnamese to retake important territory, since the teams provided the direction and assessments for the B-52 bombing runs that shattered the NVA formations.

2. Thailand Interlude

Thailand experienced increasing insurgent activity in the border changwats along the northeastern Laotian and extreme southern Malaysian frontiers by late 1965. That December, the Thai government created the Communist Suppression Operations Command and asked for emergency Special Forces assistance. Unconventional warfare assistance to Thailand fell within the realm of the 1st Special Forces Group on Okinawa, but the group was understrength as a result of the Vietnam buildup and overtaxed by other Asian commitments. The Joint Chiefs of Staff recognized these limitations and decided to activate a separate Special Forces unit dedicated purely to the Thai area of operations. In the meantime the 1st Special Forces Group was ordered to send a large task force to Thailand, primarily to offset any foreign awareness that Special Forces Asian reaction ability was strained.

The 1st Special Forces Group formed a temporary 128-man element in February 1966, and this Detachment C-101 (Provisional) arrived in Thailand by 11 April. The provisional unit was paired up with three Royal Thai Special Forces detachments to form six combined detachments, with Thai officers commanding three of them. The force was deployed into the Phitsanulok area of northern Thailand and conducted counterinsurgency operations until September. Detachment C-101 departed the country on 1 October 1966, after the advance contingent of Company D from Fort Bragg arrived to fulfill Special Forces requirements in Thailand.[4]

Company D of the 1st Special Forces Group was activated at Fort Bragg, North Carolina, on 15 April 1966 and specifically tailored for Thailand assignment. Lt. Col. Robert H. Bartelt formed the 369-man company, which he would shape and lead for two years. Bartelt was a dynamic Special Forces leader who had served in the 63d Infantry Division during World War II and had joined the 77th Special Forces Group in 1955. The main portion of the company arrived in Thailand on special flights of C-141 aircraft by 15 October. The company occupied Camp Pawai in the emerald green rice fields just outside Lopburi, the ancient Thai capital located ninety-three miles north of Bangkok.

Thailand is a large country, and the company was quickly fragmented as its three B-Detachments were sent into widely scattered regions. Detachment B-410 moved 300 miles to the northeast of Lopburi and established Camp Nam Pung Dam at Sakon Nakhon, just west of the Laotian border near the critical airbase of Nakhon Phanom. There it joined forces with the forward headquarters of the Thai Communist Suppression Operations Command, which had moved to Sakon Nakhon in September with the 1st Battalion of the 3d Thai Infantry Regiment, part of the 1st Thai Airborne Battalion, and Thai Special Forces elements to begin sweeping the northeast changwats. Numerous skirmishes had already erupted in the cave-studded jungles of the Phu Phan Mountains, typified by a 19 September 1966 encounter at Phu Pha Lek mountain against some 100 Communist Terrorists (CT). In the spring of 1967, B-410 assisted the 0910 Plan or Dry Season Campaign, which swept through ten objective areas in five northeastern changwats around Sakhon Naknon.[5]

Detachment B-420 was sent east 125 miles into the jungle at Camp Nong Takoo, Pak Chong, between the Thai Second Army headquarters at Korat and the Cambodian border. Finally, Detachment B-430 made a parachute assault on 5 November 1966 to establish its base at Trang 600 miles from Lopburi near the Malaysian border. The Thai 5th Military Circle was conducting an active anti–Communist Terrorist (CT) campaign in the Malay Peninsula. The Special Forces compound in Trang was renamed Camp Carrow in honor of the intelligence sergeant of A-434, Sfc. Billy E. Carrow, who was killed in February 1967.[6]

Company D's mission primarily involved training Royal Thai Army and Police organizations in counterinsurgency. In case of a projected U.S.–South Vietnamese invasion of Laos, contingency plans existed for Company D to organize and lead the Kha tribal groups of the Bolovens Plateau. In the meantime the company had its hands full teaching the Thais a host of subjects, ranging from HALO parachute techniques to unconventional warfare and railroad countersabotage instruction. Company D was then alerted to begin one of the most comprehensive tasks of the Special Forces in the Second Indochina War, the preparation of an entire regular armed force for frontline duty in Vietnam.

In 1966 the Royal Thai government announced it would support the war effort in Vietnam "to help oppose communist aggression when it was still at a distance from our country."[7] Initially, a regimental combat team was provided under the designation Royal Thai Volunteer Force, Vietnam, which was nicknamed the "Queen's Cobras." On 6 March 1967 Lt. Col. Zoltan A. Kollat's Task Force Slick, formed by expanding Detachment B-430, began actively training the Queen's Cobras. The Special Forces conducted infantry training at Chonburi, artillery training at Kokethiem, cavalry training at Saraburi, and engineer training at Ratburi. The success of the Thai regiment was a direct result of demonstrated Special Forces proficiency in the full spectrum of military tactics and functions, from line infantry to engineering and signal skills.[8]

The Royal Thai Army Volunteer Regiment passed its unit training test at Kanchanaburi on 27 July 1967 and deployed to Vietnam in September accompanied by several Special Forces advisors. The Special Forces maintained an active training and advisory role with the increasing number of Thai units fielded in Vietnam, to include the entire Black Panther (later Black Leopard) Expeditionary Division. The Thai forces were established at Bear Cat east of Saigon, and their area of operations generally encompassed the region between the American units in the Bien Hoa–Long Binh area and the Australian–New Zealand Task Force in Phuoc Tuy Province. Although numerous company Special Forces personnel were engaged in active Vietnam combat with the Thais, their participation was deliberately subdued by classification restrictions.[9]

Company D had always been divorced from its parent 1st Special Forces Group, and its independent achievements led to the creation of the separate 46th Special Forces Company on 15 April 1967. The headquarters relocated to Spec. Col. Tienchai Sirisumpan's Royal Thai Special Warfare Center at Fort Narai, Lopburi in December. The mission of the 46th Special Forces Company was to (1) establish a combined Special Forces training base and to assist the Royal Thai Armed Forces in improving their counterinsurgency capability, (2) provide advisory and training assistance to the Royal Thai Army Special Warfare Center, and (3) to perform such other tasks as may be assigned by the commander of Military Assistance Command, Thailand.[10]

The three original B-Detachments were renumbered B-4610 through B-4630. On 16 July 1968 the 46th Special Forces Company was authorized a special augmentation. This allowed the company to field two C-Detachments: C-4601, with company headquarters at Fort Narai; and C-4602, under Lt. Col. Kenneth C. Barclay at Kanchanaburi. The latter C-Detachment readied additional Thai troops for Vietnam deployment under Project FOLDER MARK. The company also created B-4640 at Camp Pawai for specialized missions, which included ranger, long-range reconnaissance, Police Aerial Reinforcement Unit, and Border Patrol Police duties. Initially, B-4650 (Provisional) served on the mountainous Nan Changwat front along the Laotian border, where the Thai Army was waging a full-scale antiinsurgency campaign.[11]

Although the Thai police were part of the Ministry of Interior, they served as a valuable extension of Thai combat power in contested guerrilla areas. Prior to 1965 Border Patrol Police (BPP) security was primarily aimed at apprehending or eliminating bandits and smugglers. Under Special Forces auspices, the BPP was rapidly expanded into a crack counterguerrilla organization. While the BPP General Staff Headquarters was located in Bangkok, area commanders controlled line platoons, which were backed up by mobile reserve and weapons platoons. The Police Aerial Reinforcement Unit was a battalion-size parachute reaction force with ten detachments and an air-sea rescue section. By July 1969 the authorized BPP strength was 8,344 men including the 700-man PARU. They were trained primarily by Special Forces at Hua Hin, but their operational areas encompassed most of Thailand's border regions. As early as 6 January 1968, S. Sgt. Wallace Gumbs of A-4620 was killed at Chaw Haw, Thailand, while advising a BPP unit.[12]

Combat in northern Thailand escalated sharply in early 1968. On 18 April 1968 the Border Patrol Police center at Ban Haui Khu in Chiang Changwat was overrun by an attacking force using automatic weapons, grenades, and rocket launchers. There were only two police survivors. The Special Forces escorted several sweeps, the troopers toiling up the rugged hills in tiger-striped uniforms as the Thais kept up alongside, their necks draped with chains of amulets for Buddhist protection. While there were few encounters, well-executed ambushes of roads and jeeps took a high toll of Thai casualties.

On 26 July 1968 a small CT band, armed with AK-47 assault rifles, penetrated Udorn Airbase and used satchel charges against an American C-141 and F-4D aircraft as well as an HU-43 helicopter. One Thai guard and four Americans were wounded. In exchange, two of the insurgents were killed, one of which was identified as a North Vietnamese Army sapper. The 46th Special Forces Company was immediately tasked to provide Air Force with security and mortar training at bases throughout Thailand, and this mission continued throughout the war.[13]

In the northern provinces the level of warfare had continued to escalate. While Special Forces advisors were being ordered not to accompany such operations, they were still endangered because the camps and villages they worked in were subject to attack. For instance, on the night of 20 November 1968, a CT force using flares assaulted an outpost near Ban Huai Sai Tai in Phitsanulok Province just south of Laos. The Special Forces–trained hill tribe volunteer unit repulsed the attack after a hard battle in which eight hill tribe and three Thai soldiers were killed.

Col. Stephen R. Johnson took over the 46th Special Forces Company in 1969. Under his command a SCUBA detachment was posted to Sattahip on the Gulf of Thailand, and A-Detachments worked with the BPP at Hua Hin, Bangkok, Udorn, Mai Rem, and Songkhia. The special missions detachment at Lopburi used the guise of a "proficiency course" instruction team. Five detachments, at Pranburi, Ubon, Nakhon Phanom, Lopburi, and Phitsanulok, were involved in secret operations preparing Thai and Laotian irregular infantry battalions for combat across the border. On 13 May 1970 Ubon became a permanent MACV-SOG launch site, and the 46th Special Forces Company control group used a cover story of supporting Thai field training exercises. Throughout this period the 46th Special Forces Company launched reconnaissance teams into the Bolovens Plateau of the Laotian panhandle.[14]

Col. Paul H. Combs, Jr., became the commander of the 46th Special Forces Company on 15 July 1970. All Special Forces personnel were withdrawn from the BPP regional training sites to the National Training Center at Hua Hin, where they could be dispatched to regional units as required. The Special Forces became further involved in training irregular infantry for the Laotian war. One four-battalion training camp was set up at Nam Pong, and four two-battalion training camps were established at Phitsanulok, Chieng Kham, Kanchanaburi, and Ban Nong Saeng. Each was run by an A-Detachment. One reinforced team at Lopburi was engaged in training Cambodian Special Forces on Project FREEDOM RUNNER. Other teams located at Lopburi were supporting the 1st and 2d Thai Special Forces Groups and the ranger department of the Royal Thai Special Warfare School. FTT-1 and FTT-1 (Support) were stationed on cross-border launch assignments at Ubon and Nakhon Phanom. The company also supported the Laotian requirements of Deputy Chief, JUSMAG (Joint U.S. Military Advisory Group) at Udorn. Other Special Forces troops were attached to the Defense Attaché Office, Laos, under Project 404.

The 1st Special Forces Group was still sending teams into Thailand to bolster 46th Special Forces Company efforts. For example, Project UNITY organized combat-ready Thai light infantry battalions for Laotian service. A total of eight A-Detachments from Okinawa were dispatched for six-month temporary duty tours under the control of 46th Special Forces Company elements at Phitsanulok. Led by A-123 on 18 October 1971, the training center was established at a former B-52 crash pit at Nam Phong, thirty miles south of Udorn. Four UNITY battalions were trained at a time under a twelve-week program, using Special Forces instructors with BPP members as assistant instructors and interpreters. A four-week leadership program prepared each Thai battalion cadre before the actual recruits arrived.

The 46th Special Forces Company was inactivated on 31 March 1972, and the assets were used to form the new 3d Battalion of the 1st Special Forces Group. As a consequence of Japanese sensitivity over the use of Okinawa as a "springboard" for operations in Southeast Asia, the 3d Battalion was given the cover designation of U.S. Army Special Forces Thailand, to dissociate it from open connection to the group stationed on Okinawa. In May 1972 Lt. Col. William P. Radtke assumed command of the unit, which continued its diversified missions until the cease-fire of March 1973. At that time cross-border operations were halted and the teams were reoriented to pure training assignments.

Within a year, the 3d Battalion of the 1st Special Forces Group was being tagged for inactivation because of diminished operational requirements and a desired reduction in American military presence in Thailand. On 21 February 1974, the Department of the Army ordered the battalion's redeployment to the U.S. for inactivation by 31 March. Lt. Col. George Maracek, the last commander of U.S. Army Special Forces Thailand, presented the 46th Special Forces Company flag to a small escort detachment which brought the unit colors back to Fort Bragg, North Carolina. There the battalion was officially inactivated on 31 March as ordered, and the support detachment and augmentation element remaining overseas were inactivated in Thailand on the same date. In this manner the last Special Forces unit permanently stationed in Southeast Asia was quietly folded down.

Special Forces duty in Thailand was undeniably far different from that in Vietnam. The Special Forces camps in Thailand were on friendly soil and safe from attack, except in the most remote areas. The company's civilian augmentation contained some of the most beautiful female nurses, escorts, clerks, and aides in Asia. Bangkok, one of the major rest-and-recreation centers of the Orient, was only two hours' drive from Lopburi (and less by helicopter). Many Special Forces troops married local women and kept signing up for extended duty with the company. However, it must be remembered that much of the Special Forces lifestyle in Thailand was deliberately staged as promiscuous and free of hazard, since the classified operations being conducted there were best guarded by such an impression. As honored guests of the King of Thailand, the Special Forces abided by a much stricter code of conduct than was normally demanded. Lax military appearance and troublemaking were not tolerated.

The Special Forces in Thailand performed some of the most varied duty of the war. Since there was no CIDG program to interfere with unconventional warfare tasks, the company was able to concentrate its teams on a mission-oriented basis. Unlike the general camp defense A-Detachments of 5th Special Forces Group, the 46th Special Forces Company fielded ranger, SCUBA, HALO, reconnaissance, and other specialized detachments. The Special Forces company was even authorized its own aviation section and enjoyed the organic helicopter support that the 5th Special Forces Group lacked. The 46th Special Forces Company later filled much of the void in Southeast Asian unconventional warfare requirements that was created when the 5th Special Forces Group departed South Vietnam. One constant theme of Special Forces utilization was repeated, however. As in Vietnam and Laos, the Special Forces in Thailand were used extensively to train and develop line infantry units.

3. Final Assignments

Events outside of Vietnam continued to involve Special Forces in other adjacent countries. In Cambodia, Prince Sihanouk was overthrown during March 1970, and U.S. assistance was requested in raising a new national army. President Nixon directed military aid to Cambodia commencing 22 April. During the next month, the first Cambodian recruits began arriving for training under 5th Special Forces Group auspices at Long Hai in coastal Phuoc Tuy Province and Dong Ba Thin just south of Nha Trang. Later a third camp was built at Chi Lang in the lower Delta next to the Cambodian border. From May until the end of October, when the Khmer Republic was officially declared, the Special Forces trained 4,096 Cambodians in eight battalions, four of which were ethnic Cambodians originally trained for operations inside Vietnam but diverted to Cambodia, plus four battalions of Cambodians specifically programmed as part of the FANK (Forces Armées Nationales Khmeres). Basically, all were trained along the lines of the Special Forces mobile strike force battalions.[15]

In October 1970 the Special Forces was tasked to train an additional thirty FANK battalions and 3,000 unit leaders by the next July. Colonel Healy promptly agreed to schedule the new battalions, and they started arriving at the three training sites in November.[16] However, the FANK program on the ground was sometimes hindered by old CIDG problems, especially at a post such as Chi Lang.

Chi Lang was situated in a dangerous, contested border zone. Any training venture away from camp was subject to becoming a frightening battlefield test between half-baked Cambodian trainees and hardened Viet Cong regulars, with predictable results. A bad situation was made worse by the fact that the Special Forces and Vietnamese at the post were mutually antagonistic. The Special Forces proclaimed that the Cambodian trainees were better soldiers than the ARVN border rangers, whom they openly called hoods and thieves. This incensed the Vietnamese rangers, who had formerly been the CIDG strike force under the same Special Forces troops. Major Hoa countered by refusing to punish any Vietnamese caught stealing from the Americans. The serious friction between the Detachment B-43 Special Forces and Vietnamese resulted in a series of fistfights and shootouts, which finally led to a tragic field incident.

Capt. Harry L. Purdy's instruction team was training the 6th Khmer Infantry Battalion. In January 1971 the battalion conducted a Special Forces–supervised six-day field exercise at Nui Ta Bec, five miles northwest of Chi Lang. First Lt. Gerald F. Kinsman, the tactics committee instructor, accompanied the battalion's 3d Company cadre, 1st Lt. James J. McCarty and Sgt. James A. Harwood. On 15 January, the three Special Forces troops were escorting the company's 24-man reconnaissance platoon, which was awaiting the arrival of the 8th Khmer Infantry Battalion, coming to replace them in the field.

The Special Forces–escorted platoon was moving downhill through dense bamboo thickets after searching several large rock outcroppings of Nui Ta Bec. Suddenly the pointman came under automatic weapons fire, engaging the platoon in an adverse firefight. McCarty's radioman was wounded in the leg as he frantically radioed Sergeant Stamper at the base of the hill. Major Leary, the Detachment B-43 commander, was overhead in an O-1 aircraft and relayed the request for immediate assistance to Major Hoa at Chi Lang. Hoa claimed all of his units were "busy" and no response was possible. Leary summoned a battalion from the 9th ARVN Division next, but by the time they arrived the fighting was over. In addition to the Cambodian casualties, both Lieutenant Kinsman and Sergeant Harwood were missing.[17]

The colors of Company A, 5th Special Forces Group, were sent to Fort Bragg in February 1971, but most of the Special Forces instructors remained at the Khmer training sites in Vietnam. Lt. Col. Edward S. Rybat, the former Company A commander, reorganized his men into a new command called the U.S. Army Individual Training Group (UITG) on 1 March 1971. The Bien Hoa–based UITG was initially authorized only 330 Special Forces slots. However, the overall training effort was greatly enhanced by the arrival of additional New Zealand and Australian instructor personnel. The New Zealand staff went to Dong Ba Thin, while the Australians were posted to the two southern camps. Their experience, particularly in small-unit jungle tactics, made them invaluable members of the training cadre. These allied personnel worked side by side with the Special Forces until December 1972.

The mission of UITG was "to conduct basic and advanced combat training and small-unit leadership training of individuals as directed by the Office of the Chief, Training Directorate, and perform such other missions as may be directed by the commander, MACV." The training program was completely overhauled and expanded to include a three-week leadership course given to the battalion commanders prior to the arrival of their units. The arriving battalions were actually groups of fresh recruits flown directly by C-130 aircraft from Phnom Penh to the training camps, where they were met by their battalion commanders and Special Forces advisors. In effect, the newly recruited outfits had to be completely built from scratch by UITG.

In order to produce thirty battalions, Special Forces developed a compressed training schedule that put recruits on a six-day field operation only eight weeks after getting off the plane. This exercise was conducted in an NVA/VC-contested area some distance from the training camp. During the field operation, the mobile training team (MTT) actively rehearsed them in battle drill. Many battalions participated in some type of combat during these expeditions. The Special Forces hoped that the experience gained would outweigh the casualties taken. After returning from the field, the battalions were given advanced training then sent farther into hostile territory on the final twelve-day "graduation" exercise.

During September 1971, there was a violent upsurge in North Vietnamese activity around Chi Lang. On one field operation during the month, a half-trained Khmer battalion was overrun by seasoned NVA troops. Four Special Forces personnel and sixteen Khmer trainees were killed, four supporting helicopters were shot down, and twenty-one Cambodians were captured. The only reason anyone survived was that the North Vietnamese stopped to loot the dead. The Khmer government urgently requested that the Chi Lang training camp be moved. Chi Lang was a troubled camp anyway. It ceased operations upon the graduation of the 30th Infantry Battalion, the last battalion of the 1971 program, on 23 September 1971.

The first of the forty-eight "third wave" battalions arrived at Long Hai and Dong Ba Thin in August 1971. A month later the first battalions arrived at the third center, established only two and a half miles down the road from Long Hai and known as the Phuoc Tuy Training Center. The centers also trained a host of other Cambodian groups, ranging from nurses to medium-range reconnaissance patrol cadre.

Some Special Forces troops were permanently stationed in Cambodia. The Military Equipment Delivery Team, Cambodia, (MEDTC) was officially created with sixty personnel, including Special Forces personnel, on 30 January 1971. The task of this new unit was to supervise Khmer military deliveries,which initially went through South Vietnam. The unit was doubled in size by July, and the headquarters was relocated to Phnom Penh on 9 October 1971. The American phasedown in Vietnam forced a transfer of Khmer support from South Vietnam to Camp Samae San, Thailand, in December 1972. The job of supporting Khmer field units was extremely hazardous. Valiant Special Forces missions ranged from parachuting ammunition and rice into besieged forts to guarding Mekong River ammunition convoys fighting their way from Saigon into Phnom Penh.

At the end of March 1972, the North Vietnamese launched the Nguyen Hue offensive into South Vietnam and quickly smashed through South Vietnamese defenses facing the Demilitarized Zone. Several ARVN battalions were disintegrated by the NVA onslaught, and the 3d ARVN Division completely collapsed. Col. John V. Hemler, Jr., took over the UITG on 3 April. MACV desperately ordered him to form joint U.S.-ARVN training teams for employment in Thua Thien Province on 6 May 1972.

Two days later a pair of Special Forces UITG teams arrived in the Hue-Phu Bai vicinity. Both teams (MTT) were commanded by Special Forces majors and contained twenty-five Special Forces trainers along with fifteen ARVN instructors from the Lam Son National Training Center. The two MTTs received the awesome mission of completely reequipping and retraining the badly mauled remnants of the 3d ARVN Division and 20th Tank Regiment. Most surviving ARVN officers in the units were badly shaken, and many of the good ones had been killed. As replacements and materiel arrived, the ARVN battalions were assembled behind the frontline. The Special Forces resorted to rigorous training in a crash effort to get them combat-ready. The hardest task proved to be motivation of the untried and discouraged replacement officers.

The success of these initial MTTs outside Hue caused the ARVN battalion retraining program quickly to mushroom into a major UITG commitment. Ironically, just as Hemler's group was on the verge of greatly expanding beyond the original Cambodian training mission, the Army was finally getting around to officially redesignating the UITG as the FANK Training Command, which transpired on 15 May 1972. MACV tasked the new command with both the Cambodian training and additionally "retraining, in place, ARVN infantry and ranger battalions." During the rest of the unit's existence, it conducted on-site ARVN retraining in every military region of South Vietnam. At one time the Bien Hoa headquarters supervised MTTs at more than sixteen different locations.[18] Lt. Gen. Phan Trong Chinh, chief of the ARVN Central Training Command, summed up the effectiveness of the UITG-FANK training teams in stemming the North Vietnamese advance north of Hue when he stated, "If it had not been for FANK Training Command, there would not be an I Corps today."

Each FANK Training Command team was capable of training two ARVN battalions concurrently in a two-week cycle. The Vietnamese instructors taught weapons, while the Special Forces concentrated on tactics and leadership. By late June 1972, however, the 399 assigned Special Forces trainers were hopelessly swamped by the magnitude of the dual Cambodian-ARVN projects. By that point, however, even General Abrams was pleased with the Special Forces efforts. To the absolute astonishment of his staff, Abrams actually asked for immediate Special Forces reinforcement.

The 1st Special Forces Group had been training Cambodian Special Forces troops in Vietnam since 17 April 1972, under Project FRIDAY GAP. Now it was tasked to lend full assistance to FANK Training Command. The 1st Special Forces Group formed Task Force MADDEN and sent nine operational teams and 113 Special Forces personnel to Vietnam starting on 5 July 1972, either to augment existing mobile training teams or to form entirely new teams. For example, in September 1972 the Task Force began training the Khmer

Army in medium-range reconnaissance patrols. Unfortunately, General Abrams's appreciation of Special Forces capabilities came too late to save many of the original Special Forces missions, such as protection of the Montagnards—who had now been irretrievably abandoned to their fate.[19]

In August 1972 MACV gave FANK Training Command an additional mission. The command was directed to upgrade the local security measures at thirty-eight critical ammunition and petroleum storage sites throughout South Vietnam. In response, both the command and 1st Special Forces Group formed Security Training Teams. The teams conducted intensive training in installation defense and tested the guards in the final third phase of the instruction by conducting an unannounced simulation attack. At one site near Dong Ba Thin, a North Vietnamese sapper party decided to conduct the Phase III inspection itself. They were caught in the wire perimeter of the ammunition depot on 8 January 1973 and killed. For the 1st Special Forces Group, Task Force MADDEN proved to be its last combat operation of the Second Indochina War; its teams were withdrawn to Okinawa on 31 January 1973.

The involvement of the FANK Training Command in so many other projects earned it another change of name on 1 December 1972. The Special Forces unit was redesignated the Field Training Command. The FANK Training Command had just presided over the graduation of the last scheduled Khmer light infantry battalions and closed Long Hai and Phuoc Tuy training camps on 29 November. This left only the Dong Ba Thin site actively training Cambodian infantrymen. Col. Vincent W. Lang assumed command of the Field Training Command on 12 December 1972, but the end of American military involvement in Vietnam was imminent. On the morning of 28 January 1973, the Field Training Command was ordered to cease all operations, and the unit was closed out on 22 February 1973.

The UITG-FANK-Field Training Command performed magnificently on a number of vital missions. Unfortunately, these latter Special Forces tasks are almost unknown because classifications muffled their accomplishments. The 9th, 21st, 22d, and 23d ARVN divisions had been completely retrained, and the Airborne, 3d, 5th, and 25th ARVN divisions partially retrained. In addition, fourteen ARVN ranger battalions, the 20th Tank Regiment, and eight ARVN reconnaissance companies had completed the Special Forces–led instruction. In the original Cambodian mission, a total of eighty-five Khmer infantry battalions and one Marine fusilier battalion had been trained.[20]

4. Conclusion

The Army Special Forces had fulfilled a tremendous battlefield destiny in Southeast Asia, one completely unforeseen by the originators of the Special Forces concept. The Special Forces had been raised to conduct unconventional warfare, assist escape and evasion efforts, and practice subversion against a hostile state by leading a resistance movement. During a general war in the Pacific area of Asia, the Special Forces was expected to foster and sustain national insurgent movements in the wake of Chinese military occupation of neighboring countries until the regular U.S. Army and Marine forces could strike back with conventional means. The early Special Forces reconnaissance and special missions were limited to insertions intended to resupply rebel contingents, scout out partisan targets, and emplace atomic demolitions. In a "cold war" environment the Special Forces was expected merely to train military personnel in guerrilla warfare and the techniques of combating guerrilla and terrorist activities.[21]

The actual combat role of Special Forces was far different. In the Second Indochina War, the Special Forces trained or retrained large portions of three standing national armies for frontline combat: the Forces Armées du Royaume under WHITE STAR, the Royal Thai Expeditionary Forces under FOLDER MARK, and the Army of the Republic of Vietnam in the wake of the North Vietnamese 1972 Nguyen Hue offensive. The Special Forces was also tasked with creating a new national army for the Khmer Republic and training U.S. Army long-range patrol and ranger infantry in Vietnam as well as U.S. Air Force airbase defense forces in Thailand. In addition, the Special Forces performed one of its intended missions, since it trained most of the indigenous special warfare contingents in South Korea, Taiwan, Thailand, the Philippines, and South Vietnam.

This achievement alone would have earned Special Forces a remarkable military reputation. However, the greatest Special Forces combat mission of the Second Indochina War had nothing to do with regular forces. The Special Forces created, trained, and fielded the Civilian Irregular Defense Group program troops that fought a large share of the war throughout the most threatened regions of Vietnam.

While concentrating on ethnic minorities, the CIDG program encompassed a dazzling array of various paramilitary organizations of different creeds and races that perhaps only Special Forces could have held together. Not only did Special Forces organize these troops for their intended role of local village security, but Special Forces also employed them as line infantry in the crucial battles of 1965 and Tet-68.

Yet the Special Forces was asked to accomplish even more vital military tasks. The Special Forces was directed to hold key territory and safeguard lines of communication. Special Forces was even charged with controlling the entire length of Vietnam's rugged border, where it actively pursued a campaign of hampering and interdicting the infiltration of main force Viet Cong and regular North Vietnamese Army units. The Special Forces established and defended a series of strategic forts in remote areas, which were often deliberately emplaced in Viet Cong strongholds, and formed mobile strike force brigades and battalions to reinforce and back up these citadels. Finally, the Special Forces mobile strike forces were used to assault objectives, such as mountain bastions, which defied regular South Vietnamese Army formations. The Special Forces even launched its own navy to reach otherwise-inaccessible VC sanctuaries and to control the waterways of the countryside.

The Special Forces performed a host of strategic intelligence-collection missions, which in many instances were of decisive importance to battles and campaigns. The Special Forces fielded target acquisition and damage assessment teams and provided divisional, corps, and army-level reconnaissance with Projects DELTA, OMEGA, SIGMA, and RAPID FIRE. The Special Forces staged cross-border raids, search-and-rescue missions, and other specialized tasks under the auspices of MACV-SOG. The Special Forces conducted important search-and-sweep operations under BLACKJACK and contributed to numerous major allied combat operations by screening line formations with Mike Force and mobile strike force command units.

Considering the magnitude and diversity of the Special Forces tasks during the Second Indochina War, the faults, problems, and failures of Special Forces are few. The Special Forces had only limited capabilities for static defensive or holding operations. Inevitably, several camps were overrun, and the Special Forces troops were defeated in many firefights and patrolling actions. The Special Forces–

advised CIDG natives lacked the formal training, equipment, and weapons to perform as regular line infantry, and they suffered serious battlefield reverses. The Special Forces failed in one of its primary missions: to advise the Vietnamese LLDB, although the miserable performance of the LLDB exasperated Special Forces efforts. The lack of properly qualified Special Forces replacements also added to internal difficulties that Special Forces endured.

Finally, one comment must be made in retrospect about the utilization of the Special Forces in the Second Indochina War. The liquidation of the CIDG program was naturally viewed with bitter misgivings by many Special Forces veterans, who had invested eight years of hard work and combat sacrifice in the concept. The CIDG program's dissolution, however, actually freed the Special Forces of many frustrating and futile tasks. The Special Forces was relieved of the burden of arming, training, and motivating local civilians often at war with the Saigon regime, of advising an inept and disinterested LLDB, and of maintaining and backing up a string of frontier posts along an indefensible border. No longer fettered by the shackles of civilian irregular defense requirements, the Special Forces was able to concentrate again on its primary mission of flexible unconventional warfare.

The end of an era of Special Forces combat duty was marked by the transfer of Lt. Col. Elliot P. Sydnor's 1st Special Forces Group from Okinawa to Fort Bragg, North Carolina, for inactivation during June of 1974. Due to reduced operational requirements, the redeployment also included the association elements of Security Assistance Force, Asia, of which the 1st Special Forces Group had been the nucleus. Beginning with the issuance of advance movement directives on 10 April, the group started moving back to the United States. In a solemn ceremony on 30 June 1974, the 1st Special Forces Group was officially inactivated at Fort Bragg, North Carolina.

In the wake of South Vietnam's total defeat less than a year later, the Army and its Special Forces fell in such disfavor that the country's unconventional warfare capability nearly disappeared during the late 1970s. However, less than a decade after the 1st Special Forces Group was stricken from the Army's rolls, a renewed emphasis was placed on rebuilding the Special Forces as a viable military instrument to counter terrorism and insurgency where the use of conventional forces was considered premature, inappropriate, or unfeasible. On 1 March 1984, the 1st Special Forces Group returned to active status with the creation of an advance element which was sent back to Okinawa. The group headquarters was officially reactivated at Fort Lewis, Washington, on 1 September 1984, and a full line battalion was soon stationed on Okinawa island. The Special Forces renaissance was completed during the first training exercise in Thailand, coded COBRA GOLD, marking the advent of a new era in Pacific strategy.

Notes

1. The best published source of information on the Son Tay raid is Benjamin F. Schemmer, *The Raid*, New York: Harper & Row, 1976.

2. Fifteen commandos arrived back in friendly lines at Camp Carroll four days later, having evaded two NVA companies and numerous smaller elements. Staff Sergeant Cavaiani later received the Medal of Honor, although his official cover designation as a USARV training advisor is still used by the Army awards system.

3. The personnel killed in the "EM-2" aircraft crash were: Lt. Col. Ronnie A. Mendoza (MEDTC), Lt. Col. Andrew F. Underwood (Liaison Service), Maj. Calvin T. Gore (Group 11), Maj. Nicolas Quinones-Borres (surgeon), Capt. Charlie L. Flott (Task Force 2), Capt. James F. Hollis (Operations Office), Capt. Walter S. Mullen (Liaison Service), Sfc. Amdee Chapman, Jr., (Task Force 2), S. Sgt. Thomas M. LeJeune (Liaison Service), Sgt. Kenneth L. Barnett (Task Force 1), and Sgt. Michael L. Hutson (Liaison Service).

4. USMACTHAI, *Counterinsurgency Systems Manual Overview*, 1969.

5. Research Analysis Field Paper 26, *A History of Subversive Insurgency in Thailand Through 1967*, January 1970. Like VC in Vietnam, CT was the abbreviation given all communist subversives in Thailand. The 0910 Plan derived its name from the 1966–1967 lunar calendar year 2509–2510 in Thailand.

6. 46th Special Forces Company, *The Professionals, May 66–Oct 67*, (Bangkok, Thailand: Kurusapha Ladprao Press, 1967).

7. MACV *Command History*, 1969, Vol. I, p. IV–40. This statement proved a remarkable prophecy.

8. The executive officer of Task Force Slick was Major John E. Borgman, who would later command the 5th Mobile Strike Force Command in the Battle of Nui Coto.

9. Gen. W. B. Rosson, *Assessment of Influence Exerted on Military Operations by Other Than Military Considerations*, USARPAC TS-71-1370.

10. USMACTHAI, *Command History*, 1970, p. 16.

11. The 46th Company was much larger than its authorized strength of 369 personnel. On 31 Jan 68 (Tet-68) the company had 575 assigned compared to the first SF group on Okinawa which had 740 (out of 828 authorized).

12. Joint Thai-U.S. Military Research and Development Center, *Police Organizations and Programs*, Vol. 4, 1969.

13. PACOM Intelligence Digest PID No. 16–68, p. 29.

14. AMEMB Bangkok Msg 220/060955 and COMUSMACTHAI Msg 130410z on 10 May.

15. MACJ4 Rpt, *Staff Contribution to Overview Report on MACV 1968–1970*, dtd 24 February 1971; MACMA Briefing, Subject: Cambodian MAP Summary, dtd 21 October 1970.

16. The first of the "second wave" FANK battalions arrived at Long Hai on 7 November, and Dong Ba Thin and Chi Lang received their first battalions under this program on 22 November and 4 December 1970, respectively.

17. MACV Ranger Command Advisory Detachment, Memorandum for Record, dtd 8 February 1971; Detachment B-43 AVGB Ltr, dtd 26 February 1971.

18. Special Forces MTTs were located at the following sites in Vietnam from 1972–1973: Camp Evans, Landing Zone Sally, Phu Bai, Da Nang, Hill 56, Landing Zone Baldy, Hawk Hill, Chu Lai, Kontum, Bai Gi, Pleiku, Camp Enari, Bien Hoa, Phuoc Vinh, Tay Ninh West, and Chi Lang.

19. 1st Special Forces Group, *Operational Report,* dtd 22 May 1972; and DA GAROCG, *Recommendation for Award of the Meritorious Unit Commendation,* dtd 6 November 1974.

20. Headquarters, Field Training Command, *After Action Report,* undated (final executive summary).

21. FM 31-21, *Guerrilla Warfare and Special Warfare Operations,* Headquarters, Department of the Army, September 1961.

1. Army Special Forces Presence in Vietnam

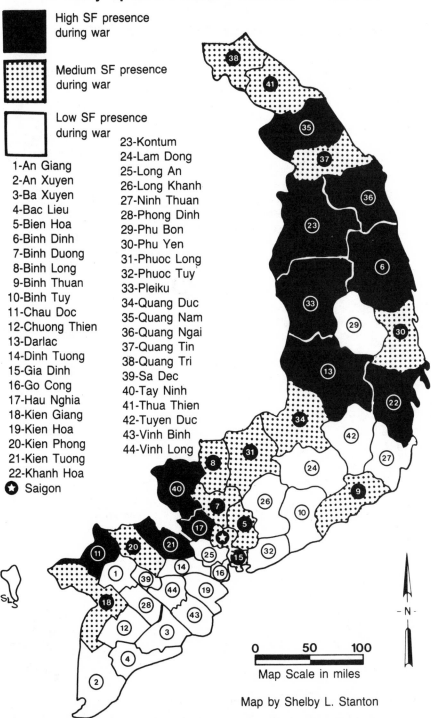

High SF presence during war

Medium SF presence during war

Low SF presence during war

1-An Giang
2-An Xuyen
3-Ba Xuyen
4-Bac Lieu
5-Bien Hoa
6-Binh Dinh
7-Binh Duong
8-Binh Long
9-Binh Thuan
10-Binh Tuy
11-Chau Doc
12-Chuong Thien
13-Darlac
14-Dinh Tuong
15-Gia Dinh
16-Go Cong
17-Hau Nghia
18-Kien Giang
19-Kien Hoa
20-Kien Phong
21-Kien Tuong
22-Khanh Hoa
⭐ Saigon

23-Kontum
24-Lam Dong
25-Long An
26-Long Khanh
27-Ninh Thuan
28-Phong Dinh
29-Phu Bon
30-Phu Yen
31-Phuoc Long
32-Phuoc Tuy
33-Pleiku
34-Quang Duc
35-Quang Nam
36-Quang Ngai
37-Quang Tin
38-Quang Tri
39-Sa Dec
40-Tay Ninh
41-Thua Thien
42-Tuyen Duc
43-Vinh Binh
44-Vinh Long

0   50   100
Map Scale in miles

- N -

Map by Shelby L. Stanton

Provinces with three or fewer SF camps are considered to have low SF presence; provinces containing from 4–9 SF camps have medium presence; and high presence provinces have ten or more SF camps or their manpower equivalent.

2.
Okinawa Island, Home of the 1st Special Forces Group

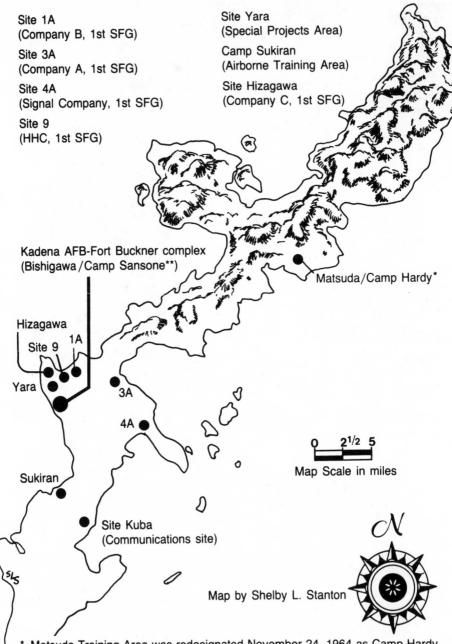

Site 1A
(Company B, 1st SFG)

Site 3A
(Company A, 1st SFG)

Site 4A
(Signal Company, 1st SFG)

Site 9
(HHC, 1st SFG)

Site Yara
(Special Projects Area)

Camp Sukiran
(Airborne Training Area)

Site Hizagawa
(Company C, 1st SFG)

Kadena AFB-Fort Buckner complex
(Bishigawa/Camp Sansone**)

Matsuda/Camp Hardy*

Hizagawa

Site 9   1A

Yara

3A

4A

Sukiran

Site Kuba
(Communications site)

0   2¹/₂   5
Map Scale in miles

Map by Shelby L. Stanton

* Matsuda Training Area was redesignated November 24, 1964 as Camp Hardy in honor of Captain Herbert F. Hardy, Jr. (A-334, 1st SFG) who was killed in Vietnam on March 4, 1964.
**Bishigawa site was redesignated on November 3, 1965, as Camp Sansone in honor of Sergeant First Class Dominick Sansone (Co B, 1st SFG) who was killed in Vietnam on December 10, 1964.

3. Exercise DALLAS II, northwest Thailand
(November 7–23, 1960)
1st Special Forces Group

AREA I

U.S. Det A-44
Royal Thai Det A-21

AREA II

U.S. Det A-42
Royal Thai Det A-22

AREA III

U.S. Det A-45
Royal Thai Det A-23

AREA IV

Royal Thai Det A-43

AREA V

Royal Thai Det A-25

AREA VI

U.S. Det A-43

AREA VII

U.S. Det A-41

⊞ Permanent Thai Border Patrol Police (BPP)
Line Platoon location

▼1 Power Station ▼2 Railroad Bridge

𝒩

0 5 10 15 20 25
Map Scale in miles

LAOS

Chang Rai

Area Boundary

Chiang Dao

IV   VI

Mae Rim

Ban Don Kaeo

III

Chiang Mai

I

Lamphun

V   2   II

1

Lampang

VII

Uttaradit

BURMA

Map by Shelby L. Stanton

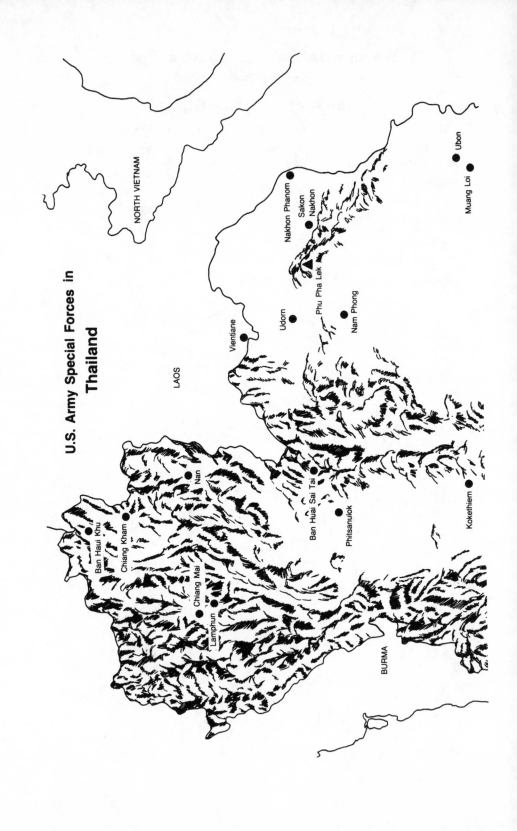

U.S. Army Special Forces in Thailand

NORTH VIETNAM

LAOS

Vientiane

Udorn

Nakhon Phanom

Sakon Nakhon

Phu Pha Lek

Nam Phong

Ubon

Muang Loi

Nan

Ban Huai Khu

Chiang Kham

Chiang Mai

Lamphun

Ban Huai Sai Tai

Phitsanulok

Kokethiem

BURMA

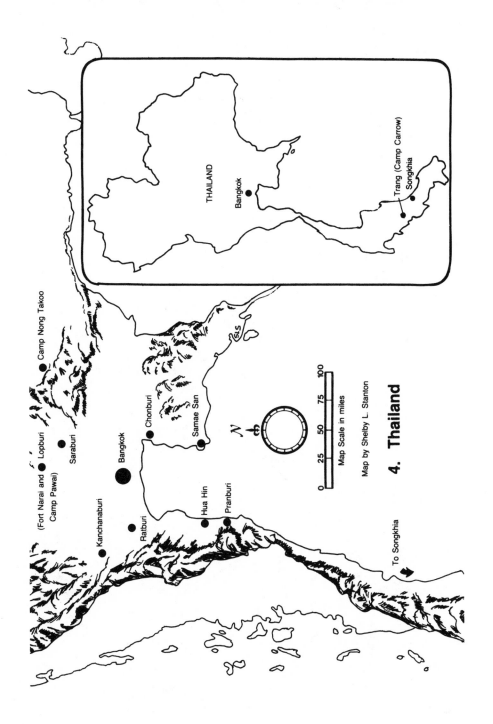

Camp Nong Takoo

(Fort Narai and   Lopburi
Camp Pawai)

Saraburi

Bangkok

Kanchanaburi

Ratburi

Chonburi

Samae San

SLS

Hua Hin

Pranburi

To Songkhia

N

Map Scale in miles

0   25   50   75   100

Map by Shelby L. Stanton

4. Thailand

THAILAND

Bangkok

Trang (Camp Carrow)

Songkhia

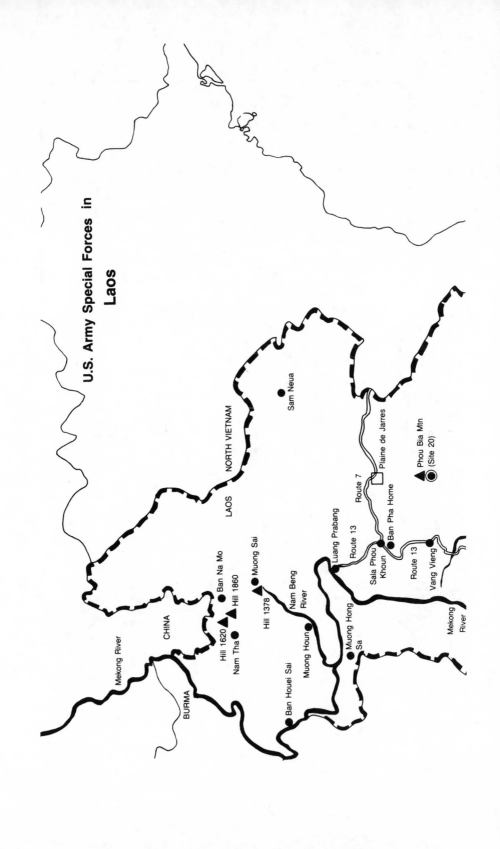

U.S. Army Special Forces in Laos

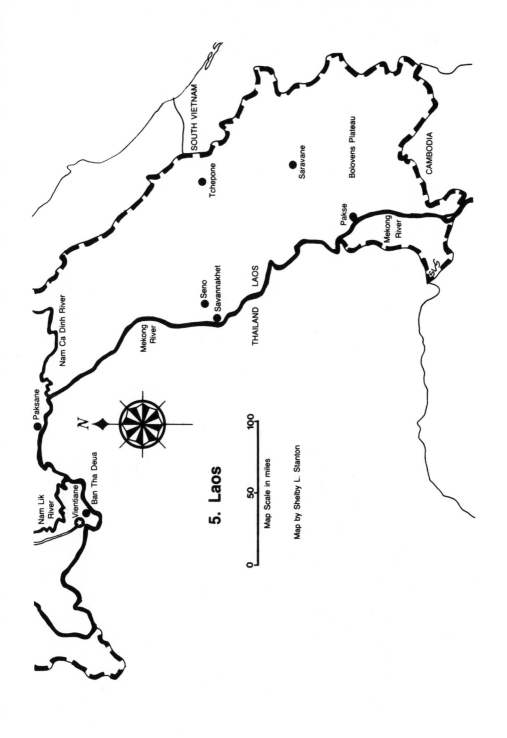

5. Laos

Map Scale in miles

Map by Shelby L. Stanton

N

SOUTH VIETNAM

Tchepone

Saravane

Bolovens Plateau

CAMBODIA

Pakse

Mekong River

Seno
Savannakhet

THAILAND   LAOS

Mekong River

Nam Ca Dinh River

Paksane

Nam Lik River

Vientiane

Ban Tha Deua

0   50   100

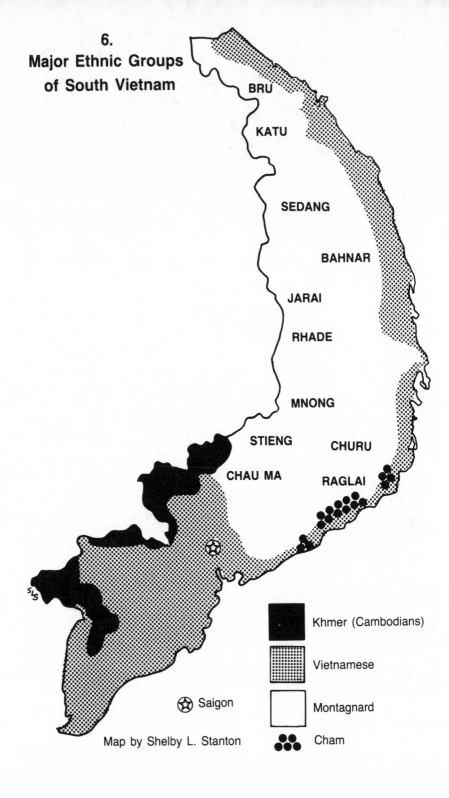

6.
Major Ethnic Groups
of South Vietnam

BRU

KATU

SEDANG

BAHNAR

JARAI

RHADE

MNONG

STIENG   CHURU

CHAU MA   RAGLAI

Khmer (Cambodians)

Vietnamese

Montagnard

⊗ Saigon

Map by Shelby L. Stanton   Cham

7. Special Forces in Vietnam, 1961–October 1962

Khe Sanh

DMZ

Nam Dong (Ruong Ruong or Ta Rau)

An Diem

An Chau

Da Nang-Hoa Cam

Tra My

Mang Buk

Tan Canh

Pleiku

Plei Do Lim

Cung Son

Buon Ho

Buon Tah

Buon Krong

Ban Enao-Buon Dan Bak

Ea Ano

Lac Thien

Nha Trang

Dam Pau
(Serignac Valley)

A Cham

Thu Duc

Long Thanh

Song Mao

Chau Lang

Vung Tau

✪ Saigon

◉ Buon Enao complex
experiment campsite

0   50   100
Map Scale in miles

N

Du Tho

Map by Shelby L. Stanton

8. Special Forces Camps Opened during Operation SWITCHBACK

(November 1962–July 1963)

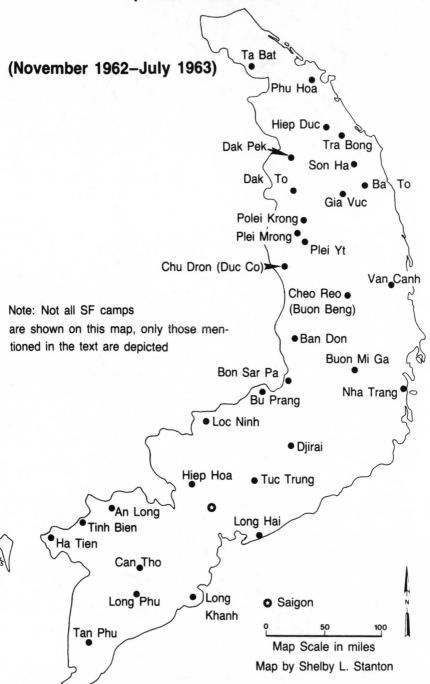

Note: Not all SF camps are shown on this map, only those mentioned in the text are depicted

Ta Bat

Phu Hoa

Hiep Duc

Tra Bong

Dak Pek

Son Ha

Dak To

Ba To

Gia Vuc

Polei Krong

Plei Mrong

Plei Yt

Chu Dron (Duc Co)

Van Canh

Cheo Reo
(Buon Beng)

Ban Don

Buon Mi Ga

Bon Sar Pa

Nha Trang

Bu Prang

Loc Ninh

Djirai

Hiep Hoa

Tuc Trung

An Long

Long Hai

Tinh Bien

Ha Tien

Can Tho

Long Phu

Long Khanh

Saigon

Tan Phu

N

0   50   100

Map Scale in miles

Map by Shelby L. Stanton

9. Montagnard Rebellion, September 19–28, 1964

II Corps Tactical Zone

1-Ammunition dump

2-Dirt airstrip

3-Buon Enao (abandoned)

4-Airfield

5-Radio station

6-Bridge

7-Power station

Map by Shelby L. Stanton

10. Battle of Mang Yang Pass
and the
Central Highlands, February 1965

A-Detachment camp

A	An Khe	**H**	Duc Co
B	Plei Do Lim	**I**	Plei Ta Nangle
C	Plei Me	**J**	Dong Tre
D	Buon Beng	**K**	Plateau Gi
E	Gia Vuc	**L**	Plei Mrong
F	Kontum	**M**	Kannack
G	Soui Doi	**N**	Plei Djereng

❶ FOB # 1

❷ FOB # 2

Map by Shelby L. Stanton

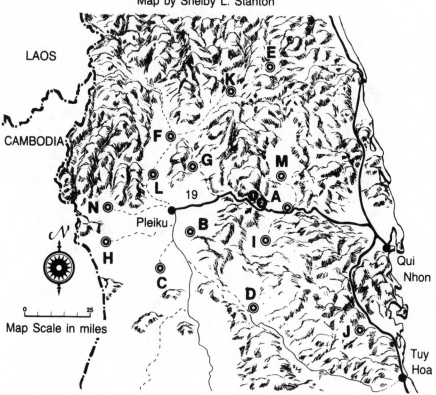

11. I Corps Tactical Zone, 1964–1971

U.S. Army Special Forces Camps in I CTZ, Vietnam, 1964–1971

1-A Loui
2-A Ro
3-A Shau
4-Ba To
5-Chu Lai
6-Con Thien
7-Da Nang
8-Gai Vuc
9-Ha Thanh
10-Kham Duc
11-Khe Sanh

12-Lang Vei
13-Mai Loc
14-Minh Long
15-Ngok Tavak Outpost
16-Nong Son
17-Ta Bat
18-Ta Ko
19-Thuong Duc
20-Tien Phuoc
21-Tra Bang

Map by Shelby L. Stanton

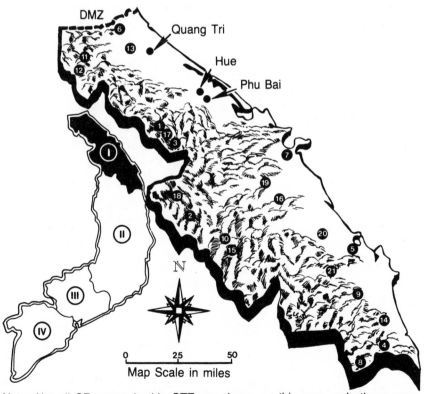

Note: Not all SF camps in this CTZ are shown on this map, only those mentioned in the text are depicted

II Corps Tactical Zone, 1964–1971

U.S. Army Special Forces Camps in II CTZ, Vietnam, 1964–1971

1-An Khe (An Tuc)

2-An Lac

3-Ban Me Thuot

4-Ben Het

5-Bong Son

6-Bu Prang

7-Buon Blech

8-Buon Ea Yang

9-Buon Brieng

10-Cung Son

11-Dak Pek

12-Dak Saeng

13-Dak Sut

14-Dak To

15-Dong Ba Thin

16-Dong Tre

17-Duc Co

18-Duc Lap

19-Ha Tay

20-Kannack

21-Kontum

22-Lac Thien

23-Mai Linh

24-Mang Buk

25-Nha Trang

26-Nhon Co

27-Phey Srunh

28-Phu Tuc

29-Plei Djereng

30-Plei Do Lim

31-Plei Me

32-Plei Mrong

33-Pleiku

34-Polei Kleng

35-Tieu Atar

36-Trang Phuc (Ban Don)

37-Vinh Thanh

Note: Not all SF camps in this CTZ are shown on this map, only those mentioned in the text are depicted.

12. II Corps Tactical Zone, 1964–1971

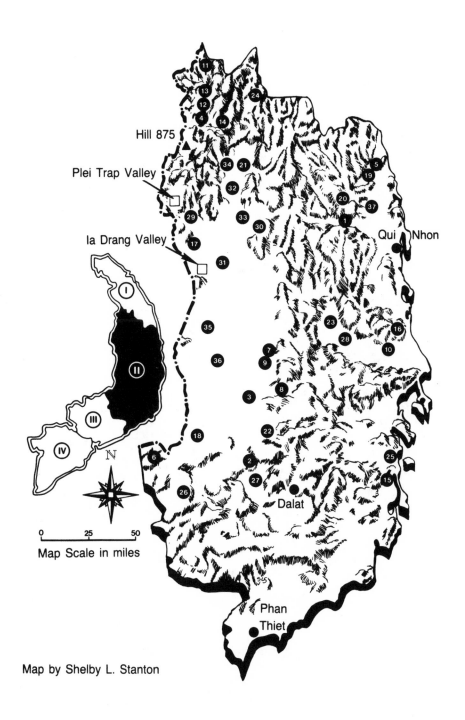

Hill 875

Plei Trap Valley

Ia Drang Valley

Qui Nhon

Dalat

Phan Thiet

N

0   25   50
Map Scale in miles

Map by Shelby L. Stanton

13. III Corps Tactical Zone, 1964–1971

U.S. Army Special Forces Camps in III CTZ, Vietnam, 1964–1971

1-Ben Soi
2-Bien Hoa
3-Bu Dop
4-Bu Ghia Map
5-Bunard
6-Chon Thanh
7-Dong Xoai
8-Duc Hoa
9-Duc Hue

10-Duc Phong
11-Go Dau Ha
12-Hiep Hoa
13-Ho Ngoc Tao-Tu Duc
14-Hon Quan
15-Katum
16-Loc Ninh
17-Long Hai
18-Long Thanh

19-Luong Hoa
20-Minh Thanh
21-Phuoc Vinh
22-Prek Klok
23-Quan Loi
24-Song Be
25-Soui Da
26-Tanh Linh
27-Tay Ninh
28-Thien Ngon
29-Tong Le Chon
30-Tra Cu
31-Trai Bi
32-Trang Sup
33-Xuan Loc
34-Chi Linh

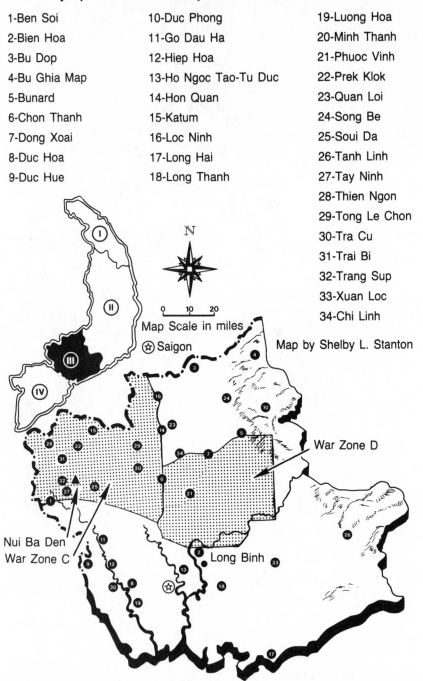

Map by Shelby L. Stanton

Note: Not all SF camps in this CTZ are shown on this map, only those mentioned in the text are depicted.

14. IV Corps Tactical Zone, 1964–1971

U.S. Army Special Forces Camps in IV CTZ, Vietnam, 1964–1971

1-An Phu
2-Ba Xoai
3-Binh Thanh Thon
4-Cai Cai
5-Can Tho
6-Cao Lanh
7-Chau Doc
8-Chi Lang
9-Don Phuc
10-Ha Tien
11-Kinh Quan II
12-Moc Hoa

13-My Dien II
14-My Phuoc Tay
15-Phu Quoc
16-Tan Chau
17-Tinh Bien
18-My Da (My An)
19-Thanh Tri
20-Thuong Thoi
21-Binh Hung
22-Tuyen Nhon
23-Vinh Gia

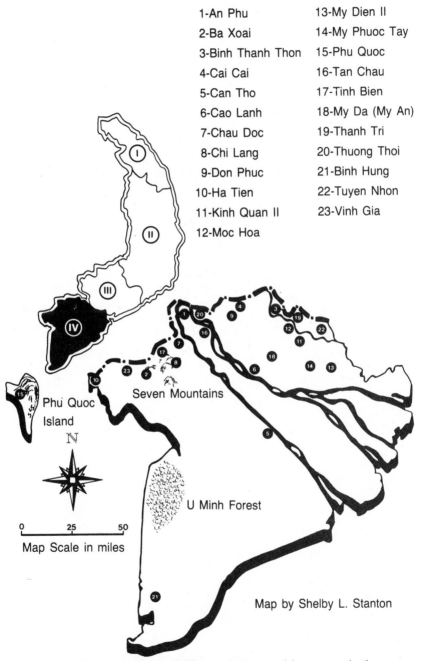

Seven Mountains

Phu Quoc
Island

N

0   25   50
Map Scale in miles

U Minh Forest

Map by Shelby L. Stanton

Note: Not all SF camps in this CTZ are shown on this map, only those mentioned in the text are depicted.

15. Pleiku and Plei Trap Valley Region, 1965–1970

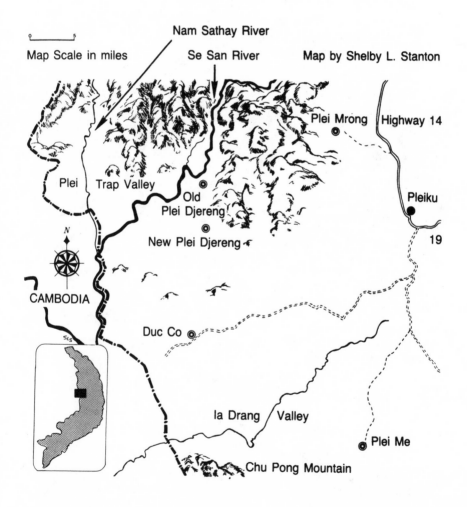

Nam Sathay River

Se San River

Map by Shelby L. Stanton

Map Scale in miles

Plei Mrong | Highway 14

Plei | Trap Valley

Old
Plei Djereng

Pleiku

New Plei Djereng

19

N

CAMBODIA

Duc Co

Ia Drang Valley

Plei Me

Chu Pong Mountain

16. Bu Prang-Duc Lap Campaign
October 28–December 24, 1969

Map by Shelby L. Stanton

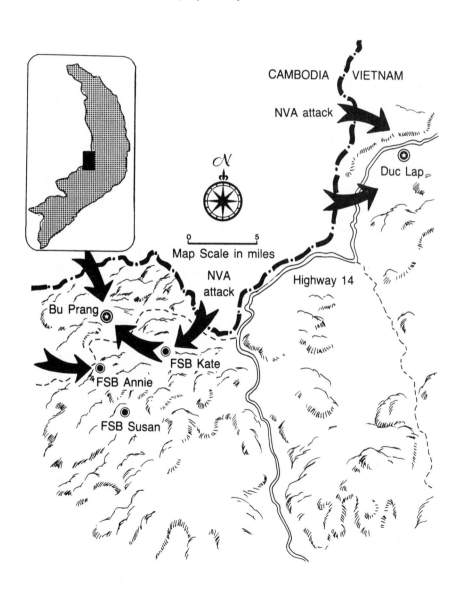

17. The Cambodian Frontier-Plain of Reeds

A Cai Cai   **F** Binh Thanh Thon

B Duc Hue   **G** Thuong Thoi

C Don Phuc   **H** Thanh Tri

D Moc Hoa   **I** Tuyen Nhon

E Kinh Quan II   **J** My Phuoc Tay

K Cao Lanh

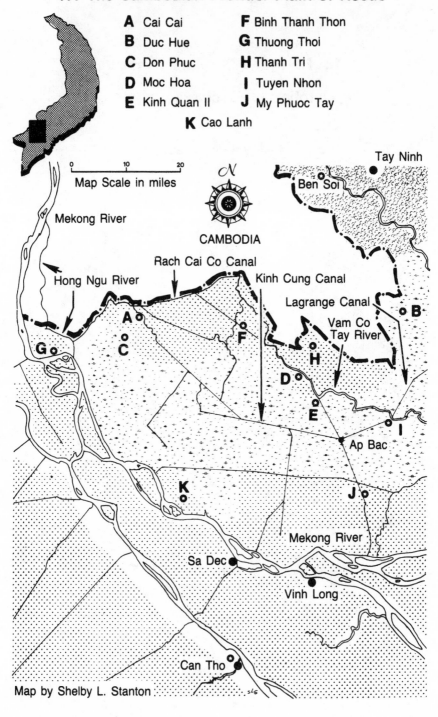

Map by Shelby L. Stanton

18. Seven Mountains Area of Vietnam, 1969–1970

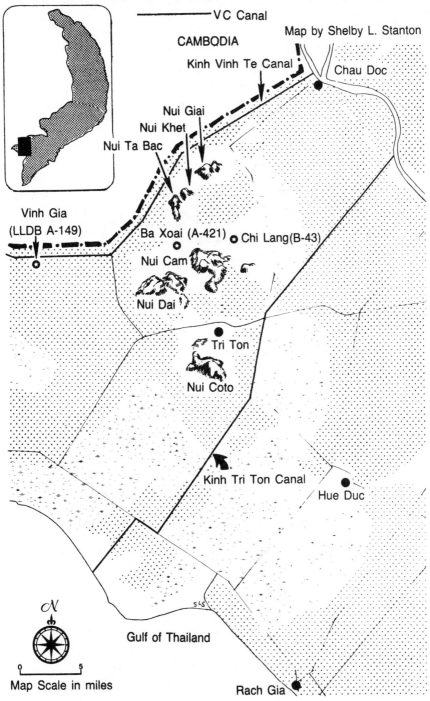

VC Canal

Map by Shelby L. Stanton

CAMBODIA

Kinh Vinh Te Canal

Chau Doc

Nui Giai

Nui Khet

Nui Ta Bac

Vinh Gia
(LLDB A-149)

Ba Xoai (A-421)

Chi Lang (B-43)

Nui Cam

Nui Dai

Tri Ton

Nui Coto

Kinh Tri Ton Canal

Hue Duc

N

Gulf of Thailand

0   5
Map Scale in miles

Rach Gia

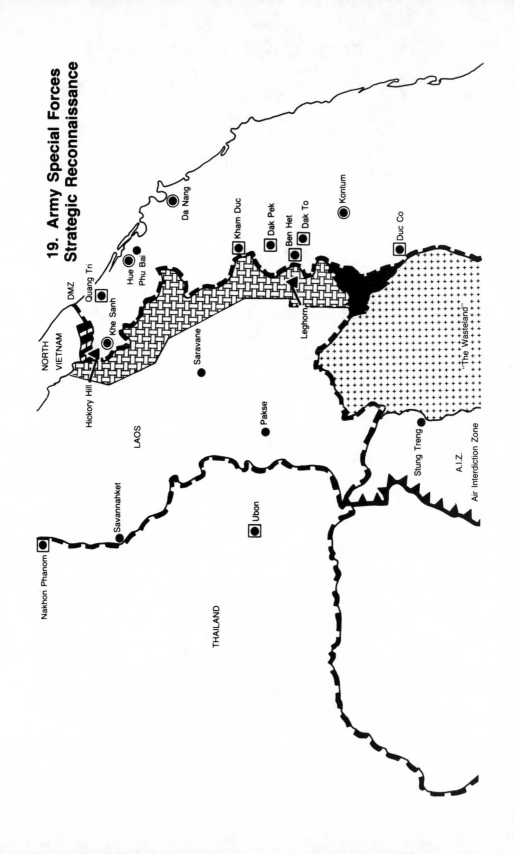

19. Army Special Forces
Strategic Reconnaissance

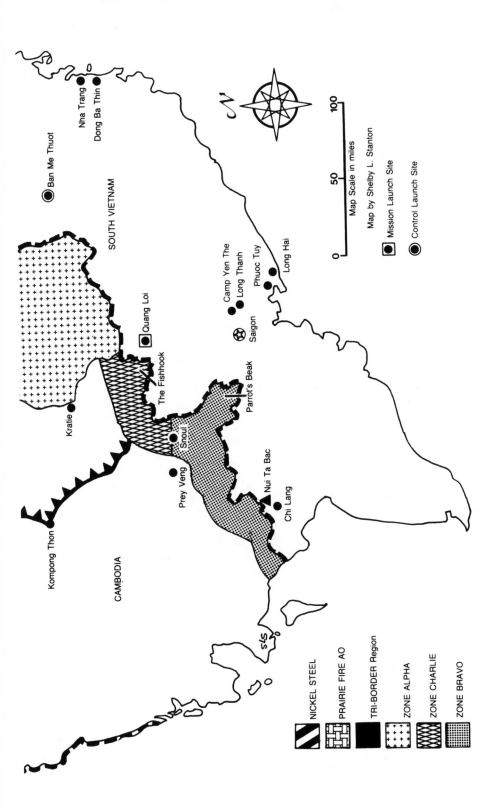

1. Hqs, Rep. of Korea forces
2. Long Van Area
3. MAAG Facility
4. Military Police Station
5. Military Prison
6. Neptune NCO Club
7. Robert Compound
8. USO Club
9. Province Chief's residence
10. High School
11. Girls High School
12. Nha Trang Hotel
13. Pagoda
14. French School
15. Shell Oil Co.
16. King Duy Tan Hotel
17. Radio station
18. Catholic Bishop's office
19. Thap Ba Temple

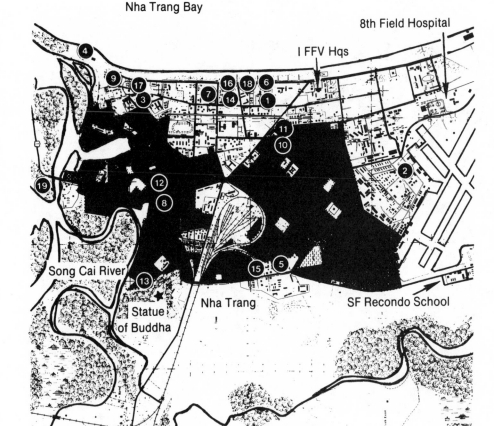

Nha Trang Bay

8th Field Hospital

I FFV Hqs

Song Cai River

Statue of Buddha

Nha Trang

SF Recondo School

N

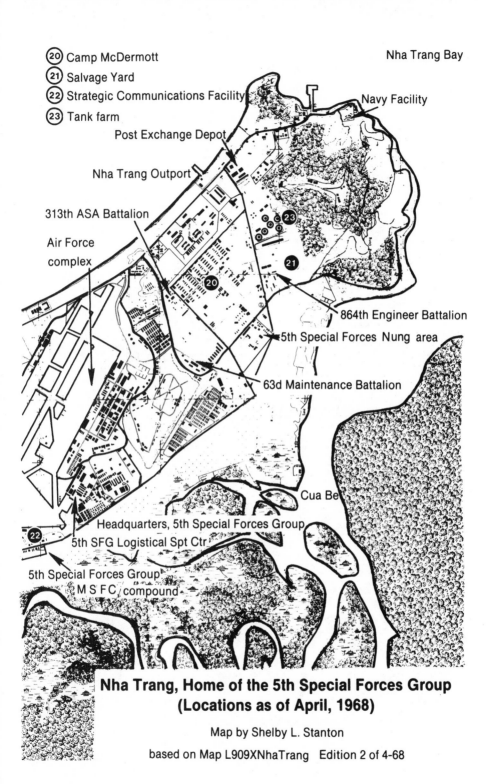

20 Camp McDermott
21 Salvage Yard
22 Strategic Communications Facility
23 Tank farm

Nha Trang Bay

Navy Facility

Post Exchange Depot

Nha Trang Outport

313th ASA Battalion

Air Force complex

864th Engineer Battalion

5th Special Forces Nung area

63d Maintenance Battalion

Cua Be

Headquarters, 5th Special Forces Group
5th SFG Logistical Spt Ctr

5th Special Forces Group
M S F C compound

**Nha Trang, Home of the 5th Special Forces Group
(Locations as of April, 1968)**

Map by Shelby L. Stanton

based on Map L909XNhaTrang   Edition 2 of 4-68

Chart 1. Standard Army Special Forces A-Detachment (1963 Type)*

1   Detachment Commander, Team Leader
    Captain (0-3)
1   Detachment Executive Officer, Team XO
    First Lieutenant (0-2)
1   Operations Sergeant, Team Sergeant
    Master Sergeant (E-8)
1   Heavy Weapons Leader, Heavy Weapons NCO
    Sergeant First Class (E-7)
1   Light Weapons Leader, Light Weapons NCO
    Sergeant First Class (E-7)
1   Intelligence Sergeant, Intel Sergeant
    Sergeant First Class (E-7)
1   Medical Specialist, Team Medic
    Specialist 7th Class or Sergeant First Class (E-7)
1   Radio Operator Supervisor, Senior Radio Operator
    Sergeant First Class (E-7)
1   Assistant Medical Specialist, Junior Medic
    Specialist 6th Class or Staff Sergeant (E-6)
1   Demolitions Sergeant, Engineer Sergeant
    Staff Sergeant (E-6)
1   Combat Demolitions Specialist, Demo Sergeant
    Specialist 5th Class or Sergeant (E-5)
1   Chief Radio Operator, Junior Radio Operator
    Sergeant (E-5)

* Dept of the Army TOE 31-107E, this standard A-Detachment organization was replaced by a revised organization authorized in 1970 but not implemented until 1972. The above type A-Detachment represented the standard team organization throughout the Second Indochina War, although Charts 2 and 3 display variants for Vietnam service. The first line of every duty position gives the official title, followed by a comma and the common position title. The second line related rank and grade allocations.
Source: Headquarters, 5th Special Forces Group (Airborne) Letter of Instructions No. 1 (First Revision), dtd 1 January 1965, Annex F; Army Concept Team in Vietnam JRATA Project No. 1B-154, Final Report, dtd 20 April 1966; 5th Special Forces Group (Airborne), Synopsis of the USASF Sector/Subsector Advisory Role, dtd 1 Decembr 1968, P. 19,20.

Chart 2. Typical Army Special Forces A-Detachment serving in a Civilian Irregular Defense Group (CIDG) role *

Command and Control:
    1   Detachment Commander, Captain (0-3)
    1   Executive Officer, First Lieutenant (0-2)
    1   Operations Sergeant, Master Sergeant (E-8)
Communications:
    1   Radio Operator Supervisor, Sergeant First Class (E-7)
    1   Chief Radio Operator, Sergeant (E-6)
Intelligence:
    1   Intelligence Sergeant, Sergeant First Class (E-7)
    1   Assistant Intelligence Sergeant, Staff Sergeant (E-6)
Tactics:
    1   Heavy Weapons Leader, Sergeant First Class (E-7)
    1   Light Weapons Leader, Sergeant First Class (E-7)
    1   Combat Engineer, Sergeant (E-5)
Medical:
    1   Medical Specialist, Sergeant First Class (E-7)
    1   Assistant Medical Specialist, Specialist 6th Class (E-6)

* Headquarters, 5th Special Forces Group (Airborne) Letter of Instructions No. 1 (First Revision), dtd 1 January 1965, Annex F, and Army Concept Team in Vietnam JRATA Project No. 1B-154, Final Report, dtd 20 April 1966. This chart displays the ideal rank structure for such an organization based on the standard 12-man A-Detachment. Note that the assistant intelligence sergeant slot was created by transfer of the demolitions sergeant position into this new role, a necessity imposed by counterinsurgency warfare in Vietnam.

Chart 3. Typical Army Special Forces A-Detachment serving in a MACV Sub-sector Advisory role *

District Advisor:
    1   Detachment Commander, Captain (0-3)
Assistant District Advisor:
    1   Executive Officer, First Lieutenant (0-2)
Pacification Advisors:
    1   Civic Action/Psychological Operations Officer, First Lieutenant (0-2)
    1   Civic Action/Psychological Operations Sergeant, Staff Sergeant (E-6)
Medical Advisors:
    1   Medical Specialist, Sergeant First Class (E-7)
    1   Assistant Medical Specialist, Specialist 6th Class (E-6)
Police Security Advisors:
    1   Operations Sergeant, Master Sergeant (E-8)
    1   Intelligence Sergeant, Sergeant First Class (E-7)
    1   Assistant Intelligence Sergeant, Staff Sergeant (E-6)
Village/Hamlet Security Force (Regional Force-Popular Force) Advisors:
    1   Heavy Weapons Leader, Sergeant First Class (E-7)
    1   Light Weapons Leader, Sergeant First Class (E-7)
    1   Combat Engineer, Sergeant (E-5)
Radio Communications:
    1   Radio Operator Supervisor, Sergeant First Class (E-7)
    1   Chief Radio Operator, Sergeant (E-5)

* 5th Special Forces Group (Airborne), Synopsis of the USASF Sector/Subsector Role, dtd 1 December 1968, P. 19 and 20. This chart displays the ideal rank structure for such an organization based on the augmented 14-man A-Detachment strengthened for utilization on a district advisory level. Such A-Detachments were still handicapped by a shortage of personnel given their increased responsibilities.

Chart 4. Typical Army Special Forces B-Detachments (Part I) *

Standard B-Detachment, 1963:

1	Detachment Commander, Major
1	Executive Officer, Captain
1	Adjutant, Captain
1	Intelligence Officer, Captain
1	Operations Officer, Captain
1	Supply Officer, Captain
1	Sergeant-Major, E-9
1	Intelligence Sergeant, E-8
1	Operations Sergeant, E-8
1	Demolitions Sergeant, E-7
1	Heavy Weapons Leader, E-7
1	Light Weapons Leader, E-7
1	Medical Specialist, E-7
1	Radio Operator Supervisor, E-7
1	Supply Sergeant, E-7
1	Administrative Supervisor, E-6
1	Assistant Supply Sergeant, E-6
1	Preventive Medical Specialist, E-6
1	Combat Demolitions Specialist, E-5
4	Chief Radio Operators, E-5

Typical B-Detachment, 5th SFG, 1965:

1	Detachment Commander, Major
1	Executive Officer, Captain
1	Adjutant, Captain
1	Intelligence Officer, Captain
1	Operations Officer, Captain
1	Supply Officer, Captain
1	Civic Action Officer, Captain
1	RF/PF Advisor, Captain
1	Sergeant-Major, E-9
1	Intelligence Sergeant, E-8
1	Operations Sergeant, E-8
1	Engineer Supervisor, E-7
1	Assistant Operations Sergeant, E-7
1	Medical Supervisor, E-7
1	Area Communications Chief, E-7
1	Supply Sergeant, E-7
1	Administrative Supervisor, E-6
1	Assistant Supply Sergeant, E-6
1	Intelligence Analyst, E-6
1	Radio Supervisor, E-6
1	Operational Clerk, E-5
3	Radio Operators, E-5

* Standard B-Detachment based on Dept of the Army TOE 31-107E. This organization proved unsuitable for Vietnam combat conditions, and Headquarters, 5th Special Forces Group Troop Change Request dtd 24 August 1965 presented modified authorized tables of organization and equipment required as depicted above. While the typical B-Detachment represented the structure of ten B-Detachments throughout Vietnam at the time, there was another B-Detachment table for three B-Detachments engaged in provincial advisory roles during 1965. Two other special B-Detachment structures are shown in Part II of this chart.

Chart 5. Typical Army Special Forces B-Detachments (Part II) *

Modified B-Detachment for
Special Operation, 1965

1	Detachment Commander, Major
1	Adjutant, Captain
1	Plans Officer, Captain
1	Intelligence Officer, Captain
1	Operations Officer, Captain
1	Supply Officer, Captain
1	Sergeant-Major, E-9
2	Intelligence Sergeants, E-8
2	Operations Sergeants, E-8
1	Reconnaissance Supervisor, E-8
1	Weapons Supervisor, E-7
1	Engineer Supervisor, E-7
1	Medical Supervisor, E-7
1	Supply Sergeant, E-7
1	Communications Supervisor, E-7
1	Administrative Supervisor, E-6
1	Assistant Supply Sergeant, E-6
16	Reconnaissance Team Advisors, E-6
1	Chief Radio Operator, E-6
3	Radio Operators, E-5

Modified B-Detachment for
Utilization by another Agency

1	Intelligence Officer, Captain
1	Operations Officer, Captain
1	Supply Officer, Captain
1	Sergeant-Major
1	Intelligence Sergeant, E-8
1	Operations Sergeant, E-8
1	Air Operations Supervisor, E-7
1	Demolitions Sergeant, E-7
1	Weapons Supervisor, E-7
1	Survival Instructor, E-7
1	Tactics Instructor, E-7
1	Assistant Operations Sergeant, E-7
1	Medical Supervisor, E-7
1	Supply Sergeant, E-7
1	Communications Supervisor, E-7
1	Assistant Intelligence Sergeant, E-6
1	Medical Specialist, E-6
1	Radio Operator, E-5
1	Demolitions Specialist, E-5
1	Clerk Typist, E-4

* Headquarters, 5th Special Forces Group Troop Change Request dtd 24 August 1965 depicting organizations already implemented. The modified B-Detachment for Special Operation was Project DELTA, and the grade allocation for the sixteen reconnaissance team advisors varied between E-7 and E-6 in practice. The modified B-Detachment for utilization by another Agency was a MACV-SOG structure. There was also a special authorization for a modified B-Detachment in support of the Vietnamese Special Forces (LLDB) Training Center not shown.

Chart 6. Standard Army Special Forces C-Detachment (1963 Type) *

1	Commanding Officer, Detachment Commander Lieutenant-Colonel (O-5)
1	Executive Officer, Detachment XO Major (O-4)
1	Adjutant, Detachment S-1 Captain (O-3)
1	Intelligence Officer, Detachment S-2 Captain (O-3)
1	Operations Officer, Detachment S-3 Captain (O-3)
1	Supply Officer, Detachment S-4 Captain (O-3)
1	Sergeant-Major, Detachment Sergeant-Major Sergeant-Major (E-9)

1	Intelligence Sergeant, S-2 Sergeant Master Sergeant (E-8)
1	Operations Sergeant, S-3 Sergeant Master Sergeant (E-8)
1	Assistant Supply Sergeant, S-4 Sergeant Sergeant First Class (E-7)
1	Radio Operator Supervisor, Communications Sergeant Sergeant First Class (E-7)
1	Administrative Supervisor, S-1 Sergeant Staff Sergeant (E-6)
1	Senior Field Radio Repairman, Communications Repairman Sergeant (E-5)
4	Chief Radio Operators, Radiomen Sergeant (E-5)

* Dept of the Army TOE 31-107E, this standard C-Detachment organization was later modified and expanded.

SOURCES AND BIBLIOGRAPHY

The research for this book was based primarily on Special Forces detachment after-action reports, officer and NCO debriefings, and other wartime historical documents, supplemented by the author's interviews of SF personnel conducted both during and after the Second Indochina War. Although much material, especially from the early Laotian and Vietnam period, has been apparently destroyed or lost, a significant body of important SF documents for the later portion of the Southeast Asian conflict is contained in Records Group 338 (Vietnam War: MACV/USARV records), currently under Army custody within the Washington National Records Center at Suitland, Maryland. Many of the documents utilized are cited in the text footnotes. The reports prepared for the 5th Special Forces Group by its attached 21st Military History Detachment proved to be indispensable references. The following is a listing of the more valuable SF-related resources available for the interested reader.

Headquarters, MACV MACJ 323, *Monthly Evaluation Reports*, for the period January–July 1965 (earlier monthly reports exist under the designation *CIDG Progress Reports*). Although sparse on detailed SF information, these provide otherwise missing data.

5th Special Forces Group, *Monthly Operational Summaries*, for the years 1965–1970. These provide the basic statistical, and historical outline data, arranged by zone and camp. The 1965 versions were printed by the 5th SFG Tactical Operations Center.

5th Special Forces Group, *Quarterly Command Report*, dtd 10 October 1965, RCS GSG-28 (R1), OACSFOR-OT-RD 650088.

5th Special Forces Group, *Command Operational Report*, dtd 10 May 1966, RCS GSGPO-28 (R1), OACSFOR-OT-RD 660557.

5th Special Forces Group, *Command Operational Report*, dtd 10 August 1966, RCS GSGPO-28 (R1), OACSFOR-OT-RD 660556.

5th Special Forces Group, *Operational Report for Quarterly Period Ending 31 October 1966*, dtd 15 November 1966 (RCS CSFOR-65), OACSFOR-OT-RD 660565.

5th Special Forces Group, *Operational Report for Quarterly Period Ending 31 January 1967*, dtd 15 February 1967, OACSFOR-OT-RD 670787.

5th Special Forces Group, *Operational Report for Quarterly Period Ending 30 April 1967*, dtd 15 May 1967, OACSFOR-OT-RD 67X012.

5th Special Forces Group, *Operational Report for Quarterly Period Ending 31 July 1967*, dtd 15 August 1967, OACSFOR-OT-RD 67X080.

5th Special Forces Group, *Operational Report—Lessons Learned*, dtd 15 November 1967, OACSFOR-OT-RD 67X205.

5th Special Forces Group, *Operational Report—Lessons Learned for Quarterly Period Ending 31 January 1968*, (RCS CSFOR-65), dtd 15 February 1968, OACSFOR-OT-RD 681210.

5th Special Forces Group, *Operational Report of 5th SFG for Period Ending 30 April 1968*, CSFOR-65 (R1), dtd 15 May 1968, OACSFOR-OT-RD 682179.

5th Special Forces Group, *Operational Report of 5th SFG for Period Ending 31 July 1968*, RCS CSFOR-65 (R1), dtd 15 August 1968, OACSFOR-OT-UT 683089.

5th Special Forces Group, *Operational Report of 5th SFG for Period Ending 31 October 1968*, RCS CSFOR-65 (R1), dtd 15 November 1968, OACSFOR-OT-UT 684314.

5th Special Forces Group, *Operational Report of 5th SFG for Period Ending 31 January 1969*, RCS CSFOR-65 (R1), dtd 15 February 1969, OACSFOR-OT-UT 691321.

5th Special Forces Group, *Operational Report of 5th SFG for Period Ending 30 April 1969*, RCS CSFOR-65 (R1), dtd 15 May 1969, OACSFOR-OT-UT 692358.

5th Special Forces Group, *Operational Report of 5th SFG for Period Ending 31 July 1969*, RCS CSFOR-65 (R1), dtd 15 August 1969, OACSFOR-OT-UT 693239.

5th Special Forces Group, *Operational Report of 5th SFG for Period Ending 31 October 1969*, RCS CSFOR-65 (R2), dtd 14 November 1969, OACSFOR-OT-UT 694287.

5th Special Forces Group, *Operational Report of 5th SFG for Period Ending 31 January 1970*, RCS CSFOR-65 (R2), dtd 13 January 1970, OACSFOR-OT-UT unlisted [date on report also inconsistent].

5th Special Forces Group, *Operational Report of 5th SFG for Period Ending 30 April 1970*, RCS CSFOR-65 (R2), dtd 15 May 1970, OACSFOR-OT-UT 702053.

5th Special Forces Group, *Operational Report of 5th SFG for Period*

Ending 31 July 1970, RCS CSFOR-65 (R2), dtd 15 August 1970, OACSFOR-OT-UT 703234.

5th Special Forces Group, *Operational Report of 5th SFG for Period Ending 31 October 1970,* RCS CSFOR-65 (R2), dtd 15 November 1970, OACSFOR-OT-UT 704176.

5th Special Forces Group, *Operational Report of 5th SFG for Period Ending 15 January 1971,* RCS CSFOR-65 (R2), dtd 1 February 1971, OACSFOR-OT-UT unlisted.

5th Special Forces Group, *Keystone Robin-C After Action Report,* dtd 28 February 1971. The final redeployment of 5th SFG from Vietnam to the United States is discussed.

Berry, John S., *Those Gallant Men,* Novato, California: Presidio Press, 1984. The infamous 5th SFG double-agent murder case as related by one of the lawyers involved.

Donlon, Roger H. C., *Outpost of Freedom,* New York: McGraw, 1965. The struggle of Camp Nam Dong as told by the SF team leader who won the Medal of Honor there.

Duncan, Donald, *The New Legions,* New York: Random House, 1967. A critical look at SF advisory effects by an SF master sergeant, which was temporarily banned at Fort Bragg during the war.

Kelly, Col. Francis J., *U.S. Army Special Forces, 1961–1971,* Washington: Department of the Army, 1973. The official Army Vietnam Studies booklet on the subject.

Marshall, Brig. Gen. S.L.A., *Ambush,* New York: Cowles Book Co., 1969. Contains a chapter on SF Operation Blackjack 22.

————, *West to Cambodia,* New York: Cowles Book Co., 1968. Contains a chapter on SF Task Force Prong.

Moore, Robin, *The Green Berets,* New York: Crown Publishers, 1965. This gripping "novel" by a famous correspondent was actually a true account of SF action in Vietnam, with only the names of individuals and minor facts changed.

Morris, Jim, *War Story,* Boulder, Colorado: Sycamore Island Books, 1979. Excellent account of an SF officer at A-team level during a tour in Vietnam from Okinawa.

Patric, Gordon M., *The Vietnams of the Green Berets,* Indiana University Northwest, 1969. Graphic account of SF operations, surprisingly accurate considering classification restrictions at the time.

Rottman, Gordon L., *U.S. Army Special Forces, 1952–84*, London: Osprey Publishing Company. The definitive work on SF uniforms, equipment, and insignia.

Research Analysis Corporation Technical Memorandum RAC-T-435, *Case Study of U.S. Counterinsurgency Operations in Laos, 1955–1962*, McLean, Virginia: RAC Publications, 1964. Excellent treatise on the Laotian conflict which preceded Vietnam.

Research Analysis Corporation Technical Memorandum RAC–T–477, *U.S. Army Special Forces Operations under the Civilian Irregular Defense Groups Program in Vietnam, 1961–1964*, McLean, Virginia: RAC Publications, 1966. Excellent account of the early CIDG period in Vietnam.

Rowe, James N., *Five Years to Freedom*, Boston: Little Brown & Company, 1971. SF officer who escaped from VC imprisonment relates his story.

Saddler, Barry, *I'm a Lucky One*, New York: Macmillan Company, 1967. Individual SF soldier's story of his A-team being deployed to Vietnam with 5th SFG.

Santoli, Al, *To Bear Any Burden*, New York: E. P. Dutton, 1985. Contains valuable material on SF participants in Vietnam, as well as the fate of Southeast Asians in the war's aftermath.

Schemmer, Benjamin F., *The Raid*, New York: Harper & Row, 1976. The classic account of the Son Tay raid.

Simpson, Col. Charles M. III, *Inside the Green Berets*, Novato, California: Presidio Press, 1983. Personal memoirs of an SF officer who later became the commander of 1st SFG.

Smith, George E., *POW: Two Years with the Viet Cong*, Berkeley: Ramparts Press, 1971. A SF sergeant's story of imprisonment after the fall of Camp Hiep Hoa in 1963.

Stanton, Shelby L., *Vietnam Order of Battle*, Washington: U.S. News Books, 1981. Contains detailed description of internal 5th SFG organization, including camp and detachment listings.

APPENDIX A

SPECIAL FORCES PERSONNEL
MISSING IN ACTION

Arthur Edward Bader, Jr., Sergeant Reconnaissance patrol member, Command & Control North, MACV-SOG. Born 12 July 1934 in Atlantic City, New Jersey. Entered service on 16 May 1964 at Atlantic City, New Jersey.
Missing in action since 30 November 1968, 10 miles inside Laos east of Tchepone, when returning from patrol aboard a Vietnamese H-34 helicopter that was hit by 37mm antiaircraft fire; aircraft fell out of control from altitude of 3,000 feet and exploded upon impact with ground. No ground search was initiated because crash site was located in a denied area.

Earl Roger Biggs, Sergeant First Class Light weapons leader, Detachment A-411, 5th Special Forces Group. Born 23 March 1932 in Concho, West Virginia. Entered service on 31 May 1950 at Colcord, West Virginia.
Missing in action since 16 January 1968, 16 miles northwest of My Tho, Vietnam, when camp strike force was involved in a firefight; CIDG and LLDB survivors reported that the Viet Cong captured and summarily executed him, but actual confirmation of death was impossible.

Klaus Yrurgen Bingham, Staff Sergeant Reconnaissance team member, Task Force 1 Advisory Element. Born 14 December 1943 in Metz, France. Entered service on 17 June 1965 at New Orleans, Louisiana.
Missing in action since 10 May 1971, after his long-range reconnaissance team "Asp" was inserted into western Quang Nam Province 12 miles from Laos on 3 May; past initial radio contact, no further contact was ever made.

John Arthur Boronski, Staff Sergeant Reconnaissance patrol member, Command & Control Central, MACV-SOG. Born 24 July 1944 in Northampton, Massachusetts. Entered service on 22 June 1964 at Springfield, Massachusetts.
Missing in action since 24 March 1970, when UH-1H helicopter lifted him and other team members from landing zone in the tri-border area 14 miles inside Cambodia; aircraft racked by explosions during ascent, continued forward aflame for 200 yards, and disappeared into the jungle, where it crashed.

Russell Peter Bott, Staff Sergeant Patrol member, Detachment B-52 DELTA, 5th Special Forces Group. Born 5 September 1936 in North Easton, Massachusetts. Entered service on 22 March 1954 at Worcester, Massachusetts.
Missing in action since 2 December 1966, 1-1/2 miles inside Laos west of the DMZ with a reconnaissance patrol which had two skirmishes with Viet Cong on 29 No-

Source: USARV USPW/CI Detainee files and MIA Board Proceedings of 5th Special Forces Group and MACV-SOG.

vember, and was last seen by Vietnamese patrol survivors attending to wounded comrade, Sfc. Willie E. Stark, whom he refused to abandon although they were surrounded by a superior force.

Alan Lee Boyer, Sergeant Reconnaissance patrol member, Command & Control, MACV-SOG. Born 8 March 1946 in Chicago, Illinois. Entered service on 11 January 1966 at Butte, Montana.
Missing in action since 28 March 1968, when last seen 15 miles inside Laos northeast of Tchpone during extraction, having started to climb a rope ladder that broke as the Vietnamese H-34 helicopter moved away because of hostile weapons fire.

George R. Brown, Sergeant First Class Reconnaissance patrol leader, Command & Control, MACV-SOG. Born 19 September 1935 in Daytona Beach, Florida. Entered service on 22 October 1952.
Missing in action since 28 March 1968, when last seen alive and unwounded with two other Special Forces sergeants and one Vietnamese sergeant awaiting extraction from an area 15 miles inside Laos northeast of Tchepone by helicopter, which was driven off by ground fire; later search of area failed to reveal any trace of the team.

William Theodore Brown, Staff Sergeant Reconnaissance patrol member, Command & Control North, MACV-SOG. Born 20 February 1945 in Chicago, Illinois. Entered service on 3 September 1965 at Whittier, California.
Missing in action since 3 November 1969, when his reconnaissance patrol was attacked by a numerically superior force 30 miles inside Laos near Ban Chakevy Tai; he was shot through the body just below the rib cage in the initial burst of automatic weapons fire and was last seen lying wounded on the ground as their position was about to be overrun, as related by an indigenous team member who evaded capture.

Michael Paul Burns, Specialist 4th Class Reconnaissance patrol member, Command & Control North, MACV-SOG. Born 25 April 1947 in Oconto Falls, Wisconsin. Entered service on 14 February 1968 at El Paso, Texas.
Missing in action since 31 July 1969, when his reconnaissance patrol was attacked 1-1/2 miles inside Laos west of Hue just prior to extraction; last seen by Pan and Comen, the surviving commandos, lying on his back with severe head wounds, possibly dead, after incurring blast of a B-40 rocket.

Johnny C. Calhoun, Staff Sergeant Reconnaissance patrol leader, Command & Control, MACV-SOG. Born 14 July 1945 in Roanoke, Alabama. Entered service on 18 January 1963 at Atlanta, Georgia.
Missing in action since 27 March 1968, when his team was attacked 1 1/2 miles south of Ta Bat in the A Shau Valley and he provided covering fire for rest of patrol while ordering the other five members to withdraw; hit several times in the chest and stomach and last seen by interpreter Ho-Thong as he slumped to the ground, pulled the pin from a grenade, and clutched it to explode among advancing enemy, but his ultimate fate was unknown because of the rapid retreat of the survivors.

Donald Gene "Butch" Carr, Captain Assistant launch officer, Mobile Launch Team 3, Task Force 1 Advisory Element. Born 10 December 1938 in East Chicago, Indiana. Entered service on 12 October 1961 at East Chicago, Indiana.

Missing in action since 6 July 1971, while flying a visual reconnaissance mission in an Air Force OV-10 aircraft from the 23d Tactical Aerial Surveillance Squadron (Tail number 634) piloted by Lt. Daniel Thomas, which disappeared 15 miles inside Laos west of Ben Het.

James Derwin Cohron, Staff Sergeant Reconnaissance patrol member, Command & Control North, MACV-SOG. Born 11 November 1938 in Leon, Iowa. Entered service on 9 January 1963, at Centerville, Iowa.
Missing in action since 12 January 1968, while a member of Spike Team "Indiana," as the second man from the rear of the team formation, when ambushed 1 mile inside Laos south of Khe Sanh; team broke contact by evading through a gully and set up defensive position on a small hill where called for helicopter extraction while waiting in vain for Cohron and two indigenous soldiers; tall elephant grass obstructed their vision, and efforts to reach him via squad radio failed.

William Michael Copley, Specialist 4th Class Reconnaissance patrol member, Command & Control North, MACV-SOG. Born 22 May 1949 in Columbus, Ohio. Entered service on 31 July 1967 at Los Angeles, California.
Missing in action since 16 November 1968, when patrol was ambushed 16 miles inside Laos west of Ben Het prior to establishing overnight positions; he was seriously wounded by automatic weapons fire and cried out to S. Sgt. Roger T. Loe, "Help me, I'm hit!"; Loe carried him on his back until he tripped after traveling a short distance, tried to administer first aid until Copley's face showed signs of death, and was forced to leave because of pursuit by hostile forces.

Douglas Edward DaHill, Specialist 4th Class Patrol member, Detachment B-52 DELTA, 5th Special Forces Group. Born 6 March 1949 in Lima, Ohio. Entered service on 28 June 1966 at Columbus, Ohio.
Missing in action since 17 April 1969, when Reconnaissance Patrol 6 was ambushed by numerically superior Viet Cong force in Thua Thien Province 9 miles from Laotian border; last heard from by radio transmission to circling aircraft requesting assistance, whereupon radio contact was lost.

David Arthur Davidson, Staff Sergeant Reconnaissance patrol member, Command & Control North, MACV-SOG. Born 8 March 1947 in Washington, D.C. Reenlisted on 18 May 1968 in the Republic of Vietnam.
Missing in action since 5 October 1970, after his patrol had established its overnight position 12 miles inside Laos west of Ta Bat and was attacked by a hostile force; according to the two surviving indigenous patrol members, Davidson was hit once in the head and fell down a ridge, after which he lay motionless with a probable fatal head wound.

Ricardo Gonzalez Davis, Sergeant First Class Reconnaissance patrol leader, Command & Control North, MACV-SOG. Born 17 March 1941 in Fort Stockton, Texas. Reenlisted on 30 May 1967 at Fort Campbell, Kentucky.
Missing in action since 20 March 1969, when his six-man patrol was attacked 11 miles inside Laos west of Kham Duc; Sgt. James C. La Motte was two feet away when Davis was hit by rifle fire in upper chest and face and said, "Jim, Jim!" and

fell; the assistant patrol leader advanced to Davis's position seven minutes later but detected no signs of life, whereupon the patrol was forced to evacuate the area because of advancing hostile soldiers.

Ronald James Dexter, Master Sergeant Reconnaissance patrol member, Command & Control, MACV-SOG. Born 23 July 1933 in Chicago, Illinois. Entered Service on 2 September 1951 at Chicago, Illinois.
Missing in action since 3 June 1967, when last seen exiting a downed CH-46 helicopter as it was being grenaded by approaching hostile forces 15 miles inside Laos west of the A Shau Valley; the Nung commander, Mr. Ky, saw several men in a large bomb crater firing red star clusters from a flare gun as Ky was lifted out on the last helicopter.

Edward Ray Dodge, Sergeant First Class Administrative supervisor, Detachment C-1, 5th Special Forces Group. Born 16 December 1933 in Norfolk, Virginia. Entered service on 21 December 1950 at Norfolk, Virginia.
Missing in action since 31 December 1964, while an observer aboard an Air Force O1-F aircraft (Number 572823) of the 336th Tactical Fighter Squadron piloted by Capt. Kurt C. MacDonald, on a reconnaissance flight over the A Shau Valley, as the aircraft failed to return to Da Nang.

Raymond Louis Echevarria, Master Sergeant Reconnaissance patrol leader, Command & Control, MACV-SOG. Born 16 September 1933 in Brooklyn, New York. Entered service on 3 December 1950 in New York City.
Missing in action since 3 October 1966, when patrol was inserted 1 mile inside Laos west of the DMZ and immediately engaged in firefight under adverse circumstances; sole survivor, interpreter Bui Kim Tien, last heard of him when Sfc. Eddie L. Williams had told Tien, "Jones is dying and Ray (Echevarria) is the same way."

Lawrence Jesse Englander, Sergeant Radio supervisor, Detachment A-109, 5th Special Forces Group. Born 19 April 1943 in Las Vegas, Nevada. Entered service on 4 August 1964 at Van Nuys, California.
Missing in action since 2 May 1968, when participated in a CIDG heliborne assault that came under intense automatic weapons fire from fortified NVA positions 8 miles southwest of Thuong Duc; last heard from by Sgt. John M. Vincent on radio stating he was wounded in foot and arm and pinned down in open field behind dead Vietnamese radio operator, refused help because he claimed to be "zeroed in," that any movement would bring heavy fire, and that he would try to crawl back to friendly lines; LLDB Lieutenant Ho Tang Dzu stated he saw him hit by machine gun fire in back and head, but attempts to reach him failed and battlefield was abandoned.

Danny Day Entrican, 1st Lieutenant Reconnaissance patrol leader, Task Force 1 Advisory Element. Born 12 August 1946 in Brookhaven, Mississippi. Entered service on 1 October 1969 at Fort Devens, Massachusetts.
Missing in action since 18 May 1971, after his reconnaissance team "Alaska" was inserted into the Da Krong Valley in Vietnam on 15 May and overwhelmed in a firefight three days later 1 mile from the Laotian border; surviving commando Truong Minh Long and interpreter Truong To Ha stated that they rolled downhill after hos-

tile search party detected them hiding in bush, at which point Entrican was apparently wounded and yelled at them to move out.

Richard Allan Fitts, Specialist 5th Class Reconnaissance patrol member, Command & Control North, MACV-SOG. Born 23 February 1946 in Weymouth, Massachusetts. Entered service on 18 January 1966 at Boston, Massachusetts.
Missing in action since 30 November 1968, 10 miles inside Laos east of Tchepone when returning from reconnaissance mission on a Vietnamese H-34 helicopter that was hit by 37mm antiaircraft fire; aircraft fell out of control from altitude of 3,000 feet and exploded upon impact with the ground. No ground search was initiated because the crash site was located in a denied area.

John Theodore Gallagher, Staff Sergeant Reconnaissance patrol member, Command & Control North, MACV-SOG. Born 17 June 1943 in Summit, New Jersey. Entered service on 25 December 1962 at New Haven, Connecticut.
Missing in action since 5 January 1968, when aboard the second helicopter transporting patrol 20 miles inside Laos south of Lao Bao, which was struck by 37mm antiaircraft fire at an altitude of 2,000 feet; it went into an uncontrollable spin and exploded in flames upon impact with ground; heavy ground fire prevented search attempts.

Fred Allen Gassman, Sergeant Reconnaissance patrol member, Command & Control North, MACV-SOG. Born 5 September 1947 at Eglin Field, Florida. Reenlisted on 10 February 1969.
Missing in action since 5 October 1970, after his patrol had established its overnight position 12 miles inside Laos west of Ta Bat and was attacked by a hostile force; Gassman radioed the overhead aircraft for emergency extraction and, as he attempted to retrieve the homing device, stated on the radio, "I've been hit, and in the worst way," followed by several groans before the radio went dead. According to the two surviving indigenous patrol members, Gassman was last seen lying motionless with a large hole in his back.

Stephen Jonathan Geist, Specialist 4th Class heavy weapons specialist, Detachment A-332, 5th Special Forces Group. Born 12 April 1946 in Philadelphia, Pennsylvania. Entered service on 9 May 1966 at Baltimore, Maryland.
Missing in action since 26 September 1967, when aboard an aircraft of the 74th Aviation company piloted by Lt. Lynn R. Huddleston on a visual reconnaissance mission north of Minh Thanh 4 miles from the Cambodian border; aircraft disappeared and never reached destination.

Douglas J. Glover, Staff Sergeant Reconnaissance patrol member, Command & Control, MACV-SOG. Born 2 May 1943 in Cortland, New York. Reenlisted on 17 October 1965 at Fort Myer, Virginia.
Missing in action since 19 February 1968, when reconnaissance team was being extracted 4 miles inside Laos west of Dak Sut; as the helicopter ascended from the landing zone, it nosed over and crashed, bursting into flames; the pilot, co-pilot, and one team member survived but left six persons missing because of hostile fire; later recovery efforts detected only five badly burned unknown remains.

Roger C. Hallberg, Staff Sergeant Platoon leader, III CTZ Mike Force (Detachment A-302), 5th Special Forces Group. Born 18 September 1944 in Visalia, California. Entered Service on 11 October 1963 at Los Angeles, California.
Missing in action since 24 March 1967, when his Mike Force company conducted a heliborne assault 7 miles east of Bu Dop; shortly after landing they were engaged by two NVA battalions armed with automatic weapons and recoilless rifles, and supported by mortars, forcing company elements to retreat under extremely heavy pressure, attempts to consolidate positions around the landing zone supported by airstrikes failed, communication was lost with the Mike Force and never regained.

Kenneth Hanna, Sergeant First Class heavy weapons specialist, Detachment A-101, 5th Special Forces Group. Born 28 April 1933 in Scranton, South Carolina. Entered service on 28 April 1951.
Missing in action since 7 February 1968, during NVA tank-infantry assault on Lang Vei Special Forces Camp, when last seen with wounds to scalp, left shoulder, and arm, administering first aid to Sfc. Charles W. Lindewald, at the mobile strike force outpost as it was about to be overrun.

Gary Alan Harned, Sergeant Reconnaissance patrol member, Command & Control Central, MACV-SOG. Born 7 July 1950 in Meadville, Pennsylvania. Entered service on 10 September 1968 at Pittsburgh, Pennsylvania.
Missing in action since 24 March 1970, when UH-1H helicopter lifted him and other team members from landing zone in the tri-border area 14 miles inside Cambodia; aircraft racked by explosions during ascent, continued forward aflame for 200 yards, and disappeared into the jungle, where it crashed.

James Arthur Harwood, Sergeant Reconnaissance team member, Detachment B-43, 5th Special Forces Group. Born 10 March 1950 in Omaha, Nebraska. Entered service on 10 October 1968 at Dallas, Texas.
Missing in action since 15 January 1971, when attached to the Reconnaissance Platoon, 2d Company, 1st (later the 6th) Cambodian Battalion, which was ambushed in thick bamboo on the slope of Hill 282 (Nui Ta Bec) northwest of Chi Lang 2 miles from the Cambodian border; last heard when he radioed 1st Lt. James J. McCarty that he was moving up toward the point, could not see anything, and was receiving direct fire from the front; communications was then lost and McCarty's shouts to him received no response.

Robert Dale Herreid, Specialist 5th Class Demolitions specialist, Detachment A-402, 5th Special Forces Group. Born 13 June 1946 in Williston, North Dakota. Entered service on 11 July 1966 at Chicago, Illinois.
Missing in action since 10 October 1968, as part of the 47th Mobile Strike Force Company advancing up Nui Coto near Chau Doc, which was blasted by heavy bunker fire and withdrew to pagoda, where set up perimeter; radio operator gave Herreid's weapon to commanding officer, stating that Herreid was dead; Nguyen Van Liet and other soldiers said Herreid was shot in left temple and lying by a leafless mangrove tree, but body never found.

Barry Wayne Hilbrich, Captain Operations Officer, Company B, 5th Special Forces

Group. Born 25 June 1947 in Cuere DeWitt, Texas. Entered service on 28 December 1965 at Corpus Christi, Texas.

Missing in action since 9 June 1970, when flying on a visual reconnaissance mission 7 miles south of Ben Het in an Air Force O-1F aircraft (Tail number 890) of the 21st Tactical Aerial Surveillance Squadron, piloted by 1st Lt. John L. Ryder, which disappeared west of Pleiku.

Cecil J. Hodgson, Sergeant First Class Patrol member, Detachment B-52 DELTA, 5th Special Forces Group. Born 28 July 1937 in Campbell, Texas. Entered service on 15 June 1955 at Greenville, Texas.

Missing in action since 29 January 1966, in An Lao Valley of Binh Dinh Province 12 miles west of Tam Quan when his reconnaissance team was split during firefight; last seen with 9mm pistol in tall grass within arm's reach of M. Sgt. Wiley W. Gray and S. Sgt. Ronald T. Terry, when they opened fire on a hostile element blocking their escape and became separated during skirmish.

James William Holt, Sergeant First Class Senior medical specialist, Detachment A-101, 5th Special Forces Group. Born 19 September 1941 in Hope, Arkansas. Entered service on 18 June 1959 at Little Rock, Arkansas.

Missing in action since 7 February 1968, when the Lang Vei Special Forces Camp was overrun by NVA tank-infantry assault; destroyed three North Vietnamese Army tanks with a recoilless rifle before forced to abandon the position; last seen by S. Sgt. Peter Tiroch running to the ammunition bunker to look for light antitank weapons.

William Balt Hunt, Staff Sergeant Replacement platoon leader, III CTZ Mike Force (Detachment A-302), 5th Special Forces Group. Born 31 July 1935 in Priest River, Idaho. Entered service on 13 November 1953 at Spokane, Washington.

Missing in action since 4 November 1966, when lifted into battle by helicopter to evacuate wounded northeast of Soui Da 10 miles from Dau Tieng and voluntarily left aircraft to reinforce remaining troops on ground; after two days of heavy fighting and numerous casualties, the Mike Force was overrun by numerically superior forces on 6 November 1966; as he carried the wounded company commander, Sfc. George H. Heaps, out of danger, he was gravely wounded by a bullet that hit him in the shoulder, penetrated his upper back, and exited his side, but still succeeded in moving Heaps to a covered position where they passed out from loss of blood; both later awoke and crawled toward landing zone, passing out periodically; Nung soldier stayed behind with Hunt and later reported that Hunt had died, but the body was never found.

Charles Gregory Huston, Sergeant Reconnaissance patrol member, Command & Control, MACV-SOG. Born 29 September 1945 in Houston, Ohio. Entered service on 5 October 1965 at Cincinnati, Ohio.

Missing in action since 28 March 1968, when last seen alive and unwounded with two other Special Forces sergeants and one Vietnamese sergeant awaiting extraction 15 miles inside Laos northeast of Tchepone by helicopter, which was driven off by ground fire; later search of area failed to reveal any traces of team.

James Emory Jones, Sergeant First Class Reconnaissance patrol member, Command & Control, MACV-SOG. Born 3 September 1939 in Enigma, Georgia. Entered service on 23 July 1957 at Milledgeville, Georgia.

Missing in action since 3 October 1966, when patrol was inserted 1 mile inside Laos west of the DMZ and immediately engaged in firefight under adverse circumstances; sole survivor, interpreter Bui Kim Tien, last heard of him when Sfc. Eddie L. Williams had told Tien, "Jones is dying and Ray is the same way."

John Robert Jones, Sergeant light weapons leader, Task Force 1 Advisory Element. Born 20 February 1949 in Louisville, Kentucky. Entered service on 1 July 1968 at El Paso, Texas.

Missing in action since 5 June 1971, at Hickory Hill Radio Relay site north of Khe Sanh in Quang Tri Province, which was overrun in heavy combat by a battalion-size North Vietnamese force in adverse weather, which prevented air support; he was not found despite search by helicopter and low-flying aircraft.

Gerald Francis Kinsman, First Lieutenant Training officer, Detachment B-43, 5th Special Forces Group. Born 12 June 1945, in Boston, Massachusetts. Commissioned on 11 July 1969, at Fort Benning, Georgia.

Missing in action since 15 January 1971, when attached to the Reconnaissance Platoon, 2d Company, 1st (later the 6th) Cambodian Battalion, which was ambushed in thick bamboo on the slope of Hill 282 (Nui Ta Bec) northwest of Chi Lang 2 miles from Cambodian border; Kinsman was severely wounded and unconscious as Lt. James J. McCarty attempted to pull him out of a bamboo thicket, but a machine gun wounded McCarty and forced him to abandon the effort.

Harold William Kroske, Jr., 1st Lieutenant Reconnaissance patrol leader, Command & Control South, MACV-SOG. Born 30 July 1947 in Trenton, New Jersey. Entered service on 29 June 1966 at Mercer, New Jersey.

Missing in action since 11 February 1969, when patrol was engaged 12 miles inside Cambodia west of Bu Dop and he killed several hostile troops along a trail; he then motioned the point man, Diep Chan Sang, to come with him; there was a sudden burst of gunfire, Kroske dropped his weapon, grabbed his stomach, and fell; Sp. 4th Class Bryan O. Stockdale tried to approach him, received no response when he called out his name from twenty feet away, whereupon the patrol was forced to withdraw because of heavy automatic weapons fire.

Frederick Krupa, Captain Platoon leader, Exploitation Company A, Task Force 2 Advisory Element. Born 2 September 1947 in Scranton, Pennsylvania. Entered service on 25 June 1965 at Wilkes-Barre, Pennsylvania.

Missing in action since 27 April 1971, when his special commando unit was about to conduct a helicopter insertion 2 miles from Laotian border northwest of Plei Djereng, Vietman; hostile forces opened up on his UH-1H helicopter when it was three feet off the ground, and he fell forward; SCU Company A commander Ayom grabbed his right shoulder but let go when Ayom's hand was struck by bullet; last seen lying next to a log sprawled out on his back, not moving or making a sound, by crew chief Sp. 4th Class Melvin C. Lew during helicopter ascent.

Gary Russell LaBohn, Specialist 4th Class Reconnaissance patrol member, Command & Control North, MACV-SOG. Born 28 December 1942 in Madison, Wisconsin. Entered service on 29 December 1966 in Detroit, Michigan.

Missing in action since 30 November 1968, 10 miles inside Laos east of Tchepone when returning from patrol aboard a Vietnamese H-34 helicopter, which was hit by 37mm antiaircraft fire; aircraft fell out of control from altitude of 3,000 feet and exploded upon impact with ground. No ground search was initiated because crash site was located in a denied area.

Glen Oliver Lane, Sergeant First Class Reconnaissance patrol leader, Command & Control, MACV-SOG. Born 24 July 1931 in Diboll, Texas. Entered service on 30 June 1951.

Missing in action since 23 May 1968, after his six-man spike team "Idaho" was infiltrated just across the Laotian border west of A Loui by helicopter on 20 May 1968, and all further contact with patrol was lost; spike team "Oregon" inserted into area for search on 22 May immediately contacted large hostile force and was extracted.

Billy Ray Laney, Sergeant First Class Reconnaissance patrol member, Command & Control, MACV-SOG. Born 21 August 1939 in Blanch, Alabama. Entered Army 3 August, 1960 with two years Navy service.

Missing in action since 3 June 1967, aboard CH-46 helicopter downed 15 miles inside Laos west of the A Shau Valley; last seen by Sergeant First Class Wilklow and Nung soldier lying wounded on floor of helicopter, between one crew member with a broken back and the door gunner with head wound, as hostile forces approached, tossing grenades at aircraft.

Charles W. Lindewald, Jr., Sergeant First Class Platoon leader, 12th Mobile Strike Force Company, Company C, 5th Special Forces Group. Born 30 July 1938 in La Porte, Indiana. Entered service on 2 August 1955 at La Porte, Indiana.

Missing in action since 7 February 1968, at Lang Vei Special Forces Camp when overrun by NVA tank-infantry assault; last seen severely wounded in chest or abdomen by automatic weapons fire and being treated at mobile strike force outpost by Sfc. Kenneth Hanna just as it was about to be overrun.

James Martin Luttrell, Staff Sergeant Reconnaissance team member, Task Force 1 Advisory Element. Born 14 December 1935 in Milwaukee, Wisconsin. Entered service on 29 March 1954 at Wamatosa, Wisconsin.

Missing in action since 10 May 1971, after his long-range reconnaissance team "Asp" was inserted into western Quang Nam Province 12 miles from Laos on 3 May 1971; past initial radio contact, no further contact was ever made.

Michael Howard Mein, Specialist 4th Class Reconnaissance patrol member, Command & Control North, MACV-SOG. Born 13 March 1945 in Oneida, New York. Entered service on 17 February 1967 at Syracuse, New York.

Missing in action since 30 November 1968, 10 miles inside Laos east of Tchepone when returning from patrol aboard a Vietnamese H-34 helicopter that was hit by 37mm antiaircraft fire; aircraft fell out of control from altitude of 3,000 feet and exploded upon impact with ground. No ground search was initiated because crash site was located in a denied area.

Michael Millner, Staff Sergeant light weapons leader, Detachment A-341, 5th Special Forces Group. Born 17 December 1942 in Alhambra, California. Entered service on 11 January 1960 at Marysville, California.
Missing in action since 29 November 1967, when accompanying a CIDG unit on a search-and-destroy operation 6 miles east of Bu Dop, which was begun 26 November; against advice of senior advisor Capt. Matthew J. Hasko, the LLDB commander stopped the troops for lunch, and unit was attacked by a Viet Cong company; the CIDG became completely disorganized and ran from field as Special Forces personnel tried to cover the rear and carry the wounded; Millner was missing when unit was finally reconsolidated.

James Leslie Moreland, Specialist 4th Class Medical specialist, 12th Mobile Strike Force Company, Company C, 5th Special Forces Group. Born 29 September 1945 in Bossemer, Alabama. Entered service on 27 September 1965 at Anaheim, California. Missing in action since 7 February 1968, at Lang Vei when overrun by NVA tank-infantry assault; severely wounded and became delirious in command bunker as it came under sapper attack, preventing his extraction when bunker was later abandoned; last seen by 1st Lt. Thomas E. Todd in the bunker ruins, apparently dead and covered by debris.

Dennis Paul Neal, Captain Reconnaissance patrol leader, Command & Control North, MACV-SOG. Born 1 February 1944 in Quincy, Illinois. Entered service on 28 June 1966 in Clearwater, Florida.
Missing in action since 31 July 1969, when his six-man patrol was attacked just prior to extraction 1-1/2 miles inside Laos west of Hue, and last seen by Pan and Comen, surviving commandos, after he was severely wounded in chest by a B-40 rocket blast, when they turned him over to take off one of his emergency UHF radios prior to retreating because of wounds and intense fire; forward air control aircraft heard the second emergency radio transmit "Help, help, help, for God's sake, help," but search teams later dispatched to area were unsuccessful.

Charles Vernon Newton, Staff Sergeant Patrol leader, Detachment B-52 DELTA, 5th Special Forces Group. Born 10 May 1940 in Canadian, Texas. Entered service on 16 December 1959.
Missing in action since 17 April 1969, when Reconnaissance Patrol #6, which had been inserted into Thua Thien Province on 14 April, was ambushed by numerically superior Viet Cong force 9 miles from Laotian border; last heard from by radio transmission to circling aircraft requesting assistance, whereupon radio contact was lost.

Warren Robert Orr, Jr., Captain Civil affairs officer, Company C, 5th Special Forces Group. Born 20 March 1943 in West Frankfort, Illinois. Entered service on 22 March 1963 at Moline, Illinois.
Missing in action since 12 May 1968, when arrived at Kham Duc Special Forces Camp to assist in evacuation efforts, and last seen loading Vietnamese civilians aboard an Air Force C-130 aircraft, which crashed one mile from the camp; Vo Dai Phung claimed he saw Orr get on aircraft after everyone was aboard before the tail

gate closed; later search of wreckage impossible because aircraft was totally destroyed except for tail boom.

Robert Duval Owen, Staff Sergeant Reconnaissance patrol member, Command & Control, MACV-SOG. Born 21 December 1938 in Lynchburg, Virginia. Entered service on 30 July 1954.
Missing in action since 23 May 1968, after his six-man spike team "Idaho" was infiltrated just across the Laotian border west of A Loui by helicopter on 20 May, and all further contact with patrol was lost; spike team "Oregon" inserted into area for search on 22 May immediately contacted large hostile force and was extracted.

Norman Payne, Sergeant Reconnaissance patrol member, Command & Control North, MACV-SOG. Born on 14 July 1939 in Greenville, Alabama. Entered service on 8 July 1957.
Missing in action since 19 December 1968, when his reconnaissance team was attacked 6 miles inside Laos west of the A Shau Valley just before nightfall; last seen by the team leader, Sp. 4th Class Donald C. Sheppard, as Payne left the team to join another group, which had slid down an embankment; Sheppard later followed this route along a creek bed, but efforts to locate Payne failed. During extraction, Sheppard heard garbled emergency radio transmission, the last word of which sounded like "bison" (the code name for Payne), but a later ground search was blocked by hostile activity.

Thomas Hepburn Perry, Specialist 4th Class medical specialist, Detachment A-105, 5th Special Forces Group. Born 19 June 1942 in Washington, D.C. Entered service on 10 March 1966 in New Haven, Connecticut.
Missing in action since 10 May 1968, when Ngok Tavak base south of Kham Duc was overrun by NVA ground assault; last seen by Sgt. Cordell J. Matheney, Jr., standing twenty feet away as Capt. John White (Australian army) formed up the withdrawal column at the outer perimeter wire on the eastern Ngok Tavak hillside; noted missing during later extraction. A ground search was prohibited by hostile activity in overrun area.

Daniel Raymond Phillips, Specialist 5th Class Demolitions specialist, Detachment A-101, 5th Special Forces Group. Born on 7 August 1944 in Philadelphia, Pennsylvania. Entered service on 18 March 1966 in Harrisburg, Pennsylvania.
Missing in action since 7 February 1968, at the Lang Vei Special Forces Camp when overrun by NVA tank-infantry assault; last seen wounded in the face and attempting to evade North Vietnamese armor by going through the northern perimeter wire.

Jerry Lynn Pool, 1st Lieutenant Reconnaissance patrol leader, Command & Control Central, MACV-SOG. Born on 2 April 1944 in Sinton, Texas. Entered service on 11 April 1964 at Austin, Texas.
Missing in action since 24 March 1970, when UH-1H helicopter lifted him and other team members from landing zone in the tri-border area 14 miles inside Cambodia; aircraft racked by explosions during ascent, continued forward aflame for 200 yards, and disappeared into the jungle, where it crashed.

Charles Francis Prevedel, Sergeant Patrol member, Detachment B-52 DELTA, 5th Special Forces Group. Born 18 November 1943 in St. Louis, Missouri. Entered service on 14 September 1965.

Missing in action since 17 April 1969, when Reconnaissance Patrol #6 was ambushed by numerically superior Viet Cong force in Thua Thien Province 9 miles from Laotian border; last heard from by radio transmission to circling aircraft requesting assistance, whereupon radio contact was lost.

Ronald Earl Ray, Staff Sergeant Reconnaissance patrol leader, Command & Control North, MACV-SOG. Born 11 August 1947 in Beaumont, Texas. Entered service on 21 June 1965 at Port Arthur, Texas.

Missing in action since 13 November 1969, when his six-man reconnaissance team was attacked and overrun 16 miles inside Laos west of Thua Thien Province; sole survivor Nguyen Van Bon stated that Ray was hit in an exchange of gunfire, fell to the ground, groaned, and then was silent; Bon shook him but received no response, and noted that Ray's weapon was smashed and that Ray had been hit in the chest and arm.

John Hartley Robertson, Sergeant First Class Operations sergeant, FOB #1, Command & Control North, MACV-SOG. Born 25 October 1936 in Birmingham, Alabama. Entered service on 15 June 1954.

Missing in action since 20 May 1968, when aboard a Vietnamese H-34 helicopter on a medical evacuation mission 4 miles inside Laos South of A Shau; as helicopter was landing it was struck by hostile fire, smashed into the trees, and burst into flames. Vietnamese ground unit could not reach the wreckage, and no survivors were spotted.

Robert Francis Scherdin, Private First Class Reconnaissance patrol member, Command & Control North, MACV-SOG. Born 14 February 1947 in Somerville, New Jersey. Entered service on 15 August 1967 at Newark, New Jersey.

Missing in action since 29 December 1968, when part of the rear element of a reconnaissance team that was split during a skirmish 4 miles inside Cambodia west of Dak To; Montagnard soldier Nguang in same element saw him fall on his right side and tried to help him stand up, but Scherdin only groaned and would not get up; Nguang was then wounded himself and realized he had been left by the other three Vietnamese of the rear element, whereupon he left Scherdin and was extracted along with the remainder of the team.

Klaus Dieter Scholz, Staff Sergeant Reconnaissance patrol member, Command & Control North, MACV-SOG. Born 20 January 1944 in Bad Warmbrunn, Rieserged, Germany. Entered service on 17 May 1965 at Amarillo, Texas.

Missing in action since 30 November 1968, 10 miles inside Laos east of Tchepone when returning from patrol aboard a Vietnamese H-34 helicopter that was hit by 37mm antiaircraft fire; aircraft fell out of control from altitude of 3,000 feet and exploded upon impact with ground. No ground search was initiated because crash site was located in a denied area.

Mike John Scott, Sergeant First Class Aerial observer, Command & Control Central, MACV-SOG. Born 2 September 1932 in Gostynin, Poland. Entered service on 13 September 1956, at Newark, New Jersey.
Missing in action since 13 May 1969, when aboard an aircraft of the 219th Aviation Company, piloted by Lt. Bruce C. Bessor, just inside the Laotian border west of Kham Duc, attempting to locate ground reconnaissance team whose members heard aircraft engine noise followed by fifteen rounds of 37mm fire and engine sputtering but no sound of crash, then a large volume of rifle fire from same direction. Efforts to locate the aircraft failed.

Lee D. Scurlock, Jr., Staff Sergeant Reconnaissance patrol member, Command & Control, MACV-SOG. Born 10 November 1943 in Restful Lake, Ohio. Entered service on 22 September 1961.
Missing in action since 21 December 1967, during extraction of team on Laotian-Cambodian boundary of the tri-border region 18 miles west of Vietnam, while climbing a rope ladder to a helicopter ("Gator 376") of the 119th Aviation Company; he climbed only three rungs on first attempt before losing grip, removed rucksack and radio, and slowly climbed ladder, appearing weak and possibly hurt as the door gunner and a Special Forces sergeant shouted encouragement; just before he reached their outstretched hands, he fell off the ladder fifty feet to the ground, landed on his neck and head, and rolled down hillside until a small tree stopped his movement. The helicopter came under automatic weapons fire and was forced from the area.

Leo Earl Seymour, Staff Sergeant Reconnaissance patrol leader, Command & Control, MACV-SOG. Born 14 May 1942 in Sayre, Pennsylvania. Entered Army 28 June 1963 with four years' Marine service.
Missing in action since 3 July 1967, when his Reconnaissance Team "Texas" was readying ambush positions near a trail junction 11 miles inside Laos northwest of Ben Het in the Dale Xow river valley; two large hostile columns converged and noticed a propaganda poster tacked to a tree that had not been there previously and began searching area, spotting the forward security element, which opened fire; team split up by skirmish, and upon rallying a distance away could not find Seymour.

Jerry Michael Shriver, Sergeant First Class Exploitation platoon leader, Command & Control South, MACV-SOG. Born 24 September 1941 in DeFuniak Springs, Florida. Entered service on 9 December 1958.
Missing in action since 24 April 1969, when his platoon was engaged by intense fire 1-1/2 miles inside Laos west of the DMZ's southern boundary of Vietnam; last seen by Capt. Paul D. Cahill, moving against machine gun bunkers and entering the woodline, whereupon he continued radio contact until transmission ceased. Ten airstrikes and 1,500 rockets were required to extract the few survivors of the platoon from the battlefield.

Donald Monroe Shue, Sergeant Reconnaissance patrol member, Command & Control North, MACV-SOG. Born 29 August 1949 in Concord, North Carolina. Entered service on 26 June 1967 at Charlotte, North Carolina.
Missing in action since 3 November 1969, when his reconnaissance patrol was attacked by a numerically superior force 30 miles inside Laos near Ban Chakeny Tai,

and he was hit by grenade fragments; last seen lying wounded on the ground as their position was about to be overrun, as related by an indigenous team member who evaded capture.

Burt Chauncy Small, Jr., Specialist 4th Class Psychological operations specialist, Detachment A-108, 5th Special Forces Group. Born 2 September 1946 in Long Beach, California. Entered service 19 January 1966 at Savannah, Georgia.
Missing in action since 6 March 1967, when accompanying a twenty-man Vietnamese patrol of the 142d CIDG Company, which was ambushed near Minh Long; during the skirmish Sgt. Jacob G. Roth, Jr., and Small tried to stop the CIDG radio operator, who was running away, when Small was wounded in the left leg, captured by North Vietnamese troops, and never seen again.

Raymond Clark Stacks, 1st Lieutenant Reconnaissance patrol leader, Command & Control North, MACV-SOG. Born 6 March 1948 in Memphis, Tennessee. Commissioned on 6 September 1966 at Memphis, Tennessee.
Missing in action since 30 November 1968, 10 miles inside Laos east of Tchepone when returning from patrol aboard a Vietnamese H-34 helicopter that was hit by 37mm antiaircraft fire; aircraft fell out of control from altitude of 3,000 feet and exploded upon impact with ground. No ground search was initiated because crash site was located in a denied area.

Willie Ernest Stark, Sergeant First Class Patrol leader, Detachment B-52 DELTA, 5th Special Forces Group. Born 7 October 1932 in Martinsburg, Nebraska. Entered service on 21 July 1950 at Waterbury, Nebraska.
Missing in action since 2 December 1966, 1-1/2 miles inside Laos west of the DMZ with a reconnaissance patrol on 29 November 1966, which had two skirmishes with Viet Cong, and last seen wounded in thigh and chest and being guarded by S. Sgt. Russell P. Bott, as related by Vietnamese patrol survivors.

Jack Thomas Stewart, Captain Commanding Officer, III CTZ Mike Force (Detachment A-302), 5th Special Forces Group. Born 30 March 1941 in Washington, D.C. Entered service on 27 February 1959 at Washington, D.C.
Missing in action since 24 March 1967, when his Mike Force Company conducted a heliborne assault 7 miles east of Bu Dop; shortly after landing they were engaged by two NVA battalions armed with automatic weapons and recoilless rifles, and supported by mortars, forcing company elements to retreat under extremely heavy pressure; attempts to consolidate positions around the landing zone supported by airstrikes failed; communications was lost with the Mike Force and never regained.

Madison Alexander Strohlein, Sergeant Parachutist commando, Task Force 1 Advisory Element. Born 17 May 1948 in Abington, Pennsylvania. Entered service on 8 July 1968 at Philadelphia, Pennsylvania.
Missing in action since 22 June 1971, after being parachuted into the Ta Ko area of Vietnam at night on a reconnaissance mission with Sgt.-Maj. William D. Waugh and Sfc. James O. Bath; last heard from by radio requesting evacuation because of injuries; his transmissions were monitored until 11:00 A.M., when he stated hostile forces were approaching, thereafter transmissions ceased. Rescue team inserted on

23 June found only his weapon, scattered gear, and indications that his parachute had been pulled from a tree.

William Wentworth Stubbs, Staff Sergeant Reconnaissance patrol member, Command & Control Central, MACV-SOG. Born 6 August 1949 in Oak Harbor, Washington. Entered service on 26 October 1967 at Newport, Washington.
Missing in action since 20 October 1969, when his reconnaissance team was attacked 20 miles inside Laos northeast of Nakhon Phanom and he was at the point of immediate contact; according to surviving indigenous patrol members, three bursts of automatic fire were directed at him from a distance of two feet, striking him in the head, followed by three grenades thrown onto his position. The rest of patrol was unable to move up the steep slope to reach him and were forced to withdraw five minutes later because of renewed hostile assault.

Randolph Bothwell Suber, Sergeant Reconnaissance patrol member, Command & Control North, MACV-SOG. Born 22 May 1947 at Albuquerque, New Mexico. Entered service on October 26, 1967, at Albuquerque, New Mexico.
Missing in action since 13 November 1969, when his six-man reconnaissance team was attacked and overrun 16 miles inside Laos west of Thua Thien Province; sole survivor Nguyen Van Bon stated that he last saw Suber trying to gain contact on his URC-10 emergency radio, then pick up his weapon and aim at four approaching hostile soldiers, but that the rifle did not fire because it became jammed, and Suber was hit immediately afterwards and fell to the ground; Bon called to him, but he did not move or answer, and Bon was forced to evade from the area.

Samuel Kamu Toomey, Major Special mission officer, Headquarters, MACV-SOG. Born 30 December 1935 in Honolulu, Hawaii. Entered Army on 13 April 1956 after service with the Marines.
Missing in action since 30 November 1968, 10 miles inside Laos east of Tchepone when returning from patrol aboard a Vietnamese H-34 helicopter that was hit by 37mm antiaircraft fire; aircraft fell out of control from altitude of 3,000 feet and exploded upon impact with ground. No ground search was initiated because crash site was located in a denied area.

Glenn Ernest Tubbs, Staff Sergeant Reconnaissance patrol member, Command & Control South, MACV-SOG. Born 24 January 1940 in Sulphur Springs, Texas. Entered service on 21 June 1959 at Olton, Texas.
Missing since 13 January 1970, when his reconnaissance team was crossing the Se San River close to the Cambodian border 12 miles northwest of Duc Co; Tubbs was the last member of the team to cross; near the center of the channel he was swept from the rope by the swift current, tried to swim against the current, and was last seen when he went under for the sixth time while being carried over some deep rapids about fifty feet downstream from the rope. Team members chased after him, two by swimming back across the stream, but he had disappeared.

Gunther Herbert Wald, Staff Sergeant Reconnaissance patrol member, Command & Control North, MACV-SOG. Born 7 January 1944 in Frankfurt, Germany. Entered Army on 13 June 1967 with four years Marine service.
Missing in action since 3 November 1969, when his reconnaissance patrol was at-

tacked by a numerically superior force 30 miles inside Laos near Ban Chakevy Tai whereupon he was hit by a grenade while trying to make radio contact; last seen lying on the ground with multiple wounds and possibly dead as their position was about to be overrun; related by an indigenous member Pong, who evaded capture.

Lewis Clark Walton, Staff Sergeant Reconnaissance team member, Task Force 1 Advisory Element. Born 13 May 1934 in Providence, Rhode Island. Entered service on 21 June 1952 at Providence, Rhode Island.
Missing in action since 10 May 1971, after his long-range reconnaissance team "Asp" was inserted into western Quang Nam Province 12 miles from Laos on 3 May; past initial radio contact, no further contact was ever made.

Charles Edward White, Sergeant First Class Reconnaissance patrol member, Command & Control North, MACV-SOG. Born on 18 May 1933 in Union Town, Alabama. Entered service on 23 May 1950 at Columbus, Georgia.
Missing in action since 29 January 1968, when he was being extracted by McGuire Rig hoist by helicopter 16 miles inside Cambodia west of Kontum along with team members Nang and Khong; after being radioed by White that the trio was ready to be lifted out, the pilot increased his altitude to 200 feet, at which point White fell into the jungle. Later ground search on 31 January found path that falling body made through jungle canopy into thick bamboo, which was surmised as being enough foliage to have safely broken his fall, but no trace was ever found of him.

Eddie Lee Williams, Sergeant First Class Reconnaissance patrol member, Command & Control, MACV-SOG. Born 10 February 1935 in Miami, Florida. Entered service on 30 November 1953.
Missing in action since 3 October 1966, when patrol was inserted 1 mile inside Laos west of the DMZ and immediately engaged in firefight under adverse circumstances; sole survivor interpreter Bui Kim Tien last saw him on 4 October while they were trying to evade capture; Williams sent him to investigate some caves, at which point Tien was spotted by hostile forces and forced to run from area.

Peter Joe Wilson, Staff Sergeant Reconnaissance patrol leader, Command & Control Central, MACV-SOG. Born 23 August 1938 in Ridley Park, Pennsylvania. Entered service on 17 February 1961 at Long Beach, New York.
Missing in action since 19 October 1970, when his reconnaissance patrol was attacked 2 miles inside Laos in the tri-border area southwest of Ben Het and forced to abandon the battlefield with hostile forces in close pursuit; last seen by Sgt. John M. Baker when Wilson directed him to the front of the patrol and told him to continue to the east if the column was split; at that time Wilson was covering the rear of the patrol and assisting a wounded indigenous soldier, Djuit; later Baker heard Wilson transmit "May Day, May Day" on his emergency radio and the sounds of a firefight from the direction of the separated patrol element.

Remains Recovered

Frank Collins Parrish, Sergeant First Class Senior medical specialist, Detachment A-411, 5th Special Forces Group. Born 19 September 1931 in Big Springs, Texas. Entered service on 14 October 1948 at Cleburne, Texas.

Missing in action since 16 January 1968, near My Phuoc Tay, when camp strike force was involved in a firefight; CIDG and LLDB survivors reported that the Viet Cong captured and summarily executed him, but remains were not recovered until 30 April 1973.

George Quamo, Major Deputy commander, FOB #3, Command & Control North, MACV-SOG. Born 10 June 1940 in Lynn, Massachusetts. Entered service on 23 October 1958 at Averill Park, New York.

Disappeared on 14 April 1968, when aboard a Vietnamese U-17 aircraft (Tail number XT), flown by Chinese contract pilot, as courier enroute from Khe Sanh to Da Nang. Remains recovered on 28 June 1974.

APPENDIX B

SPECIAL FORCES MEDAL OF HONOR RECIPIENTS

*Eugene Ashley, Jr.,** Sergeant First Class Intelligence sergeant, Detachment A-101, 5th Special Forces Group. Born 12 October 1931 in Wilmington, North Carolina. Entered service at New York, New York.
Personally led five counterattacks on 7 February 1968 at Camp Lang Vei, Quang Tri Province, Vietnam, in effort to break through to comrades in overrun camp before he was killed.

Gary B. Beikirch, Sergeant Medical specialist, Detachment B-24, 5th Special Forces Group. Born 29 August 1947 in Rochester, New York. Entered service at Buffalo, New York.
Retrieved and treated disabled soldiers on 1 April 1968 at Camp Dak Seang, Quang Duc Province, Vietnam, under heavy fire despite serious wounds.

Roy P. Benavidez, Staff Sergeant Headquarters, B-56 (Project SIGMA), 5th Special Forces Group. Born 5 August 1935, on a small farm near Cureo, Texas. Entered service in June 1955.
Voluntarily accompanied evacuation force from his forward headquarters on 2 May 1968 and rescued several isolated patrol members in heavy combat near Loc Ninh, Binh Long Province, Vietnam.

***William M. Bryant,** Sergeant First Class Advisor, 321st CIDG Company, 32d Mobile Strike Force Battalion, Detachment B-36, 5th Special Forces Group. Born 16 February 1933 at Cochran, Georgia. Entered service at Detroit, Michigan.
Enabled his surrounded company to escape by charging several Viet Cong positions before he was killed by a rocket on 24 March 1969 in Long Khanh Province, Vietnam.

***Brian L. Buker,** Sergeant Advisor, 513th CIDG Company, 1st Battalion, 5th Mobile Strike Force Command, Detachment B-55, 5th Special Forces Group. Born 3 November 1949 in Benton, Maine. Entered service at Bangor, Maine.
Led the attack against a heavily defended mountain fortress on 5 April 1970 at Nui Khet, Chau Doc Province, Vietnam, during which he was mortally wounded assaulting a bunker.

Jon R. Cavaiani, Staff Sergeant Platoon leader, Task Force 1 Advisory Element. Born 2 August 1943 in Royston, England. Entered service at Fresno, California.
Defended Hickory Hill Radio Relay site (Hill 953) in Quang Tri Province, Vietnam, on 4–5 June 1971 against a North Vietnamese Army battalion until overwhelmed and captured.

*Posthumous award.

Drew D. Dix, Staff Sergeant Reconnaissance team leader (mixed LLDB/U.S. Navy SEAL) MACV Combined Studies Division (Central Intelligence Agency). Born 14 December 1944 at West Point, New York. Entered service at Denver, Colorado.
Helped lead repulse of Viet Cong from Chau Phu, Chau Duc Province, Vietnam, with jeep mounting machine gun from 31 January to 1 February 1968, single-handedly assaulted building and rescued personnel inside.

Roger H. C. Donlon, Captain Commanding officer, Detachment A-726, 7th Special Forces Group. Born 30 January 1934 Saugerties, New York. Entered service in Fort Chaffee, Arkansas.
Heroically defended Camp Nam Dong, Thua Thien Province, Vietnam, on 6 July 1964 despite serious wounds.

*Loren D. Hagen, 1st Lieutenant Reconnaissance patrol leader, Task Force 1 Advisory Element. Born 25 February 1946 in Fargo, North Dakota. Entered service in Fargo, North Dakota.
Courageously defended patrol perimeter inside Demilitarized Zone on 7 August 1971 and repelled numerous charges until killed extracting comrades from imperiled bunker.

*Charles E. Hosking, Jr., Sergeant First Class Advisor, 3d Mobile Strike Force, 5th Special Forces Group. Born 12 May 1924 in Ramsey, New Jersey. Entered service at Fort Dix, New Jersey.
Wrestled a Viet Cong prisoner with a live grenade to the ground and saved his men by absorbing the blast on 21 March 1967 in Phuoc Long Province, Vietnam.

Robert L. Howard, Sergeant First Class Reconnaissance patrol leader, MACV Studies & Observation Group. Born 11 July 1939 in Opelika, Alabama. Entered service at Montgomery, Alabama.
Rallied surrounded platoon and covered its aerial extraction despite severe injuries on 30 December 1968 in Laos.

*John J. Kedenburg, Specialist 5th Class Reconnaissance patrol leader, MACV Studies & Observation Group. Born 31 July 1946 in Brooklyn, New York. Entered service at Brooklyn, New York.
Defended landing zone and covered team aerial extraction on 13 June 1968 in Laos, giving his place to another team member, who suddenly came to pickup zone, and remained alone on LZ until overwhelmed and killed.

Franklin D. Miller, Staff Sergeant Reconnaissance patrol leader, MACV Studies & Observation Group. Born 27 January 1945 in Elizabeth City, North Carolina. Entered service at Albuquerque, New Mexico.
Repelled several attacks on his patrol despite serious wounds, on 5 January 1970 in Laos.

*George K. Sisler, 1st Lieutenant Exploitation force leader, MACV Studies & Observation Group. Born 19 September 1937 in Dexter, Missouri. Entered service at Dexter, Missouri.
Destroyed machine gun and personally counterattacked into NVA assault, at which point he was killed on 7 February 1967 in Laos.

Charles Q. Williams, 2d Lieutenant Executive officer, Detachment A-342, 5th Special Forces Group. Born 17 September 1933 in Charleston, South Carolina. Entered service at Fort Jackson, South Carolina.

Directed defense of beleaguered compound at Camp Dong Xoai, Phuoc Long Province, Vietnam, on 9 and 10 June 1965 despite grievous wounds, destroying numerous key Viet Cong positions.

*Gordon D. Yntema, Sergeant Platoon advisor, Detachment A-431, 5th Special Forces Group. Born 26 June 1945 in Bethesda, Maryland. Entered service at Detroit, Michigan.

Carried several personnel to safety from 16 to 18 January 1968 near Thong Binh, Kien Tuong Province, Vietnam, and returned to trenchline, which he defended until ammunition was exhausted, after which he used his rifle as a club until he was killed.

Fred W. Zabitosky, Staff Sergeant Reconnaissance patrol leader, MACV Studies & Observation Group. Born 27 October 1942 in Trenton, New Jersey. Entered service at Trenton, New Jersey.

Defended landing zone against determined NVA attack on 19 February 1968 in Laos and rescued pilot from downed helicopter before he passed out because of multiple wounds and burns.

INDEX